ASPECTS OF ANCIENT INDIAN ADMINISTRATION

ASPECTS OF ANCIENT INDIAN ADMINISTRATION

DILIP KUMAR GANGULY
M.A., P.R.S., Ph.D.

Department of Ancient Indian History, Culture and Archaeology, Visva-Bharati University

abhinav publications

First Edition: 1979

PUBLISHER Shakti Malik
Abhinav Publications
E-37 Hauz Khas
New Delhi-110016

PRINTER Sunil Composing Co.
at S.P. Printers
1067 Ajay Palace, Naraina
New Delhi-110028

Dedicated to my Mother

Kamala Ganguly

Contents

Chapter II

THE QUEEN

Chapter III

THE CROWN PRINCE

Chapter IV

THE ROYAL CHAPLAIN

Chapter V

THE MINISTER

Chapter VI

THE *SANDHIVIGRAHIKA*

Chapter VII

THE AMBASSADOR

Chapter VIII

THE JUDGE

Chapter IX

THE CHIEF DISTRICT OFFICER

Chapter X

THE SPY

Chapter XI

THE VILLAGE HEADMAN

Preface

Study of ancient Indian administrative systems has been engaging the attention of scholars since the days of the great Indologist K.P. Jayaswal but there is no gainsaying the fact that a comprehensive, systematic and connected treatment of the administrative machinery of early Indian kingdoms from the Ṛgvedic period onwards down to the thirteenth century A.D. has long been a *desideratum.* The present work, which is based on the author's prolonged study of the existing source-materials, both literary and archaeological, indigenous and foreign, partly fulfils that need.

Chapter I deals with the king, who was the supreme head of the executive, judicial, revenue and military departments of the government of ancient Indian kingdoms, which were, generally speaking, monarchical in character and composition. The ascendancy of royal authority was clearly visible in the Ṛgvedic period, while the later Vedic age witnessed its crystallisation. For our knowledge about the king in the post-Vedic period, we turn to Jātaka literature but the information it supplies is too inadequate to enable us to reconstruct a full picture. The early *Dharmaśāstra*-writers unanimously point out that the preservation of the caste system was the foremost duty of the king; they, likewise, provide us with a wealth of information about his sources of income. The Maurya rulers, who had no pretensions to divinity, possessed imperial grandeur and dignity and were the supreme heads of the executive, judicial and military branches of administration. The *Arthaśāstra,* which was probably composed during the reign of Candragupta Maurya, throws welcome light on the office of the king. The Bactrian kings at first adopted the title of *Basileos* but with the augmentation of power, they assumed more dignified epithets. The Scytho-Parthian rulers adopted more dignified titles as compared to those of their Indo-Greek predecessors and popularised the system of dual monarchy. During the period of the Kuṣāṇa kings, an exalted conception of monarchy was introduced, deification of kingship was claimed and the title 'Sons of Heaven' came to be used. The early Guptas were called *Mahārāja* but from the time of Candragupta I onwards, the higher title of *Mahārājādhirāja* came to be applied to them. They advocated the divinity of kingship and usually followed the system of primogeniture. The period following the downfall of the Imperial Guptas witnessed the emergence of the Maukharis, Later Guptas and Puṣyabhūtis, who began with the use of the modest title of *Mahārāja* but subsequently assumed the title of *Mahārājādhirāja.* The little that we know about them makes it abundantly clear that they were at the head of the civil and military administration. The royal office remained practically the same in both principle and practice in the Pratīhāra and Pāla kingdoms, the king being at the head of all the executive, judicial and military functions of the state and enjoying the sole right to dismiss any officer and appoint any person to any post he liked. On turning to South India, we find that the Śātavāhana kings, in spite of their great victories, generally called themselves *Rājan* and *Svāmin.* The Bṛhatphalāyana, Śālaṅkāyana and Viṣṇukuṇḍin kings indifferently used the titles of *Rājā* and *Mahārāja.* The king was at the head of the administration in both the Cālukya and Pallava dominions. *Mahārājādhirāja*, *Mahārāja*, *Dharma-Mahārāja* and *Dharma-Mahārājādhirāja* were some of the titles borne by the Pallava monarchs. Monarchy was hereditary in the Rāṣṭrakūṭa kingdom and usually the eldest son inherited the throne of his father. The king was the fountainhead of all power; he commanded the army, carried on the administrative functions with the help of subordinates and acted as the supreme court in legal disputes.

In Chapter II, we have made a detailed study about the queen who, though almost passed over in silence in the *Ṛgveda*, finds prominent mention in the later Vedic texts which would imply that in this period the king usually had four queens, the *Mahiṣī*, *Parivṛktī*, *Vāvātā* and *Pālāgalī*. We hardly meet with a trustworthy account of queens in the *Jātakas* but the Classical authors record some genuine traditions about them. The edicts of Aśoka, Buddhist legends and *Arthaśāstra* furnish us with valuable information about the Maurya queens. Coins would disclose that the queens wielded enormous influence in the Indo-Greek principalities in the north-western part of India. Coming to the Gupta age, we find that while Kumāradevī, whose name and effigy appear on the Candragupta I-Kumāradevī coins along with those of her husband, held a high status in the kingdom; other queens never attained the same pinnacle of glory as she. The *Harṣacarita* implies that at the time of coronation, both the king and the chief queen were consecrated but it leaves us in the dark about her participation in administration. The Chinese pilgrim Hiuen Tsang refers to two *strīrājyas* in the seventh century A.D. The *Rājataraṅgiṇī* reveals that the queens of Kashmir assumed great power; they sometimes helped their husbands in administration, while others governed the kingdom either in their own name or as regents on behalf of minor rulers. The queens in the Bhañja kingdom were entrusted with the important task of maintaining the royal seal and scrutinising the genuineness of documents. Rajasthan has produced a galaxy of valiant queens who not only actively participated in administration, but also threw their phalanx behind their husbands to fight against the enemies. Turning to South India, we find that while the Śātavāhana queens were sometimes associated with administration, those in the Ikṣvāku kingdom did hardly occupy such an important status. The Vākāṭaka queens were generally known as *Devīs*, while the chief ones among them were called *Mahādevīs*. The queens of the Cālukya kingdom are known to have issued records, administered divisions, made handsome gifts and installed images of gods and goddesses. We know very little about the Pallava queens, excepting, of course, their religious charities and the foundation of monuments for their favourite deities. The queens were not entitled to any special privilege in the Rāṣṭrakūṭa realm but as we approach the time of the Cālukyas of Kalyāṇī, we at once notice to our great satisfaction that most of the Cālukya queens shouldered administrative responsibilities.

Chapter III delineates the crown prince about whom some useful accounts are preserved in the Vedic and Jātaka texts. The Mauryas followed the practice of governing provinces with the help of princes who were called both *Kumāras* and *Āryaputras*. Puṣyamitra continued the Maurya tradition of associating the prince in administration. In the Gupta kingdom, the heir-apparent discharged a great deal of administrative work and often led the imperial army in the face of any foreign aggression. The *Yuvarāja* was an important limb of the administrative machinery of the state in the age of Harṣavardhana. The Pāla and Sena records take prominent notice of the crown prince but in regard to the duties and functions that he discharged during this period, we are almost left in the dark. A perusal of the Gāhaḍavāla epigraphs would show that the Gāhaḍavāla crown prince, called *Yuvarāja* or *Mahārājaputra*, was more powerful than his counterpart in other contemporary North Indian kingdoms. An attempt has also been made in this chapter to ascertain, with the help of epigraphic and other evidence, the position of the crown prince in different South Indian kingdoms.

The antiquity of the office of the *Purohita* goes back to pre-Ṛgvedic times, although it is with the Ṛgvedic period and onwards that we possess definite material about the institution. In those early days, the priesthood had attained a high position and it maintained an equally important status in the succeeding age. The *Jātakas* show that in the post-Vedic period the office was generally hereditary and held by the same family for generations. The *Dharmasūtra*-writers provide us with an interesting insight into the office. The epics would create the impression that the priestly profession was not an honourable one. The *Arthaśāstra* gives us useful information about the *Purohita*. The Gupta inscriptions do not take any notice of the *Purohita* but mention a class of officers who might have taken over some of the priestly functions. The royal priest in the Pratīhāra and Gāhaḍavāla kingdoms was entrusted with various functions, including the education of princes. The *Purohita* figures prominently in the inscriptions of the Kāmboja, Varman and Sena kings of Bengal but the Pāla records hardly take any notice of him. In the *Śukranīti,* the priest, called *Purodhā*, is included in the council of ministers.

Chapter V deals with ministers who constituted an important wheel of the administrative machinery of the state. The ministers in ancient India were broadly divided into a twofold group, comprising counsellors and executive ministers who, to deduce from the testimony of literary and archaeological materials, coming from different areas and periods, helped the king to perform the works and responsibilities of the state. But these ministers were not the representatives of the people but were actually royal servants who worked under constant threat of dismissal. Some ministers, no doubt, were destined to play a commanding role in the formulation and execution of the state's policies and programmes, but they were few and far between in number.

Chapter VI deals with the foreign minister, called *Sandhivigrahika*, who was entrusted with the important tasks of peace, war, neutrality, marching, seeking refuge and dual policy. But it is rather strange that we do not hear of any foreign minister in Indian kingdoms till we come to the age of Manu. The *Sandhivigrahika* finds prominent mention in Indian inscriptions and literature from the Gupta period onwards.

Chapter VII deals with the ambassador. The term *dūta* in the sense of an envoy occurs in the *Ṛgveda* but there are reasons to believe that the science of diplomacy was in its infancy in the Vedic period. Whereas, we seldom come across any detailed information about *Dūtas* in the early Buddhist and Jaina sources, welcome light on the position of these officers in the pre-Maurya epoch is thrown by the accounts of the Classical authors. In the section entitled *Dūta-praṇidhiḥ* of the *Arthaśāstra*, Kauṭilya has elaborately discussed the problem of *Dūtas*. Manu, whose writings appear to reflect the condition of the country during the early centuries of the Christian era, is aware of the importance of the institution of ambassadors. As we approach the seventh century A.D., we come across evidence which would testify to ambassadors being employed time and again by Indian kings to cultivate diplomatic ties with foreign powers. The *Nītiśāstra*-writers of early mediaeval India have made important observations on ambassadors but it is far from being known at present how far the recommendations of these authors were accepted by the governments of those days.

In Chapter VIII, we have made a thorough study of the different categories of judges in ancient India. In the Buddhist literature, mention is made of two classes of judges, called *Vinicchayāmaccas* and *Vohārikamahāmattas*. The writers of the

Dharmasūtras mention the *Prāḍvivāka* and provide us with valuable information about him. Kauṭilya refers to the *Dharmasthas* and *Pradeṣṭṛs* and brings out their respective functions. The *Dharmaśāstras* constitute a mine of information regarding the qualifications and duties of a judge and the sources of law. Inscriptions of the Gupta period mention some officers like the *Pramāṭrs* and others, who were, in all probability, connected with the judicial department. Śukra and Jīmūtavāhana deal at great length with the constitution of the court of justice, grades of courts, different stages of judicial proceedings, role of agents, order of hearing suitors, time allowed for filing plaints, four kinds of reply and various kinds of proof.

Chapter IX deals with the chief officer of the district about whom we hardly possess any reliable information for the period preceding the advent of the Mauryas on the political chessboard. In the inscriptions of Aśoka, mention is made of the *Rājūkas* who have been identified with the chief officers of districts. Kauṭilya mentions some administrative divisions and it is not unlikely that his *droṇamukhas* correspond to districts. The *Śāntiparvan* of the *Mahābhārata* and the *Manusaṁhitā* refer to a number of officers who were in charge of different kinds of administrative units like the lord of one village, lord of ten villages, lord of twenty villages, lord of one hundred villages and lord of one thousand villages. We have identified the lord of one hundred villages with the chief officer of the district. In the period of Gupta supremacy the officer, who was administering the district, was designated as *Kumārāmātya*, *Āyuktaka* and *Viṣayapati*. The *Viṣayapati* finds mention in the inscriptions of many North Indian dynasties of the later period and we have discussed how his functions differed in different kingdoms. The districts of the Śātavāhana kingdom were called *āhāras* which were usually placed under officers, bearing the designation of *Amacca*. The district officers of the Bṛhatphalāyana kingdom were known as *Vyāpṛtas*. The *nāḍus* of the Pallava kingdom corresponded to the *āhāras* under the Śātavāhana kings. They were generally placed under the officers who were called *Āyuktakas* and *Adhyakṣas* in the early period and *Nāṭṭuviyavans* in later days. The districts of the Rāṣṭrakūṭa kingdom were placed under the supervision of the *Viṣayapatis* who sometimes enjoyed the status of feudatories.

In Chapter X, we have made a detailed study of the spy. In Vedic literature, there are some indications which would testify to the prevalence of the institution of espionage in the contemporary period. The combined testimony of the Classical authors and Kauṭilya proves beyond doubt the existence of spies in the Maurya kingdom. An elaborate account of spies is to be met with in the epics. Manu speaks of as many as five categories of spies but unfortunately does not mention them. Important notices of spies during the Gupta period may be found in some contemporary works like the *Mṛcchakaṭika*, *Mudrārākṣasa*, *Yājñavalkya-Smṛti* and *Raghuvaṁśa*. For our knowledge about spies during the post-Gupta period, we may turn to the testimony of the *Kādambarī* and *Śiśupālavadham*. As we approach the early mediaeval period, we are delighted to find abundant materials on spies in the contemporary documents, literary as well as epigraphic.

In Chapter XI we have traced the growth and development of the office of the village headman from the Vedic age onwards down to the thirteenth century A.D. and have pointed out how the duties and responsibilities of this functionary varied in different kingdoms.

In Chapter X we have made a detailed study of the spy. In Vedic literature there are some indications which would clearly point to the existence of the institution of espionage in the [illegible] period. The combined testimony of the Classical authors and Kautilya proves beyond doubt the existence of spies in the Mauryan regime. An elaborate account of spies [illegible] is given in the epics. Manu mentions as many as five [illegible] of spies. Unfortunately [illegible] do not mention them. [illegible] of spies during the Gupta period may be found in some contemporary works like the Mrcchakatika, [illegible] and Raghuvamsa. For our knowledge about spies during the post-Gupta period we may [illegible] the Kathasaritsagara and [illegible] Harsacarita. [illegible] we are [illegible] to find [illegible] in the contemporary [illegible] [illegible].

In Chapter XI we have traced the growth and development of the office of the village headman from the Vedic age onwards down to [illegible] A.D. and have pointed out how the duties and responsibilities of this functionary varied in different kingdoms.

Abbreviations

AAHI	*Aśoka And His Inscriptions* (Calcutta, 1955) by B.M. Barua.
AAILFSS	*Aspects of Ancient Indian Life From Sanskrit Sources* by S.C. Banerji.
AAIP	*Aspects of Ancient Indian Polity* (Calcutta, 1960) by N.N. Law.
AI	*Aśokan Inscriptions* (Calcutta, 1959) by R.G. Basak.
AI	*Ancient India.*
AIDMA	*Ancient India as Described by Megasthenes and Arrian* (Calcutta, 1960) by McCrindle.
AIK	*The Age of Imperial Kanauj* (Bombay, 1955) edited by R.C. Majumdar.
AIU	*The Age of Imperial Unity* (Bombay, 1960) edited by R.C. Majumdar.
APIIAI	*Aspects of Political Ideas and Institutions in Ancient India* (Banaras, 1959) by R.S. Sharma.
ASI (*ASR*)	*Annual Report of the Archaeological Survey of India.*
ASLUP	*Administrative and Social Life Under the Pallavas* (Madras, 1938) by C. Minakshi.
CA	*The Classical Age* (Bombay, 1954) edited by R.C. Majumdar.
CAI	*The Classical Accounts of India* (Calcutta, 1960) by R.C. Majumdar.
CGE	*The Coinage of the Gupta Empire* (Banaras, 1957) by A.S. Altekar.
CHI	*The Cambridge History of India*, I (First Indian Reprint) edited by E.J. Rapson.
	A Comprehensive History of India, II (Calcutta, 1957) edited by K.A.N. Sastri.
CII	*Corpus Inscriptionum Indicarum.*

DHNI — *Dynastic History of Northern India*, I-II (Calcutta, 1931, 1936) by H.C. Ray.
EC — *Epigraphia Carnatica.*
EHCK — *Early History and Culture of Kashmir* (Calcutta, 1957) by S.C. Ray.
EHD — *The Early History of the Deccan* by G. Yazdani.
EHI — *The Early History of India* (Oxford, 1924) by V.A. Smith.
EI — *Epigraphia Indica.*
EIP — *Evolution of Indian Polity* (Calcutta, 1920) by R. Shamasastry.
GBI — *The Greeks in Bactria and India* (Cambridge, 1951) by W.W. Tarn.
GP — *The Gupta Polity* (Madras, 1952) by V.R. Ramachandra Dikshitar.
HA — *The History of Civilisation of the People of Assam* (Gauhati, 1959) by P.C. Choudhury.
HB — *History of Bengal*, I (Dacca, 1943) by R.C. Majumdar.
HD — *History of the Dharmaśāstras* (Poona, 1946) by P.V. Kane.
HG — *History of Greece* by J. Bury.
HIPI — *A History of Indian Political Ideas* (Bombay, 1959) by U.N. Ghosal.
HK — *History of Kanauj to the Muslim Conquests* (Banaras, 1959) by R.S. Tripathi.
IA — *Indian Antiquary.*
IAB — *India of the Age of the Brāhmaṇas* (Calcutta, 1963) by J. Basu.
IB — *Inscriptions of Bengal*, III by N.G. Majumdar.
IC — *Indian Culture.*
IDETBJ — *India as Described in Early Texts of Buddhism and Jainism* (London, 1941) by B.C. Law.
IDRW — *India's Diplomatic Relations With The West* (Bombay, 1958) by B.A. Saletore.
IE — *Indian Epigraphy* (Banaras, 1965) by D.C. Sircar.
IF — *Indian Feudalism: c. 300-1200* by R.S. Sharma.
IHQ — *Indian Historical Quarterly.*
IKP — *India as Known to Pāṇini* (Lucknow, 1953) by V.S. Agrawala.

ILISRAI	*International Law And Inter-State Relations In Ancient India* (Calcutta, 1958) by H.L. Chatterjee.
JAOS	*Journal of the American Oriental Society.*
JASB	*Journal of the Asiatic Society of Bengal.*
JBBRAS	*Journal of the Bombay Branch of the Royal Asiatic Society.*
JBORS	*Journal of the Bihar and Orissa Research Society.*
JBRS	*Journal of the Bihar Research Society.*
JDL	*Journal of the Department of Letters* (Calcutta University).
JIH	*Journal of Indian History.*
JNSI	*Journal of the Numismatic Society of India.*
JRASB	*Journal of the Royal Asiatic Society of Bengal.*
KA	*The Kauṭilīya Arthaśāstra* (Bombay, 1963) by R.P. Kangle.
KA	*Kauṭilya's Arthaśāstra* (Mysore, 1919) by R. Shamasastry.
KST	*Kālidāsa—His Style And His Times* (Bombay, 1966) by S.A. Sabnis.
LGAI	*Local Government in Ancient India* (Delhi, 1958) by R.K. Mookherji.
OUBK	*Orissa Under the Bhauma Kings* (Calcutta, 1934) by B. Misra.
PAP	*Polity In The Agni Purāṇa* (Calcutta, 1965) by B.B. Mishra.
PBI	*Pre-Buddhist India* (Bombay, 1939) by R.N. Mehta.
PHAI	*Political History of Ancient India* (Calcutta, 1950) by H.C. Raychaudhuri.
PHNI	*Political History of North India From Jain Sources* (Amritsar, 1954) by G.C. Choudhury.
PIA	*The Political Institutions and Administration* (Delhi, 1969) by P.B. Udgaonkar.
PIHC	*Proceedings of the Indian History Congress.*
RG (*HG*)	*History of the Gāhaḍavāla Dynasty* (Calcutta, 1959) by Roma Niyogi.
RSPMGT	*Revenue System in Post-Maurya and Gupta Times* (Calcutta, 1967) by D.N. Jha.
RT	*The Rāṣṭrakūṭas And Their Times* (Poona, 1934) by A.S. Altekar.

RTA *Rajasthan Through the Ages* (Bikaner, 1966) by D. Sharma.

SE *Struggle for the Empire* (Bombay, 1957) edited by R.C. Majumdar.

SGAI *The State and Government in Ancient India* (Banaras, 1955) by A.S. Altekar.

SHAIB *Some Historical Aspects of the Inscriptions of Bengal* (Calcutta, 1942) by B.C. Sen.

SI *Select Inscriptions* (Calcutta, 1965) by D.C. Sircar.

SIP *South Indian Polity* (Madras, 1955) by T.V. Mahalingam.

SLA *The Sacred Laws of the Āryas*, II by G. Bühler.

SONEI *The Social Organisation in North-East India* (Calcutta, 1920) by S.K. Maitra.

SSAAMI *Studies in the Society and Administration of Ancient and Mediaeval India*, I (Calcutta, 1967) by D.C. Sircar.

STLH *Studies in Tamil Literature and History* (London, 1930) by V.R. Ramachandra Dikshitar.

TSELT *Thirumathi Sornammal Endowment Lectures on Tirukkural* (Madras, 1971).

VA *The Vedic Age* (Bombay, 1951) edited by R.C. Majumdar.

VGA *The Vākāṭaka-Gupta Age* (Lahore, 1946) by R.C. Majumdar.

VI *Vedic Index*, I and II (London, 1912) by A.A. Macdonell and A.B. Keith.

ZDMG *Zeitschrift der Deutschen Morgenlandischen Gessel·schaft.*

1

The King

Notwithstanding the undoubted existence of republics from the Ṛgvedic times to about the fourth century A.D., there is hardly any gainsaying that monarchy was the usual form of government prevalent in ancient India. Whereas in republics the power of the state was vested in many, in a monarchial kingdom the king was the supreme head in all matters of administration, executive, military, revenue and judicial. But circumstances being diverse in different ages and the personality of rulers being constantly variable, the power of the king varied from time to time and kingdom to kingdom. Thus while in the early Vedic period the royal power was considerably circumscriptive, in the days of the Imperial Mauryas it reached the summit of its glory. From about the post-Gupta period onwards, if not from a still earlier date, there was a steady decline of the central authority which culminated in the dethronement of most of the indigenous ruling houses and installation of the Delhi Sultanate.

I

The King in the Ṛgvedic Period

The king in the Ṛgvedic period was generally styled *Rājan*,[1] although he was also sometimes called *Viśpati*, head of the *viś*. In the *Ṛgveda* we come across terms like *samrāṭ*,[2] *ekarāṭ*[3] and *adhirāṭ*[4] which would indicate the existence of different gradations of monarchy in those days of hoary antiquity. This is quite natural in an age which was characterised by frequent outbreaks of war among kings either for survival or extension of hegemony. The victorious and ambitious kings would justifiably adopt more dignified titles in contrast to the colourless epithets, usually assumed by rulers of ordinary stature.

Kingship was normally hereditary. In the *Ṛgveda* we can trace at least three lines of succession[5] like that of Vadhryaśva, Divodāsa, Pijavana and Sudās; or Durgaha, Girikṣit, Purukutsa and Trasadasyu; or Mitrātithi, Kuruśravaṇa and Upamaśravas. A passage[6] of the *Ṛgveda*, which credits the people (*viśas*) with the election of their king, presupposes that the Ṛgvedic monarchy was occasionally elective. It cannot be definitely ascertained whether the general public or the elite alone were entitled to franchise. Similarly it is far from being known whether in the event of any such election the choice was limited to the royal family or was left open. It may be noted in this connection that the theory of the prevalence of elective monarchy in the early Vedic period has been opposed by some competent Indologists, including Geldner,[7] on the ground that the passages cited are not indicative of choice by the cantons but of acceptance by the subjects.

The king's exchequer derived its revenue from the tribute of the conquered tribes as well as the gifts given by his people. The gifts of the people, known as *bali*,[8] which apparently consisted of agricultural produce and the stock of cattle, were at first voluntarily offered, but in the course of time, they developed into fixed payments, 'which the king could exact, if denied'.

In the *Ṛgveda*, we hardly come across a passage which alludes to the king's administration of justice. But it is not improbable that he, with the aid of assessors, exercised criminal and civil jurisdiction. Despite being the pivot in the realm of administration, the Ṛgvedic king could hardly wield his power unabated. Generally speaking, the state in those days was tribal in character and tiny in dimension, as was the case with the city states of ancient Greece, in consequence of which the leading men maintained a strict vigil upon his activities. The royal power was moreover checkmated by an assembly, called *Samiti*, which, if the view of A.S. Altekar[9] is accepted, 'consisted of the heads of the few military and aristocratic families which occupied a prominent position in the political and social life of the community'. A passage[10] in the *Ṛgveda* which refers to king Trasadasyu as a demi-god (*ardha-devatā*) seems to imply that the divinity of kingship was not altogether unknown. Since this is the solitary passage alluding to the divine character of the king, it appears that the doctrine of the deification of kingship was not widely approved in contemporary society.

II

The King in the Later Vedic Age

The age of the later Vedic *Saṁhitās*, the *Brāhmaṇas*, the *Āraṇyakas* and the *Upaniṣads* witnessed an appreciable growth of royal power and prestige. This was because, first, the state grew larger than the Ṛgvedic kingdom; second, the newly emerged warrior class became a tower of strength to the king; and third, the *Samiti*, which proved to be a healthy check upon royal authority in the earlier epoch, could hardly wield its power so effectively in this age.[11] Even then we hear of the expulsion of kings from their dominions. The Sṛñjaya king Duṣṭaṛtu Pauṁsāyana was deposed; Dīrghaśravas was banished and Sindhukṣit was exiled. In the later Vedic literature, we meet with terms which are indicative of different grades of kingly power. The view that the *Bhoja*, the *Rājan*, the *Svarāṭ*, etc., belonged to the different categories of kings in accordance with their military renown and the extent of their kingdom is not in agreement with a passage in the *Aitareya Brāhmaṇa* which states that the kings of the east were called *Samrāṭ*, those of the south were known as *Bhoja*, the monarchs of the Nicyas and the Apācyas were called *Svarāṭ*, the sovereigns of Uttara-Kuru and Uttara-Madra in the north were termed as *Virāṭ* and the suzerains of the central region were designated as *Rājan*. But the view that words like *samrāṭ*, *bhoja*, etc., have only a regional significance, as advocated in the above passage of the *Aitareya Brāhmaṇa*, is unfortunately contradicted by other evidence. The importance of kingly rank is emphasised by the performance by the king of sacrifices like the *Vājapeya*, the *Aśvamedha* and the *Rājasūya*.

At the time of his accession to the throne, the king is 'clad in the ceremonial garments of his rank, is formally anointed by the priest, steps on tiger-skin to attain the power of the tiger, takes part in a mimic cattle-raid, assumes the bow and arrow, and steps as a conqueror to each of the four quarters, an action paralleled in the coronation of the Hungarian king'.[12] The nature and form of coronation (*rājy=ābhiṣeka*) have raised a lot of controversy among scholars. P.B. Udgaonkar[13] maintains that coronation consisted of several rituals including *Rājasūya*, *Vājapeya* and *Sarvamedha.* Coronation, properly so called, means rites which 'are designed to endow the personage selected for the office of king with the attributes and power required for kingship'.[14] Judged in this context, *Rājasūya* and *Vājapeya*, which were undertaken to achieve universal dominion and kingship, respectively, were not parts of the ceremony of the installation of a king; nor did *Sarvamedha* form a part of it. K.V. Rangaswami Aiyangar[15] seems to be right when he observes, 'The ordinary ceremony of installation of the king was also a *rājasūya*, because the king was ceremonially 'born' of it, but the two must be distinguished. The sacrifice of *Rājasūya* took about two years to finish, and was therefore a *dīrgha-sattra.* The installation ceremony, on the other hand, lasted only some days.' The statement of the *Śatapatha Brāhmaṇa*[16] that 'to the king doubtless belongs *Rājasūya.* for by offering *Rājasūya* he becomes king' (*Rājña eva Rājasūyaṁ| Rājā vai Rājasūyen=eṣṭvā bhavati|*) does not go against this presumption, for the word *rājasūya* of the passage does not denote the great Vedic sacrifice of the same name but the consecration of the king.

The theory of the divinity of kingship became fairly popular in this age. King Parīkṣit is described in the *Atharva Veda*[17] as a 'god who is above mortals' (*yo devo martyām=adhi*) while a newly elected king is extolled in the same text[18] as an Indra in human form (*Indr=endra manuṣyāḥ*). The same feeling is echoed in the *Śatapatha Brāhmaṇa* wherein the king is represented as a visible symbol of god Prajāpati.

It is quite in conformity with the augmentation of the kingly power that his office should be hereditary. The *Śatapatha Brāhmaṇa*[19] mentions that the Sṛñjaya king Duṣṭaṛtu Pauṁsāyana inherited his kingdom through ten generations (*daśa-puruṣaṁ rājyaṁ*). That kingship was occasionally elective is vouchsafed by a passage in the *Atharva Veda*[20] which states that the people were sometimes empowered to elect their king (*tvāṁ viśo vṛṇatāṁ rājyāya*). If the opinion of R.N. Dandekar[21] be accepted, it was a smaller body, constituting what may be called the electoral college, and not the whole community, that elected the king.

Insofar as the functions of the king are concerned, there is hardly any evidence to show that these underwent any fundamental change in this age. He still led his men in war and took an active part in the administration of justice. There are references in the contemporary literature to show that he controlled the land of the tribe, but there is hardly any conclusive evidence in favour of the royal ownership of all the land in the kingdom. It is sometimes argued that land was a communal property throughout the Vedic period and that the concept of royal and private ownership of land was of much later origin.

III

The King in the Post-Vedic Period

For our knowledge in regard to the kingship in the post-Vedic period we may turn to the testimony of the Jātaka and Dharmasūtra literature, although admitting that the information, as is supplied by it, is far from being adequate. The *Jātakas* imply that the people sometimes jealously guarded their rights and privileges and revolted against the tyrannical rule of their king. The *Padakusalamānava Jātaka*,[22] for example, speaks of an unrighteous monarch who was dethroned by the people who later on selected a suitable Brāhmaṇa[23] as their king. The *Saccaṁkira Jātaka*[24] similarly states how a bad king was deposed and a Brāhmaṇa was placed on the throne.

In some of the *Jātakas*[25] we find the enumeration of the tenfold duty of the king (*dasa-rāja-dhamme*) which comprised munificence, a moral course of life, sacrifice, truthfulness, mildness, self-denial, forgiveness, nonviolence, forbearance and a yielding disposition. But these aforesaid qualities, as has been rightly pointed out by Fick, 'give us no idea of the essence of the kingly power, the obligations or functions of the *Rājan*, because they contain universal prescriptions of morals applicable to the whole Buddhist laity.'[26] It is worth noting that the Buddhist sources do not refer to the maintenance of castes which, according to the Brahmanical sources, constituted one of the fundamental duties of the king. This is what is exactly expected of the Buddhists who are most critical of the caste system.

Turning to the Dharmasūtra writers, we find Gautama[27] laying down that the king is the master of all, with the exception of the Brāhmaṇas. Āpastamba[28] similarly enjoins that the king rules over all the people, excepting the Brāhmaṇas. As regards the duty of the king, Gautama[29] observes: 'He shall protect the castes and orders in accordance with justice. And those who leave the path of duty, he shall lead back to it . . . His administration of justice shall be regulated by the *Veda*, the Institutes of the Sacred Law, the *Aṅgas* and the *Purāṇas*.' With this may be compared the following statement of Āpastamba: 'If any persons, other than Brāhmaṇas, transgress their orders, the king, after having examined their actions, may punish them even by death. But such Brāhmaṇas should be sent to the domestic priest for trial. Let him not live better than his *Gurus* or ministers. He should take care of the welfare of his subjects.'[30] Vasiṣṭha[31] also says an identical thing when he says, 'The particular duty of a king is to protect all beings; by fulfilling it, he obtains success in this world and in the next. Let the king pay attention to all the laws of countries, subdivisions of castes (*jāti*) and families and make the four castes (*varṇa*) fulfil their respective particular duties.'

It is evident from the discussion above that the Dharmasūtra writers are unanimous in upholding the preservation of the order of castes as the foremost duty of the king.[32] They further furnish us with useful information about the king's revenue. Gautama[33] refers to the king's levy of taxes. Vasiṣṭha[34] points out that the king should receive one-sixth of the crops. But more details on this issue are, however, provided by Baudhāyana[35] who says, 'Let the king protect his subjects, receiving as his pay a sixth part.' This may be taken as implying that the king was entitled to receive the sixth part of the produce of the people on the ground that he was charged with the duty of protecting the people. The view that taxes are the king's dues for the service of protection favourably compares with the fashionable doctrine, propounded in Europe in the seventeenth and eighteenth centuries that taxes are the fees paid for the services of the public authorities. The Brāhmaṇas, no doubt, were exempted from taxation but the king derived a sixth part of their spiritual merit. That the king had other sources of income is evidenced when Baudhāyana[36] further observes, 'the duty on goods imported by sea is, after deducting a choice article, ten *paṇas* in the hundred'. This statement has generally been taken to mean that[37] 'the king may take one article which particularly pleases him out of each consignment, and impose on the rest an *ad valorem* duty of ten per cent.' Baudhāyana[38] elsewhere remarks, 'Let him also levy just (duties) on other (marketable goods) according to their intrinsic value without oppressing the traders.' The commentator Govinda interprets the term *anupahatya* as meaning 'without deducting (*anudhṛtya*) a choice article'. It is thus clear from the testimony of Baudhāyana that the king was entitled to receive from the people the sixth part of the produce in addition to certain other taxes imposed on mercantile commodities.

IV

The King in the Maurya Period

It was in c. B.C. 324 that Candragupta[39] (c. B.C. 324-c. B.C. 300) founded the Maurya dynasty in Magadha by supplanting the Nandas. Both he and his illustrious grandson Aśoka (c. B.C. 272-c. B.C. 232) exercised their political suzerainty over the major part of India and Afghanistan. The former probably adopted the title *Devānāṁpriya*,[40] while the latter assumed the titles of *Devānāṁpriya*, *Pripadarśī* and *Rājā*. As known from the Junagadh inscription of Rudradāman, the title *Rājan* was also used by one of Aśoka's officers named Tuṣāspa, who appears to have enjoyed a certain amount of autonomy. The title *Devānāṁpriya*, which was continued by Daśaratha,[41] the grandson of Aśoka, etymologically denotes 'beloved of gods'. Pāṇini's aphorism *ṣaṣṭhyā ākrośe*[42] seems to imply that the word *devānāṁpriya* is abusive in meaning. Other writers including Bhaṭṭoji Dīkṣita, Rāmacandra and Kaiyaṭa have likewise used the word as meaning a fool (*Devānāṁpriya iti ca mūrkhe*). The Maurya rulers, however, appear to have used it as a complimentary title, comparable with *bhavān*, *āyuṣmān* and *dīrghāyuḥ*. The term Priyadarśī means 'one who glances amiably', 'one who looks on all as dear' and finally, 'one who looks after the welfare of all'.

The Maurya rulers, as suggested by the adoption of the title *Devānāṁpriya*, were averse to the doctrine of the divinity of kingship. Nevertheless, they did not lack in any imperial grandeur and dignity and were the supreme heads of the executive, judicial and military departments of administration. For efficient administration, they divided their kingdom into a number of provinces which were again subdivided into a number of smaller units. As has been revealed by the witness of the classical writers and the testimony of contemporary epigraphs, the Maurya kings were ever alert in the discharge of their duty and debt to the people. Megasthenes[43] points out that 'the king does not sleep in daytime but remains in the court the whole day for the purpose of judging cases and other public business which was not interrupted even when the hour arrived for massaging the body. Even when the king has his hair combed and dressed, he has no respite from public business. At that time he gives audience to his ambassadors.' The First Separate Rock Edict shows that the Mauryas, particularly Aśoka, were inspired by a lofty ideal of royal duties, for Aśoka declares in that edict, 'All men are my children. Just as I desire for my children that they may be associated with all kinds of welfare and happiness both in this world and in the next, so also I desire the same for all men'[44] (*Save munise pajā mamā| Athā pajāye ichāmi hakaṁ kiṁti savena hita-sukhena hida-lokika pāla-lokikāyekena yūjebuti, tathā munisesu pi ichāmi hakaṁ|*).

The *Arthaśāstra*,[45] which was probably composed by Kauṭilya under the patronage of Candragupta Maurya, throws welcome light on the royal office. There is hardly any indication in the *Arthaśāstra* which would suggest that its author regarded the king as divine, but that the king's power was extensive admits of no doubt. He presides over the executive, revenue and judicial departments of government and is expected to lead the army in the battle-field. Among the executive functions of the king Kauṭilya mentions the appointment of ministers and other important functionaries, consultation with the council of ministers, sending out of spies and attending to them, taking care of the learned Brāhmaṇas, the distressed, the helpless and women, reception of envoys, etc. The king is further the chief guiding factor in the formulation of foreign policy and the undertaking of military operations and programmes. As the head of the judicial department, he should not only organise the *Kaṇṭakaśodhana* and *Dharmasthīya* courts, but he sometimes personally decides cases as the highest court of appeal without unnecessary delay. He looks into the revenue and expenditure of the kingdom and is ever alert to increase the revenue by taking an active part in the furtherance of trade, agriculture and industries.

Referring to the sources of judicial laws, Kauṭilya[46] observes, 'A matter in dispute has four feet, law, transaction, custom and the royal edict; (among them) the latter one supersedes the earlier one. Of them the law is based on truth, a transaction, however, on witnesses, custom on the commonly held view of men, while the command of kings is the royal edict'[47] (*Dharmaś=ca vyavahāraś=ca caritraṁ rāja-śāsanaṁ/ vivād=ārthaś= catuṣpādaḥ paścimaḥ pūrva-bādhakaḥ// Tatra satye sthito dharmo vyavahāras=tu sākṣiṣu/ caritraṁ saṁgrahe puṁsāṁ rājñām= ājñā tu śāsanaṁ//*). Kauṭilya thus includes *Rāja-śāsana* among the sources of law and extols it as superior to the rest. Although we are far from being certain, discrepancy among the law books might have induced Kauṭilya to impose a stamp of inferiority on the authoritativeness of *Dharma* in judicial matters. Still under the Kauṭilīya system the king could seldom turn out to be an unbridled autocrat. He says, '(Carrying out) his own duty by the king, who protects the subjects according to law, leads to heaven; of one who does not protect or who inflicts an unjust punishment, (the condition) is the reverse of this'. Kauṭilya further enjoins the king to rule in accordance with *Dharma*, to accept and enforce the *Varṇāśrama* system, to show regard to the laws of communities, professions and guilds and to fix the rate of taxes in agreement with the customary law and usage of the communities and region. Kauṭilya emphasises that the paramount duty of the king lies in promoting the welfare of the people. 'In the happiness of his subjects,' says he, 'lies his happiness; in their welfare his welfare; whatever pleases him he shall not consider as good[48] but whatever pleases his subjects he shall consider as good' (*Prajā-sukhe sukhaṁ rājñaḥ prajānāṁ ca hite hitaṁ/ n=ātma-priyaṁ hitaṁ rājñaḥ prajānāṁ tu priyaṁ hitaṁ//*).

Kauṭilya further points out that the life of the king is not one of comfort and leisure but is crowded with packed programmes throughout the day and the night. The king should divide the day and the night each into eight parts by means of *nālikās* or by the measure of the shadow of the sun[49] (*Nālikā-bhir=ahar=aṣṭaahā rātriṁ ca vibhajet chāyā-pramāṇena vā*) and discharge during each of these parts the following assignments:

Day:

(i) Receiving reports about the measures taken for defence and accounts of income and expenditure[50] (*Tatra pūrve divasasy=āṣṭabhāge rakṣā-vidhānam=āya-vyayau ca śṛṇuyāt*/);

(ii) Looking into the affairs of the people of both the rural and urban areas;

(iii) Bath, meals and study;

(iv) Receiving revenue in cash and attending to the heads of departments;

(v) Holding consultations with the council of ministers and receiving secret information brought in by spies;

(vi) Recreation at his pleasure or deliberation on state affairs;

(vii) Inspection of elephants, horses, chariots and troops;

(viii) Discussion with the commander-in-chief about military plans.

Night:

(i) Interview with the secret agents;

(ii) Bath, meals and study;

(iii-v) Sleep;

(vi) Contemplation upon the teaching of the science of politics as well as the work to be done;

(vii) Consultation with the councillors and despatching of spies;

(viii) Receiving blessings from priests, preceptors and chaplain and seeing his physician, chief cook and astrologer.[51]

V

The King in the Post-Maurya Period

By about the middle of the third century B.C., the Bactrian kings began their rule. These kings generally adopted the title of *Basileos* but with the augmentation of their power, they assumed more dignified epithets. Eucratides, for instance, at the beginning of his reign, when his dominions probably did not include any part of India, assumed the title of *Basileos*, but later on he styled himself as *Basileos Megalou* (Prākṛt *Maharajasa*), probably in imitation of the Achaemenian kings of Iran who described themselves as great kings. Demetrius was originally called *Basileos* but in the course of time with the expansion of his conquests in India, he took the titles of *Basileos* and *Aniketou* in Greek, and *Maharajasa* and *Aparajitasa* in Prākṛt.

The claim of divine origin did not find favour with the majority of the Bactrian kings, for we do not come across any title on their coins which would indicate any such pretension on their part. It cannot escape notice that queen Agathocleia prided herself on being simply called *Theotropou*, 'god-like'. The case was, however, different with Antimachus who assumed the title *Theos*.

These kings sometimes followed the Seleucid practice of appointing the heir-apparent as joint-king. Thus Euthydemus II and after him Demetrius II ruled jointly with their father, Demetrius I; queen Agathocleia reigned conjointly with her son Strato I; and Strato I, in turn, was associated with his grandson, Strato II.[52] It is again interesting to note that the king occasionally allowed his younger son to rule a definite part of the kingdom as a sub-king with the right of coining in his own name. Antimachus served as a sub-king first under his father Euthydemus I and subsequently under his brother Demetrius I; Demetrius II, Pantaleon, Agathocles and Apollodotus were sub-kings under Demetrius I, and both Menander and Strato I are known to have had under them many sub-kings.[53]

The Śaka kings, who gradually eliminated Greek rule from the north-western part of India, adopted more dignified titles than those of their Indo-Greek predecessors. Maues, the earliest known Śaka king in India, at the beginning of his rule, adopted the usual Greek title *Basileos* or *Basileos Megalou*. When he succeeded in conquering Gandhāra from the Greeks, he styled himself as *Basileos Basileon Megalou* in imitation of the famous Parthian king Mithridates, ruling at Ctesiphon. This set of titles was adopted by Azes I, Azilises and Azes II on the obverse of their coins without any modification, but there is a slight variation of the corresponding Prākṛt equivalent on the reverse of their coins. Thus while for Maues the Prākṛt titles were *Rajatirajasa* and *Mahatasa*, for his successors those were *Maharajasa*, *Rajarajasa* and *Mahatasa*. The titles of the Parthian kings like Vonones, Spalirises, Orthagnes, Gondopharnes, Pacores, etc., were the same as those of Maues' successors.

The system of dual monarchy was popularised in India by the Scytho-Parthian rulers. Like the Seleucid kings of Western Asia, most of these rulers associated their heirs with them as joint kings; the name of the senior partner in Greek occupies the place of honour on the obverse of their coins and that of the junior in Prākṛt appears on the reverse. We may refer, for instance, to the joint issues of Azes I and Azilises which show the legend *Basileos Basileon Megalou Azou* on the obverse and *Maharajasa Rajarajasa Mahatasa Ayilisasa* on the reverse. The institution of joint kingship must have acted as a healthy check upon the power and authority of the king. Another check was provided by the Satraps who were charged with the administration of many of their Indian possessions, with full autonomy for all practical purposes.

VI

The Kuṣāṇa King

It was during the time of the Kuṣāṇa monarchs that an exalted conception of kingship was introduced in India. Kujula Kadphises (c. A.D. 25-c. A.D. 55) at first took the humble title of *Yavuga*[54] but later on used such imperial titles as *Mahārāja*, *Mahānta*, *Rajadiraja*,[55] etc. Wema Kadphises, who was destined to conquer the Indus region, assumed more high sounding titles like *Basileos*, *Basileon*, *Soter* and *Megas* in Greek, and *Maharajasa*, *Rajadirajasa*, *Sarvaloga Iśvarasa*, *Mahiśvarasa* and *Tradara* in Prākṛt. He is given in the Mathura inscription the epithets of *Devaputra* and *Ṣāhi*. Kaṇiṣka I (c. A.D. 78-A.D. 102) adopted the proud title of *Shaonano Shao*, probably based on old Persian *Khshāyathiyānām Khshāyathiya* on some of his coins and those of *Maharaja, Rajatiraja,* and *Ṣāhi* in others. Kaṇiṣka I's titles were continued by his successors like Vāsiṣka and Huviṣka, while Kaṇiṣka II of the Ara inscription used, in addition to the usual ones, the title of *Kaisara* which is evidently of Roman origin.

The above titles would unmistakably point out that the Kuṣāṇa kings had imbibed a lofty idea of the royal office. Notwithstanding their Buddhist affiliation in the generality of cases, they claimed deification, representing themselves as 'Sons of Heaven'. There has been a great deal of controversy on the significance of the term *Devaputra*, as used by the Kuṣāṇa kings. F.W. Thomas[56] and U.N. Ghosal[57] opine that it was not an official designation of the Kuṣāṇa kings but a complimentary epithet applied to them by their grateful subjects. This view does not appear to be tenable, because, first, *Devaputra* is mentioned along with other official designations in the Kuṣāṇa inscriptions; second, it is applied, along with other official titles, to the contemporary Kuṣāṇa king by the Gupta monarch Samudragupta; third, the Chinese sources often describe the Yueh-chi kings as 'Son of Heaven';[58] and last, the absence of the title on the Kuṣāṇa coins[59] may be ascribed to the lack of space but cannot be treated as a positive proof in favour of Thomas' contention. It is generally believed, though opposed by Thomas, that the title was derived from the Chinese *Tien-tie* or *Tien-tzu*. But it may be remembered that the two Parthian kings, Pharates II and Pharates III, who flourished in the first part of the first century A.D. and preceded the Kuṣāṇas, assumed the title of '*god-fathered*'. R.S. Sharma[60] observes in this connection, 'Apparently when Parthia had been conquered by the early Kuṣāṇas, the Parthian titles and dominions alike were appropriated by Kaṇiṣka and his successors.' It thus seems that the Kaṇiṣka group of kings borrowed this title from their Parthian predecessors, who, of course, might have been inspired to adopt this title after the practice of the Chinese emperors. But the Kuṣāṇa royal title *Devaputra*, which merely alludes to the divine parentage of the king but does not actually identify him with the god or gods, was not in accord with Indian tradition; as a result, it went out of use consequent upon its non-recognition by indigenous kings, subsequent or contemporary. The title *Shaonano Shao* appears to be of Śaka origin, as may be inferred from the fact that it is written on the Kuṣāṇa coins in pure Khotani Śaka language and, further, their Prākṛtised form *Ṣāhānuṣāhi* is ascribed to the Śakas by the author of the *Kālakācārya Kathānaka.*

The Kuṣāṇa kings' claim to divinity is manifest in their adherence to the practice of erecting *devakulas* in which the statues of their deceased predecessors were preserved and worshipped as those of gods.[61] Thus the repair of the dilapidated *devakula* of his grandfather at Mathura was undertaken during the reign of Huviṣka for the increase of his life and strength. It is held by some scholars that the Kuṣāṇas in this respect followed the Roman practice on the bank of the river Tiber. But the cult of the dead king was also prevalent in Mesopotamia and Egypt, 'where mortuary temples were built to enshrine the statues of the Pharaos. Probably the Romans derived this idea from these predecessors and passed it on to the Kuṣāṇas either through direct commercial contacts or through some intermediaries.'[62] The deification of kingship, as claimed by the Kuṣāṇa monarchs, is further borne out by the evidence of numismatics. 'On the gold pieces of Kadphises II the shoulders of the king are surrounded by luminous rays or flames, and his bust appears to issue from the clouds like the gods of Greece . . . Nimbus appears only on some pieces of Kanishka; on certain gold pieces of Huvishka the sovereign is at once ornamented with nimbus, flames and clouds . . . Vāsudeva had simply the nimbus round his head which is itself surmounted by a pointed tiara. This last type remained that of the Indo-Scythian Kushan kings called the later Kushans.'[63]

Notwithstanding their keen interest in the deification of the institution of kingship, the Kuṣāṇa kings appear to have encouraged the idea of the decentralisation of power. They governed their kingdom through subordinate rulers who enjoyed the status of Kṣatrapas and Mahākṣatrapas. The great Satrap Kharapallāna and Satrap Vanaspara governed the eastern part of Kaṇiṣka's empire as subordinate rulers. If Nahapāna's contemporaneity with the Kuṣāṇa rulers is to be accepted, it would follow that Nahapāna was a Satrap under them. He was virtually independent and issued coins in his own name. If it is conceded that the so-called 'Nameless King' of the copper coins was a subordinate chief, placed in charge of his Indian conquests by Wema Kadphises, we have to assume that these subordinate rulers were not only empowered to strike coins but they also assumed full imperial titles. There are some indications in favour of the belief that the practice of joint rule was popular with the Kuṣāṇa kings. If the suggestion of D.C. Sircar[64] be accepted, Vamatakṣama of the Mathura inscription and Vaskuṣāṇa of the Sanchi record were junior partners of Kaniṣka I. There seems to be little room for doubt that Huviṣka (years 28-60) actually ruled jointly with Vāsiṣka (years 24-28) and Vajhiṣka's son Kaṇiṣka (year 41). 'Just as the high-sounding titles of the Kuṣāṇa rulers,' writes R.S. Sharma,[65] 'indicated nothing more than the reality of decentralisation, so also the device of deification was nothing more than an attempt to conceal and remove their political weakness.' But the view that the weakening of the central government is the corollary of decentralisation appears to be far-fetched. The weakness or strength of a monarchical state was determined by the ability of the king, loyalty of the subordinates and efficacy of the administrative machinery. Power was delegated to the subordinates in order to maintain the effectiveness of administration in every nook and corner of the far-flung kingdom but not to preside over the liquidation of the state. There is no evidence to show that during the days of the early Kuṣāṇa kings the governors proved to be insubordinate and set up independent principalities at the expense of their masters.

VII

The Indigenous and Śaka Kings

While grandiloquent titles were being assumed by the foreign kings of India, indigenous rulers remained contented with the use of simpler epithets. Puṣyamitra, the founder of the Śuṅga dynasty, called himself a *Senāpati*, although he twice asserted his claim to paramount sovereignty by performing the *Aśvamedha* sacrifice. His successors were simply called *Rājan*. The Besnagar inscription of Heliodorus mentions the Indo-Greek king Antialkidas of Taxila as a *Mahārāja*, but it applies the designation of *Rājā* to the contemporary Indian monarch Bhāgabhadra of Vidiśā. Amoghabhūti, who founded a short-lived kingdom in the region around the Siwalik hills during the second half of the first century B.C., took the titles of *Rājā* and *Mahārāja*. The Audumbara kings were similarly called *Rājā*. One of their kings, Mahādeva, bore the unusual title of *Rājarāja*.[66]

The Śaka kings of Western India used the titles of *Kṣatrapa*, *Mahākṣatrapa* and *Rājā*. From the time of Nahapāna onwards, they began adopting the designation of *Svāmin*. The early Śaka kings followed the system of conjoint rule, according to which the king with the title of *Mahākṣatrapa* and his son or brother, in the capacity of a *Kṣatrapa*, jointly carried on the administration of the country. From c. A.D. 200 a peculiar mode of succession came to be established under which system the crown passed from the eldest brother to the younger ones in succession. When the youngest brother died after enjoying his turn to rule, he was generally succeeded by the surviving eldest son of the eldest brother. It is pointed out by some scholars that the Śaka kings were familiar with the practice of elective kingship. The statement on the Junagadh inscription that Rudradāman was appointed king to protect them by the people of all castes (*sarva-varṇair=abhigamya rakṣaṇ=ārthaṁ patitve vṛtena*) lends colour to such a hypothesis. But this statement does not appear to be true, for, it occurs in eulogistic document, composed by a panegyrist, and secondly, it is contradicted by the fact that the Junagadh inscription elsewhere refers to Rudradāman as earning the title of *Mahākṣatrapa* through his own prowess (*svayam=adhigata-Mahākṣatrapa-nāmnā*).

The writings of Manu throw light on the royal office during the early centuries of the Christian era. He maintains that one of the most important functions of the king is to uphold the observance of the respective duties of the four castes. Manu says that the king is the protector of the four castes and of the four *Āśramas* and he should see that the people are engaged in their own duties[67] (*Sve sve dharme niviṣṭānāṁ sarveṣām=anupūrvaśaḥ| varṇāṇām=āśramāṇāñ=ca rājā sṛṣṭ=obhirakṣitā*). Referring to the administration of justice, which is another important function of the king, Manu[68] says, 'Rightly considering the place, time, offenders' power and knowledge of the law of administration, the king should inflict, according to the *Śāstras*, punishment on persons, doing wrong' (*Taṁ deśakālau śaktiñ=ca vidyāñ=c=āvekṣya tattvataḥ| tath=ārhataḥ sampraṇa-*

yen=nareṣv=anyāyavartiṣu). Manu further points out that in return for his service to the people, the king should receive revenue from them. As the leeches, the calves and the bees suck their food little by little, similarly the king should realise from his kingdom the annual revenue little by little[69] (*Yath=ālp=ālpa-madanty=ādyaṁ vāryokovatsa-ṣaṭpādāḥ/ tath=ālp=ālpo grahītavyo rāṣṭrād=rājñ=āvdikaḥ karaḥ//*). He should take one-fiftieth part of the surplus cattle and gold; similarly, he must take the sixth, eighth or twelfth part of the paddy[70] (*Pañcāśad-bhāga ādeyo rājñā paśu hiraṇyayoḥ/ dhānyānām=aṣṭamo bhāgaḥ ṣaṣṭho dvādaśa eva vā//*). The king, though faced with a monetary crisis, should not impose taxes upon a Brāhmaṇa, versed in the *Vedas*; nor should a true Brāhmaṇa suffer from hunger in his kingdom.[71]

Manu declares that the king is divine being created by the Lord out of the particles from the bodies of Indra, Vāyu, Yama, Sun, Fire, Varuṇa, Moon and Kuvera[72] (*Indr=Ānila Yam=Ārkāṇām=Agneś=ca Varuṇasya ca/ Candra-vitteśayoś=c=aiva mātrā nirhṛtya śāśvatīḥ//*). Manu points out, 'Being a man the king should not be slighted though young; for he is some great god come in the form of a man'[73] (*Vāl=opi n=āvamantavyo manuṣya iti bhūmipaḥ/ mahatī devatā hy-eṣā nara-rūpeṇa tiṣṭhati//*). There is then a significant difference in the attitude of Manu and his predecessor Kauṭilya towards the king's divinity, both betraying the sentiment of two different epochs.

VIII

The Gupta King

The early Gupta kings like Śrīgupta and Ghaṭotkaca were simply called *Mahārāja*, but from the time of Candragupta I onwards, the higher title of *Mahārājādhirāja*,[74] evidently derived from the titles *Mahārāja* and *Rājātirāja*, as used in the Mathura inscriptions of Huviṣka and Vāsudeva, came to be applied to them. In some private records and coins, the Gupta emperors were sometimes described as *Mahārāja*[75] and *Rājā*, but there is no doubt that in the Gupta empire the official designations of a paramount ruler were *Paramabhaṭṭāraka* and *Mahārājādhirāja*, and the title of a subordinate king was *Mahārāja*. The Gupta rulers from the time of Candragupta II Vikramāditya generally described themselves as *Paramabhāgavata* which is indicative of their Vaiṣṇava affiliation. There is no consensus among scholars on the meaning of the term *paramadaivata*, which was also applied to them. H.C. Raychaudhuri[76] rightly interprets it as an imperial title meaning the supreme deity. The term *paramadaivata* has sometimes been taken as referring to an avowed adherent of Viṣṇu, but this explanation is probably untenable.[77] In the Allahabad pillar inscription, Samudragupta is described as a god dwelling on the earth (*Lokadhāma-deva*), the Incomparable Being (*Acintya-puruṣa*) and the equal of Kuvera, Varuṇa, Indra and Yama (*Dhanada-Varuṇ=Endr=Āntakasama*). The high-sounding epithets did not always imply increasing power, for a weak ruler like Narasiṁhagupta had assumed the title of the rising sun (*Bālāditya*). The doctrine of the divinity of the king, as claimed by the Gupta rulers, is corroborated by the evidence of contemporary literature. The *Viṣṇu* and the *Bhāgavata Purāṇas*, which were probably composed during the time of the Guptas, state that a number of gods reside in the person of the king[78] (*Brahmā Janārdano Rūdra Indro Vāyur=Yamo Riviḥ| Hṛtabhug=Aruṇo Dhātā pūṣā bhūmir =niśākaraḥ| Ete c=ānye ca ye devāḥ śāp=ānugrahakāriṇaḥ| nṛpasy=aite śarīrasthāḥ sarva-devamayo nṛpaḥ*). The contemporary Sanskrit work *Mudrārākṣasa*[79] declares the king as an image of god Viṣṇu, whereas its commentator Ḍhuṇḍirāja[80] quotes an anonymous *Smṛti* text to the effect that the king is a human incarnation of Viṣṇu. It may be mentioned in this connection that Sanskrit dramatists time and again have used the word *deva* as a synonym for king. 'But the divine origin,' writes T.V. Mahalingam,[81] 'claimed for monarchy in India is not in any way analogous to the divine right claimed by the early Stuarts in England. The British sovereigns of the early seventeenth century claimed divine origin for their power to support their absolutism. But the Hindu theory was propounded not as a claim for absolutism or autocracy. The view was that the king was an incarnation of God on earth for the support of the people by ruling over them righteously.'

The succession was hereditary, the crown being usually passed on to the eldest son. Occasions were not rare when a junior son was selected by the father to succeed him when he was considered the best among his brothers to occupy the privileged position.

This was most probably the case with Candragupta II, as may be guessed from the epithet *tatparigṛhīta* (accepted as his successor), applied to him in the genealogical passages of the Gupta inscriptions. A clear indication of the custom of the selection of the king by the predecessor is afforded by the Allahabad pillar inscription which shows how Candragupta I selected Samudragupta from among his several sons to succeed him on the throne. V.R. Ramachandra Dikshitar[82] is of opinion that under the Guptas the nomination of the successor to the throne by the predecessor was never considered final till it was legally approved by the court and the people. Rāmagupta, he argues, succeeded Samudragupta as the candidature of Candragupta II, though supported by his father, was not finally ratified by the court and the public. But there is no cogent evidence in support of the contention of Dikshitar.

The Gupta kings, as usual, were the centres of all military, political, administrative and judicial powers. They governed their kingdom with the help of ministers and officers of different ranks, but the ultimate responsibility rested with them. They were often their own commanders-in-chief, personally spearheading important military engagements. Indian tradition, however, asserts that the real object of the king is to win the heart of the people by impartial discharge of his duty. He is father to the poor and helpless and a terror to miscreants. The Gupta, nay, Indian ideal of kingship has been remarkably reflected in the writings of the great poet Kālidāsa, who lays down that the king is so called for he pleases his subjects (*Rājā prakṛti-rañjanāt*). As a father affectionately looks after his children, the king should likewise protect his subjects (*Prajāḥ prajānātha pit=eva pāsi*).

The writings of Kālidāsa enlighten us on many aspects of kingship. The kings are painted in his works as being well-tutored in arts and sciences, including the science of warfare and political strategy. Their prime duty was to maintain the established order of social life with the utmost care. The people were required to pay to the king one-sixth of their cumulative income (*ṣaṣṭh=āṁśa-vṛtti*). The *Abhijñānaśakuntalam*[83] discloses that even ascetics were to make over to the king one-sixth of their corn, in addition to the usual contribution in the shape of religious merit. But the taxes, thus collected, were to be distributed for the good of the people, 'just as the sun by his rays draws up to the skies the water of the ocean only for the purpose of pouring it down a thousand times for the fructification of the earth'.[84] Needless to emphasise that only a few kings could have reached the lofty ideal of kingship, outlined in Kālidāsa's works, in their personal rule.

IX

The King in the Post-Gupta Period

Among the dynasties of the period, following the downfall the Imperial Guptas, mention may be made of the Maukharis, the Later Guptas and the Puṣyabhūtis. The Maukharis and the Later Guptas began with the modest title of *Mahārāja* but subsequently assumed the imperial title of *Mahārājādhirāja.* The records of these ruling houses offer us scanty notices of the king's functions[85] but he was undoubtedly the live-wire of the civil and military administration.

The first three kings of the Puṣyabhūti dynasty assumed the simple title of *Mahārāja*, but it was Prabhākaravardhana who was the first king to call himself *Paramabhaṭṭāraka* and *Mahārājādhirāja.* The same titles were also applied to Rājyavardhana and, with more justification, to Harṣa.[86] Harṣa's ideal of kingship and the benevolence of his rule are remarkably brought out by Hiuen Tsang[87] in the following words, 'He (Harsha) was just in his administration and punctilious in the discharge of his duties. He forgot sleep and food in his devotion to good works . . . The king's day was divided into three periods of which one was given up to affairs of state and two were devoted to religious works. He was indefatigable and the day was too short for him.' The Chinese pilgrim states that in order to ensure good government in the kingdom, Harṣa made tours of inspection throughout his dominions during the three months of the rainy season. But Hiuen Tsang's account would make it abundantly clear that with all his vigilance, Harṣa was not destined to bring about such peace and security as had been accomplished by the Imperial Guptas centuries earlier. We are told by the Chinese pilgrim[88] that the Puṣyabhūti king performed a great ceremony every five years at Prayāga on which occasion he distributed in one day the accumulated wealth of five years. This shows that, first, the royal treasury was often misused as a private property of the ruling authority, and second, the king was not possessed of the political wisdom that the treasury was not a charitable dispensary but would be kept ever replenished to combat any financial crisis, imperilling the security of the state.

It may be mentioned that Bāṇa does not believe in the divinity of the king, which, according to him, is an invention of unscrupulous flatterers who surround the monarch. In ridiculing the king's claims to divinity, Bāṇa[89] says, 'Though subject to mortal conditions, they look on themselves as having alighted on earth as divine beings with a superhuman destiny; they employ a pomp in their undertakings only fit for gods and win the contempt of all mankind. They welcome this deception of themselves by their followers. From the delusion as to their own divinity established in their minds, they are overthrown by false ideas, and they think their own pair of arms have received another pair;[90] they imagine their forehead has a third eye buried in the skin.'[91] Bāṇa's dislike for the divinity of the king may reasonably be ascribed to his detestable attitude to some of the monarchs of his time like Pulakeśin II and Śaśāṅka.

X

The Pratīhāra and Pāla Kings

The Pratīhāras came into prominence of Indian history from about the second quarter of the eighth century A.D. Whereas, in the records of their feudatories they are given the titles of *Paramabhaṭṭāraka*, *Mahārājādhirāja* and *Parameśvara*, the Pratīhāra kings chose to be called *Rājā* or *Mahārāja* in their own inscriptions. The attention of the Pratīhāra kings was probably 'not so much on their political achievements as on their cultural aspirations and fight for the preservation of Indian freedom'.[92] Bhoja I of this family, and, his grandson Vināyakapāla, to judge from their Ādivarāha coins, describing them as *Śrīmad=Ādivarāha*, adopted the title of *Ādivarāha* which was indicative of a 'certain missionary zeal that they had the power and capacity to save the country from the raids of the *Mleccha* hordes'. The epithet *Ādivarāha*, as assumed by these Pratīhāra monarchs, is a further proof of their claim to divinity, which is also corroborated by the Gwalior inscription where two of their predecessors, Nāgabhaṭa I and Nāgabhaṭa II, are represented as incarnations of the god Nārāyaṇa. The usual titles of the Pāla kings, who ruled almost contemporaneously with the Pratīhāras, were *Parameśvara*, *Paramabhaṭṭāraka* and *Mahārājādhirāja*. It may be noted that the order of the three designations in the compound *Parameśvara-Paramabhaṭṭāraka-Mahārājādhirāja* is differently arranged in the Pratīhāra and Pāla records. In the records of the Pratīhāras, *Paramabhaṭṭāraka* comes first in the compound, while in the Pāla inscriptions we find the term *Parameśvara* at the beginning.

The office of the king remained practically the same in principle and practice in both the Pratīhāra and Pāla kingdoms. Kingship continued to be hereditary, although there is a reference in a contemporary document to a king's election to the royal office. Gopāla, the founder of the Pāla dynasty, is described in the Khalimpur inscription[93] as being appointed their king by the Prakṛtis, who have been differently identified with the people, ministers or high officials. It is sometimes held that the people did not elect Gopāla but they enthusiastically welcomed his rule which had put an end to the state of lawlessness in Bengal.[94]

The king was at the head of all the executive, judicial and military functions of the state, enjoying the sole right to dismiss any officer and appoint any person to any post he liked. The records of our period usually describe the kings as possessing many qualities of head and heart, prescribed, as would be shown later, by the *Nīti*-works. The Pratīhāra kings are eulogised in their records as being endowed with bravery, valour and modesty. King Kakka was the master of prosody, grammar, logic and astronomy. He was also a store of arts and had the ability to compose poetry in many languages.[95] The Pāla king Vigrahapāla III was acquainted with fine arts.

Now, as one turns to contemporary literary evidence, one meets with abundant material on the institution of kingship in the *Nītivākyāmṛta*, composed by the Jaina author, Somadeva Sūri. Somadeva identifies the king with the Brahmanical trinity, Brahmā, Nārāyaṇa and Śiva, and states that there is no other visible god than the king himself who is a supreme deity (*Rājā hi paramaṁ daivataṁ*). As regards the king's functions, he lays down that the protection of his subjects is the king's sacrifice (*prajā-pālanaṁ hi rājño yajñaḥ*), and he is not a king who does not protect his people (*sa kiṁ rājā yo na rakṣati prajāḥ*). The dangers against which protection has to be provided have been identified as thieves, exiled Kṣatriyas, those who use weights and measures, those who fix the price of commodities, royal favourites, foresters, frontier-guards, officers in charge of gambling, officers of the state, headmen of villages and hoarders of grain. The king is further called upon to see that the *Varṇ=āśrama* rules are observed by the people and the prescribed code of conduct is not violated. That kingdom is best, he says, where there is strict adherence to the *Varṇ=āśrama-dharma* and where the mixed caste is conspicuous by its absence.

The *Agni Purāṇa*[96] of about the same period tells us that the welfare of the people is more important to the king than the performance of sacrifices and penance. It[97] further states that the king is like the Sun because of his prowess, like the Moon on account of giving pleasure to the people, like Vāyu because of pervading the whole world through his spies, like Yama as he brings offenders to book, like Fire for the reason that he burns people having propensities, like Kubera on account of the gifts he gives away to the Brāhmaṇas, like Varuṇa as he showers money, like Pṛthvī because of his patience and forgiveness and like Hari on account of the protection he renders to the people by means of the threefold energies. The author of these passages of the *Agni Purāṇa* then does not accept the divinity of the king in a literal sense but postulates the functional resemblance between the king and some deities. In this respect his attitude is quite different from that of Manu who regards the king as divine, being created by the particles of different gods.

The duties[98] to be performed by the king daily (*prātyahika-karma*) are enumerated in the following order:

(i) Rising two *n uhūrtas* before sunrise;
(ii) Audience with spies;
(iii) Hearing the report on income and expenditure;
(iv) Worship of god and making suitable gifts to the Brāhmaṇas;

(v) Wearing dresses and ornaments and seeing auspicious things;
(vi) Consultation with the astrologer and the physician and receiving blessings of his elders and superiors;
(vii) Attending his court and receiving the Brāhmaṇas, high officers, ministers and the people;
(viii) Hearing daily reports of works and determining the routine of business for the day;
(ix) Adjudication of law-suits;
(x) Consultation with ministers;
(xi) Gymnastics and physical exercises;
(xii) Mid-day bath, visit to temples, etc.;
(xiii) Meal and rest;
(xiv) Study of religious scriptures;
(xv) Inspection of treasury, army, armoury and stores;
(xvi) Evening prayer;
(xvii) Deputing spies to various assignments; and
(xviii) Supper and sleep amidst songs and music.

A comparison of the daily routine, prescribed by the *Agni Purāṇa*, with the time-table, enumerated in the *Arthaśāstra* would show that the former account is primarily based on the latter, although a few minor points of disagreement between the two cannot escape notice. Thus, whereas, according to the *Agni Purāṇa* the king is expected to consult the astrologer and the physician during the day, Kauṭilya urges the king to do the same at night. Again, the *Agni Purāṇa* does not emphasise the importance of the king's consultation with the commander-in-chief, as we find in the *Arthaśāstra*. The *Agni Purāṇa*, further, does not divide the day and night into various parts for performing different duties, as is done by Kauṭilya. Furthermore, while the *Agni Purāṇa* advises the king to rise only two *muhūrtas* before sunrise, Kauṭilya expects him to get up a little earlier.

XI

The King of the Post-Pratīhāra Period

The decline and fall of the Imperial Pratīhāras of Kanauj led to the rise of new powers in different parts of Northern

India like the Kalacuris[99] of Cedi, the Candellas of Jejākabhukti, the Paramāras of Malwa and the Caulukyas of Gujarat. In Eastern India the Pālas were succeeded by the Senas. The Kalacuris assumed the usual imperial titles of *Parameśvara*, *Paramabhaṭṭāraka* and *Mahārājādhirāja*. Karṇa, Yaśaḥkarṇa and Jayasiṁha of this family added to these titles the epithets *Aśvapati*, *Gajapati*, *Narapati* and *Rājatray=ādhipati*. The Candellas, likewise, used the conventional imperial titles. Some of their kings bore the well-known Kalacuri titles of *Paramamāheśvara*, *Śrīmad=Vāmadevapād=ānudhyāta*, *Trikaliṅg=ādhipati*, *Aśvapati*, *Gajapati*, *Narapati* and *Rājatray=ādhipati*. The Paramāras also adopted the usual imperial titles. The early Gāhaḍavāla kings assumed the usual imperial titles of *Paramabhaṭṭāraka*, *Mahārājādhirāja* and *Parameśvara*. But Govindacandra adopted the additional epithets of *Aśvapati*, *Gajapati*, *Narapati* and *Rājatray=ādhipati*, which were continued by his successors. The Caulukya kings, besides being assigned the usual royal titles, are sometimes called *Laṅkeśvara-Nārāyaṇ=āvatāra* or *Abhinava-Siddharājadeva-Bāla-Nārāyaṇ=āvatāra* which would envisage an honoured position for them, being looked upon as human incarnations of Viṣṇu, as was the case with the Pratīhāra kings. The Sena kings used the usual titles from the time of Vijayasena, but the later scions of this family adopted the additional titles of *Aśvapati*, *Gajapati* and *Narapati*. The commonplace expression *Parameśvara-Paramabhaṭṭāraka-Mahārājādhirāja* or *Paramabhaṭṭāraka-Mahārājādhirāja-Parameśvara* was often condensed in the East Indian medieval records to *Parameśvar=ety=ādi-rāj=āvalī-pūrvavat* or *Paramabhaṭṭārak=ety=ādi-rāj=āvalī-pūrvavat.*[100]

There has been no unanimity among Indologists regarding the interpretation of the terms, *aśvapati*, *gajapati* and *narapati*. Rapson[101] is inclined to regard them as one title, meaning 'overlord of the three *rājās*, the lord of horses, the lord of elephants, the lord of men', and points out that the assumption of this title by a king indicates his possession of the Allahabad region, the region of the once-famous kingdom of Kauśāmbī. This is hardly tenable for the simple reason that these titles were sometimes adopted by kings of other regions. Some scholars are of opinion that *Narapati* was the title assumed by the kings of Telangana and Karnata and *Gajapati* was the one assumed by the kings of Kaliṅga, but it is not likely that all the bearers of these titles were in possession of Telangana and Orissa. It is reasonable to accept the expressions *aśvapati*, *narapati* and *gajapati* in the sense of kings, strong in cavalry, infantry and elephantry, respectively.

In this period, as in the earlier days, primogeniture was the normal form of succession of the throne. 'The crown therefore usually passed from the father to the eldest son, who was installed to the office of the heir-apparent, when he had come of age and finished his education and training. That the heir-apparent was selected during the life-time of the ruling king is evident not only from the epigraphical evidence but also from the accounts of foreign travellers.'[102] This is in consonance with the injunction of the *Nīti*-writers that an heir-apparent should be selected in the life-time of the ruling king. But the eldest son was denied the crown if he suffered from any physical or mental shortcoming. If the king had no son, the crown usually passed to his younger brother. The Candella king Devavarman, being childless, appointed his younger brother Kīrtivarman as heir to the throne;[103] the Cedi Lakṣmaṇarāja, who left no issue, was succeeded by his younger brother Yuvarāja II;[104] the Cedi Narasiṁha, who had no issue, was followed on the throne by his younger brother Jayasiṁha; the Paramāra rulers Lakṣmadeva and Jaitugi were succeeded by their younger brothers Naravarman and Jayavarman II,[105] respectively; the Cāhamāna Vigraharāja was succeeded by his younger brother Durlabharāja[106] and Jājalla by his younger brother Āśarāja[107] or Aśvarāja. In the absence of a son or a brother, an uncle was sometimes selected for the throne, as was the case with Pṛthvīvarmadeva who succeeded his nephew, the Candella king Jayavarmadeva who died without leaving any issue.[108]

The contemporary inscriptional records afford us interesting glimpses into the qualities of royal personages, although their reliability in most cases stands uncorroborated. Many Gāhaḍavāla kings are known to have assumed the title *vividha-vidyā-vicāra-vācaspati*, 'sound scholar engaged in pondering over the different branches of learning', which is indicative of their scholarship or patronage of learning. The Ratanpur inscription[109] of the Cedi king Jājalladeva dated A.D. 1114 informs us how king Pṛthvīdeva was endowed with nobility, bravery and depth. The Khajuraho inscription[110] states that Harṣa combined in himself eloquence, statesmanship, heroism, ambition, modesty and self-confidence. The Candella king Sallakṣaṇavarman is described as 'a master of the sacred lore, a kinsman of the virtuous, a store of arts and an abode of good conduct.'[111] Intelligence, bravery, religiousness, truthfulness and gratitude were the qualities that characterised the Candella king Devavarman, 'who had full control over *all his* senses.'[112] King Jayavarmadeva of this family possessed generosity, truthfulness, statesmanship and heroism.[113] The Paramāra king Bhoja[114] was a great poet, being described in the Udayapur record as a prince among poets.

Kings normally used to occupy the throne till their death but there were occasions when they abdicated the throne in favour of their sons, probably either under the influence of *Vānaprastha* and *Sannyāsa* or due to infirmity or disease. The *Prabhāvakacarita*[115] informs us that king Āma, a son of Yaśovarman of Kanauj of the earlier period, abdicated the throne in favour of his son Duṇḍuha and spent his life in religious devotions. The Jodhpur inscription[116] of Bauka tells us how Bhillāditya entrusted the reins of government to his son and went to the river Ganges where he lived as an ascetic for eighteen years. Jāṭa,[117] a member of the family of Pratīhāra Bauka, likewise, retired to the pious hermitage of Māṇḍyava to practise penance after entrusting the administration to his younger brother Bhoja. The Pāla king Vigrahapāla[118] entrusted the reins of government to his son Nārāyaṇapāla and became an ascetic. The Kalanjar inscription[119] informs us that the Candella king Jayavarman, being wearied of the administrative burden, handed over the government to Pṛthvīvarman and went to the Ganges. The Cedi king Lakṣmīkarṇa[120] probably abdicated the throne in favour of his son. The *Dvyāśraya Kāvya*[121] states that the Caulukya king Durlabharāja abdicated the throne in favour of his nephew Bhīma who likewise abdicated the throne to be succeeded on the throne by his son Karṇa. The *Hammīra-mahākāvya*[122] also states that Jaitrasiṁha handed over the administration to his son Hammīra and himself went to the forest. In commenting on the cases of abdication on the part of kings, P.B. Udgaonkar[123] observes, 'All this evidence clearly indicates that some of the pious rulers of our period actually followed the teachings of Hinduism and Jainism which lay down that a person should retire from life at the advent of old age in order to realise the spiritual ideal of human life. In the earlier periods, such instances are relatively few. This may perhaps indicate that the ideal of renunciation was becoming more popular in Hinduism in our period.'

The *Śukranīti** constitutes a store-house of materials about the king of this period, although it is sometimes held to be a work of a much later period. Śukra regards the king of divine. 'The king is made,' says he,[124] 'out of the permanent elements of Indra, Vāyu, Yama, Sun, Fire, Varuṇa, Moon and Kuvera and is the lord of both the immovable and movable worlds.' He reminds the king of his eightfold function which consists of punishment of the wicked, charity, protection of the subjects, performance of Rājasūya and other sacrifices, equitable realisation of revenue, conversion of princes into tributary chiefs, quelling of enemies and extraction of wealth from land.[125] While administering justice 'the king should attentively look after law-suits (*Vyavahāras*) by freeing himself from anger and greed according to the dictates of *Dharma Śāstras*, in the company of the Chief Justice, *Amātya*, Brāhmaṇa and Priest.'[126] He is enjoined to 'perform his duty by carefully studying the customs that are followed in countries and that are mentioned in the *Śāstras*, as well as those that are practised by castes, villages, corporations, and families.'[127] Śukra[128] lays down that the king should realise funds by any means in order to maintain the commonwealth, the army as well as sacrifices. The collection of revenue is not meant for wives and children, nor for the self-enjoyment of the king himself but is for the maintenance of the army and the subjects and the observance of sacrifices. Śukra[129] observes, 'The best king is he who, by following the

*Whereas Pradhan (*Modern Review*, 1916, February) and K.P. Jayaswal (ibid) have placed the work in the fourth and eighth centuries A.D. respectively, U.N. Ghosal (*A History of Indian Political Ideas*, p. 249), P.B. Udgaonkar (*The Political Institutions and Administration*, pp. 3-12) and Rajendralal Mitter (*The Positive Background of Hindu Sociology*, p. 64) have respectively assigned it to A.D. 1200-A.D. 1625, A.D 800-A.D. 1200 and the sixteenth century. R.C. Majumdar (*Ancient India*, p. 442) is inclined to attribute the text to the latest phase of the early period, although Lallanji Gopal (*BSOAS*, 1962, XXV, pt. iii) is of opinion that the work was compiled in the first half of the nineteenth century.

practice of the weaver of garlands, protects his subjects, makes the enemies tributaries and increases the treasure by their wealth. The middling king is he who does this by following the practice of the Vaiśya. And the worst by service and receipts from fines, holy places and lands consecrated by gods.'

XII

Checks on Royal Despotism

It cannot escape notice that by the early medieval period the Indian king, though still looked upon as the supreme head of his dominions, stood, in respect of both grandeur and power, in sad contrast with his predecessors. Since the post-Gupta days there had been developing in India an elaborate feudal system that contributed, in no small measure, to the general weakening of the central authority. Titles like *Mahāmaṇḍaleś-vara*, *Mahāmaṇḍalādhipati*, *Māṇḍalika*, *Sāmanta*, *Rāṇaka*, *Rāuta*, *Ṭhakkura*, etc., denoting feudal lords, occur time and again in literary documents and epigraphic records. The kingdom was transformed into a conglomeration of feudal estates and the king was hardly destined to exercise an effective control over these potentates who wielded their authority almost like an independent sovereign within their respective jurisdiction. The royal power was further on the wane in consequence of the king's dependence, in most cases, on the military service of his vassals. The Indian king of this period had seldom any standing army, and on the outbreak of a war or emergency, he used to summon his subordinate chiefs to come forward with their armed forces to join hands with him. He was often helpless in the face of an external aggression or any other serious danger, and even when he secured timely and adequate assistance from his feudatories, his army, which was composed of heterogeneous elements, was incapable of being welded into a composite whole. In the circumstances he was not emboldened to assume the character of an unbridled monarch of all he surveyed.

There were also other factors which were likely to check the arbitrary powers of the king to a considerable extent. Hindu political writers have popularised the idea that the king was not above *Dharma* which comprised *deśa-dharma* (local customs), *jāti-dharma* (caste rules), *kula-dharma* (family traditions) and *śreṇi-dharma* (guild regulations) but was to act according to its dictates. Moreover, he is urged to act at every step in consonance with the advice of his ministers,[130] preceptors and Brāhmaṇas. Furthermore, public opinion, which found its expression through local non-official councils that effectively supervised and controlled the district, town and village administrations, likewise served as a check on royal power. Even then there were in ancient India, as in all other parts of the world, some tyrants who oppressed the subjects and ruled arbitrarily, although their percentage to good and benevolent rulers cannot be ascertained.

But what could the people do in the event of despotism on the part of their kings? The *Śāntiparvan*[131] says, 'That king who disregards righteousness and desires to act with brute force soon falls away from righteousness and loses both righteousness and profit. That king who acts according to the counsels of a vicious and sinful minister becomes a destroyer of righteousness and deserves to be slain by his subjects with all his family.' With this may be compared Kauṭilya's[132] statement to the effect that 'When a people are impoverished, they become greedy, when they are greedy, they become disaffected, when disaffected, they voluntarily go to the side of the enemy or destroy their own master.' Śukra[133] lays down that 'the monarch who follows his own will is the cause of miseries, soon gets estranged from his kingdom and alienated from his subjects.' These and other warnings to kings about the possible consequences of misrule occur quite frequently in ancient Indian literature. Do these extracts prove that a theory of the moral justification of revolt against a bad king was developed in ancient India?[134]

XIII

The Śātavāhana King

When we turn to South India, we find that the Śātavāhana kings, notwithstanding their grand victories and possession of an extensive kingdom, generally called themselves *Rājan*[135] and sometimes also *Svāmin*,[136] probably emulating the Śaka kings of Western India. Gautamī Balaśrī, the mother of Gautamīputra Śātakarṇi and grandmother of Vāsiṣṭhīputra Pulumāyi, is described in a Nasik inscription as *Mahārāja-mātā* and *Mahā-*

rāja-pitāmahī. This shows that the title *Mahārāja*[137] was also sometimes adopted by the Śātavāhana kings. Some of these kings, including Gautamīputra Śātakarṇi and his son Vāsiṣṭhīputra Pulumāyi, are known to have borne metronymics along with their personal names. Although various suggestions have been advanced on this issue, it seems that these kings used metronymics in order to 'distinguish themselves from their predecessors bearing their name as well as from their numerous step-brothers.'[138] Succession was usually in the male line. During the minority of the crown prince, either the queen-mother or the brother of the deceased king normally governed the kingdom. It is held that both the Śātavāhanas and the Mahāmeghavāhanas of Kaliṅga followed the practice of conjoint rule by the ruling chief and his heir, but there is no positive evidence in support of this contention.

The early kings of the Śātavāhana dynasty were staunch followers of the Vedic religion. The Nanaghat inscription[139] refers to the performance of a number of sacrifices by Śātakarṇi I and to his gifts of cows, elephants and money to the Brāhmaṇas, proving thereby 'the great hold which the Vedic rituals had on their courts and entourage.'[140] The second Nasik cave inscription gives us an insight into the ideal of kingship as visualised by the Śātavāhana monarchs. It states that Gautamīputra Śātakarṇi 'properly devised time and place for the pursuit of the *Tivaga* (i.e., *Trivarga*), and sympathised fully with the weal and woe of the citizens.'[141] This is in complete agreement with Kauṭilya's recommendation that the king may 'enjoy in equal degree the three pursuits of life—*dharma, artha*, and *kama*—which are interdependent upon one another.'[142] Another inscription from Nasik reveals how Gautamīputra succeeded in arresting the forces that jeopardised the caste system.

XIV
Kingship in the Kural

Interesting details about the various aspects of the institution of kingship are preserved in the *Kural.* Unlike most of the early Indian political thinkers, the author Tiruvalluvar does not believe in the divine origin of kingship but points out that the king becomes divine with the impartial administration of justice and protection of his subjects.[143] The *Kural* makes the king the most important of the seven elements of sovereignty and considers the rest to be subordinate to him. The importance of the royal office has not been unduly emphasised, because the king was the main pivot of administration and the strength and durability of the government very much depended on his personality. We have spoken of many necessary qualities of the king like diligence, valour, learning, courage, alertness, virtue, righteousness, gracefulness, liberality and impartiality. He is enjoined to be accessible to all his subjects and never to be harsh of word.[144] He is to develop the resources of his kingdom by the utilisation of natural resources and production, enrich his treasury and properly distribute his wealth.[145] Before any action is taken, the king has to size up the situation by weighing the magnitude of the action, his own strength and the strength of both the enemy and his allies.[146] In assigning duties to different individuals, 'the right man for the right job should be selected and left alone to do his duty and in making the selection there should be no favour or partiality.'[147]

XV

The King in the Pre-Cālukya Period

Pravarasena I, the greatest of the Vākāṭaka king of the Deccan and a part of Central India, assumed the title of *Samrāṭ*, while his successors reverted to the simple title of *Mahārāja*. The reason that led to the change of the title from *Samrāṭ* to *Mahārāja* is not far to seek. If the evidence of the *Śatapatha Brāhmaṇa*[148] that the performance of *Vājapeya* entitles its performer to the title of *Samrāṭ* (*samrāṭ-sava*) is accepted, it would follow that Pravarasena I was called *Samrāṭ* on account of his performance of the *Vājapeya* sacrifice, and since none of his successors was credited with it, they, being orthodox Brāhmaṇas, were content with the title of *Mahārāja*. Pravarasena I was further called *Dharma-Mahārāja* which was justified by his performance of many sacrifices, including *Aśvamedha*. The kings of this family were particularly proud of their right of hereditary descent, as is illustrated by the statement that their royalty was obtained in course of succession, appearing in their seals. They, at least on one occasion, followed the practice of dividing the kingdom among the royal princes, in order to avoid a civil war. This probably happened after the death of Pravarasena I when his kingdom was partitioned among his four sons.

The kings of the Bṛhatphalāyana, Śālaṅkāyana and Viṣṇukuṇḍin dynasties indifferently used the titles *Rājā* and *Mahārāja.* The Viṣṇukuṇḍin king Mādhavavarman I performed eleven *Aśvamedha* sacrifices and flourished at a time when the title of *Mahārājādhirāja* was popular with the kings of Northern India. Still he was content with the modest title of *Mahārāja.* Some of the Śālaṅkāyana kings, like the Kadamba rulers of a slightly later period, claimed themselves to be the fifth Lokapāla, the divine protector.[149] In the Hidahadagalli grant, the Pallava king Śivaskandavarman is called *Dharma-Mahārāja*, while his unnamed father is mentioned therein as *Mahārāja bappa-svāmin* (i.e., *Mahārāja*. the father, the lord). The title *Dharma-Mahārāja* is sometimes taken to mean 'a *Mahārāja* who at the time of issue of the record, was engaged in an act of religion or merit'. Fleet[150] understands it to mean 'a *Mahārāja* by or in respect of religion', 'a pious or righteous *Mahārāja*'. C.R. Krishnamacharlu[151] supports the view that the successors of the Aśokan *Dharma-Mahāmātras* assumed the title of *Dharma-Mahārāja* and *Dharma-Mahārājādhirāja* after they had asserted their independence, but there is no sufficient evidence in support of this suggestion. The opinion of Fleet may be provisionally accepted at present. It is interesting to note that this title occurs in the Pallava grants only in connection with the names of the ruling kings. The Kadambas derived this title from the early Pallavas, but in their inscriptions this title is applied to both deceased and reigning monarchs. Kaṅgavarman, the greatest ruler of the house, assumed the title of *Dharma-Mahārājādhirāja.* Cases of division of kingdom in order to accommodate the claims of the rival groups are few and far between in the history of the Kadamba dynasty, and only one such case is recorded. When Kākutsthavarman died, his kingdom was divided between his two sons, Śāntivarman and Kṛṣṇavarman.[152]

The early kings of the Eastern Gaṅga family of Kaliṅga assumed the title of *Mahārāja* and very rarely the title of *Tri-Kaliṅgādhipati* (Lord of Tri-Kaliṅga) was applied to them. The exact meaning of Tri-Kaliṅga is far from certain. Some are of opinion that it signified three divisions of Kaliṅga, while others take it to mean the amalgamation of three countries, one of which was Kaliṅga. The statement, 'Veṅgīdeśa together with the Tri-Kaliṅga forest' (*Veṅgīdeśaṁ Tri-Kaliṅg=āṭavī-yuktaṁ*), which is met with in the Eastern Cālukya records possibly helps us to locate the country in the buffer region between the dominions of the later Eastern Cālukyas of Veṅgī and those of the Gaṅgas of Kaliṅganagara.[153]

XVI

The King in the Cālukya-Pallava Period

All the early Cālukya kings of Badami, including Pulakeśin II (c. A.D. 610-42) called themselves *Mahārāja.* Pulakeśin II was also called *Parameśvara.* It is stated in the records of his successors that he assumed this title after having defeated the 'glorious Harṣavardhana, the warlike lord of all the regions of the North' but this statement appears to be unwarranted. It is not improbable that Pulakeśin II assumed the title of *Parameśvara* 'after saving his homeland from enemies and restoring Cālukya sovereignty in the territories of the disaffected neighbours, but . . . an additional significance was later attached to it after his victory over *Parameśvara* Harṣavardhana'.[154] From the time of Vikramāditya I, the Cālukyas began to describe themselves as *Mahārājādhirāja*, *Parameśvara* and *Bhaṭṭāraka* (usually not *Paramabhaṭṭāraka*). An interesting title of these kings was *Śrī-Pṛthivī-vallabha,* often contracted into *Śrī-Vallabha* or *Vallabha,* which seems to allude to their claim of being incarnations of Viṣṇu. In some early records, the Cālukyas are described as meditating on the feet of Svāmi-Mahāsena, identified with Kārttikeya.

The king was the fountain-head of administration in the Pallava dominions. But until we come to the reign of Siṁhaviṣṇu we do not definitely know whether kingship descended from father to son and, if so, whether the rule of primogeniture was in vogue. From the time of Siṁhaviṣṇu's son Mahendravarman till the reign of Parameśvaravarman II we find that a father was generally succeeded by his eldest son on the throne. It seems that the election of the king by the subjects was not altogether unknown. The Vaikunthaperumal temple inscription[155] shows that when, with the demise of Parameśvaravarman II, the Pallava kingdom was subjected to anarchy, the important subjects of the kingdom elected a king.[156] *Mahārājādhirāja*, *Mahārāja*, *Dharma-Mahārāja* and *Dharma-Mahārājādhirāja* were some of the titles borne by the Pallava monarchs. Some of them were fond of assuming new names at the time of their coronation. Thus Rājasiṁha bore the *abhiṣekanāma* Narasiṁhavarman II, and Parameśvara *alias* Pallava Malla called himself Nandivarman.[157] These Pallava kings had further a passion for titles. Mahendravarman I (c. A.D. 600-630), for instance, bore a number of titles like *Cetthakāri* (temple-builder), *Mattavilāsa* (addicted to enjoyment), *Citrakārappuli* (tiger among painters) and *Vicitravitta* (myriad-minded).

XVII

The Rāṣṭrakūṭa King

Monarchy was hereditary in the Rāṣṭrakūṭa kingdom and usually the eldest son inherited the throne of his father. But cases of supersession are not altogether unknown in the Rāṣṭrakūṭa history. This happened when Dhruva chose his third son Govinda III to succeed him on the throne on the ground of the latter's superiority to his other brothers. The occurrence of such statements as *sāmantair=atha Raṭṭa-rājyam=ahimālam=ambārtham=abhyarthitaḥ*, 'He was requested by the feudatories to accept the throne for supporting the glory of the Rāṣṭrakūṭa empire', appearing in the Rāṣṭrakūṭa records, may lend colour to the assumption that feudatories had sometimes a determining voice in deciding the question of succession to the throne, but such statements need not be taken too seriously, and even on those occasions when Govinda II was deposed or Amoghavarṣa III was installed king, Dhruva and Amoghavarṣa III owed their position more to their 'own exertions than to the votes of the feudatories'.[158] The Rāṣṭrakūṭa history provides us with a few cases of abdication of the throne by the reigning king, as did Dhruva in his old age in favour of Govinda. When the ruling kings were old and of a religious disposition, as were Amoghavarṣa I and Amoghavarṣa II, the heir-apparents wielded all the powers of the ruling chiefs. This explains why there was the overlapping of the reigns of the above kings and their successors.[159] During the minority of the king, usually a male member of the house was appointed to act as regent. When Amoghavarṣa I was a minor, his cousin Karkka was appointed to rule the kingdom.

As it was in all the contemporary kingdoms, the king was the centre and fountain-head of all power in the Rāṣṭrakūṭa realm. He commanded the army, shouldered the administrative responsibility with the help of trusted and competent officers and acted as the supreme authority in legal affairs. Still it will be a mistake to look upon a Rāṣṭrakūṭa king as an autocrat Sultan. The following observations of A.S. Altekar[160] may be quoted in this connection: 'It may be pointed out that the Hindu monarchy was in theory always limited, but the constitutional checks thought of in our period by the theorists on the subject were of a different nature from those to which we are accustomed in the present age. Spiritual sanctions, effects of careful and proper education, force of public opinion, division of power with a ministry, supremacy of established usage in the realm of law and taxation, devolution of large powers to local bodies whose government was democratic in substance, if not always in form—these were the usual checks on monarchy relied on by the Hindu political writers.'

XVIII

The Western Cālukya King

The kings of the Cālukya dynasty of Kalyāṇī adopted titles like *Samasta-bhuvan=āśraya* (asylum of all the worlds), *Śrī-Pṛthivī-vallabha* (beloved of the goddess of prosperity and earth), *Mahārājādhirāja*, *Parameśvara*, *Paramabhaṭṭāraka*, *Saty=āśraya-kula-tilaka* (the chief of the line of Satyāśraya) and *Cāluky=ābharaṇa-śrīmat* (the ornament of the Cālukyas). These kings were fond of the *Malla* title, and sometimes the same ruler bore a couple of such titles, as was the case with Someśvara I, who was called both *Āhavamalla* (wrestler in war) and *Trailokyamalla* (wrestler in the three worlds).

Someśvara I is reputed to have composed a text in Sanskrit called *Mānasollāsa* which embodies the king's own views about the responsibilities and privileges of the royal office. Recommending the *ātm=āyattva-rājya* or absolute rule of the king, the text says that the best ruler is one who relies on himself and the worst is he who depends on his ministers. It further adds that only that king deserves to be called a *Prabhu*, master, who is capable of doing things on his own, wields unbridled commands and is blessed with powers of his own. The king is, however, enjoined not to use his high position to act against the interest of the people and the *dharma* and *deś=ācāra* of the country.

XIX

The King in the Post-Cālukya Period

With the decline and fall of the Cālukya kings of Kalyāṇī, the Hoysalas of Dorasamudra became the leading power in the Mysore region. During the period of their allegiance to the Cālukya paramountcy the Hoysalas were content with the assumption of the feudatory title of *Mahāmaṇḍaleśvara*. But Vīra Vallāla II bore a number of titles like *Samasta-bhuvan=āśraya*, *Śrī-Pṛthivī-vallabha*, *Mahārājādhirāja* and *Parameśvara*, no doubt, in imitation of the Western Cālukya kings. The Pāṇḍya kings, during the palmy days of their rule, assumed the titles of *Mahārājādhirāja*, *Parameśvara*, etc. A characteristic feature of the later Pāṇḍya kingship was the system of co-regency which attracted the attention of some contemporary foreign travellers.[161]

It is from about the middle of the twelfth century A.D. that the Kākatīyas of Warangal came to occupy a prominent place in the political firmament of the Deccan. The later kings of this family usually made the heir-apparents their partners in the governance of the kingdom. Gaṇapati appointed his daughter Rudramadevī his co-regent during the closing years of his reign, and Rudramadevī, in her turn, emulated her father by associating her grandson and heir Pratāparūdra with herself in the administration of the kingdom. The crown usually descended in the male line from father to son. The kings of the Kākatīya dynasty, particularly Gaṇapati and Pratāparūdra, as a perusal of their inscriptions would suggest, enjoyed a high degree of popularity in their life-time. Still the monarch was the source of all power, and it was he who was the pivot about which the entire structure of government moved. An idea about the kingship of the contemporary period may be gleaned from some treatises on politics like the *Nītisāram* by Pratāparūdra and the *Nītiśāstramuktāvalī* of Baddena which lay down that a king should be proficient in the *Vedas*, *Dharmaśāstras*, political science, art and literature, be possessed of wisdom and integrity, be impartial in the discharge of his duty and ever alert to rule the kingdom for the welfare of his subjects. The king should be kind, considerate and fatherly towards the people who should be granted frequent audiences so that he may be apprised of their grievances. The king is further urged to enforce the caste laws among the people and bring the culprits to book.[162]

As was the case in North India, land yielded the bulk of revenue for the king in South India. Burnell is of opinion that the royal share in the produce of land was not uniform in North and South India. He[163] says, 'There is ample evidence to show that Manu's proposition of one-sixth was never observed, and that the land tax taken not only by the Muhammadan but by the Hindu sovereigns also was fully one-half of the gross produce.' But an unequivocal reference to the king's one-sixth share of the produce in the commentary of Parimelazhagar,[164] coupled with the unambiguous statement of the *Mānasollāsa*[165] that the king is entitled to the sixth, eighth, or twelfth part of the yield of grain from land would make us sceptic about the soundness of Burnell's hypothesis.[166]

XX
Epilogue

It may be observed in conclusion that ancient Indian thinkers, most of whom, without any shadow of doubt, enjoyed royal patronage, had time and again denounced unfettered autocracy of a king and emphasised that it was his bounden duty to rule the country in accordance with the sacred law, the *varṇ=āśrama* system, the laws of communities, professions and guilds, to follow, in levying taxation, the customary law and usage of the communities and regions, and to treat the people he ruled as his own offspring.[167]

References and Notes

1. The *Śabdakalpadrumaḥ* (Chapter IV, p. 126) takes the term *rājan* in the sense 'to shine' (*rajate śobhate iti*), deriving it as *rāj kanin*. The *Vācaspatyam* points out that the term is capable of being derived

from the root *rañj*, 'to please', as well. R.C.P. Singh (*Kingship in Northern India*, 1968, pp. 38-39) derives the word *rājan* from the root *rāj*, which, according to him, means 'to rule, to govern, to be king', etc., but this hypothesis in regard to the etymological meaning of the root *rāj* is incompatible with the canons of Sanskrit grammar. Generally speaking, the term *rājan* denoted kings but sometimes it was applied to the elders of the state that established the *Saṅgha* form of government. Kauṭilya (XI, 1, 5) speaks of the *Saṅghas* of the Licchavis, Vṛjis, Mallas, Madras, Kukuras, Kurus and Pañcālas as *Rāja-śabd=opajīvin*, i.e., those whose members bore the title of *Rājā* (*Licchavika-Vṛjika-Mallaka-Madraka-Kukura-Kuru - Pañcāl = ādayo rāja-śabd=opajīvinaḥ*). The Licchavis are said to have claimed 7,707 *Rājans*, each of whom, to suggest from the testimony of the *Lalita-vistara*, thought 'I am the king, I am the king' (*Ek=aiva eva manyate ahaṁ rājā ahaṁ rāj=eti*).

2. III.55.7; 56.5; IV.21.2; VI.27.8; VIII.19.32.
3. VIII.37.3.
4. X.128.9.
5. *CHI*, p. 84.
6. X.124.8.
7. *Vedische Studien*, II, p. 303. An opposite view has been propounded by Dikshitar (*Kuppuswami Sastri Commemoration Volume*, p. 119), who opines that in Vedic India the very election of the king was in the hands of the people.
8. The term *bali*, though used in the *Vedas* in the sense of a tribute to the king or to a god, is explained by Bhaṭṭasvāmin (*JBORS*, XI, p. 83) as denoting a local tax of one-tenth or one-twentieth other than the ordinary one-sixth (*Baliḥ ṣaḍ-bhāgād=anyo yathā-deśa-prasiddho daśa-viṁśati-bandh=ādhikaḥ*).
9. *SGAI*, p. 134.
10. IV.42.9.
11. It would, however, be wrong to suppose that in the later Vedic period the *Samiti* lost all its power. A passage in the *Atharva Veda* (VII.12.1) describes it as one of the twin daughters of Prajāpati, the Creator (*Sabhā ca māṁ Samitiś=c=āvatāṁ Prajāpater duhitarau saṁvidāne*). That the king was sometimes eager to cultivate amity with the *Samiti* is further vouchsafed by another passage (VI.88.3) in the *Atharva Veda* (*Dhruvāya te Samitiḥ kalpatām=iha*). This shows that the *Samiti* had some control over the king, but its importance was, no doubt, diminished.
12. *CHI*, p. 116.
13. *PIA*, p. 52.
14. Gaekwad's Oriental Series, C, p. 26.
15. K.V.R. Aiyangar, *Kṛtyakalpataru*, XI, *Rājadharmakāṇḍa*, Baroda, 1943, p. 27.
16. V.1.1.12.
17. XX.127.7.

18. III.4.6.
19. XII.9.1.
20. III.4.2.
21. *Professor Birinchi Kumar Barua Commemoration Volume*, p. 34.
22. III.501.
23. *SONEI*, pp. 103-04.
24. I.326.
25. *SONEI*, p. 101.
26. Ibid., p. 101.
27. XI.1.
28. II.5.11.1.
29. XI.9; XI.10; XI.19.
30. II.5.11.1; II.5.10.14; II.10.25.10; II.10.25.15.
31. XIX.1; XIX.7.
32. R.S. Sharma (*APIIAI*, p. 41) draws the attention of scholars to almost a similar idea, expressed by Plato in his *Republic* to the effect that 'Any meddlesome interchange between the three classes would be most mischievous to the state and would properly be described as the height of villainy.' (Ibid.)
33. X 27.
34. I.42.
35. I.10.18.1.
36. I.10.18.14.
37. Edited by Bühler, p. 200.
38. I.10.18.15.
39. Candragupta is called a *Vṛṣala* in the drama entitled *Mudrārākṣasa*. H.C. Seth (*IHQ*, XIII, pp. 641ff) has taken it as a kingly title, being the Sanskritised form of Greek *Basileus*. But the word generally means one belonging to a non-Brahmanical and heretical sect and subsequently it came to signify a Śūdra.
40. In Babylon, however, the title 'favourite of the gods' is found as early as the age of Hammurabi (*IC*, 1946, p. 241).
41. Luders' List, No. 954-6.
42. VI.3.21.
43. *AIU*, p. 63.
44. *AI*, p. 119.
45. The date of the *Arthaśāstra* is a moot question among Indologists. Some scholars assign this work to the early centuries of the Christian era. It is argued on the other hand, on the basis of its references to *Cīnabhūmi* and *Cīnapaṭṭa* and the *bhāṣya* style of its composition, that the *Kauṭilīya Arthaśāstra* was finally composed by Viṣṇugupta in c. A.D. 600 (*Prācī-Jyoti*, VII, p. 101).
46. *KA*, II, p. 225.
47. III.1.39-40.
48. I.19.
49. I.19.6.
50. I.19.9.
51. *KA*, II, pp. 51-2; I.19.9-24.

52. *GBI*, pp. 37, 157-8.
53. *CHI*, II, p. 340.
54. The real meaning of the term *yavuga* is far from being certain. D.C. Sircar (*SI*, p. 110) takes it to be a Turkish word meaning a 'prince'. J.N. Banerjea and Jagannath (*CHI*, II, p. 230) interpret the term to mean a chief. S.N. Ghosal (*Prācī-Jyoti*, 1967 (December), pp. 361-2) interprets it as standing for Sanskrit *yuvaka* to mean a 'young man'.
55. While commenting on the titles, borne by the Kuṣāṇa kings, R.S. Sharma (*The Quarterly Review of Historical Studies*, IV, p. 180) points out that they 'demonstrate some kind of decentralisation which began during this period. The Kuṣāṇas called themselves the king of kings and the chief of chiefs, which presupposes that they ruled over lesser kings and lesser chiefs. As a conquering minority, they naturally had to build this type of feudal organisation.'
56. *B.C. Law Volume*, II, p. 313.
57. *CHI*, II, p. 345.
58. *B.C. Law Volume*, II, pp. 314-5, 318. It is interesting to note that the *Suvarṇaprabhāsottamasūtra*, a Mahāyānist Buddhist text of the third century A.D., justifies the divine origin of kings on the grounds that, first, before being born as a man, the king was living in the company of the gods, and second, the thirty-three gods had contributed to his substance (*Api vai deva-saṁbhūto deva-putraḥ sa ucyate/ Trayas=triṁśair=deva-rājendrair=bhāgo datto nṛpasya hi/ putratvaṁ sarva-devānāṁ nirmito manuj=eśvaraḥ// B.C. Law Volume*, II, p. 314; *The Quarterly Review of Historical Studies*, IV, p. 180).
59. Cunningham (*B.C. Law Volume*, II, p. 307) reads the title *Devaputra* on a coin of Kuyula Kara Kaphsa, identified with Kadphises II, although Thomas does not accept the reading as correct.
60. *APIIAI*, p. 177.
61. The custom of enshrining royal images in temples for worshipping them regularly was also followed by the Cola kings as well as by some Hinduised rulers of South-East Asia (Sastri, K.A.N.—*The Cholas*, II, p. 223).
62. *APIIAI*, p. 178.
63. *IA*, XXXII, pp. 427-32.
64. *AIU*, p. 148.
65. *APIIAI*, p. 180.
66. The name of king Mahādeva is known to us from some coins bearing the legend *bh(a)gavato Mahādevasa rājarājasa*. The legend on these coins has generally been interpreted to refer to a king named Mahādeva. S.K. Chakrabortty (*A Study of Indian Numismatics*, Mymensingh, 1931, pp. 161ff) takes this legend as applicable to god Mahādeva.
67. VII.35.
68. VII.16.
69. VII.129.
70. VII.130.
71. VII.133.

72. VII.4.
73. VII.9.
74. The independent rulers of some kingdoms like the Licchavis, the Maghas, the Bhāraśivas and the Vākāṭakas, on the other hand, still preferred to be called *Mahārāja.*
75. In the Mankuwar stone inscription, Kumāragupta I is given the subordinate title of *Mahārāja* instead of the paramount title of *Mahārājādhirāja.*
76. *PHAI*, p. 559.
77. The term *daivataḥ* is interpreted by Amara in the sense of a god (*devatā ity=Amaraḥ*). V.S. Apte (*Sanskrit-English Dictionary*, p. 261) thinks that the term may mean (i) a god, deity, divinity, (ii) a number of gods, the whole class of gods and (iii) an idol.
78. *Viṣṇu*, 1.13-14.
79. VII.19.
80. On above.
81. *Administration And Social Life Under Vijayanagar*, Madras, 1940, p. 22.
82. *The Gupta Polity*, Madras, 1952, p. 111.
83. Act II.
84. S.A. Sabnis, *Kālidāsa, His Style And His Times*, 1966, p. 207; *Raghuvaṁśa*, I.18.
85. The Asirgarh copper seal inscription (*CII*, III, No. 47) testifies to the fact that the preservation of the *Varṇ=āśrama-dharma* constituted an important duty of the Maukhari kings.
86. Harṣa ascended the throne of Thanesar according to the rule of hereditary descent but was offered the crown of the Maukhari kingdom of Kanauj to which he had no claim. Since there was no competent heir to succeed Grahavarman, the Maukhari ministers offered the crown to the brother of their widowed queen. This instance, therefore, does not show that kingship was normally elective in the Maukhari kingdom but proves that in the event of the absence of a legitimate heir, the ministers, along with other high functionaries, used to elect a suitable successor from among the relations of the deceased king.
87. *CA*, p. 350.
88. Ibid., p. 118.
89. C.M. Ridding, *The Kādambarī Of Bāṇa*, London, 1896, p. 82.
90. Like Viṣṇu.
91. As is the case with Śiva.
92. *RTA*, p. 306.
93. *EI*, IV, p. 248.
94. *PIA*, p. 34. There is, however, a definite reference to an election in the *Rājataraṅgiṇī* which informs us how at the end of the Utpala dynasty in Kashmir in A.D. 939 the assembly of the Brāhmaṇas elected a Brāhmaṇa named Yaśaskara as king. Kalhaṇa (V.454-60) pooh-poohs the election as a foolish procedure.
95. *EI*, XVIII, p. 95.

96. Chapter 223.
97. Ibid., 226.
98. *PAP*, pp. 55-56.
99. The Kalacuri kings Karṇa and his successors described themselves in their own records as *śrī-Vāmadeva-pād=ānudhyāta*, implying thereby that they regarded their dominions as belonging to the saint Vāmaśambhu and themselves as the latter's deputies, just as the Guhilots of Chitor and the kings of Travancore looked upon themselves as viceroys, respectively, of the gods Ekaliṅga and Padmanābhasvāmin.
100. *EI*, XXX, p. 79.
101. *Woolner Commemoration Volume*, pp. 196ff.
102. *PIA*, p. 36.
103. *EI*, I, p. 195.
104. Ibid., XI, p. 142.
105. *DHNI*, II, p. 795.
106. *EI*, V, pp. 180-95.
107. *DHNI*, II, p. 1067.
108. Ibid., p. 1109.
109. *EI*, I, p. 35.
110. Ibid., p. 131.
111. *PIA*, p. 46; *EI*, I, p. 195.
112. *IA*, XVI, p. 205.
113. *EI*, I, p. 205.
114. Ibid., V, p. 18.
115. *SIGM*, XIII, p. 108.
116. *EI*, XVIII, p. 95.
117. Ibid.
118. *IA*, XV, p. 306.
119. *DHNI*, II, p. 704.
120. *EI*, XII, p. 205.
121. 8, 5, 20.
122. VIII, 54-57; 106-08.
123. *PIA*, p. 68.
124. I.143-44.
125. I.245-48.
126. *Śukranīti* (Edited by B. Sarkar), p. 183.
127. Ibid., p. 187.
128. Ibid., p. 138.
129. Ibid., p. 139.
130. Somadeva (*Nītivākyāmṛta*, p. 114) points out that the king, who does not pay any heed to the advice of the council of ministers, would cease to be king (*Sa khalu na rājā yo mantriṇ=otikramya varteta*).
131. *Śāntiparvan*, XCIII.
132. VII.4.
133. II.7-8.
134. Benoy Kumar Sarkar (*The Śukranīti*, Allahabad, 1914, p. 54) observes, 'Ancient Hindu statesmen and philosophers placed restraints upon the king not simply by devising rules of morality and

social etiquette to be strictly followed by him as by all other men but also by prescribing regular courses of instruction and training as well as by imposing what may be regarded as the positive and direct checks of a constitutional government.'

135. The title *Rājan* was sometimes borne by subordinate rulers as was the case with Vāsiṣṭhīputra Vilivāyakura of Kolhapur.
136. *SI*, pp. 184-85, 191, 193, 195.
137. Khāravela who ruled in Kaliṅga in the second half of the first century B.C. assumed the title of *Mahārāja*. He seems to be the first Indian king to adopt this title.
138. *SSAAMI*, I, p. 208.
139. *EI*, VIII, p. 91.
140. *EHD*, p. 141.
141. *EI*, VIII, p. 60.
142. *EHD*, p. 131.
143. 388.
144. 386.
145. 385.
146. 471.
147. *TSELT*, p. 579.
148. V.1.1.13.
149. *EI*, VIII, p. 234; *IA*, V, p. 15.
150. *EI*, V, p. 163.
151. Ibid., XXIV, p. 140.
152. *CA*, p. 272.
153. Ibid., p. 215.
154. Ibid., p. 237.
155. *SII*, IV.
156. *ASLUP*, p. 38.
157. Ibid., p. 39.
158. *RT*, p. 151.
159. Ibid., p. 153.
160. Ibid., p. 157.
161. *SE*, p. 284.
162. *EHD*, p. 671.
163. *South Indian Paleography*, p. 112.
164. *TSELT*, p. 92.
165. II, 3, 163.
166. Of the system of land revenue, as in vogue in the ancient South Indian kingdoms, Kanakasubbai Pillai (*Tamils Eighteen Hundred Years Ago*, p. 112) writes, 'One-sixth of the produce on land was the legitimate share of the king, and for water supplied by the state a water cess was levied from the farmers.'
167. The word *prajā* etymologically means both subjects and children.

APPENDIX I

THE CASTE OF THE KING

Invaluable information in regard to the problem of the caste of kings is supplied to us by the Dharmaśāstra and the epic literature, while epigraphs, no doubt, supplement our knowledge with stray information. In referring to the time-honoured duties of the four castes Manu observes that teaching (*adhyāpanaṁ*), study (*adhyayanaṁ*), performance of sacrifices (*yajanaṁ*), officiating as priests at others' sacrifices (*yājanaṁ*), charity (*dānaṁ*) and acceptance of gifts (*pratigrahañ=c=aiva*) are the duties of the Brāhmaṇas;[1] protection of the people (*prajānāṁ rakṣaṇaṁ*), gift-making (*dānaṁ*), performance of sacrifices (*ijyā*), study (*adhyayanam=eva ca*) and abstention from luxury[2] (*viṣayeṣv=aprasaktiñ=ca*) are the concerns of the Kṣatriyas;[3] rearing of cattle (*paśūnāṁ rakṣaṇaṁ*), charitable deeds (*dānaṁ*), performance of sacrifices (*ijyā*), study (*adhyayanam=eva*), trade and commerce (*vaṇik-pathaṁ*), money-lending (*kusīdañ=ca*) and agriculture (*kṛṣim=eva*) are the duties of the Vaiśyas[4] and an ungrudging service to the upper castes is the sole job of the Śūdras[5] (*Ekam=eva tu Śūdrasya prabhuḥ karma sam=ādiśat| eteṣām=eva varṇāṇāṁ śuśrūṣām=anasūyayā||*). As is evident from the foregoing enumeration of the respective duties of the four social orders, as envisaged by the *Varṇāśrama* scheme, the duty of protecting the subjects, which is the corner-stone of kingship and denied to the members of the other castes, was the prerogative of the Kṣatriyas.

It is in tune with the *Varṇāśrama* system that we find so much insistence in the *Smṛti* literature on the Kṣatriyas for being entitled to rulership. 'The protection of the kingdom in accordance with justice and law', says Manu, 'should be undertaken by the Kṣatriya who has been initiated with all the initiatory rites, inculcated in the *Vedas*'[6] (*Brāhmaṁ prāptena saṁskāraṁ Kṣatriyeṇa yathā-vidhi| sarvasy=āsya yathā-nyāyaṁ kartavyaṁ parirakṣaṇaṁ||*). Manu and, following him, Harīta[7] and Kāmandaka have used the terms *rājā* and *kṣatriya* as synonyms. Manu[8] is not unaware of the existence of the Śūdra kings of his times but he interdicts residence in their dominions (*na Śūd-*

ra-rājye nivaset). Gifts[9] from such a king as is not born of the Kṣatriya lineage are banned (*Na rājñaḥ pratigṛhnīyād=arājanya-prasūtitaḥ*), because a non-Kṣatriya king is equal to ten brothels[10] (*Daśa-veśa-samo nṛpaḥ*) and would adequately compare with a butcher who maintains ten thousand slaughter-houses[11] (*Daśa-sūnā-sahasrāṇi yo vāhayati saunikaḥ| tena tulyaḥ smṛto rājā ghoras=tasya pratigrahaḥ||*).

The *Mahābhārata* prefers the Kṣatriyas to men of the other communities for the royal office, although it does not altogether rule out the possibility of non-Kṣatriya kingship, particularly in times of storm and stress. On being enquired by Yudhiṣṭhira about the legitimacy of a non-Kṣatriya man for being anointed a king, consequent upon his success in protecting the people righteously from the insurrection of robbers[12] (*Brāhmaṇo yadi vā Vaiśyaḥ Śūdro vā rāja-sattama| dasyubhy=otha prajā rakṣed=daṇḍaṁ dharmeṇa dhārayaṇ||*), Bhīṣma replies that any person, irrespective of the caste he may belong to, who gives evidence of his indispensability in the hour of need, richly deserves the crown[13] (*Apāre yo bhavet pāram=aplave yaḥ plavo bhavet| Śūdro vā yadi v=āpy=anyaḥ sarvathā mānam=arhati||*).

It cannot escape notice that some of the commentators of the *Manu-saṁhitā* do not agree with their master on the issue of the eligibility of individuals to the royal title, as they could not overlook the undoubted existence of the non-Kṣatriya kings of early and contemporary times. Medhātithi, for instance, points out that the term *rājā* does not refer exclusively to a Kṣatriya but is used in the sense of any territorial ruler, blessed with consecration (*Rājā-śabdas=tu n=eha Kṣatriya-jāti-vacanaḥ kiṁ tarhi abhiṣek=ādi-guṇa-yogini-puruṣaṁ vartate*?). Medhātithi's view about the wider connotation of the term *rājā* finds favour with Kullūka who points out that the word is seldom used in the sense of the Kṣatriyas alone but signifies such consecrated persons as are in possession of rural and urban units (*Rāja-śabd=opi n=ātra kṣatriya-jāti-vacanaḥ kintv=abhiṣikta-janapada-purapālayitṛ-puruṣa-vacanaḥ|*). It is the profession that determines kingship (*yathā vṛtto bhaven=nṛpa iti|*). Viśvarūpa is, likewise, of opinion that the royal title belongs to one who possesses a kingdom, and not to a Kṣatriya alone.

Nīlakaṇṭha Bhaṭṭa accepts the early Smṛti tradition that the expression *rājā* is applicable to the Kṣatriyas but not to a *de facto* king (*Rāja-śabdaḥ Kṣatriya-mātre śakto na rājya-yogini*). The same view is expressed by Mitramiśra[15] (*Rāja-śabdaḥ Kṣatriya-jāti-vacanaḥ*/). Caṇḍeśvara[16] holds a contrary view as he points out that the *Rājā* is he who is the overlord of subjects by virtue of his protection to the latter and consecration (*Vastu-tas=tu prajāpālana-pravṛtty=abhiṣek=āday=osya kāraṇamā-traṁ prajā-svāmitve rājatvena prasiddho rājā*/). Thus Caṇḍeśvara, unlike Nīlakaṇṭha Bhaṭṭa and Mitramiśra, calls a *de facto* king *Rājā*. Lakṣmīdhara does not raise the problem of the caste of the king at all, 'but the drift of his treatment is to confine lawful kingship to men of the Kṣatriya caste'.[17] The commentator Mādhavācārya,[18] who flourished in the fourteenth century A.D., maintains that one is not entitled to kingship by virtue of one's possession of a kingdom; *rājā*, in the principal meaning of the term, means the Kṣatriyas. He adds that in those cases where the Brāhmaṇa or Vaiśya crown-holders are called *Rājā*, the term is employed figuratively, and not in its literal sense (*Na rājya-yogād rājatvaṁ kṣatriyatvaṁ tu tattvataḥ*/ *Rāja-śabdaḥ kṣatriya-jātau rūḍhaḥ na tu rājya-yogas=tasya pravṛtti-nimittaṁ*/).

But whatever view the framers of Indian society might have taken, there is no doubt that the Brāhmaṇas, Vaiśyas and Śūdras sometimes founded kingdoms and assumed rulership. A number of such cases are cited below:

Mahāpadma,[19] the founder of the Nanda dynasty, was a man of low origin, being born, according to the *Purāṇas*, of a Śūdra mother, and described in Greek accounts as the son of a Śūdra father. Candragupta Maurya is represented in Brahmanical traditions as base-born, while Buddhist traditions describe him as a Kṣatriya. Puṣyamitra, who founded a new line of rulers by bringing about the downfall of the Mauryas, belonged to the Śuṅga family of the Brāhmaṇa clan of the Bhāradvāja lineage. Vasudeva, who founded a new dynasty after having supplanted the Śuṅgas, was a Kāṇva Brāhmaṇa. The Sātavāhana kings were Brāhmaṇas with a little admixture of Nāga blood. Gautamīputra Sātakarṇi of this royal family is called in the Nasik inscription an *eka Bamhaṇa*, i.e., the unique Brāhmaṇa. Vindhyaśakti, the founder of the Vākāṭaka dynasty, was a Brāhmaṇa (*dvija*) of the Viṣṇuvṛddha or Bhāradvāja gotra. Mayūraśarman, the progenitor of the

Kadamba dynasty, was an orthodox Brāhmaṇa of the Mānava gotra. The Pallavas, who are referred to as Kṣatriyas in the Talagunda inscription of the fifth century A.D., had probably in their veins an admixture of the blood of a Brāhmaṇa family of the Bhāradvāja gotra. *Mahārāja* Mātṛviṣṇu,[20] who flourished during the time of the Gupta emperor Budhagupta, is described in the Eran stone pillar inscription of A.D. 484 as a great grandson of a Brāhmaṇa saint named Indraviṣṇu. *Mahāsāmanta* Pradoṣaśarman[21] was likewise a scion of an orthodox Brāhmaṇa family. The kings of the Puṣyabhūti dynasty of Thanesar belonged to the Vaiśya caste. The Chinese pilgrim Hiuen Tsang[22] refers to the Brāhmaṇa kings of Ujjayinī, Jijhoti and Maheśvarapura, the Vaiśya king of Pāryātra and the Śūdra rulers of Matipura and Sindh. The Pratīhāra dynasty was founded by a Brāhmaṇa named Haricandra. Kallar,[23] who founded the Hindu Ṣāhi dynasty in the ancient Gandhāra country in the ninth century A.D., was a Brāhmaṇa. Bappa,[24] the founder of the Guhila dynasty of Mewar, is mentioned in the Chitorgarh and Achaleswar inscriptions as a Brāhmaṇa. The Cāhamānas were likewise originally Brāhmaṇas, as Sāmanta, an early member of the house of Śākambharī is called in the Bijolia inscription a Brāhmaṇa of the *Vatsa* gotra. Almost all these rulers assumed full regal titles, as befitted independent sovereigns, thus demonstrating their strong disapproval of the view of the orthodox school of social thinkers in favour of the limitation of rulership to members of the Kṣatriya caste. But the case was entirely different with a few kings like Puṣyamitra and Vindhyaśakti who, notwithstanding their independent status, seem to have adhered to the traditional view by refraining from adopting any royal title.

References and Notes

1. I.88.
2. The commentator Kullūka interprets *viṣayeṣu* to mean non-attachment to music, women, dancing and articles of luxury (*gīta-nṛtya-vanit=opabhog=ādiṣu*).
3. I.89.

4. I.90.
5. I.91.
6. VII.2.
7. II.2. *Rājyasthaḥ kṣatriyaś=c=āpi prajā-dharmeṇa pālayam.*
8. IV.61. In commenting on this passage, Kullūka says, 'one should not live in a country where the king belongs to the Śūdra caste' (*Yatra deśe Śūdro rājā, tatra na vaset*). The *Viṣṇu Purāṇa* (72, 64), likewise, lays down that a Brāhmaṇa should not live in the kingdom of a Śūdra.
9. IV.84.
10. Ibid., 85.
11. Ibid., 86.
12. *Śāntiparvan*, 76, 36.
13. Ibid., 76, 38.
14. *Nītimayūkha*, p. 1.
15. *Rājanītiprakāśa*, p. 11.
16. *Rājanītiratnākara*, pp. 2-3. Aparārka (*Rājanītiprakāśa*, pp. 14-15) also calls a *de facto* king *rājā*.
17. K.V. Rangaswami Aiyangar, *Kṛtyakalpataru*, XI, *Rājadharmakāṇḍa*, p. 22.
18. S. Bhattacharya Sastri, *Jaiminīya-Nyāyamālā vistaraḥ* (B.S. 1358), p. 236.
19. The *Saccaṁkira Jātaka* (I, pp. 324-26) speaks of a Brāhmaṇa having been anointed king. The *Padakulamānava Jātaka* (III, pp. 313-14) tells us how a Brāhmaṇa was placed on the throne by the people. Another *Jātaka* (*PBI*, p. 104) refers to a Brāhmaṇa as being installed on the throne that was lying vacant consequent upon the death of a king. A son of a woodgatherer is made a king in the *Kaṭṭhahārī Jātaka* (I, pp. 134-36). But all these references are not historical.
20. *SI*, pp. 334ff.
21. *EI*, XIV, pp. 306ff.
22. *CA*, p. 271.
23. *AIK*, p. 111.
24. *IHQ*, XXVIII, p. 83.

2

The Queen

I

The Queen in the Vedic Period

In the absence of any worthwhile information about her in the *Ṛgveda*, it is wellnigh impossible to ascertain the status of the queen in Ṛgvedic times. The queen, however, finds prominent mention in the later Vedic texts. It seems that in this period the king was usually allowed to have four[1] queens, the *Mahiṣī*,[2] the *Parivṛktī*,[3] the *Vāvātā* and the *Pālāgalī*. Sāyaṇa, while commenting on a passage of the *Aitareya Brāhmaṇa*,[4] observes that the king had three wives, comprising the *Mahiṣī*, the *Vāvātā* and the *Parivṛktī*. This observation can hardly be taken as authentic, on the ground that it does not take any notice of the *Pālāgalī*, whose existence as one of the royal consorts is indubitably vouchsafed by several texts. We cannot similarly agree with Sāyaṇa when he says that the *Mahiṣī*, the *Vāvātā* and the *Parivṛktī* came from the higher, middle and lower castes, respectively (*Rājñāṁ hi trividhāḥ striyah tatr=ottama-jāter=Mahiṣ=īti nāma madhyama-jāter=Vāvāt=aiti adhama-jāteḥ parivṛktīr=iti*). A passage of the *Śatapatha Brāhmaṇa*[5] implies that the lady who was married to the king first was called the *Mahiṣī*, chief queen. The *Parivṛktī* was the discarded wife, being relegated to ignominy on account of her barrenness.[6] Whereas, the *Vāvātā*[7] was the favourite wife, the *Pālāgalī* was the daughter of the last of the court officials.

The *Mahiṣī* was superior in power and position to the other queens. This is suggested, in the first place, by the fact that while the *Mahiṣī* is assigned the third position in almost all the lists of the *Ratnins*, the *Parivṛktī* is usually accorded the fourth position and the *Vāvātā* figures as a *Ratnin* only in the *Tai-*

ttirīya Brāhmaṇa. Again, the description of the royal consecration and the *Aśvamedha* sacrifice, as given in the *Śatapatha Brāhmaṇa*, would indicate a higher status of the *Mahiṣī*, as compared with the other wives of the king. The *Mahiṣī* had an active part to play in the *Rājasūya* sacrifice. As soon as the chariot race was over, the king, along with the *Mahiṣī*, used to ascend the sacrificial post, saying, 'We have become the children of Prajāpati'[8] (*Prajāpateḥ prajā abhūma*). Owing to her participation in *Rājasūya*, the *Mahiṣī* came to be vested with divinity. The *Śatapatha Brāhmaṇa* tells us that at the time of the *Aśvamedha* sacrifice the chief queen was attended by one hundred princesses[9] (*tasyai śataṁ rāja-putryaḥ anucaryo bhavanti*), the favourite queen was accompanied by a hundred women of royal descent[10] (*tasyai śataṁ rājanyā anucaryo bhavanti*), the *Parivṛktī* was followed by one hundred daughters of heralds and village headmen[11] (*tasyai śataṁ sūta-grāmaṇyā duhitaro='nucaryo bhavanti*) and the *Pālāgalī* was escorted by one hundred daughters of chamberlains and charioteers[12] (*tasyai śataṁ kṣātra-saṁgrahītṛṇāṁ duhitaro='nucaryo bhavanti*). This clearly shows the respective positions of the different queens.

Referring to the functions of the queens, K.P. Jayaswal[13] observes that the queens had seldom any functions other than religious. In the Vedic period, women had to perform sacrifices jointly with their husbands. The *Aitareya Brāhmaṇa*[14] declares that spiritually, a man cannot be considered complete unless he is accompanied by his wife (*tasmād puruṣo jāyāṁ vittvā kṛtsnataram=iv=ātmānaṁ manyate*). The *Śatapatha Brāhmaṇa*[15] echoes the same feeling when it forbids a bachelor to offer oblations (*a-yajñīyo v=aiṣa yo='patnīkaḥ*). The queen then as a life-long partner of her husband co-operated with the latter in religious rites and ceremonies. The presence of the queen was obligatory even at the time of the *Aśvamedha* sacrifice. When the horse would return from its journey, queens washed the horse and decorated its body. The horse was next killed and laid on a blanket. The chief queen would lie by its side and the priest would cover both the queen and the horse with a piece of cloth. While lying thus the queen used to catch the genital organ of the animal and get united with it at the time the priest uttered the verse, 'O horse, ejaculate your semen'[16] (*Aśvasya śiśnaṁ mahiṣī upasthe nidhatte vṛṣā 'vājī retodhā reto dadhātu iti'*).

When the chief queen performed her rites, different priests indulged in conversing in abusive dialogue with different female characters; the *Brahman* conversed with the chief queen, the *Adhvarju* with the attendants of the *Mahiṣī*, the *Udgātṛ* with the *Vāvātā*, the *Hotṛ* with the *Parivṛktī* and the *Kṣattṛ* with the *Pālāgalī*.[17]

But it would not be correct to hold that the activities of the queens did not transcend the limits of the religious arena. Jogiraj Basu[18] observes that the queens, particularly the favourite one, 'enjoyed an important position as a go-between between the king and his officers or the king and the people'. But in Vedic literature there is hardly any evidence which is in agreement with this contention. Further, it is quite unlikely that the people, particularly the commoners, had developed such intimate relations with the queens as to influence them to persuade the king to redress the grievances of the aggrieved. As *Ratnins*[19] of the kingdom, the queens were undoubtedly entrusted with some administrative functions, the details of which are, unfortunately, not known.

II

The Queen in Buddhist and Classical Accounts

The Buddhist sources preserve interesting accounts about queens of the post-Vedic period, although the authenticity of some of these accounts may justifiably be called in question. That polygamy was in vogue in the vast majority of the royal houses during this period is unmistakably revealed by the Jātaka texts which tell us how kings' harems were always overcrowded with glamorous girls. The *Cullasutasoma Jātaka*[20] speaks of a king who had 700 wives, while another[21] refers to another claiming as many as 84,000 queens. The figures, as mentioned in these texts, are, however, conventional and not actual. It is of interest to note that kings like Bimbisāra, Prasenajit, Udayana and Ajātaśatru were all polygamists. The chief queen is called *Aggamahesī* who 'commanded a respectable status both in and out of the palace, being presumably the mother of the heir-apparent'.[22] The post of the chief queen does not seem to have been permanently reserved for one and the same lady only; the final say in the selection for such a post rested with the king.

The *Jātakas* record numerous cases of infidelity of queens. We are told in a Jātaka text[23] how a wicked queen was granted pardon by her husband at the instance of the chaplain; the queen Kinnarā is reported in another text[24] to have been discarded by her lord due to her misconduct and the examples of queens, misbehaving themselves—Kaṇhā, Kākāṭī and Karuṅgavī—may be met with in the *Kuṇāla Jātaka*.[25] But the Jātaka narratives, which vouchsafe the low standard of queenly morality, have to be carefully scrutinised, as they are primarily intended to caution the Bhikṣus against the danger of falling from the ideal of celibacy. One of the *Jātakas*[26] refers to a queen of Kāśī who was entreated by the subjects to assume the reins of administration consequent upon the renunciation by her husband of the world.

The writings of the Classical authors appear to preserve some genuine traditions about queens. While referring to the Pāṇḍya kingdom, Megasthenes[27] says, 'Next come the Pandae, the only race in India ruled by women. They say that Hercules having but one daughter, who was on that account all the more beloved, endowed her with a noble kingdom. Her descendants rule over 300 cities and command an army of 150,000 foot and 500 elephants.' It appears from Megasthenes' accounts that during his time, the Pāṇḍya country was governed by a queen who exercised her authority over 300 villages and had at her command a powerful army. The use of the term women in plural by the Greek ambassador would further bring out the fact that the rule of the queens was quite commonplace in the history of this country.

The Classical authors tell us about Kleophis, the queen of the Assakenoi in the Punjab. When the king of the Assakenoi laid down his life in the course of his fight with Alexander the Great, Kleophis assumed the charge of the fortress of Massaga and offered a gallant resistance until she was overpowered and captured by the Macedonian army. Q. Curtius[28] says that after the conclusion of the war she was reinstated in her own kingdom as a reward for her bravery, and she afterwards gave birth to a son, named Alexander.[29] The queens of the Assakenoi, as is suggested by the example of Kleophis, were not mere consorts of their husbands, but, faced with an adverse situation, they could rise to the occasion with display of administrative and martial skill.

III

The Maurya Queen

From Pillar Edict VII[30] we learn that the Maurya queens were called *Devīs*. It says, *ete ca aṁne ca bahukā mukhā dāna-visagasi viyāpaṭā, se mama c=eva devinaṁ ca.* R.G. Basak[31] translates the passage thus, 'These and many other *mukhyas* (chiefs or heads of departments) are engaged in the distribution of charities and this too on my own behalf and that of my queens.' It is evident that Aśoka's queens were not only designated as *Devīs* but they also had their private funds to make charities on their own account. In Pillar Edict VII[32] we also read the following passage, *dālakānāṁ pi ca me kaṭe aṁnānaṁ ca devi-kumālānāṁ*, which R.G. Basak[33] renders into English as: 'I have also ordered this to be done with regard to my sons, and other princes born of the queens.' The interpretation of the expression *devi-kumālānāṁ* is, it must be admitted, baffling. Now, it is almost certain that *dālakānāṁ*[34] refers to the sons of Aśoka himself, and the expression *devi-kumālānāṁ*, accordingly, cannot be taken as denoting the sons of Aśoka's queens. Bühler rightly points out that the *devi-kumālās* were not the sons of Aśoka's queens but were those born of the queens of his father. It may accordingly be concluded that during the period of the Maurya rule, the wives of both the reigning and deceased kings were called *Devīs*.

The Maurya emperors were polygamists.[35] A study of the *Mahāvaṁsa*,[36] *Divyāvadāna*[37] and other texts[38] shows that Aśoka had the following queens:

1. Devī. She was married to Aśoka at Vidiśā, identified with Besnagar, and gave birth to Mahendra and Saṅghamitrā. The *Samanta Pāsadikā*[39] represents her as a Vaiśya, while she is described as *Vedisa-mahādevī* and *Śākyānī* (i.e., *Śākya-Kumārī*) in the *Mahābodhivaṁsa*.[40]
2. Āsandhimitrā. The *Mahāvaṁsa* represents her as Aśoka's chief queen (*piyā aggamahisī*) who died in the twenty-sixth year of Aśoka's consecration.

3. Padmāvatī. She is mentioned in the *Divyāvadāna*[41] as the mother of Dharmavivardhana who became famous as Kuṇāla in later years.
4. Tiṣyarakṣitā. The *Divyāvadāna*[42] states that she was raised to the position of Aśoka's chief consort four years later than the death of Āsandhimitrā. If legends[43] have any credence, she plucked out the eyes of prince Kuṇāla out of jealousy and was burnt to death as a punishment for this crime.

To the above list of queens may be added the name of Kāruvākī who is mentioned in one of Aśoka's edicts as the second queen (*dutiyāye deviye*).

It is difficult to evaluate the veracity of the above details of Aśoka's queens, as derived from several Buddhist texts, but if they be accepted as trustworthy, then the following facts emerge:

First, the senior wife of the king could not necessarily be anointed as the chief queen. Āsandhimitrā became the chief consort, though Aśoka married Devī first.

Second, the chief queen was called *Aggamahisī*. Here we probably notice a discrepancy in the accounts between the epigraphic and literary evidence, for inscriptions imply that the chief queen was called *Prathamā-devī*, as may be guessed from the expression *dutiyāye deviye*, applied to Kāruvākī.

Third, the post of the chief queen did not remain vacant for long. With the death of the occupant, another queen stepped into the post in no time.

Fourth, it seems that there were several family establishments for individual wives at different places. The Pāli texts tell us that Devī did not accompany the emperor to Pāṭaliputra but continued to stay at Vidiśā. The testimony of the Pāli texts regarding the separate establishment of different queens at different places appears to be corroborated by inscriptional evidence. The Queen's Edict[44] suggests that Kāruvākī had her residence at Kauśāmbī. That many of Aśoka's queens did not live with him at Pāṭaliputra but resided at other places is conclusively proved by the following statement in P.E. VII, 'In all my harems, they become acquainted in many ways with all the (proper) objects where satisfaction is to be arranged, here (in the capital) and in the (different) quarters (of the country).'[45]

The information about the Maurya queens, supplied to us by the edicts of Aśoka and Buddhist legends, is, however, by no means complete, and for fuller details we may turn to the *Arthaśāstra.* Kauṭilya includes the queen mother and the chief queen in the list of the highest paid state officials who received 48,000 *paṇas* as their emolument. Kauṭilya warns the king not to confide in his queen greatly and advises him to visit her only 'after she is cleared (of suspicion) by old women'. He cites a few cases of treachery on the part of queens. The Kāśī monarch was killed by his queen who served him poisonous fried grain under the guise of honey; the king Vairantya was killed by his queen by means of an anklet smeared with poison; Viduratha was murdered by his queen who kept a weapon concealed in the braid of her hair. Kauṭilya[46] lays down that the king should keep the queens under strict vigil. He says, 'He should forbid (the queen's) contact with ascetics with shaven heads or matted hair and with jugglers as well as with female slaves from outside. No members of their families should visit these queens except in establishments for maternity and sickness.' In the circumstances, the queen, as envisaged by Kauṭilya, hardly enjoyed any scope to participate in public life and administration. Even we are not sure whether the Maurya queens had any direct control over the ladies of the royal household; for, inscriptions speak of the *Stryadhyakṣa Mahāmātras*[47] who were, in all probability, appointed to look after matters concerning the ladies of the palace.

Vasiṣṭha,[48] who is generally believed to have flourished in an earlier epoch, points out that the queen mother should receive maintenance, and the other queens of the deceased king should be provided with food and raiment but they are at liberty to go elsewhere, according to their desire. An incidental reference to a queen, who being concealed from the public gaze, attended a sitting of the royal court, is to be met with in the Jaina *Kalpa-sūtra,* which was, in all probability, composed during the early days of Maurya rule Here we read that when the king Siddhārtha summoned his ministers and courtiers for the interpretation of the queen's dream, he took his seat on the throne in the hall of audience, whereas, the queen was seated behind a curtain. It is extremely difficult to deduce any conclusion on the evidence of this story the authenticity of which is not beyond dispute.

IV

The Queen in the Indo-Greek, Scytho-Parthian and Kuṣāṇa Kingdoms

That the queens wielded enormous influence in the Indo-Greek principalities in the north-western part of India is evidenced by coins. Numismatic evidence implies that Menander considered himself to be the husband of the goddess Athena whose figure appears on some of his coins. But the goddess is represented in the form of his queen Agathocleia. This shows the great esteem in which Agathocleia[49] was held by her husband. But it was after the death of her husband that she seized the opportunity to demonstrate her skill as an administrator. The so-called joint-issues of Agathocleia and her son Strato I, which bear the portrait of Agathocleia alone, show that they were issued at a time when Agathocleia assumed the reins of administration as regent for her minor son, consequent upon the death of her husband Menander. She assumed the title of 'god-like' on coins.[50] The period of her regency proved to be of long duration, as may be inferred from her second series of coins which shows jugate busts of herself and Strato I.[51]

The case of Laodice, who was the mother of Eucratides, also deserves to be considered. Eucratides struck a series of coins on which figure his parents Heliocles and Laodice. Laodice, to judge from her name, was a Seleucid princess, and if the theory of Tarn[52] is accepted, she was a daughter of Seleucus II and sister of Antiochus III. It is of interest to note that on coins Laodice wears the diadem, while her husband is found bare-headed. The use of the diadem, the symbol of royal power, by Laodice may be regarded as a proof of her being the real mistress of the satrapy with which her husband was associated either as a general or a governor.

Attention may further be drawn to some silver pieces on which Hermaeus and Calliope appear side by side, both wearing the diadem. This shows that Calliope, who was related to Hippostratus of the Euthydemid family, as is upheld by Tarn,[53] was a queen in her own right, and it seems quite likely that, although corroborative evidence is not forthcoming, she shouldered the administrative responsibilities jointly with her husband who was the last descendant of Eucratides.

Our knowledge of the queens in the Scytho-Parthian and Kuṣāṇa kingdoms is extremely meagre. When the Parthian king Mithridates I died in B.C. 138-7, his queen Ri . . . mu acted as regent for his young son Phrates II.[54] But our sources do not disclose the existence of a Ri . . . mu in any Parthian kingdom in India proper. The Mathura lion capital inscriptions[55] speak of Ayasi Kamuia as the chief queen of the *Mahākṣatrapa* Rajula and daughter of the *Yuvarāja* Kharaosta. It was this Buddhist queen at whose behest some religious endowments (*dharma-dāna*) were made in a cave monastery (*guhā-vihāra*), as the records tell us. Some scholars[56] are inclined to read the name of the queen as Nada Di(or Si)aka, taking her to be the mother of the *Yuvarāja* Kharaosta. According to this view, Arta, the father of Kharaosta, was the first husband of Rajula's chief queen who married Rajula consequent upon Arta's death. If this view be accepted, it would follow that remarriage of widow-queens was not entirely unknown in Scytho-Parthian ruling houses.

V

The Queen in Epics and Other Early Texts

The evidence of the *Rāmāyaṇa* and the *Mahābhārata* may be utilised as reflecting the condition of India for the period between the fourth century B.C. and the fourth century A.D., which witnessed the final composition of the epics, as well as for some earlier centuries. There are a few passages in the epics which show that at the time of emergency, women were allowed to ascend the throne. The *Ayodhyā-kāṇḍa*[57] of the *Rāmāyaṇa* states that there was a proposal to place Sītā on the throne when Rāma was banished to the forest (*Ātmā hi dārā sarveṣāṁ dāra-saṁgrahavartināṁ| ātm-eyam=iti Rāmasya pālayiṣyati medinīṁ||*). But generally speaking, the *Rāmāyaṇa* would leave the impression that the royal ladies did not ordinarily move out of the precincts of the palace, and occasions were few and far between when they came under public gaze. When Sītā, along with her husband, set out for the forest through the public thoroughfares of Oudh, the people lamented that the lady, yet to be seen by the spirits of the sky, would be seen by the people walking on the road.[58] There are also other indications in the *Rāmāyaṇa* to show that women of a higher stratum avoided public eyes. Thus, after Rāvaṇa's defeat, when Sītā was brought before Rāma, Vibhīṣaṇa tried to drive away the common soldiers, crowding the place but Rāma forbade him to do so, saying,[59] 'The public appearance of a woman does not spoil her in misery, in extraordinary circumstances, in war, in *svayamvara* and in marriage.' Similarly, when, after the great battle at Kurukṣetra, the Kaurava queens appear on the battle-field, lamenting for their deceased husbands, a regret is expressed to the effect that 'Those queens, whom even the gods could not see formerly, are now seen by common people, after the death of their husbands.'[60]

In regard to the prevalence of the *purdah* system in those days, it may be observed that no evidence is forthcoming from the *Rāmāyaṇa* about the prevalence of the system among the Ikṣvāku princesses. S.N. Vyas[61] has shown on the basis of a statement[62] of Maṇḍodarī, the wife of Rāvaṇa, that the observance of *purdah* or *avaguṇṭhana* was in vogue among the Rākṣasas. D.P. Vora[63] points out that a sort of *purdah* must have been adopted by the royal ladies, while facing the general public, excluding, of course, high officials and ministers.

The *Śāntiparvan*[64] of the *Mahābhārata* implies that in the event of the absence of any male heir, women were offered the throne (*Kumārī n=āsti yeṣāṁ kanyās=tatr=ābhiṣecaya*). It is to be remembered in this connection that the *Mahābhārata* in a different context decries the rule of women as the harbinger of misery[65] (*Yatra strī yatra kitavo vālo yatr= ānuśāsitā| majjanti te='vaśā rājan=nadyām=aplavā iva||*).

The epics envisage that the kings were reverential to their consorts. The king is enjoined to take care of his queen as his mother and respect her as his elder sister[66] (*Iyaṁ ca naḥ priyā bhāryā prāṇebhyo='pi garīyasī| māt=eva paripālyā ca pūjyā jyeṣṭh=eva ca svasā||*). Still, the well known example of Yudhiṣṭhira staking Draupadī in the gambling hall may suggest that the husband was considered to have had a proprietary right in the wife. In the epics, there are also passages where some of the queens are treated with scorn. The *Rāmāyaṇa*[67] brings to light in no uncertain manner the meanness of Kaikeyī's nature and tells us how her mother was banished for preferring widowhood to the satisfaction of her curiosity. The curse of Yudhiṣṭhira[68] to the women of the world for the folly of his mother is well known. The diversified opinion of the compilers of the epics towards the queens probably indicates the absence of a universally accepted status of women.

The *Mahābhārata* shows the prevalence of the custom of levirate in the royal harem. When the kings were physically incapable, the queens were urged by their husbands or relatives to procreate offspring with the help of other persons, according to the *niyoga* system. Dhṛtarāṣṭra and Pāṇḍu were born to Vicitravīrya as a result of such a union of his queens Ambikā and Ambālikā with Kṛṣṇa Dvaipāyana Veda Vyāsa. Mādrī gave birth to her sons through the grace of the twin Aśvinas. It, however, cannot be definitely said whether the *niyoga* marriage was current among any of the royal families in India during the period between the fourth century B.C. and the fourth century A.D.

The *Mahābhārata* refers to the self-immolation of Mādrī; it, likewise, speaks of four wives of Kṛṣṇa as burning themselves with their royal husband. There is, however, no definite indication in favour of the wide prevalence of *Suttee* in the royal houses with which the custom might have originated.

While referring to the qualifications of the queen, Manu[69] points out that she should be of equal caste (*varṇa*), be born in a great family, and be possessed of auspicious marks on her body, charms and many other excellent qualities. Manu scorns the idea of the queen being consulted by the king in matters of government, as would be clear from his following observations:[70] 'At the time of consultation, let him cause to be removed idiots, the dumb, the blind and the deaf, animals, very aged men, women, the sick and those deficient in limbs. (Such) despicable (persons), likewise animals and particularly women betray secret counsel, for that reason he must be careful with respect to them.' Although queens are denied participation in governmental matters as consorts of kings, they must have enjoyed an honoured position in the palace, being the custodians of household ceremonies and upbringers of the family[71] (*Yatra nāryas=tu pūjyante ramante tatra devatāḥ/ yatr=aitās=tu na pūjyante sarvās=tatr=āphalāḥ kriyāḥ//*). Manu recommends women to inherit some kinds of property. If this right of inheritance, as suggested by Manu, applies to all classes of women, then it may be held that queens had their own property which comprised the gifts offered by parents and brothers at any time, gifts of affection bestowed by husbands after marriage, and presents given by anybody either at the time of marriage or at the time they are taken to their new home.[72] It may be mentioned that the above six varieties of *strī-dhana* are supplemented by Viṣṇu[73] with the addition of three more categories, including the gifts given by the son or any other relative and the compensation paid to the wife at the time of her supersession on the occasion of her husband's second marriage.[74]

But when we compare the evidence of the epics with that of the *Arthaśāstra* and the *Manu-saṁhitā* on the position of queens, we hardly meet with any appreciable discrepancy in them. Both Kauṭilya and Manu are unanimous in decrying the idea of investing queens with the right to assist kings in administrative matters; the movements and activities of queens, according to them, are strictly restricted within the bounds of the palace. Whereas, in some passages of the epics we, no doubt, find a more liberal attitude being adopted towards queens and women, as compared to the *Arthaśāstra* and the *Manu-saṁhitā*, views like those of Kauṭilya and Manu and even more drastic ones are also reflected both in the *Rāmāyaṇa* and the *Mahābhārata*. It is interesting to note in this connection that Pāṇini, whose date is variously estimated between the seventh and fourth centuries B.C., in the *Kṛd=anta-kṛtya-prakaraṇam* section of his *Aṣṭādhyāyī*, has used the expression *a-Sūrya-lalā-ṭayor=dṛśitapoḥ*. The commentators, including Patañjali and Bhaṭṭojī Dīkṣita, have interpreted it in the sense of queens (*Sūryāṁ na paśyant=īty=asūryampaśyā rājadārāḥ*). It may accordingly be safely presumed that the eminent grammarian knew of the royal ladies 'who lived in the seclusion of the palace where they could not see even the sun'.[75]

VI

The Queen in the Gupta Age

We now come to the Gupta age. Dikshitar[76] is of opinion that the Gupta queens were generally called *Devīs* and he cites, in support of his contention, the cases of Kumāradevī and Dattadevī. But it may be argued that Kumāradevī and Dattadevī were the personal names of the chief queens of Candragupta I and Samudragupta, respectively, and that the official charters of the Gupta kings describe both of them as *Mahādevīs*.[77] Dikshitar[78] further opines that queens in the Gupta period held in administration an equally important status with their husbands, but this suggestion, likewise, cannot be definitely proved. It is true that the name and effigy of Kumāradevī appear on the so-called Candragupta I-Kumāradevī coins along with those of her husband, and this may indicate that Kumāradevī held a high position in the kingdom, but there is hardly any ground in support of the contention that queens of other kings rose to the same pinnacle of glory, as did the Licchavi princess.

But how would we explain the presence of the name and the portrait of Kumāradevī on the Candragupta I-Kumāradevī coins? An answer to this question is not possible unless the issue of their authorship is resolved first. If it is conceded that they were issued by Samudragupta to commemorate the marriage of his parents, the presence of the queen's portrait on coins then would not indicate any political or administrative significance. If, on the contrary, we assume that they were the joint issues of Candragupta I and Kumāradevī, then the conclusion becomes inevitable that 'Kumāradevī was a queen by her own right, and the proud Licchavis, to whose stock she belonged, must have been anxious to retain their individuality in the new Imperial state'.[79] But the absence of any reference to Samudragupta's name on these coins proves that they were not commemorative medals but were issued by Candragupta I, and when it is remembered that the latter owed his rise to the imperial position to his marriage with the Licchavis, the appearance of Kumāradevī's figure on his coins may be explained by suggesting that 'the coins . . . bearing the joint names and portraits of Candragupta I and Kumāradevī were really issued when these two were ruling the Gupta empire'.[80]

Besides Kumāradevī, two other Gupta queens, viz., Dattadevī and Anantadevī, are found represented on coins. The Aśvamedha coins of Samudragupta show on the reverse 'the crowned queen, standing on a circular pearl bordered mat, with *chouri* in r. hand and towel in l. hand'.[81] The similar coins of Kumāragupta I depict on the reverse his crowned queen, Anantadevī. But the chief queens of Samudragupta and Kumāragupta I appear on these two series of coins not because of any political reasons but for the fact that they, as wives, as laid down by the sacred literature, played an important role in the rituals of the horse-sacrifice, performed by their husbands.

Were the Gupta kings polygamists? The question has to be answered probably in the affirmative. That Samudragupta had his chief queen in Dattadevī is well known. The Allahabad inscription states that Samudragupta was presented maidens (*kany=opāyana-dāna*) by some foreign potentates. These maidens were either married to the Gupta ruler or stayed in the Gupta palace as opera girls. If the first suggestion is accepted, it would follow that Samudragupta had a plurality of queens. It is certain that Candragupta II had no fewer than two queens, Dhruvadevī or Dhruvasvāminī and Kuberanāgā. The existence of the former is disclosed by the *Devīcandraguptam* as well as by inscriptions, while the Poona plates of Prabhāvatīguptā refer to Kuberanāgā. The chief queen of Kumāragupta I was Anantadevī who gave birth to Purugupta. The mother of Skandagupta appears to have been different from Anantadevī and was probably named Devakī, as first suggested by Sewel[82] and subsequently endorsed by H.C. Raychaudhuri.[83] Kumāragupta I had evidently at least two wives. On the basis of the above evidence, it may be concluded that the Gupta kings were normally polygamists.

Turning to contemporary literature, we find that the great poet Kālidāsa refers to the prevalence of the custom of polygamy[84] in royal families (*Bahu-vallabhā rājānaḥ śruyante*). Śakuntalā is advised by Kaṇva to be courteous to her co-wives[85] (*Kuru priya-sakhī-vṛttiṁ sapatnījane*). The husband is represented in Kālidāsa's works as the absolute master of his wife's destiny. This is indicated by the exile of Sītā by Rāma as well as by the statement[86] of Sāradvata that authority over wives is admitted to be unlimited (*Upapannā hi dāreṣu prabhūtā sarvato-mukhī*). There is a reference to a queen's accession to the throne in Canto XIX of the *Raghuvaṁśa*.

VII

The Queen in the Post-Gupta Period

We know very little about the queens of the Maitraka kings who succeeded the Imperial Guptas in parts of Western India. Princess (*rāja-duhitṛ*) Bhūpā or Bhūvā acted as the *dūtaka* for both the Alina and Kaira plates[87] of Dharasena IV. It is clear from her role in these records that she 'accompanied the king in his tour or march of war and was entrusted with considerable responsibilities'.[88] When a daughter of a Maitraka king played a significant role in the kingdom, it is not unlikely that their queens were also granted similar, if not greater, prerogatives.

There is an inscriptional evidence in favour of the assumption that some of the queens of contemporary Nepal were more powerful than those in other North Indian kingdoms. One of the Nepal inscriptions[89] tells us that queen Rājyavatī, the widow of Dharmadeva, on the death of her husband, directed her son Mānadeva to reign so that she would follow her deceased husband. The inscription, in question, then recognises the right of the widow of a deceased king to decide the issue of succession to the throne.

The *Harṣacarita* seems to imply that at the time of coronation, both the king and the chief queen were consecrated. When Yaśomatī was consecrated, 'wives of hundreds of Prabhākaravardhana's feudatories poured on her water from gold pitchers and her forehead was adorned with a tiara indicative of her august position'.[90] But the *Harṣacarita* does not portray queens as playing any important part in administration. In this connection we may note the following statement by Patralatā on behalf of Rājyaśrī, 'A husband or a son is a woman's true support; but to those who are deprived of both, it is immodesty even to continue to live.'[91] The statement appears to contain a veiled allusion to the custom of *Suttee* in the days of Bāṇa who refers in unambiguous terms to Yaśomatī as ascending the funeral pyre of her husband. The earliest epigraphical reference to the self-immolation of widows is to be found in the Eran inscription of Bhānugupta dated A.D. 510, which tells us how Goparāja's wife became a Suttee at the death of her husband in the battle of Eran. In the accounts of Bāṇa, there is no evidence which would show that queens of his times actively participated in administration. Bāṇa speaks of Rājyaśrī as an intelligent and accomplished lady, but whether she had any role to play in the government is nowhere mentioned in the *Harṣa-carita.* The Chinese text *Fang-chih*[92] states that Rājyaśrī administered the government in conjunction with her brother Harṣavardhana. It must be admitted that there is no evidence to corroborate the Chinese account in regard to Rājyaśrī's role in Harṣavardhana's administration.

The writings of Hiuen Tsang[93] prove the existence of a couple of *Strī-rājyas* in the seventh century A.D. One of them was called 'the Eastern Women's Country', being located in the present Kumaon-Garhwal region in the Himalayas. The other *Strī-rājya,* known as 'the Western Women's Country', was situated in the present Baluchistan region. Unfortunately, Hiuen Tsang does not give us any precise information about the administrative and political activities of the queens of the above two *Strī-rājyas.*

Some of the Later Gupta queens are described as *Mahādevī, Paramabhaṭṭārikā* and *Rājñī* in contemporary epigraphs like the Mandar hill[94] and the Deo-Baranark[95] inscriptions of Ādityasena and Jīvitagupta II, respectively, although we are hardly provided with any information concerning the rights and responsibilities that they may have enjoyed.

VIII

The Queen in the Pāla and Pratīhāra Kingdoms

We possess meagre information about the queens in the Pāla kingdom. It is worth noting that queens are not mentioned in the long list of officers, appearing in the official charters of the Pāla kings from the time of Dharmapāla onwards. This may reasonably imply that the queens of the Pāla kings did not occupy an important position.[96] But the condition of the Pratīhāra queens may be said to have been somewhat better, as may be suggested by the fact that the seals of the Imperial Pratīhāras invariably mention the *Mahādevīs* of whom they were born. Śīlābhaṭṭārikā, many of whose verses are found quoted in the anthologies, was probably a queen of king Bhoja I.

IX

The Queen in Other Contemporary and Later Kingdoms

But more enviable was the status of the Cāhamāna queens. Somaladevī, the queen of Ajayarāja, is known to have issued coins in her own name. Her silver coins,[97] which are very rare, bear the crude representation of the king's head on the obverse, and the legend *Śrī-Somaladevī* in Nāgarī on the reverse. Her copper coins, which are more numerous than the silver pieces, contain the figure of a Chauhan horseman on their obverse and the legend, giving her own name, on the reverse. Someśvara's queen Karpūradevī[98] assumed the reins of government during the minority of her grandson Pṛthvīrāja III. Of the queens of this dynasty, performing benevolent acts, mention may be made of the wife of king Candana,[99] who is known to have laid the foundation of some religious buildings at Puṣkara. Epigraphs suggest that the queens in the Cāhamāna kingdom were sometimes granted assignments of land as pin-money. Thus, an inscription,[100] dated A.D. 1143, describes queen Tihuṇaka as being in enjoyment of a village as her *girāsa* (e.g., *grāsa*), while another record[101] of A.D. 1179 refers to the *bhukti* of queen Jālhaṇadevī. P.B. Udgaonkar[102] is of opinion that sometimes taxes were assigned to the queens as part of their income, probably in addition to the *Grāsa-bhūmi* lands, but others may not agree with this view.

The queens of the Gāhaḍavāla kings[103] were generally designated as *Rājñī and Mahiṣī*, while the chief ones among them were called *Agramahiṣī*, *Paṭṭamahiṣī*, *Paṭṭamahādevī* and *Mahārājñī*. The Hatiyadah pillar inscription[104] of V.S. 1207 mentions one Bellana who was the *Bhāṇḍāgārika* of queen Gosalladevī. It is evident from the above record that some of the Gāhaḍavāla queens had their own personal *bhāṇḍ=āgāra* or treasury which, as has already been observed, consisted of the different categories of *strī-dhana*. P.B. Udgaonkar[105] has shown that the Gāhaḍavāla queens were often granted land allotments, known as *Rājakīya-bhoga*, for their personal expenditure but it is not possible to say definitely whether they enjoyed full proprietary rights over these lands. The Gāhaḍavāla queens are mentioned in the copper-plate grants as making land grants. Queen Pṛthvīśrīkā donated the village of Bahuvarā to the *Purohita* Devavarman and other Brāhmaṇas with the consent of the emperor Madanapāla;[106] the Kamauli copper-plate inscription[107] speaks of Nayanakelidevī, the queen of Govindacandra, as supplicating for the king's permission while granting a village to the *Mahāpurohita* Jāguśarman; and Gosalladevī, another queen of Govindacandra, as known from the Bangavan copper-plate inscription,[108] secured her husband's approval while granting the village of Ghāṭiyārā to a donee, named Kulhe. All this evidence would clearly indicate that the Gāhaḍavāla queens were hardly empowered to grant land in their own right; whenever a queen desired to make a grant, she had to obtain the prior approval of the ruling monarch.[109] Kumāradevī, the Buddhist queen of Govindacandra, is reputed in her Sarnath inscription[110] to have repaired the Dharmacakra-Jina, originally set up by Dharmāśoka, and placed it in a newly-built *vihāra* at Sarnath.

It is not definitely known whether the Gāhaḍavāla queens had ever played any important part in administration. In two of the records[111] of Madanapāla, the crown-prince Govindacandra is stated to have taken the consent of a few persons, including the ministers, the *Purohita* and the queen mother Rālhaṇadevī at the time of the land grant (*Eteṣāṁ saṁmatiṁ prāpya samyag=likhitavān=idam| nāmnā Vijayadās=ākhyaḥ śāsanaṁ rāja-śāsanam||*); but it is difficult to say whether the permission of the queen was a mere formality or it was due to her being a member of the government.[112]

Queens, in particular, and women, in general, are held in great distrust by the contemporary or nearly contemporary writers, including the authors of the *Agni Purāṇa* and the *Nītivākyāmṛta* who, being too much obsessed with the patriarchal conception, have denounced the right of women in the case of succession to the throne. The *Agni Purāṇa*[113] advises the king not to repose trust in queens, especially those who are blessed with sons (*Na c=āsāṁ viśvaset=jātu putra-mātur=viśeṣataḥ| na svapet strī-gṛhe rātrau viśvāsaḥ kṛtrimo bhavet||*). It, however, admits that the nomination of the chief queen is a prerequisite for the king's coronation[114] (*Rājā bhaṭṭārako devaḥ s=ābhiṣekā devy=api*), but this would only imply the importance of queens for religious purposes, since no sacrifice was considered complete without the wife's participation in it. The idea of placing implicit faith in women is likewise deprecated by Somadeva Sūri,[115] who, however, urges the king against antagonising the queen. 'He is so distrustful of women that he asks the king neither to appoint any women to look after things used by him nor to partake of anything sent from his wife's apartment.'[116]

But the *Rājataraṅgiṇī*, the chronicle of Kashmir, composed by Kalhaṇa about the middle of the twelfth century A.D., reveals that the queens of Kashmir assumed enormous power. They sometimes helped their husbands in administration and some of them are known to have ruled the country either in their own name or as regents on behalf of minor kings. A passage of the *Rājataraṅgiṇī*[117] implies that some queens were authorised to issue written orders to ministers who were subjected to punishment for the transgression of such orders. Sugandhā, for instance, dominated the political stage of Kashmir in the first quarter of the tenth century A.D. She held the reins of administration during the minority of her son Gopālavarman who ascended the throne after the death of king Śaṅkaravarman shortly before A.D. 900.[118] Gopālavarman was later on treacherously murdered and the throne passed on to an alleged son of Śaṅkaravarman named Saṅkaṭa whose rule lasted a few days only. Sugandhā, who was responsible, in no small measure, for these palace intrigues, finally assumed royalty, though Kalhaṇa states that she did so at the behest of the people. She was, however, not destined to reign for long, being overthrown and killed by the Tantrins.

Sugandhā was not the lone queen to guide the political destiny of Kashmir in the tenth century A.D. Diddā, the queen of Kṣemagupta, too, is known to have played a decisive role in the history of the province during the second half of the same century. Kalhaṇa states that Diddā exercised considerable influence upon her husband who 'became known by the humiliating appellation Diddā-Kṣema'.[119] Attention may be drawn to some of the copper coins of Kṣemagupta which bear the legend *Di-Kṣema*, apparently a contraction of *Diddā-Kṣemagupta*. It is interesting to note that while the coins of the above type are quite numerous, those containing the name of Kṣemagupta alone are rare. This unmistakably points to the prominent position held by the queen in the government of her husband (A.D. 950-A.D. 958). Kṣemagupta was succeeded by his young son Abhimanyu who ruled for fourteen years. Abhimanyu was followed, respectively, by his three sons, Nandigupta, Tribhuvanagupta and Bhīmagupta, all of whom were mere puppets in the hands of Diddā who finally killed Bhīmagupta by a stratagem and herself ascended the throne of Kashmir in A.D. 980. She governed the kingdom with extraordinary ability till her death in A.D. 1003.[120]

The other queen who is reputed to have exercised no mean influence upon the history of Kashmir is Sūryamatī. She was in reality the *de facto* ruler of the kingdom during the rule of her husband, the Lohara king Ananta and even persuaded the latter, notwithstanding the opposition of the wisest counsellors, to abdicate the throne in favour of her unworthy son Kalaśa. In VII.197 of the *Rājataraṅgiṇī*[121] we have the expression, 'by giving up the accumulation in her own treasury', which is used with reference to the queen Sūryamatī. This implies that, like their Gāhaḍavāla sisters, the queens of Kashmir sometimes owned private treasuries. The *Rājataraṅgiṇī* speaks of another lady named Koṭādevī, who adorned the throne of Kashmir for a short while about A.D. 1338.[122]

If the queens of any royal family matched the prestigious position of their Kashmiri sisters, then it was the queens of the Bhauma-Kara royal house of Orissa. To start with, Tribhuvanamahādevī I *alias* Sindagaurī whose Dhenkanal plate,[123] issued in the Bhauma year 120, states that she assumed the reins of government on the persuasion of her feudatories. According to the testimony of one of the Talcher grants,[124] she subsequently abdicated the throne in favour of her grandson Śāntikara II *alias* Gayāḍa II or Loṇabhāra (Lavaṇabhāra) when the latter became sufficiently grown up. A similar role on the political stage of Orissa was played by Pṛthvīmahādevī, the widowed queen of Śubhākara IV. She informs us in her Baud plates[125] of the Bhauma year 158 that since both her husband and the latter's younger brother Śivakara III died without leaving any male issue, she ascended the Bhauma throne. But as Śivakara III had at least a couple of sons, viz., Śāntikara III *alias* Lavaṇabhāra II and Śubhākara V, as is disclosed by inscriptions, Pṛthvīmahādevī was evidently lukewarm to recognise the sons of Śivakara III as rightful heirs and successfully occupied the throne for some time. Tribhuvanamahādevī and Pṛthvīmahādevī were not the only Bhauma-Kara queens to shoulder the administrative responsibilities; some other queens are known to have discharged administrative functions. Queen Gaurīmahādevī succeeded her husband Śubhākara V who probably left no male heir and she was followed by her daughter Daṇḍīmahādevī who issued charters in the years 180 and 187. The Taltali plates[126] of Dharmamahādevī tell us that Daṇḍīmahādevī was followed by her step-mother Vakulamahādevī[127] who, in her turn, was succeeded by Dharmamahādevī,[128] the wife of Śāntikara III. It is, therefore, evident that the last four rulers of the Bhauma-Kara family were all women who reigned in the capacity of *de facto* and *de jure* rulers. The ruling queens of the Kara dynasty generally assumed all the imperial titles in accordance with their power and position. Queen Daṇḍīmahādevī, for instance, called herself *Paramabhaṭṭārikā*, *Mahārājādhirāja* and *Parameśvarī*.

The queens in the Bhañja kingdom are represented in inscriptions as being entrusted with the important task of maintaining the royal seal and scrutinising the genuineness of documents. Some grants of king Vidyādharabhañja Amoghakalaśa are known to have been registered with the royal seal by his own queen Jayamahādevī. A charter[129] of king Neṭṭabhañja III Tribhuvanakalaśa was similarly registered by queen Jīvalokamahādevī. The queens of the Gaṅga kings of Śvetaka are known to have discharged similar functions. A grant of Pṛthvīvarman was registered by his queen; a charter of Anantavarman was likewise registered by his queen Śrīvāsabhaṭṭārikā.

The Brahmeśvara inscription speaks of Kolāvatī, the queen of the Somavaṁśī king Yayāti III Caṇḍīhara and mother of Udyotakesarin, as erecting the temple of Brahmeśvara (Śiva) at Ekāmra. The Ratnagiri charter registers a grant in favour of *Rāṇī* Śrī-Karpūraśrī. Karpūraśrī is generally supposed to have been a *Devadāsī*, attached to the Buddhist Mahāvihāra of Saloṇapura[130] but her designation suggests that she might have been a queen of the last Somavaṁśī king Karṇadeva.

Rajasthan has produced a galaxy of valiant queens who not only actively participated in administration, but also joined hands with their husbands to fight the enemies. The *Pṛthvīrājarāso* of Cand Bardāī speaks of the Caulukya princess Karma-devī who governed the kingdom of Mevāḍa following the death of her son Samarasiṁha at the hands of Muhammad Ghūrī. Tod[131] observes, 'She headed her Rājputs and gave battle to Qutbuddin near Ambar, when the viceroy was defeated and wounded. Nine *Rājās* and eleven chiefs of inferior dignity with the title of *Rāvat* followed the mother of their prince.' Modern scholars are, however, loath to accept most of these traditions as historically genuine.

X

The Queen in the Pre-Vākāṭaka Period

Having surveyed the position of queens in different North Indian kingdoms in different periods, we may now turn our attention to South India. Some useful information about the queens in the Śātavāhana kingdom may be derived by a careful study of the inscriptions of the family. Nāganikā or Nāyanikā,[132] queen of Śātakarṇi I, who flourished about the close of the first century B.C., is called *Devī*, while another queen of the same dynasty, flourishing a few generations later, is styled as *Mahādevī*. It would then follow that the Śātavāhana queens were generally called *Devī* and *Mahādevī*. Notwithstanding her less pretentious title of *Devī*, Nāganikā played an important part in the annals of the Śātavāhana house by acting as regent during the minority of her son Vedaśrī. The Nanaghat record would tend to suggest that it was during the period of her regency that she performed a number of Vedic sacrifices and made liberal donations to learned Brāhmaṇas. It has to be noted that Jaimini, a contemporary of Nāganikā, declares that women are incompetent to perform a sacrifice for the reason that 'the woman is inferior to man. The sacrificer is learned, his wife is ignorant[133] (*atulyā hi strī puṁsā/ yajamānaḥ pumān vidvāṁś=ca/ patnī strī c=āvidyā ca/*). Nāyanikā's performance of Vedic sacrifices at a time when women were discouraged to do so demonstrates how the cry of social reformers in ancient India often went unheeded by the mighty. T.V. Mahalingam[134] opines that the Śātavāhana kings often ruled their kingdom in association with their queen mothers. This contention is based on the evidence of a Nasik cave inscription[135] which, according to him, shows that 'Gautamīputra Śātakarṇi and his mother Gautamī Balaśrī made a joint order in the 24th year of the former's reign to an officer who was in charge of Govardhanāhāra'. But it may be pointed out that the Nasik inscription only proves that the queen-mother Balaśrī was associated with her son Gautamīputra in a gift in favour of certain Buddhist monks, but we have no positive evidence to ascertain that she helped her son in administration.[136]

The Ikṣvākus were not far removed from the later Śātavāhanas in point of time but their queens could stand no comparison with those of the Śātavāhanas. Insciiptions do not associate them with any administrative duty. The mention of the *Antaḥpura-mahattarikā* in an inscription[137] of Ehuvula Cāntamūla would seem to indicate that the Ikṣvāku queens were even relieved of the charge of the harem. Some of the Ikṣvāku queens like Mahādevī Rudradhara-bhaṭṭārikā, Bāpi Siriṇikā, *Mahādevī* Cāṁthisiri and Bhaṭidevā are, however, known to have pooled their donations in favour of the Buddhist establishments at Nagarjunakonda.

XI

The Queen in the Vākāṭaka Kingdom

The Vākāṭaka queens were generally known as *Devīs*, while the chief ones among them were called *Mahādevīs*. Prabhāvatīguptā, who was the *Agra-mahiṣī* of king Rudrasena II (*Mahārāja-śrī-Rudrasenasy=āgramahiṣī*), bore the designation of *Mahādevī* (*Jīva-putra-pautrā śrī-mahādevī Prabhāvatīguptā*). Her Poona plates[138] seem to imply that Prabhāvatī, following the death of her husband, assumed the reins of administration as regent, first on behalf of the minor king Divākarasena, and later, with the death of the former, for her young son Dāmodarasena. A.S. Altekar[139] points out that the period of her regency lasted for a term of about twenty years. Prabhāvatī, however, lived for a few years more as we find her mentioned in the Tirodi plates, issued in the twenty-third year of the reign of her son Pravarasena II.[140] D.C. Sircar[141] has advanced the view that Prabhāvatīguptā ruled the Vākāṭaka kingdom as a *de jure* ruler and not as regent. The factor that contributed to her assumption of power was either 'her love of power or some unknown reason that might have prevented Divākarasena from occupying the throne as in the case of the Pallava *Yuvamahārāja* Viṣṇugopavarman'.[142] This theory, it must be admitted, does not appear to be unlikely, as there are reasons to believe that the Poona plates were dated in her own regnal year. In any case, there is hardly any doubt that Prabhāvatīguptā was a dominating personality in the Vākāṭaka kingdom for a few years about the beginning of the fifth century A.D.

XII

The Queen in the Cālukya and Pallava Kingdoms

That the queens of the Cālukya kings of Badami were no less powerful is evidenced by inscriptions which represent them as issuing records, administering divisions, making generous gifts and installing images of gods and goddesses. Vijayabhaṭṭārikā, the senior queen of Candrāditya Pṛthivīvallabha Mahārāja, the elder brother of Vikramāditya I, was ruling over, as may be inferred from one of her charters,[143] which is dated in the fifth year of her reign, a portion of the Cālukya kingdom by the middle of the 7th century A.D. Her records extol her as a poetess, who 'won high rank in the esteem of literary critics'. She has been identified with Vijayāṅkā who is extolled as 'Sarasvatī incarnate and as a peer of Kālidāsa in the Vaidarbhī style of composition' in some verses attributed to Rājaśekhara in Jalhaṇa's *Suktimuktāvalī* (A.D. 1258). The cultivation of literature was evidently one of the hobbies of the queens. Among other Cālukya queens to attain glorious heights, mention may be made of Vikramāditya II's wife Lokamahādevī who built a temple at Paṭṭadakal.[144] The Kuntakoti inscription[145] of Vijayāditya refers to one Lokatinimmadi as administering the Kuruttakuṇṭa region. If Lokatinimmadi was identical with Lokamahādevī, which does not appear to be improbable, it would follow that she wielded great power during the reign of her father-in-law. The queen-mother Vinayavatī[146] is known to have set up the images of Brahmā, Viṣṇu and Maheśvara in the capital city of Vātāpī. The Kundur plates[147] of Kīrtivarman II, which speak of the presence of the chief queen (*Mahādevī*) of the said Cālukya monarch in the military camp at Raktapura, leave the impression that queens sometimes accompanied their husbands during their military operations. We are reminded of the Turk-Mongol royal ladies of the sixteenth and seventeenth centuries A.D. who used to accompany their husbands to the war-fields and took an active part in the actual fight.[148]

We know very little about the Pallava queens, barring, of course, their religious endowment and the foundation of monuments in honour of their favourite deities. Cārudevī, the queen of the heir-apparent Vijayabuddhavarman, issued an inscription[149] recording the grant of a piece of land in favour of a Viṣṇu temple at Dalūra. The inscription does not take notice of either her husband or her father-in-law whose sanction was necessary in normal cases. The omission of their approval was probably due to some carelessness on the part of the writer of the grant. It is sometimes held that Cārudevī held such an influential position in the kingdom that she hardly required the permission of the reigning king to make an endowment[150] but this, in the absence of any corroborative evidence, does not seem to be a reasonable presumption. Raṅgapatākā, the queen of Narasiṁhaviṣṇu, is mentioned in a Pallava charter[151] as being the beloved of her husband as Pārvatī was to Śiva and as having obtained the everlasting favour of her husband. This shows that it was the affection of the husband and not a voice in administration, that the Pallava queen prized most. Indeed, we have hardly any evidence at our disposal which would disclose that the queens participated in administration. Mādevī Adigal, the queen of Aparājita, is known to have 'endowed 30 *Kalañjus* of gold for lamps to the Śiva temple at Tiruvorriyūr'.[152] It may be remembered that though like their Cālukya sisters the Pallava queens made various endowments, they did not claim the same status as the former. No inscriptions associate any Pallava queen with administrative responsibility, while a few Cālukya queens were definitely entrusted with administration of at least parts of the kingdom.

XIII

The Queen in the Rāṣṭrakūṭa Kingdom

The queens did not claim any special privilege in the Rāṣṭrakūṭa realm. We do not see them occupying administrative posts[153] or running the government during the minority of the king. An inscription[154] of A.D. 786 mentions Śīlamahādevī, the crowned queen of Dhruva, as making a grant of land 'without any express mention of her husband, Dhruva, as permitting the transaction'. This has led A.S. Altekar[155] to surmise that Śīlamahādevī 'felt that being the crowned queen, she had an inherent right to issue routine administrative orders without any reference to her husband; or, the latter may have expressly invested her with certain ruling powers, including the important power of making land grants'. It is difficult to agree with A.S. Altekar, since we are inclined to treat the omission of her husband's sanction more as accidental than as deliberate.

XIV

The Queen in the Western Cālukya Kingdom

When we come to the time of the Cālukyas of Kalyāṇī, we find that the kings were usually polygamists. Someśvara I had, for instance, at least six queens, viz., Candalakabbe or Candrikādevī, Mailaladevī, Līlādevī, Hoysaladevī, Ketaladevī and Bācaladevī. Of the wives of Vikramāditya VI,[156] mention may be made of Ketaladevī II, Lakṣmīmahādevī, Jekkaladevī, *Paṭṭamahādevī* Mailalamahādevī, Padmaladevī, Candaladevī, Mālaladevī, Bhāgalamahādevī and Sāvaladevī. Most of the Cālukya queens were entrusted with administrative responsibilities.[157] Mailaladevī[158] was ruling in A.D. 1053 Banavāsi 12,000; Ketaladevī II was administering in A.D. 1054 the Ponnavāḍa-*agrahāra*; another queen[159] was the ruler of Siruguppe and Kolanūru in Bellary district in the sixteenth regnal year of her husband Vikramāditya VI; Lakṣmīmahādevī[160] governed first eighteen *agrahāras* along with Dharmapuram and subsequently[161] Niṭṭasingi; Jekkaladevī[162] ruled the village of Inguṇige; Mailalamahādevī[163] was in charge of Kaṇṇavalle in A.D. 1095 and Padmaladevī[164] held sway over the Mamgoli-*agrahāra* in A.D. 1116. It is far from being definitely known whether these queens ruled over their respective divisions from the capital city of Kalyāṇī or were stationed in the areas of their jurisdiction. It is more likely that they lived in Kalyāṇī in the constant company of their husbands and governed their territories with the help of some trusted officers.

Inscriptions also refer to queens making handsome donations on appropriate occasions. Hoysaladevī[165] is known to have made a grant in A.D. 1055; Ketaladevī II,[166] likewise, made a gift to the shrine of Caṇḍeśvara at Kumbittige in Bijapur district; Mālaladevī constructed a Maheśvara temple and Bhāgalamahādevī[167] made a gift of gold in Sirur. G.H. Khare[168] has brought to light a few coins that bear the legend *Śrī-Lakṣumā.* He has attributed these pieces to the queen Lakṣmīmahādevī, although A.S. Altekar[169] holds a contrary view. We thus see that queens played a prominent role in the Western Cālukya kingdom. They patronised the learned, championed the cause of their religion and governed, either personally or through their agents, several divisions of their husbands' kingdom. Indeed, Indian queens reached the pinnacle of their glory in the Cālukya age.

XV

The Queen in the Post-Cālukya Period

The history of the Kākatīya royal family provides us with one of the very few instances of a female ruler exercising royal authority over the entire kingdom in her own right. She was Rudramadevī or Rudrāmbā, being nominated by her father Gaṇapatideva as his successor. On her accession to the throne, she took the masculine name of Rudradeva Mahārāja and ruled the kingdom for nearly four decades with such ability as to win the admiration of the contemporary Venetian traveller Marco Polo.[170]

As would appear from the study of their records, the queens of the Ālūpa kings of South Canara held an honoured position in their husbands' kingdom. T.V. Mahalingam observes that the chief queens of the Ālūpa kings were allowed to rule jointly with their husbands. Mahalingam, in support of his contention, cites the case of Vīra Pāṇḍyadeva Ālūpendradeva who 'is said to have jointly ruled with his senior queen Paṭṭadevī from his capital (*rājadhānī*) Bārahakanyāpura'. But this epigraphic statement, which may aptly be compared with a statement in the Sudi record[172] that Lakṣmīdevī ruled the Western Cālukya kingdom along with her husband Vikramāditya VI from Kalyāṇī, should not be taken seriously, particularly in view of the fact that no other chief queen of the dynasty is represented as playing the role of a joint ruler in the Ālūpa inscriptions, hitherto discovered. The inscription of A.D. 1261-62 only shows that Paṭṭadevī was held in high esteem by her husband. One Ālūpa queen, viz., Ballamahādevī,[173] is known to have held the reins of government for at least fourteen years from Śaka 1201 to Śaka 1214. Like the Kākatīya queen Rudramadevī, she assumed masculine titles like *Mahārāj=ādhirāja*, *Para-bala-sādhaka*, etc. The adoption of male titles by a reigning queen demonstrates that the people, in general, were averse to the rule of women.

We have no means to ascertain whether it was a usual practice with a queen in ancient India to undergo a ceremony for being invested with chief queenhood, as was the case with Harṣavardhana's mother Yaśomatī. This, however, appears to have been a regular feature in the Vijayanagar kingdom, for, we find at least two kings, viz., Kṛṣṇadeva Rāya and Acyuta Rāya, being crowned, respectively, along with their wives, Tirumalādevī and Varadāmbikā, at the time of their coronation.[174]

XVI

Epilogue

It is evident from the foregoing discussion that whereas, among the queens in ancient India only a few were destined to play an active role in administration, and fewer still assumed rulership of kingdoms, the activities of the vast majority remained confined to the precincts of the palace. The reason why the number of the ruling queens was so limited in ancient India, as in all other countries in the contemporary world, is a fascinating subject for investigation. Polygamy which was the usual practice with men in those days and ineligibility of women to family property must have adversely affected the social and economic status of women in general. The society in those days was absolutely predominated by men, and the people were so much obsessed with the patriarchal concept that they were hardly prepared to accept an eve as the supreme head of government. The patriarchal tempo of the people has been clearly reflected in early Indian literature, which, generally speaking, decries women's participation in matters concerning state policies. The commonly accepted belief in the superiority of men to women has so profoundly prejudiced the vision of the Nīti-writers in India that they have strongly denounced the claim of the queen to the throne of her deceased childless husband in favour of the latter's uncle, younger brother, nephew and even the sister's son. Furthermore, it should be noted that the circumstances in those primeval days were hardly conducive to the rule of women. Women, who could not match the military skill and physical hardship of their male counterparts, were seldom expected to provide a stable government in those days of political uncertainty and instability when the issue of leadership was dependent more on brute force than on diplomatic manoeuvres.

References and Notes

1. *VI*, I, p. 478. It, however, seems that the number of queens varied from kingdom to kingdom. In order to safeguard the continuity and honour of the family, a king might have been induced to practise polygamy but the number of his queens undoubtedly depended on his attitude towards life.
2. The term *mahiṣī*, which literally means the chief queen, proves that the king had a plurality of wives.
3. She is called *Parivṛktā* in the *Ṛgveda* (X.102.11), *Atharva Veda* (VII.113.2; XX.128.10-11) and *Śatapatha Brāhmaṇa* (XIII.2.6.6; 4.1.8; 5.2.7).
4. 12.11.
5. VI.5.3.1.
6. Jogiraj Basu (*IAB*, p. 120) quotes from the *Śatapatha Brāhmaṇa* the following passage, *a-putrā vai patnī Parivṛktā*.
7. *VI*, I, p. 478.
8. *Śatapatha Brāhmaṇa*, V.2.1.11.
9. Ibid., XIII.5.2.5.
10. Ibid., XIII.5.2.6.
11. Ibid., XIII.5.2.7.
12. Ibid., XIII.5.2.8.
13. *HP*, p. 201.
14. I.2.5.
15. V.1.16.10.
16. *Śatapatha Brāhmaṇa*, XIII.5.2.2.
17. For a detailed account of the *Aśvamedha* sacrifice, see *IAB*, pp. 207-08.
18. *IAB*, p. 121.
19. The *Ratnins*, who comprised royal relatives, ministers, courtiers and departmental heads, were the high functionaries of the state, forming the king's council. The *Taittirīya Brāhmaṇa* (I.7.3) expressly describes them as the bestowers of the kingdom (*Ete vai rāṣṭrasya pradātāraḥ*).

20. V.178.
21. I.392.
22. *PBI*, p. 117.
23. I.437-40.
24. V.437-40.
25. V.424-31.
26. IV.487.
27. *AIDMA*, pp. 150-51.
28. VIII.10.
29. *EHI*, p. 55.
30. *AI*, pp. 107ff.
31. Ibid., p. 112.
32. Ibid., p. 108.
33. Ibid., p. 112.
34. *AAHI*, p. 52.
35. Ibid., pp. 51ff.
36. Eng. trans. (*The Great Chronicle of Ceylon*) by W. Geiger.
37. Ed. by E.B. Cowell and R.A. Neil, Cambridge, 1886.
38. This has been elaborately discussed by B.M. Barua in his *Aśoka And His Inscriptions* (pp. 51-54).
39. *AAHI*, p. 51.
40. Pp. 98, 110.
41. XXVII.
42. Ibid.
43. *Prācī-Jyoti*, III.I, p. 109.
44. *AI*, pp. 151ff.
45. *AI*, p. 112. The original text reads, *savasi ca me olodhanasi te bahuvidhena ā kālena tāni tāni tuṭhāyatanāni paṭipādayaṁti hida c=eva disāsu ca.*
46. I.XX.18.
47. They may be identified with the *Antarvaṁśikas, Antaḥpurādhyakṣas, Ābhyantarikas, Antaḥpurikas* and *Antaḥpuravergaḍes,* mentioned in contemporary and later documents, as officers, connected with the harem of the king. B.M Barua (*AI*, p. 183) is of opinion that the *Stryadhyakṣa Mahāmātras* were instituted to guard the interests of women, in general, not excluding courtesans, prostitutes, actresses and the like.
48. XIX, 30; XIX, 33; G. Bühler, *The Sacred Laws of the Āryas,* II (1965), p. 100.
49. Several Greek and Roman rulers claim to have wedded goddesses. Antiochus IV wedded Atargatis, Antony married Isis (*GBI*, p. 265), and so on.
50. *Corolla Numismatica* (1906), p. 245.
51. Ibid., p. 245; *CHI*, I, p. 553. It has been suggested by some scholars that Agathocleia was the queen of Strato I. Agathocleia is shown on the left side of Strato I and it is suggested that the convention was to represent the wife on the left of the husband. But the example of the Candragupta I-Kumāradevī type of gold coins, representing

queen Kumāradevī on the right side of king Candragupta, goes against this presumption. The similarity of names and coin-types indicates that Agathocleia was the sister or daughter of the Indo-Greek king Agathocles (*AIU*, pp. 113-14).

52. *GBI*, p. 177.
53. Ibid., p. 337.
54. A.T. Clay, *Babylonian Records in the Library of J. Pierpont Morgan*, II, p. 53.
55. *CHI*, II, p. 270.
56. *JRAS* (1894), pp. 451ff; *EI*, IX, pp. 135ff.
57. II.37.38.
58. II.33.8.
59. D.P. Vora, *Evolution Of Morals In The Epics* (Bombay, 1959), p. 122.
60. *Mahābhārata*, XI.10.8 (Bomb. Ed.); *Evolution Of Morals In The Epics*, p. 122.
61. *Journal of the Oriental Institute*, Baroda, V, p. 332.
62. The original verse of the *Rāmāyaṇa* (*Laṅkā-kāṇḍa*, 113, 61) reads: *Dṛṣṭvā na khalv=asi kruddho mām=ih=ānavaguṇṭhitāṁ| nirgatāṁ nagara-dvārāt padbhyām=ev=āgatāṁ prabho||.*
63. *Evolution Of Morals In the Epics*, p. 122.
64. XIII.32.33.
65. V.38.92. The *Mahābhārata* (III.51.25) refers to a women's kingdom.
66. *Virāṭaparvan*, 3.17.
67. *Ayodhyā-kāṇḍa*, 35.18-26.
68. *Mahābhārata*, XII.6.10.
69. VII.77.
70. G. Bühler, *Laws of Manu*, p. 239.
71. III.56.
72. *Adhyagny=adhyāvāhanikaṁ dattañ=ca prīti-karmaṇi| bhrātṛ-mātṛ-pitṛ-prāptaṁ ṣaḍ-vidhaṁ strī-dhanaṁ smṛtam||* (Manu, IX.194). The commentator Kullūka interprets *adhyagni* and *adhyāvāhanikaṁ* in the sense of the gifts at the time of marriage (*vivāha-kāle agni-sannidhau yat pitr=ādi-dattaṁ tad=adhyagni*) and departure for the husband's home (*yat=tu pitṛ-gṛhād=bhartṛ-gṛhaṁ nīyamānayā labdhaṁ tad=adhyāvāhanikaṁ*) respectively.
73. XVII.18.
74. Yājñavalkya gives a more extended list of *strīdhana—Pitṛ-mātṛ-pati-bhrātṛ-dattam=adhyagny=upāgatam| ādhivedanik=ādyañ=ca strī-dhanaṁ parikīrttitam* (II. 143); *Bandhu-dattaṁ tathā śulkam=anvādheyakam=eva vā| atītāyām=aprajasi bāndhavās=tad=avāpnuyuḥ* (II.144).
75. *IKP*, p. 405.
76. *GP*, p. 124.
77. *Mahādevī*, which literally means a 'great goddess', appears to have been always a technical title of the principal wives of paramount sovereigns from about this period onwards. It cannot escape notice that junior queens were sometimes called *Mahādevīs*. Kuberanāgā,

for example, is called *Mahādevī* in the Poona plates of Prabhāvatīguptā.

78. *GP*, p. 124.
79. *JRASB* (1937), *Num. Suppl.*, XLVII, pp. 105ff.
80. *CGE*, p. 32.
81. Ibid., p. 62.
82. *Historical Inscriptions of Southern India*, p. 345.
83. *PHAI*, p. 570.
84. *Abhijñānaśakuntalam*, Act III.
85. Ibid., Act IV.
86. The full statement is as follows: 'Śakuntalā is your wife, either abandon her or take her, for authority over wives is admitted to be unlimited' (Act V).
87. *IHQ*, IV, p. 465.
88. Ibid., p. 465.
89. *IA*, IX, pp. 164ff; *GI*, p. 12.
90. *RTA*, p. 315.
91. Cowell and Thomas, *Harṣacarita* (English Translation), p. 254.
92. *HK*, p. 35.
93. Watters, *On Yuan Chwang's Travels in India*, I, p. 330; ibid., II, p. 257.
94. *CII*, III, Nos. 44-45. The title *Paramabhaṭṭārikā* is the feminine form of *Paramabhaṭṭāraka*, which literally means 'one who is supremely entitled to reverence or homage'.
95. Ibid., No. 46.
96. That the kings, ruling in Bengal during this period, were polygamists is proved, besides other evidence, by the Belava copper-plate grant of king Bhojavarman which refers to Sāmalavarman's seraglio as being full of the daughters of many kings (*HB*, I, p. 282).
97. C.R.S. Singhal, *Bibliography of Indian Coins*, Part I (Bombay, 1950), p. 101; D. Sharma, *Early Chauhan Dynasties*, p. 41.
98. *Early Chauhon Dynasties*, p. 72.
99. *AIK*, p. 106.
100. *EI*, XI, No. 4 (V), R.S. Sharma (*JESHO*, IV, p. 87) explains *girāsa* as being for food and clothing. K.K. Gopal (*University of Allahabad Studies*, Ancient Section, 1963-64, p. 94) points out that in modern usage *girās* stands for the landed property of a ruling tribe.
101. *EI*, XI, No. 4 (XVII).
102. *PIA*, pp. 73-74.
103. It seems that the Gāhaḍavāla kings were polygamists. The king Madanapāla had at least two queens in Pṛthvīśrīkā and Rālhaṇadevī, while his son Govindacandra is known to have had at least four queens, viz., Nayanakelidevī, Gosalladevī, Kumāradevī and Vasantadevī.
104. *ASR*, I, pp. 95-96.
105. *PIA*, p. 73.
106. *JRAS* (1896), pp. 787-88.

107. *EI*, IV, pp. 107-09.
108. *EI*, V, pp. 117-18.
109. *HK*, p. 338.
110. *EI*, IX, pp. 319ff.
111. *IA*, XIV, pp. 103-04; *EI*, II, pp. 359-61.
112. Women's participation in administration during this period is probably proved by the Sarnath inscription of Kumāradevī (*EI*, IX, pp. 325ff) which refers to a female officer named Jambukī in charge of a *Paṭṭala* (*Sā Jambukī sakalapaṭṭalik=āgrabhūtā*) which denotes a territorial unit larger than a village.
113. 224.42.
114. 360.76.
115. 24.10.
116. *PAP*, pp. 70-71.
117. VII.1206.
118. *AIK*, p. 117.
119. *SSAAMI*, I, p. 243.
120. *AIK*, p. 120.
121. R.S. Pandit, *Rājataraṅgiṇī* p. 234.
122. *DHNI*, I, pp. 158, 179-80.
123. *JIH*, XXXIV, pp. 296ff.
124. B. Misra, *Orissa Under The Bhauma Kings*, pp. 32ff.
125. *EI*, XXIX, pp. 210ff.
126. *IHQ*, XXI, pp. 213ff.
127. Vakulamahādevī issued a charter in the year 204 (*EI*, XXXVI, pp. 307ff).
128. We have two copper-plate grants issued by Dharmamahādevī (*OUBK*, pp. 59ff; *IHQ*, XXI, pp. 287ff).
129. *EI*, XXVIII, pp. 335-36.
130. D.C. Sircar, *Early Indian Political And Administrative Systems* (Calcutta, 1972), p. 87.
131. Tod, *Annals and Antiquities of Rajasthan*, I, p. 270.
132. *SI*, p. 185.
133. The passage is quoted by A.S. Altekar in his *WAI*, p. 205.
134. *The South Indian Polity*, p. 38.
135. *EI*, VIII; Nasik inscription no. 5.
136. D.C. Sircar (*SSAAMI*, pp. 249-50) suggests that for a short period about the twenty-fourth regnal year of Gautamīputra Śātakarṇi the king was ill and 'that the reins of government were temporarily assumed by his mother Gautamī Balaśrī'.
137. *EI*, XXXV, pp. 4ff.
138. *SI*, pp. 411ff.
139. *VGA*, p. 104.
140. *EI*, XXII, pp. 167ff.
141. *SSAAMI*, I, pp. 234-35.
142. Ibid., pp. 234-35.
143. *IA*, VII, p. 163.

144. *EHD*, p. 235.
145. BK. 127 of 1926-27.
146. R.S. Panchamukhi, *Karnatak Inscriptions*, p. 3.
147. *EI*, IX, p. 205.
148. Rekha Misra, *Women in Mughal India* (Allahabad, 1967), pp. 16ff.
149. *EI*, VIII, p. 146.
150. *ASP*, p. 166.
151. *SII*, I, p. 23.
152. *ASP*, p. 163.
153. Revakaṁmadi, a daughter of Amoghavarṣa I and wife of Erragaṅga, was appointed governor of Edatore district (*PIA*, p. 74) but she was not a Rāṣṭrakūṭa queen.
154. *EI*, XXII, p. 98.
155. *WAI*, p. 189.
156. Bilhaṇa mentions two queens of Vikramāditya VI; one of them was the daughter of the Cola king Vīrarājendra and the other was the Silāhāra princess Candralekhā who is usually identified with the Candaladevī of the epigraphic records (*EHD*, I, p. 368).
157. The wives of some of the feudatory chiefs under the Cālukyas are likewise known to have enjoyed a high official status. An inscription records a petition being addressed through a *Mahāmaṇḍaleśvara* and his wife to the emperor for the grant of an estate (*EI*, XV, p. 27), while another speaks of the wife of a chief as granting land to a temple (Ibid., p. 331).
158. *SII*, XI, I, 83; BK. 72 of 1932-3; *SII*, IX, 1, 119, 121.
159. *SII*, IX, 1, 159.
160. *IA*, X, pp. 185-90.
161. Local Records (in the Government Oriental Manuscripts Library, Madras), VV.
162. BK. 105 of 1932-3.
163. BK. 56 of 1936-7.
164. *SII*, IX, 1, p. 195.
165. *EC*, VII, HL. 1.
166. BK. 67 of 1936-7.
167. BK. 90 of 1927-8.
168. *JNSI*, III, p. 53.
169. Ibid., XXIII, p. 76.
170. R.C. Majumdar, *The Struggle for the Empire*, p. 484.
171. *SIP*, p. 37.
172. *EI*, XV, p. 102.
173. *EI*, III, pp. 306ff; ibid., XXII, pp. 189ff.
174. *SIP*, pp. 43ff.

3

The Crown Prince

I

The Crown Prince in the Vedic Period

It is only once that the term *rāja-putra* is mentioned in the *Ṛgveda*[1] in the sense of a prince, although it occurs time and again in later Vedic literature.[2] The *Aitareya Brāhmaṇa*[3] sometimes applies the appellation *Rāja-pitṛ*, father of a king, to the reigning monarch, implying thereby the important status that the crown prince enjoyed in the kingdom. The *Pañcaviṁśa Brāhmaṇa*[4] includes the *Rājaputra* in the list of eight *Vīras*, heroes, who constituted the supporters and entourage of the king. That the king's son, possibly the eldest, was entitled to an important constitutional status in the later Vedic period is further borne out by the *Śatapatha Brāhmaṇa*,[5] which states that during the sprinkling ceremony the king's son consecrates the king with the holy water and that, later on, on being anointed, the king hands over a vessel, filled with holy water, to his dearest son, exclaiming, 'May this son of mine perpetuate the vigour of mine'.[6]

II

The Crown Prince in the Pre-Maurya Period

The *Jātakas* provide us with useful information about the *Uparāja* who may be tentatively identified with the crown prince, although there are views identifying him with a deputy king[7] or a provincial administrator.[8] Usually, the eldest son of the king was entitled to this post but there are indications that brothers were occasionally preferred to incompetent sons. Again, in the absence of any male descendant, the eldest among the younger brothers of the king would have been the natural choice. One of the *Jātakas*[9] speaks of two brothers, of whom the elder was made *Uparāja* and the younger *Senāpati*. The commentary of the *Mahāparinibbāna-sutta*[10] points out that every matter in the administration of justice must go to the *Uparāja* before the final judgement is pronounced by the king. The *Khaṇḍahāla Jātaka*,[11] likewise, speaks of the important role that an *Uparāja* used to play in the administration of justice.

The crown prince helped the reigning king in the discharge of administrative responsibilities. We see Bimbisāra[12] assuming the charge of the province of Aṅga during the reign of his father, whereas, at a still later date, he nominated his son Ajātaśatru[13] as the viceroy of the same province. If the story of malevolence of the last-named king be regarded as authentic, it would follow that occasions were not few and far between when princes misused their position to usurp the throne for themselves. The *Jātakas* record a few instances of princes being sent to distant places for higher education. In those days Takṣaśilā was a renowned centre of learning, being the resort not only for princes but also for students from other classes and ranks of society.[14] The conventional list of the subjects of study for princes includes, as we learn from some of the *Jātakas*,[15] the three *Vedas* and the eighteen or all the arts (*tayo Vede aṭṭhārasa vijjh=āṭṭhānāni*).

III

The Crown Prince in the Maurya Period

Literary and epigraphic evidence proves the continuity of the practice of governing provinces with the help of princes in the Maurya period. The Pāli tradition[16] tells that when Bindusāra was on the throne of Pāṭaliputra, he appointed his two sons, Susīma (or Sumana) and Aśoka, viceroys at Takṣaśilā and Ujjayinī, respectively. Subsequently, Takṣaśilā fell a prey to popular uprising, whence Aśoka was deputed by his father to suppress the revolt. The *Divyāvadāna*[17] records the incident in the following words:

'*Atha rājño Bindusārasya Takṣaśilā-nāma-nagaraṁ viruddham/ Tatra rājñā Bindusāreṇ=Āśoko visarjitaḥ ... yāvat kumārś=caturaṅgena balakāyena Takṣaśilāṁ gataḥ, śrutvā*

Takṣaśilā-nivāsinaḥ paurāḥ . . . praty=ud-gamya ca kathayanti, 'na vayaṁ kumārasya viruddhāḥ, n=āpi rājño Bindusārasya api tu duṣṭ=āmātyā asmākaṁ paribhavaṁ kurvanti'.' The passage has been translated into English thus, 'Now Taxila, a city of king Bindusāra, revolted. The king Bindusāra despatched Aśoka there . . . while the prince was nearing Taxila with his four-fold army, the resident, *pauras* (citizens of Taxila), on hearing of it . . . came out to meet him and said, 'We are not opposed to the prince nor even to king Bindusāra. But these wicked ministers insult us'.'[18]

The following facts emerge from the above accounts:

First, the Maurya princes served as viceroys of provinces;

Second, the posts of the *Kumāra*-viceroys were subjected to transfer;

Third, the *Kumāras* had their own council of ministers who, if left to themselves, would generally prove to be oppressive.

Leaving aside the *Divyāvadāna*, we may now turn to the edicts of Aśoka for fuller information about princes who were called both *Kumāras* and *Āryaputras*. Kaliṅga Edict I refers to a *Kumāra* who was entrusted with the administration of Ujjayinī (*Ujenite pi cu kumāle*) and a second prince, who was in charge of Takṣaśilā (*Takhasilāte*), the headquarters of Gandhāra, whereas Kaliṅga Edict II tells us of one such prince placed in charge of a part of Kaliṅga with its headquarters at Tosalī (*Tosaliyaṁ kumāle*). The existence of another prince-viceroy is vouchsafed by Minor Rock Edict I which refers to an *Āryaputra* at Suvarṇagiri (*Suvaṁnagirīte ayaputasa*) which is generally identified with a locality near Erragudi, where a complele set of the Rock Edicts has been found, in Kurnool district in Andhra Pradesh.[19] D.R. Bhandarkar[20] suggests its location in Rājagṛha, the old capital of Magadha, and points out that this prince, who was in all likelihood the crown prince, administered the Maurya empire from Suvarṇagiri in Rājagṛha during Aśoka's temporary cessation of rule, possibly when the latter went on pilgrimage to Bodh Gaya. But both the location of Suvarṇagiri and the interpretation of the word *āryaputra*, as suggested by D.R. Bhandarkar, are, by no means, certain. Nevertheless, the testimony of the literary evidence about the appointment of the Maurya princes as viceroys for outlying provinces stands corroborated by epigraphic records.

There are reasons for the belief that all the *Kumāra*-viceroys did not claim any uniform status and position. The *Kumāra*-viceroy at Tosalī was not empowered to exercise unfettered power which was the prerogative of those stationed at Ujjain and Taxila. This would be evident from the facts enumerated below:

First, the *Kumāras* of Ujjain and Taxila were to send on tour their own *Mahāmātras* every three years to ensure the proper administration of justice, whereas in the case of Tosalī the *Mahāmātras* were deputed by Aśoka himself.

Second, in connection with the despatch of such an officer, the *Kumāras* of Ujjayinī and Takṣaśilā are mentioned by themselves and not associated with any state dignitaries, whereas in Separate Kaliṅga Edict II (Ḍhauli version), where alone the Kumāra of Tosalī is referred to, he is mentioned not by himself but associated with the *Mahāmātras*.

And last, Aśoka issued orders to the *Nagara Vyāvahārikas* and others of Tosalī directly, even though the *Kumāra* was placed in charge of the province, and not through the *Kumāra* himself.

It would become clear from the foregoing discussion that Aśoka hardly empowered the *Kumāra* of Tosalī to enjoy a large measure of freedom in administration which he was pleased to grant to the *Kumāras* placed at Ujjain and Taxila. This disparity in position among princes justifies the assumption that, although corroborative evidence is lacking, the viceroyalty of Taxila and Ujjain was reserved for the *Yuvarāja* and other important princes.

A meticulous treatment of princes, not excluding their boyhood days, is found in the *Kauṭilīya Arthaśāstra*. We may take into consideration the following observations of Kauṭilya:

'. . . when the chief queen is in her *ṛtu*(-period), priests should offer a *caru*-oblation to Indra and Bṛhaspati. When she is pregnant, a children's specialist should arrange for the nourishment of the foetus and for delivery. When she has given birth, the chaplain should perform the sacraments for the son. When he is ready for it, experts should train him.'[21]

'One possessed of sagacity, one with intellect requiring to be goaded and one of evil intellect—these are the different kinds of sons. He, who, when taught, understands spiritual and material good and practises the same is one possessed of sagacity. He who understands but does not practise (them) is one with intellect requiring to be goaded. He who is even full of harm and hates spiritual and material good is one of evil intellect' (*Buddhimān=āhārya-buddhir=durbuddhir=iti putra-viśeṣāḥ| Śiṣyamāṇo dharm=ārthāv=upalabhate c=ānu-tiṣṭh-ati ca buddhimān| Upalabhamāno n=ānutiṣṭhaty=āhārya-buddhiḥ| Apāyanityo dharm=ārtha dveṣī c=eti durbuddhiḥ||*).[22]

'If such be the only son, he should endeavour to get a son born of him. Or, he should get sons begotten on an appointed daughter' (*Sa yady=eka-putraḥ putr=otpattavasya viyatet| Putrikā-putrān=utpādayed=vā|*).[23]

'An old or diseased king, however, should get a child be-gotten on his wife by one of the following (viz.), his mother's kinsman, a member of his own family, and a virtuous neigh-bouring prince. But he should not install on the throne an only son, if undisciplined' (*Vṛddhas=tu vyādhito vā rājā matṛ-bandhu-tulya guṇavat-sāmantānām=anyatamena kṣetre vījam=utpādayet| Na c=aika putram=avinītaṁ rājye sthāpayet|*).[24]

'Of many (sons, who are undisciplined) confinement in one place (is best); (however), the father should be beneficently disposed towards the sons. Except in case of a calamity, sovereignty passing on to the eldest son is praised'[25] (*Bahūnām=eka-saṁrodhaḥ pitā putra-hito bhavet| Anyatr=āpada aiśvar-yaṁ jyeṣṭha-bhāgī tu pūjyate||*).[26]

In referring to the education of princes, Kauṭilya[27] observes, 'when the ceremony of tonsure is performed, the prince should learn the use of the alphabet and arithmetic. When the initia-tion with the preceptor is performed, he should learn the three Vedas and philosophy from the learned, economics from the heads of departments (and) the science of politics from theore-tical and practical exponents. And (he should observe) celibacy till the sixteenth year. Thereafter (should follow) the cutting of the hair and marriage for him. And (he should have) constant association with elders in learning for the sake of improving his training, since training has its root in that.'[28] It would appear from the above remarks of Kauṭilya that first, princes were trained in different branches of learning by different experts, and second, they were given in marriage at the end of their sixteenth year. Even with the completion of their studies, the princes were not placed in independent situations but were to undergo a period of apprenticeship as subordinates to the administrative heads.[29] When they proved to be competent and worthy of occupying an independent position, they were appointed to responsible posts like the commander-in-chief of the army, governor of a province or were raised to heir-apparency.[30]

In the *Arthaśāstra*, we meet with a somewhat graphic treatment of the problem pertaining to the king's relations with his sons. If an honest prince apprehends insecurity from his father, he is advised to take to forest-life,[31] leave the state and work in gold and ruby mines or, if possible, join hands with his maternal relatives in order to bring about the dethronement of his father.[32] If, on the contrary, the prince himself misbehaves with his father, he should be conciliated, in the first instance, by diplomacy, and if he does not get rectified, he may be sent on distant expeditions that may spell disaster for him, be imprisoned, or, as the last resort, be put to death.[33] It is worth noting that whereas Bhāradvāja advocates secret murder of really refractory princes, the sage Viśālākṣa recommends only imprisonment in certain deserted places.[34] The crown prince, nevertheless, occupied an honoured position in the state, being entitled to a monthly (or annual) allowance of 48,000 *paṇas*, the highest remuneration, equal to that of the chief priest, commander-in-chief, queen-mother and chief queen, and to the rare privilege of being not watched by the Intelligence Department.

As we compare the accounts of princes, as found in the Pāli texts, epigraphic records and the *Arthaśāstra*, we find that whereas the first two sources are primarily concerned with the princes' role in administration, the *Arthaśāstra* deals with their upbringing and conduct as well. In all these accounts, the princes are represented as being entrusted with the administration of provinces. The appointment of princes as provincial governors in lieu of those not related to the royal family was, no doubt, in harmony with the interest of the ruling monarch who was always apprehensive of the machinations of his ministers and generals. But the selection of princes for such a prestigious post would sometimes prove detrimental to the state, for it would lead to the fragmentation of the kingdom, as it did in the later days of the Imperial Guptas.

IV

The Crown Prince in the Epics

The princely curriculum, as prescribed in the *Śāntiparvan*[35] of the *Mahābhārata*, includes a variety of subjects like knowledge of the family laws, the *Veda*-of-the-bow, the *Veda*, elephant-riding, horse-riding, chariot-driving, rules of propriety, word-science, music and the fine arts, legends and tales. In the *Rāmāyaṇa* we, likewise, meet with a detailed list of subjects the king was expected to study, comprising *Dhanurveda*, *Veda*, *Nītiśāstra*, the art of elephants and cars, the art of painting (*ālekhya*), writing (*lekhya*), jumping (*laṅghana*) and swimming. The *Ādiparvan*[36] shows that the Pāṇḍavas had studied all the *Vedas* and the various treatises (*te=dhītya nikhilān vedān śāstrāṇi vividhāni ca*). It seems that the royal princes were primarily concerned with the science of arms, which required years of patient study and paid scant attention to the holy writings the mastery of which 'must have been peculiar to the man of leisure, the priest', as is implied by a glance at the list of the branches of study pursued by the model prince Abhimanyu. 'The *Veda*-of-the-bow, in four divisions and ten branches, he, the *Veda*-knower, learned complete from Arjuna, both the divine (weapons) and the human. Then Arjuna taught him the special points in the knowledge of different weapons, in dexterity of use, and in all arts; and both in science and practice made him equal unto himself; and he rejoiced as he beheld him.'[37] In explaining the term *Dhanurveda*, R.K. Mukherji[38] observes that the 'entire military science and art of the age seems to have been comprehended by the generic term *Dhanurveda*, the *dhanu* or bow being regarded as the type or symbol of all weapons or methods of warfare'.

The *Sabhāparvan* mentions the crown prince as one among the eighteen[39] high functionaries of the state[40] (*Mantrī purohitaś =c=aiva yuvarājaś=camūpatiḥ| pañcamo dvāra-pālaś=ca ṣaṣṭh= ontarveśikas=tathā||*). The king is urged to keep these officers watched by spies, except the chief councillor, the high-priest and the crown prince.[41] If the crown prince happened to be a minor on the king's death, the kingdom was kept for the prince by an elder relative who governed it as if he were the king, as did Bhīṣma[42] on the death of his brother Citrāṅgada when Vicitravīrya, the real successor to the throne, was still a boy-prince (*Hate Citrāṅgade Bhīṣmo bāle bhrātari . . . pālayāmāsa tad=rājyaṁ Satyavaty=āmate sthitaḥ*). The age of sixteen[43] was probably the terminus of boyhood and the princes of that age were looked upon as fully equipped knights.

The *Mahābhārata* speaks of a few senior princes like Dhṛtarāṣṭra, Devāpi and Yadu whose claims to the throne were passed over in favour of those of younger brothers like Pāṇḍu, Śāntanu and Pūru, respectively, the cause of supersession being either their physical defect or the father's disapproval.[44] A prince, selected for heir-apparency, had to go through the whole gamut of ceremonies (*abhiṣecanaṁ*) before he was officially declared the crown prince. A practical instance of the *abhiṣecanaṁ* of the *Yuvarāja* may be found in the preparations made for Rāma's consecration by king Daśaratha.[45] The princes led an idle life in the time of peace, taking part in tournaments and trials of skill but such intervals, it must be admitted, were, indeed, rare as most of their life was spent in the military camps in response to their commitments to the state.

The *Rāmāyaṇa* speaks of princes ruling over territorial units over which they were the heads but still answerable to the monarch. Bharata's two sons, Takṣa[46] and Puṣkala, were appointed governors of Takṣaśilā and Puṣkalāvatī (*Takṣaṁ Takṣaśilāyāṁ=tu Puṣkalaṁ Puṣkalāvate*); Śatrughna's two sons[47] were the governors of Mathurā and Vidiśā (*Subāhur=Mathurāṁ lebhe Śatrughātī ca Vidiśāṁ*); Lakṣmaṇa's two sons[48] were heads of two cities in the country of Kārupatha and Rāma's two sons[49] ruled over Kośala and the northern region (*Kośaleṣu Kuśaṁ vīram=uttareṣu Lavaṁ tathā*) with their headquarters at Kuśāvatī and Śrāvastī, respectively.

V

The Crown Prince in the Post-Maurya Period

Puṣyamitra, who succeeded the Mauryas on the throne of Pāṭaliputra, followed the Maurya practice of appointing princes as viceroys of provinces. The *Mālavikāgnimitram* tells us how the crown prince Agnimitra governed Vidiśā, identified with Besnagar in eastern Malwa, as his father's viceroy. It cannot be ascertained whether the example of Puṣyamitra was emulated by his successors.

Manu does not refer to the crown prince. Yet as regards the education of the king, he[50] says that 'the king should learn the three *Vedas* from Brāhmaṇas, versed in those *Vedas*, should learn politics which is ever useful to him, should also study metaphysics, *Upaniṣads* and agriculture from experienced men' (*Trai-vidyebhyas=trayīṁ vidyāṁ daṇḍanītiṁ ca śāśvatīṁ| Ānvīkṣikīṁ c=ātma-vidyāṁ vārtarambhāṁś=ca lokataḥ||*). It is quite likely that the proficiency in all these branches of learning was acquired by the king even before his accession to the throne. Manu elsewhere points out that 'devoid of diseases, the lord of the earth will himself do all these duties; but at the time of illness he will entrust all these to fit ministers'[51] (*Etad=vidhānam=ātiṣṭhed=arogaḥ pṛthivī-patiḥ| Asvasthaḥ sarvam=etat=tu bhṛtyeṣu viniyojayet||*). It would thus be apparent that Manu has denounced the idea of the crown prince being appointed regent during the life-time of the reigning monarch even in a time of emergency.

The inscriptions of the Indo-Greek, Scytho-Parthian and Kuṣāṇa kings do not mention the term *yuvarāja*, excepting, of course, the Mathura Lion capital inscriptions which apply the designation twice to one Kharaosta, who is almost unanimously identified by scholars with the *Kṣatrapa* Kharaosta of the coins.[52] The so-called Takht-i-Bahi inscription of the time of Gondophares speaks of one *Erjhuna* Kapa who is identified by Sten Konow with Kujula Kadphises. The epithet *erjhuna* is the Prākṛt transliteration of the old Śaka term *alysānai* which was used as a synonym of the Sanskrit word *kumāra*. The title also occurs in a Brāhmī record[53] at Mathura, engraved on the pedestal of a Buddha statuette and dated in the year 36. But these epigraphs hardly supply us with any information in regard to the position of the princes in administration.

Princes are known to have played a pivotal role in administration in the Scytho-Parthian kingdoms, as is suggested by the joint issues of coinage by Azes I and Azilises, Azilises and Azes II, Gondophares and Gad, and Gondophares and Abdagases. The Andhau inscriptions suggest that the Śaka chief

Caṣṭana ruled in the capacity of a *Mahākṣatrapa* conjointly with his grandson *Kṣatrapa* Rudradāman. But in these cases, the princes were not heirs-apparent but co-rulers or subordinate colleagues of kings.

There are, however, reasons to believe that the institution of heir-apparency was in vogue in the Kuṣāṇa kingdom, at least, in the latter part of the reign of the first Kuṣāṇa monarch, Kujula Kadphises. When one looks at the discovery of Kujula Kadphises' coins in Taxila in the context of the statement of the *Hou-Han shu*, crediting Wema with the conquest of India, one has to conclude that Kadphises I associated himself in the latter part of his life with the crown prince Wema Kadphises who conquered India and put in circulation in the newly-annexed territories the currency of the old king who was then leading a retired life.[54] Marshall[55] is of opinion that the coins bearing the legend, *Maharayasa Rayatirayasa Kujula Kara Kaphasa Sacadhramaṭhitasa*, were plausibly issued by Wema when he was still a crown prince.

VI

The Crown Prince in the Gupta Period

Our knowledge about the *Yuvarāja* during the Gupta period is derived from the combined testimony of the contemporary inscriptions and the *Nītisāra* of Kāmandaka, which was, in all probability, composed during this epoch. The Allahabad *praśasti* probably gives us an account of the selection of Samudragupta, plausibly as a *Yuvarāja*, by Candragupta I.[56] We are told that Candragupta I selected him for the august post in an open assembly. We are further informed that when this selection was announced, his kinsmen of equal birth (*tulya-kulaja*) became pale-faced with disappointment. This description leaves the impression that for heir-apparency the claims of the elder sons were sometimes passed over in silence in favour of those of the younger princes, otherwise the deep disappointment of the kinsmen of equal birth would remain inexplicable. This supposition is corroborated by the fact that Candragupta II, to judge from the expression '*tat-parigṛhīta*', 'accepted as his chosen successor', applied to him, was selected by his father to succeed the latter on the throne, though he was not the eldest son. The reason behind the selection of a younger prince as *Yuvarāja* was due not so much to favouritism on the part of the royal father as to the character and ability of the candidate.

It is quite likely that the heir-apparent discharged a great deal of administrative work and even led the imperial army in the face of any external invasion. When the Puṣyamitras, who 'had great resources in men and money', invaded the Gupta dominions in the closing years of Kumāragupta I's reign, Skandagupta fought hard with them 'to restore the fallen fortunes of his family'[57] (*Vicalita-kula-lakṣmīs=tam=abhanāy=odyatena| Kṣiti-tala-śayanīye yena nītā triyāmā| Sam-udita-bala-Kośān Puṣyamitrāṁś=ca jitvā kṣitipa-caraṇa-pīṭhe sthāpito vāma-pādaḥ||*).

Some welcome light on the office of the crown prince is shed by a few seals from Basarh in which we have the following legends:

(i) *Yuvarāja-pādīya-Kamārāmāty=ādhikaraṇasya*; and

(ii) *Śrī-Yuvarāja-bhaṭṭāraka-pādīya-Kumārāmāty=ādhi-karaṇasya.*

Unfortunately, there is no consensus among scholars on the meaning and interpretation of the above legends. U.N. Ghosal[58] takes the word *pādīya* as equivalent to *pād=ānudhyāta* and denoting the relations between father and son. According to this interpretation, the *Kumārāmātyas* of the Basarh seals were related as sons to the crown prince, a theory which is hardly conclusive. R.D. Banerji[59] interprets the word *pādīya* as a synonym of *kalpa*, meaning 'equal to' and suggests that some of the *Kumārāmātyas* were equal in rank to the heir-apparent but this is equally untenable. Fleet has shown that the expression *pād=ānudhyāta* is used in inscriptions to mean different kinds of relations. The word *pādīya* in the Basarh seals, which literally means 'belonging to the foot of', implies, in all probability, that the *Kumārāmātyas*, in question, were attached to the department of the heirs-apparent. The *Yuvarāja* had evidently under him a body of officers who helped him to carry on his duties. While dealing with these inscriptions, Dikshitar[60] observes, 'This class of seals betrays clearly that the crown prince was distinguished from other princes of the royal family. While the crown prince was entitled *Yuvarāja Bhaṭṭāraka*, ordinary princes were merely *Yuvarājas* and did not have the appellation *Bhaṭṭāraka* attached to their names.' It seems that both '*Yuvarāja*' and '*Yuvarāja Bhaṭṭāraka*' have been used indiscriminately in the sense of heir-apparent, and that the expression *Bhaṭṭāraka* is used in one case and omitted in the other because of the carelessness on the part of the scribes who incised the seals.

From Basarh has been discovered another seal containing the legend, *śrī-Yuvarāja-bhaṭṭāraka-pādīya-bal=ādhikaraṇasya*, 'the (seal) of the office of the army commander, attached to the *Yuvarāja*'. It is clear that the crown prince, who was sometimes entrusted with the administration of a part of the kingdom, was also responsible for leading the forces to the battle-field, and further that, a contingent was placed at his disposal to assist him in his military operations.

Kāmandaka, who probably flourished in this age, points out that the eldest among the princes should be appointed *Yuvarāja* (*Avinītaṁ kumāraṁ hi kulam=āśu vivasyati| Vinītam=aurasaṁ putraṁ yauva-rājye=bhiṣecayet||*). As regards the princely curriculum, Kāmandaka[61] lays down that he is to be well-versed in economics and politics as well as in the *Vedas* and philosophy. It may be noted that the Bārhaspatya school forbids the king from Vedic study which is supposed to act as a screen to obscure the vision of the person who has to know the hard world around him. That the Gupta princes hardly minimised the cultivation of fine arts is possibly indicated by the statement in the Allahabad inscription that Samudragupta 'put to shame the preceptor of the lord of gods, Tumburu, Nārada and others by his sharp and polished intellect and choral skill and musical accomplishments[62] (*Gāndharva-lalitair-vrīḍita-Tridaśapatiguru-Tumburu-Nārad = āder = vidvaj - jan= opajīvy = āneka-kāvya - vikrayābhiḥ pratiṣṭhita - kavirāja - śabdasya*). That princes had to undergo a period of rigorous training at the hands of experts is also borne out by the *Raghuvaṁśa*[63] (*Upātta-vidyaṁ vidhivad=gurubhyas=taṁ*).

The *Bṛhatsaṁhitā*, which was probably a work of the Gupta period, preserves some interesting details about the crown prince. It states that the *paṭṭa* of the *Yuvarāja* contained three crests but the width and length of the queen's were more than those of the crown prince's. The rod of the umbrella of the crown prince measured four and a half cubits.[64] Varāhamihira further says that the *Yuvarāja* occupied a house which was bigger than that of the queen. The commentator Bhattotpala describes the *Yuvarāja* as a partner in the enjoyment of the kingdom[65] (*Yuvarāj=ardha-rājya-bhāg rājā*; *Yuvarāj-ordha-bhogī rājā*; *Yuvarājaḥ prasiddh=ordha=rājya-bhāk*).

VII

The Crown Prince in the Puṣyabhūti Kingdom

The heir-apparent was an important member of the administrative machinery of the state in the age of Harṣavardhana. Rājyavardhana was sent by his father Prabhākaravardhana as the leader of the army to fight against the Hūṇas. If literature reflects the picture of contemporary society, then Bāṇa's account of prince Candrāpīḍa, as found in the chapter entitled *Candrāpīḍasya Yauvarājy=ābhiṣekaḥ* of the *Kādambarī* may be taken into consideration for ascertaining the condition of the princes in the seventh century A.D. Bāṇa provides us with the following details about Candrāpīḍa:

First, during the childhood days, various rites such as tonsure, etc., were performed.

Second, the boyhood days of the prince having passed by, king Tārāpīḍa constructed a school-house on the outskirts of the capital city where his son was placed. Professors of every branch of knowledge were appointed to train the prince. The king, along with his queen Vilāsavatī, used to go to the school every day in order to acquaint himself with the progress of the prince. Candrāpīḍa[66] gained proficiency in grammar, *Mīmāṃsā*, logic, politics, use of weapons such as the bow, etc., driving a chariot, riding on elephant's back, riding horses, instrumental music, works on dancing, various musical treatises, art of training elephants, science of ascertaining the age of a horse and the characteristic marks on the body of a person, fine arts, calligraphy (making clay-dolls), engraving, arts of gambling, various systems of music, interpreting the omens from the cries of birds, astronomy, testing precious stones, carpentry, ivory-carving, art of building, science of medicine, use of the proper *yantras*, use of antidotes against poison, swimming, rowing, jumping, climbing, erotic arts, magic, study of romances, dramas, tales, poetry, *Mahābhārata*, *Purāṇas*, historical works and *Rāmāyaṇa*, all the alphabet and dialects of the country, all the mechanical arts, *Vedas* and many other different accomplishments.

Third, the prince took a period of ten years to complete his course of study, and then he was brought home.

Fourth, he was later on crowned as the heir-apparent. Bāṇa vividly describes how Candrāpīḍa's consecration ceremony as *Yuvarāja* was observed with grandeur. The king himself, accompanied by his prime minister and a host of subordinate kings, rained water on Candrāpīḍa's head (*Rājā svayam=utkṣipta-maṅgala kalaśaḥ saha Śukanāsena puṇy=ehani purodhasā sampādit=āśeṣa - rājy=ābhiṣeka - maṅgalam=aneka - narapati-sahasra-parivṛtaḥ sarvebhyas=tīrthyebhyaḥ sarvābhyo nadībhyah sarvebhyaś=ca sāgarebhyaḥ sam=āhṛtena sarva-auṣadhibhiḥ sarva-phalaiḥ sarvam=ṛddhiḥ sarva-ratnaiś=ca parigṛhīten=ānanda-vāṣpa-jala-miśreṇa mantra pūtena vāriṇā sutam=abhiṣeṣe ca*/). Next the queen-mother herself anointed his body from the soles of his feet upwards with fragrant sandal-paste. 'On his head he wore a chaplet of newly-blossomed white flowers, his body had a sprinkling of the *gorocanā* paint, he wore ear-ornaments, made of the blades of the *durvā* grass, he put on a new pair of silken garments, his hand was adorned with a wrist-thread and he had on his chest a pearl necklace, looking as if it were the circle of (the stars of) the seven (heavenly) sages, come there to witness the coronation ceremony.'[67] Thus being decorated, Candrāpīḍa arrived at the assembly hall and ascended the royal throne of gold (*sabhā-maṇḍapam=upagamya kāñcanamayaṁ śaś=īva meru-śṛṅgaṁ Candrāpīḍaḥ siṁh=āsanam=āruroha*). Just as Kālidāsa has painted the picture of Raghu on the model of Samudragupta, similarly it is not unlikely that Bāṇa has portrayed the crown prince Candrāpīḍa in imitation of either prince Rājyavardhana or a son of Harṣa.

Daṇḍin, who according to some scholars flourished in about the same epoch, speaks in *Ucchvāsa* I of the *Daśakumāracarita* of the princes who acquired proficiency in all scripts (*sakala-lipi-jñānaṁ*), languages, *Vedas* and their six *Aṅgas*, *Purāṇas*, *Kāvyas*, *Nāṭakas*, *Ākhyānas*, *Ākhyāyikās*, *Itihāsas*, *Citrakathā* (*Kāvyanāṭak=ākhyānak=ākhyāyik=etihāsa - citrakathā - sahita-purāṇagaṇa-naipuṇyaṁ*), *Dharmaśāstras*, *Vyākaraṇas*, astrology, logic, *Mīmāṁsā* (*Dharma-śabda jyotiṣka-mīmāṁs=ādi-samasta-śāstra-nikara cāturyaṁ*), treatise on politics by Kauṭilya and

Kāmandaka, musical instruments, music, poetics, magical sciences, riding all vehicles, use of various weapons and different crooked arts such as thieving, gambling, etc.[68] The combined evidence of both Bāṇa and Daṇḍin would indicate that the princes of their times were not only trained in politics and military science but also they had to be acquainted with other branches of knowledge, not excluding fine arts.

VIII

The Crown Prince in the Pāla-Pratīhāra Period

The *Yuvarāja* finds frequent mention in the Pāla records. The king's eldest son, as usual, was selected as the heir-apparent but in regard to his duties and functions during this period, we do not possess detailed information. Tribhuvanapāla, who served as *Yuvarāja* under his father Dharmapāla, acted as the *Dūtaka*, messenger, in connection with the Khalimpur grant. Another Pāla crown prince, viz., Rājyapāla (*sthira-yauvarājyaṁ*) was entrusted with similar business in respect of the Monghyr grant.[69] The advice of the crown prince on important issues was sometimes solicited by the king, as would appear from the fact that Rāmapāla often held consultations with his son Rājyapāla 'in connection with his war-preparations against the Kaivartas'.[70] The history of the Pāla dynasty furnishes us with a few instances to show that the heirs-apparent did not always succeed their fathers on the imperial throne. Tribhuvanapāla, as we have already seen, was the crown prince during the reign of Dharmapāla, but the prince who succeeded Dharmapāla on the throne was his younger brother Devapāla. Are we to suppose that the rightful claims of Tribhuvanapāla were challenged by Devapāla who occupied the throne after defeating his brother in a fratricidal struggle? But the possibility of an internecine war after the death of Dharmapāla is ruled out in the presence of the statement in the Monghyr grant that Devapāla ascended the throne peacefully (*nir=upaplavaṁ*). Tribhuvanapāla did not ascend the Pāla throne probably because he predeceased his father. Similarly, Devapāla, after his demise, was followed by Śūrapāla, and not by his worthy son Rājyapāla (*ātm=ānurūpa-caritaṁ*) probably because he outlived the latter. The crown prince normally inherited the throne after the death of the ruling monarch but Nārāyaṇapāla ascended the throne during the life-time of his father Vigrahapāla, who abdicated the throne to lead a life of austerities.[71]

Inscriptions are not of much value in knowing the position of the *Yuvarāja* in the contemporary Pratīhāra kingdom. But the little that we know about him would make it abundantly clear that generally the eldest son was selected for the post. We have, however, a few cases of younger brothers being elevated to the rank of *Yuvarāja*. The Daulatpura copper plates of Bhoja I mention Nāgabhaṭa as *Yuvarāja* and *Dūtaka* of the grant but this Nāgabhaṭa was probably a brother of Bhoja I.[72] For our knowledge of the education of the princes of the contemporary period, we may turn to the testimony of the *Nītivākyāmṛta*, composed by Somadeva Sūri, who tells us that they were trained in the four branches of learning[73] (*Ānvīkṣikī trayī vārtā daṇḍanītir=iti catasro rāja-vidyāḥ*), comprising *Ānvīkṣikī* (the knowledge of self), *Trayī* (three *Vedas*), *Vārtā* (the science of agriculture, cattle-breeding and commerce) and *Daṇḍanīti* (the principles of politics). In emphasising the importance of education for princes, Somadeva[74] says that a prince, howsoever well born, should not be selected as the heir-apparent unless he is properly qualified for the great trust. The *Agni Purāṇa*[75] prescribes that the prince should be taught *Dharmaśāstra*, *Kāmaśāstra*, *Arthaśāstra*, science of archery and various arts and crafts by competent teachers (*Dharm=ārtha-kāma-śāstrāṇi dhanur=vedañ=ca śikṣayet| śilpāni śikṣayec=c=aivam-āptair mithyā-priyaṁvadaiḥ|*) and be separated from wrathful, avaricious and ill-reputed persons[76] (*na c=ānya saṅgo dātavyaḥ kruddha-lubdha-vimānitaiḥ*). With the completion of his studies, he would assume charge of different departments but an uneducated prince merits confinement[77] (*Aśakyaṁ=tu guṇā-dhānaṁ kartuṁ taṁ bandhayet sukhaiḥ| Adhikāreṣu sarveṣu vinītaṁ viniyojayet||*).

The *Yuvarāja* finds mention in the inscriptions of the early Gaṅga kings of Kaliṅganagara. One such prince, Rājendravarman II,[78] is known to have issued the Pattali and Nampali grants from the city of Kaliṅganagara, although the circumstances leading to the issue of these charters in the name of the crown prince instead of the reigning king himself cannot be determined.

IX

The Crown Prince in the Post-Pāla-Pratīhāra Period

Generally speaking, during the period, following the decline of the Pāla and Pratīhāra kingdoms, the crown prince assumed a position of greater importance in administration, as compared to his predecessor in the earlier kingdoms. A perusal of the Gāhaḍavāla epigraphs reveals that the Gāhaḍavāla crown princes, called *Yuvarājas* and *Mahārājaputras*, enjoyed the special prerogative of making grants of land, no doubt, with the approval of the ruling monarch, and issuing records of such gifts. When the *Yuvarāja* Jayacandra,[79] for example, made a grant, he did so with the consent of king Vijayacandra. They announced their grants in their own names unlike the queens whose gifts were to be announced by kings.[80] The seals of these princes contain their own insignia (*lāñchana*) which consists of a conch-shell and an arrow below with the name of the *Yuvarāja* across the centre, as distinct from the royal seal which shows Garuḍa above, a conch-shell below and the name of the king, written across the centre.[81] Sometimes the crown prince seems to have enjoyed a position of extraordinary importance and influence in administration, as did Govindacandra during the reign of his father Madanapāla, as may be guessed, in the first instance, from the use of the royal seal in his own name in the inscriptions which he issued during the reign of his father, and secondly, from the occurrence of extravagant praise for his military achievements which we hardly come across in the grants of the other princes of the dynasty. The *Yuvarāja* Āsphoṭacandra[82] issued a copper plate in A.D. 1134, bearing his father Govindacandra's seal. The younger princes, likewise, appear to have held important administrative posts in the Gāhaḍavāla kingdom, as was the case with Rājyapāla,[83] a younger son of Govindacandra, who is described as being endowed with all the royal prerogatives (*śrī-mad=Govinda-candradeva-pāda-padma-saṁmatyā samasta-rāja-prakriy=opeta-mahārāja-putra-śrī-mad-Rājyapāla-devo*). Rājyapāla is known to have issued an inscription, using his own seal, containing the legend, *mahārāja-putra-śrīmad-Rājyapāladevaḥ*, and recording the king's consent to his grant of a piece of land in favour of a Brahmin scholar named Dāmodaraśarman.

The Sena inscriptions take notice of the princes some of whom gave a good account of themselves by participating in the reigning kings' military campaigns. The Madhainagar grant[84] seems to imply that Lakṣmaṇasena, while he was still a *Kumāra*, took part in some victorious expeditions. In his two extant grants, viz., the Sahitya Parisat and Madhainagar grants, Viśvarūpasena is described as being 'engaged in wars since the days of his viceroyalty[85] (*ā-kaumāram=apāra-saṅgar . . . a-hara-vyāpāra-tṛṣṇā*). The Sahitya Parisat grant[86] discloses the names of two princes, Sūryasena and Puruṣottamasena, who are said to have made a gift of two plots of land to Halāyudha.

As was the case with their Gāhaḍavāla brethren, the Cāhamāna princes were frequently appointed to some important posts in administration. The Jalor stone inscription[87] of Samarasiṁhadeva refers to prince Jojala as looking after the administration of the kingdom (*rājya-cintaka*) and successfully dealing with the unsettled tribes (*taskara*) of the whole district of Pīlvāhikā,[88] the Kiradu stone inscription[89] informs us how the king Ālhaṇadeva used to take help from his two sons, Gajasiṁha and Kelhaṇadeva, in important administrative matters (*śrī-mahārāja-putra-śrī - Kelhaṇadeva - matam=etat/ mahārāja - putra-Gajasiṁhasya mataṁ*); the prince Cāmuṇḍarāja was appointed governor of Māṇḍyavapura by his father Gajasiṁha in A.D. 1170; the two sons of the king Kelhaṇa, Vikramasiṁha[90] and Soṭala,[91] were appointed to the same post in A.D. 1180 and 1185, respectively. The example[92] of the prince Sallakṣaṇapāla, who was appointed a senior minister by his father Vīsaladeva, shows that the younger princes were sometimes inducted in the ministry. P.B. Udgaonkar[93] has shown that for their personal enjoyment and expenses, the Cāhamāna princes were usually given fiefs, known as *Sejā*, their size being dependent 'upon the extent and resources of the kingdom and the importance of the grantee'. Thus whereas, the prince Kīrtipāla,[94] for instance, enjoyed twelve villages as his fief, the princes Lākhaṇapāla and Abhayapāla, as known from the Lalrai stone inscription,[95] simultaneously enjoyed one and the same village as a fief in A.D. 1177. The princes' appointment being temporary, they did hardly enjoy the proprietary right over their fiefs, and the central government reserved its power to assign revenues out of these lands.[96]

Some records of the Cāhamānas of Nadol refer to the rule of both the king and the crown prince at the beginning as in the case of the Sevadi stone inscription[97] which refers both to *Mahārājādhirāja* Aśvarāja and the *Yuvarāja* Kaṭukarāja (*Mahārāj=ādhirāja-śrī-Aśvarāja rājye śrī-Kaṭukarāja-yauvarājye*) and of another inscription[98] from the same place, referring to the king Kaṭukadeva along with the heir-apparent Jayatasīha (*mahārāj=ādhirāja-śrī - Kaṭukadeva - vijay=odayīta - sat - suta-Jayatasīha-yuvarāja-bhujyamāna-samīpātyāṁ*).

The title *Mahākumāra* is known to have been borne by some later princes of the Paramāra dynasty like Lakṣmīvarman, Hariścandra and Udayavarman. While confirming a grant in V.S. 1200, originally made by his father Yaśovarmadeva, Lakṣmīvarman describes himself in his Ujjain inscription[99] as a Mahākumāra who owed sovereignty to his own valour (*nija-kara-kṛta-karāvāla-prasād=āvāpta-nij=ādhipatya . . . Mahā-kumāra-śrīmad=Lakṣmīvarmadevaḥ*) and was entitled to the five great sounds (*sam=adhigata-pañca-mahā-śabd=ālaṅkāra-virājamāna*). The Piplianagar grant[100] speaks of his son Hariś-candra, also called a *Mahākumāra*, as obtaining sovereignty of his own through the grace of the illustrious Jayavarmadeva (*śrī-Jayavarmadeva ity=etasmāt pṛṣṭhatama-prabhoḥ prasād=āvāp-ta-nij=ādhipatyaḥ . . . mahākumāra-śrī - Hariścandradevaḥ*), earning the status of a *Pañca-mahāśabda Sāmanta* and making a gift of land in favour of a scholar named Daśarathaśarman. Hariścandra's son Udayavarman is, likewise, described as a *Mahākumāra* in his Bhopal inscription which records the grant of a village by him in favour of a Brahmin named Mūlaśar-man.[101] The reason why these *de facto* independent chiefs claimed for themselves the title of *Mahākumāra* for generations is not definitely known. It might be, as suggested by Kielhorn, that they looked upon the deposed Paramāra king Jayavarman as the rightful ruler of Malwa or the threat of a Caulukya in-vasion might have forced them to assume a subordinate title in their own official records.

Some of the records[102] from Bangla near Narwar in Madhya Pradesh speak of a *Mahākumāra* named Jaitravarmadeva who seems to have been the eldest son of the Yajvapāla king Gopāla who flourished in the thirteenth century A.D. This crown prince was the *de facto* ruler[103] of the Yajvapāla kingdom during the later years of his father's reign and the Mahāpradhāna Rāuta Dejai served directly under him. Jaitravarmadeva appears to have predeceased his father as the latter was succeeded by his younger son Gaṇapati.[104]

X

The Crown Prince in the Śukra-nīti

In the *Śukra-nīti,* we have the following details about the crown prince:

'The crown prince and the body of councillors are the hands of a monarch. They are also known to be his eyes and ears, in each case right and left, respectively[105] (*Yuvarāj=omātya-gaṇ=obhuj=āvetau mahībhujaḥ| Tāv=eva-nayana-karṇo dakṣasavyau kramāt smṛtau||*). Without these two, the ruler would be deprived of his arms, eyes and ears (i.e., without any means of action). Hence he should appoint them on careful considerations. Otherwise there would be great calamity[106] (*Bāhu-karṇ=ākṣi-hīnaḥ syād=vinā tābhyām=ato nṛpaḥ| Yojayet=cintayitvā tau mahān=āśāya c=ānyathā*). The ruler should select as crown prince the offspring of the legally married wife who can perform the tasks of the state without idleness'[107] (*Mudrāṁ vin=ākhilaṁ rāja-kṛtyaṁ kartuṁ kṣamaṁ sadā| Kalpayet Yuvarāj=ārtham=aurasaṁ dharmapatnījam||*).

'He may select as crown prince his uncle younger than himself or younger brother or son of his elder brother, his own son or one treated as son or an adopted child or daughter's son or sister's son, successively according to failure.' The *Śukra-nīti*[109] further says that the king 'should keep the royal children very near to himself and always know their minds by employing craft through good servants. He should make the children of his family well up in the *Nīti Śāstras,* proficient in archery, capable of undergoing strains, and of bearing harsh words and punishments, habituated to the feats of arms, master of all arts and sciences, upright in morals as well as well-disciplined through his ministers and councillors. He should appoint them to crown-princeship after having brought them up with good dolls, clothed them in good dress, respected them with good seats, nourished them with good food and thus made them worthy of being crown princes.'

The following facts emerge from the above accounts of Śukra:

First, the crown prince was an important administrative machinery in the state, rendering the same, if not more useful, service as the body of councillors.

Second, he had to undergo a period of training in the *Nīti-śāstras* as well as in statecraft at the hands of ministers and councillors.

Third, he lived with the reigning king who was thus well informed of his activities. Śukra evidently decries the idea of deputing the *Yuvarāja* and other princes as governors of administrative divisions.

XI

The Crown Prince in the Pre-Cālukya-Pallava Period

An attempt may now be made to ascertain, with the help of the available material, the position of the crown prince in the South Indian kingdoms.

R.G. Bhandarkar and D.R. Bhandarkar[110] are of opinion that the Śātavāhana kings followed the practice of conjoint rule by the reigning king and the heir-apparent. According to them, Gautamīputra Śātakarṇi reigned simultaneously with his son Pulumāyi. This theory is mainly based on the argument that if at the time of issue of Gautamī's Nasik inscription Pulumāyi alone was reigning, the exploits of the latter would have been eulogised in the record. But H.C. Raychaudhuri[111] points out that 'although it is not customary for an ordinary subject to extol a dead king and pass over a reigning monarch in silence, still it is perfectly natural for a queen-mother in her old age to recount the glories of a son who was associated with her in a previous gift. That Gautamīputra and Pulumāyi did not rule conjointly appears abundantly clear when it is remembered that, in the first instance, the former is described in an inscription as the lord of Beṇākaṭaka, located in Govardhana in Nasik district, secondly, he addressed the official at Govardhana directly, and finally, the 'inscription of Gautamī Balaśrī was recorded in the year of Pulumāyi's reign, and not in that of his father who is supposed to have been the senior partner.'

The Hathigumpha inscription[112] gives us an interesting

insight into the education and responsibilities of the crown prince in the Cedi kingdom of Kaliṅga in the first century B.C. Referring to the accomplishment of prince Khāravela, the epigraph says, '*Paṁdarasa-vasāni siri-kaḍāra-sarīra-vatā kiḍitā kumāra-kīḍikā| Tato lekha-rūpa-gaṇanā-vyavahāra-vidhi-visāra-dena sava-vij=āvadātena nava-vasāni yovarajaṁ va sāsitaṁ*'. This passage has been translated by B.M. Barua[113] as follows: '. . . were played for fifteen years the sports befitting the young age of the prince with a handsome body of fair-brown complexion. Thereafter, for nine years, just the office of a Crown Prince was administered by (His Royal Highness) who was well-versed in (matters relating to) writing, coinage, accounting, procedure, and approved principle of action, whose self was purified by proficiency in all (Indian) polite learning.' We thus see that serious attention was paid to the training of the crown prince in order that, on accession to the throne, he would be able to discharge the duties of kingship efficiently.

XII

The Crown Prince in the Cālukya-Pallava Kingdoms

When we come to the time of the Cālukya kings of Badami, we see that the princes held an important position in the kingdom. The Nerur grant[114] creates the impression that the education and training of princes were carefully attended to, for Pulakeśin I is described in that record as an expert in the *Manusaṁhitā*, *Purāṇas*, *Mahābhārata*, *Rāmāyaṇa* as well as the art of politics. The crown prince took an active part in administration and often led the royal army against enemies. The *Yuvarāja* Vijayāditya is said to have defeated the hostile forces and acquired the Gaṅgā and Yamunā symbols, along with the *Pālidhvaja* standard during the reign of his father Vinayāditya.[115] Again, we come to learn from the Ulchala stone inscription[116] that the *Yuvarāja* Vikramāditya conquered Kāñcī and levied tribute on the Pallava king Parameśvaravarman II. The *Yuvarāja* Śryāśraya Śilāditya issued an inscription[117] from Navasārikā in Surat district, recording the donation of the village of Āsaṭṭi in favour of a Brahmin named Bhogikkasvāmin. The *Yuvarāja* Śryāśraya also issued the Surat plates,[118] making a grant of a plot of land on behalf of his father during the reign of king Vinayāditya. But Śryāśraya Śilāditya was the son of Dhārāśraya Jayasiṁha who was placed by Vikramāditya I in charge of South Gujarat. This would only show that the sons of provincial governors sometimes assumed the title of *Yuvarāja.*

We, however, possess much more information about the crown princes in the Pallava kingdom who were generally called *Yuvamahārāja.* They were sometimes entrusted with provincial administration and enjoyed the privilege of issuing records in their own names, as was the case with Śivaskandavarman, who issued an order, as is known from the Mayidavolu grant,[119] to his officers at Dhānyakaṭa. Viṣṇugopa, another Pallava crown prince, issued a grant,[120] but the record is dated in the regnal year of the ruling monarch Siṁhavarman. Śivaskandavarman, no doubt, enjoyed a greater amount of freedom as compared with Viṣṇugopa but still it may be admitted that generally speaking, the Pallava princes more actively participated in administration than the princes of the Cālukya dynasty.

XIII

The Crown Prince in the Rāṣṭrakūṭa Kingdom

That the crown prince held a high position in the Rāṣṭrakūṭa realm is indisputably proved by the epigraphic records of the family.[121] The eldest son was usually appointed the crown prince. Govinda II, for example, succeeded his father Kṛṣṇa I to the throne after the latter's death. If the father was sceptic about his abilities or was ill-disposed, a young son was chosen for the post. Stambha Raṇāvaloka was the eldest son of king Dhruva but his claims for heir-apparency were brushed aside in favour of those of his second or third brother Govinda III.[122] The Western Gaṅga king Avanīta Koṅgaṇi *Mahārājādhirāja,*[123] likewise, set aside the claims of his son Durvinīta by his first wife in favour of a younger prince, very probably by a different queen. But unlike Stambha Raṇāvaloka, Durvinīta rose equal to the occasion and succeeded in occupying the throne by dragging to himself 'the Lakṣmī of sovereignty by her hair'. It is worth noting that the practice of selecting a younger person in place of the legitimate claimant was at times fraught with grave danger, encouraging 'palace feuds and court intrigues among the members of the royal family and their partisans'.[124] The selection of his younger son Govinda by Dhruva as the *Yuvarāja* in preference to Stambha led to the outbreak of a civil war in the Rāṣṭrakūṭa realm after the father's demise. In the Talegaon plates[125] of Kṛṣṇa I Govindarāja is simply mentioned by his name only, whereas the same prince is described as a *Yuvarāja* in the Alas plates[126] which were issued two years later. This would reasonably point to the fact that the position of the crown prince was to be legalised by a consecration ceremony and that he was not recognised as a *Yuvarāja* until the ceremony was observed.

The *Yuvarāja* generally ascended the throne after the death of the ruling king, but sometimes the latter would abdicate the throne to make room for him.

The testimony of the Radhanpur plates of Govinda III implies that at the time of consecration the *Yuvarāja* was invested with a necklace (*kaṇṭhikā*) which was presumably the insignia of his office. As regards the prerogatives of princes, it may be pointed out on the evidence of the Alas plates that they sometimes exercised the right of granting villages. They normally did not actively participate in administration during the reign of their fathers but assumed the reins of administration when the ruling kings were old or of a retiring or religious disposition, as it happened in the reign of Amoghavarṣa I and Amoghavarṣa III. The *Yuvarāja* usually stayed in the capital. We hardly come across a Rāṣṭrakūṭa heir-apparent being deputed as a governor of an outlying province, the administration of which was generally entrusted to the younger princes and cousins. The Rāṣṭrakūṭa practice of stationing the crown prince in the capital was, no doubt, in harmony with the interest of the *Yuvarāja* himself whose constant presence in the capital helped him to safeguard successfully his prospect of succession by nipping palace feuds and court intrigues of other aspirants to the throne in the bud. The Rāṣṭrakūṭa inscriptions suggest that the *Yuvarāja* was sometimes entitled to the status of a *Pañca-mahāśabda Sāmanta*.[127]

XIV

The Crown Prince in Other South Indian Kingdoms

The copper plate grants[128] of the Kadamba kings would

indicate that the *Yuvarāja* enjoyed a high status in the kingdom, enjoying the right of making important appointments. He carried the main bulk of administrative burden during the old age of the ruling monarch, as was the case in the closing years of the reign of Kṛṣṇavarman.[129]

The *Yuvarāja* in the kingdom of the Cālukya kings of Kalyāṇī was called *Irivabeḍaṅga*. The *Vikramāṅkadevacarita* tells us that the prince had to learn the *Vedas*, *Āgamas*, *Itihāsas*, different scripts (*sarvāsu lipiṣu*), composition of poems and oratory. The choice for such an exalted post generally fell upon the eldest son, and in case of absence of any direct descendant, one amongst the brothers was nominated as *Yuvarāja*. The *Vikramāṅkadevacarita*[130] states that when Vikramāditya VI was crowned king in A.D. 1076, his younger brother Jayasiṁha was appointed the *Yuvarāja*.[131] When there was no properly qualified prince in the royal family, the heir-apparency was temporarily conferred on a trusted official.[132] As was the custom in the Rāṣṭrakūṭa kingdom, the *Yuvarāja* of the Western Cālukya kingdom was invested with a *kaṇṭhikā* or necklace at the time of his coronation, but unlike the Rāṣṭrakūṭa prince, he generally stayed outside the capital and was charged with the administration of a part of the kingdom. Taila's son and successor Irivaveḍaṅga Satyāśraya governed the province of Raṭṭapāḍi, as suggested by the Kharepatan grant.[133] Jayasiṁha, who became the *Yuvarāja* during the reign of his brother Vikramāditya VI, was appointed the governor of Banavase.[134] The crown prince was usually placed in charge of the administration of the two central divisions of Belvola Three Hundred and Purigere Three Hundred.[135]

As proved by the testimony of inscriptions, the practice of investing the crown prince with a *kaṇṭhikā* was likewise in vogue in the Eastern Cālukya kingdom of Veṅgī, but it is interesting to note that some of the Cālukya crown princes were at the same time adorned with a *paṭṭabandha*, i.e., diadem. A copper plate grant[136] of Bhīma II Viṣṇuvardhana, for example, mentions that Vijayāditya, the eldest son of Ammarāja, was invested with a necklace and a diadem (*paṭṭabandha*). Such was, however, not the case with the *Yuvarāja* Vikramāditya I, the younger brother of Vijayāditya III, who was adorned with a glittering necklace (*kaṇṭhikā*) round his throat.[137] The case of Vikramāditya I may further be cited to illustrate how the younger brothers were sometimes chosen for heir-apparency, presumably to ensure the continual good governance of the kingdom under a strong person. The case of Vijayāditya, the younger son of Vimalāditya, who usurped the throne by setting aside the claim of his elder brother Rājarāja, shows that the succession of a legitimate heir-apparent to the throne was sometimes challenged by ambitious claimants. The selection of a younger son for the throne in preference to the elder one often led to the outbreak of a civil war. Thus when the claim of Dānārṇava[138] was superseded in favour of his twelve-year-old brother Amma II, Dānārṇava acquiesced in this arrangement of his father Bhīma II for the time being but finally took possession of the kingdom by slaying Amma. D.P. Karmarkar[139] opines that the title *Yuvarāja* was bestowed even on persons outside the royal family in the Cālukya kingdom of Veṅgī. He refers in this connection to the *Yuvarāja* Ballāladeva Velābhaṭa, the son of Pammavā of the Paṭṭavardhinī family, who is known to have been granted a plot of land by Ammarāja II Vijayāditya.[140] But Ballāladeva appears to have been a subordinate ally under Ammarāja II rather than a proud crown prince in the Cālukya territory.

It may not be out of place here to mention that the absence of any direct heir had often induced the Cola kings to nominate their younger brothers for heir-apparency. When Rājādhirāja, the eldest son of Rājendra Gaṅgaikoṇḍa Cola, ascended the throne, he, being childless, appointed his younger brother Rājendra II the crown prince and associated him with administration. Rājendra II, likewise, selected his younger brother Vīra Rājendra for heir-apparency which fell vacant in consequence of the death of his own son Rājamahendra Rājakeśari,[141] the original incumbent of the post.

When we turn to the Hoysala kings, we find that they usually nominated the *Yuvarāja* during their own life-time. The Hoysala Narasiṁha III[142] was made the crown prince during the reign of his father. As would appear from the testimony of the inscriptions of the family, there was no lower age-limit for the appointment of a prince as a *Yuvarāja*. Narasiṁhadeva,[143] the son of Viṣṇuvardhana, was crowned *Yuvarāja* even on the very day of his birth. The reason why a prince at his infancy was declared to be the *Yuvarāja* might be that the reigning king feared some trouble over the question of succession to the throne after his death. It cannot escape notice that Tirumala was appointed *Yuvarāja* in A.D. 1524 by his father king Kṛṣṇadeva Rāya when he was but six years old.[144]

The *Yuvarāja* finds prominent mention in the Kākatīya inscriptions. During the rule of the later kings of the dynasty we find that the crown prince was often taken by the ruling monarch into partnership in the governance of the kingdom. Gaṇapati appointed his daughter Rudramadevī his co-regent during the closing years of his reign and Rudramadevī, in her turn, emulated her father by associating the *Yuvarāja* Pratāparūdra with herself in the administration of the kingdom.[145]

References and Notes

1. X.40.3.
2. *Aitareya Brāhmaṇa*, VII.17.6; *Pañcaviṁśa Brāhmaṇa*, XIX.1.4; *Kāṭhaka Saṁhitā*, XIV.8; *Taittirīya Brāhmaṇa*, III.8.5.1; *Śatapatha Brāhmaṇa*, XIII.4.2.5.
3. VIII.12.5; 17.5.
4. XIX.1.4.
5. V.3.5.12.
6. V.4.2.8.
7. D.C. Sircar, *Early Indian Political And Administrative Systems* (Calcutta, 1972), p. 122.
8. Ibid., p. 123.
9. Jāt., VI.30.
10. Sircar, *op. cit.*, p. 123.
11. VI.131.
12. *AAHI*, p. 35.
13. *PHAI*, p. 209.
14. R.N. Mehta, *Pre-Buddhist India* (1939), p. 89.
15. I.259, 356; II.87; III.115, 122.
16. *Dīpavaṁsa*, VI.15; *Mahāvaṁsa*, XIII.8.
17. P. 371.
18. *PHAI*, p. 363. The *Divyāvadāna* (pp. 407-08) further states that Aśoka once sent his son Kuṇāla to Takṣaśilā to pacify the citizens who had been offended by the arrogance of the *Amātyas*.
19. *AI*, XVI-VII.
20. *CHA*, II, p. 29.
21. *KA*, II, p. 46.
22. I.16.
23. I.16.

24. Ibid.
25. Ibid.
26. Ibid.
27. I.13.
28. *KA*, II, p. 12.
29. I.18.
30. I.17.
31. Ibid.
32. Ibid.
33. IX.3.
34. I.17.
35. XIII.104.125, 146ff.
36. I.1.124.
37. E.W. Hopkins, *The Social and Military Position of the Ruling Caste in Ancient India* (Varanasi, 1972), p. 55.
38. *Lucknow University Journal*, II, p. 57.
39. The eighteen *tīrthas* (*tīrthāni aṣṭādaś=aiva ca*) are the *Mantrī* (chief minister), *Purohita* (chief priest), *Yuvarāja*, *Camūpati*, also called *Senāpati* (commander-in-chief), *Dvārapāla*, also known as *Dauvārika* (chief warden), *Antarveśika* or *Antarvaṁśika* (overseer of the harem), *Kārāgārādhikārī* (overseer of prisons), *Dravyasañcayakṛt*, identified with *Samāhartā* of other texts (chief steward), *Sannidhātṛ* (collector of the exchequer), *Pradeṣṭṛ* (chief police officer or judge), *Nagarādhyakṣa* (overseer of the city), *Kāryanirmāṇakṛt* (chief engineer), *Dharmādhyakṣa* (overseer of justice), *Sabhādhyakṣa* (president of the assembly), *Daṇḍapāla* (leader of the army or criminal judge), *Durgapāla* (officer-in-charge of fortresses), *Antapāla* (chief of frontier guards) and *Aṭavīpāla* (guardian of the forest).
40. II.5.38.
41. E.W. Hopkins, *op. cit.*, pp. 72-73.
42. I.102.1.
43. E.W. Hopkins, *op. cit.*, p. 53.
44. Ibid., pp. 83-86.
45. *Ayodhyākāṇḍa*, 3.6.
46. VII.114.11.
47. VII.121.20.
48. VII.115.1-14; 102.1.
49. VII.120-17; 121.4-5.
50. VII.43.
51. VII.116.
52. *CHA*, II, p. 270.
53. *JBRS*, XXXVIII, p. 231.
54. B. Chattopadhyay, *Kushāṇa State And Indian Society* (Calcutta, 1975), p. 96.
55. Marshall, *Taxila*, I, pp. 67-68.
56. Chhabra (*IC*, XIV, p. 141) offers a new reading and interpretation of the corresponding passage of the Allahabad inscription. The passage

Āryoh=ity=upaguhya is read by him as *ehi eh=īty=upaguhya*, which means 'Come, come. Protect thou the whole earth.' If we accept this reading, it would follow that Candragupta I abdicated in favour of Samudragupta.

57. *SI*, p. 322.
58. *GP*, p. 156.
59. *HB*, I, p. 284.
60. *GP*, p. 155.
61. *Kāmandakīya*, VII.5-6.
62. *SI*, p. 267.
63. V.39.
64. LXXII.4.
65. XXX.19; XXXIV.10; XXXVI.1; LII.17; LXXII.4.
66. M.R. Kale, *Bāṇa's Kādambarī* (1968), p. 105.
67. Ibid., p. 153.
68. V. Satakopan, *Daṇḍin's Daśakumāracarita* (Madras, 1966), p. 18.
69. *EI*, XVIII, pp. 304ff.
70. *SHAIB*, p. 529.
71. Ibid., p. 359.
72. *RTA*, p. 314.
73. *Nītivākyāmṛta*, p. 60.
74. Ibid., p. 56.
75. 225.1-2.
76. 225.3.
77. 225.3.
78. D.K. Ganguly, *Historical Geography and Dynastic History of Orissa* (Calcutta, 1975), p. 239.
79. *EI*, IV, pp. 118 and 120.
80. *RG*, p. 145.
81. *EI*, VIII, pp. 156-66; *RG*, p. 146.
82. *EI*, VIII., 155-56.
83. Ibid., pp. 157-58.
84. *SHAIB*, p. 475.
85. Ibid., p. 478.
86. Ibid., pp. 483-84.
87. *EI*, XI, pp. 52ff.
88. The prince Jojala is described as *tiraskṛta-sakala-Pīlvāhikā-maṇḍala-taskaraḥ* (Ibid., pp. 53-54).
89. Ibid., p. 45.
90. *JASB*, X, p. 209.
91. Ibid., XIV, p. 104.
92. *IA*, XIX, p. 218.
93. *PIA*, pp. 76-77.
94. *EI*, IX, p. 68.
95. Ibid., XI, p. 50.
96. *PIA*, pp. 76-77.
97. *EI*, XI, p. 29.
98. Ibid., p. 34.

99. *IA*, XIX, pp. 351-53.
100. *DHNI*, II, p. 890.
101. Ibid., pp. 892-93.
102. *EI*, XXXI, pp. 326ff.
103. This is implied by the passage, occurring in an inscription from Bangla: *śrī Gopāladeva-vijaya-rājye tasmin kāle varttamāne rāvata-Jayatabrahmadeva - mahāpradhāna-Dejai-parigrahī-gadani - vyaparita-samaye*. As D.C. Sircar (*EI*, XXXI, p. 331) points out, the language of the passage is defective but it apparently refers to the time when Jaitravarman and Dejai were conducting the affairs of administration during the reign of Gopāla.
104. *EI*, XXXI, p. 329.
105. II.12.
106. II.13.
107. II.14.
108. B.K. Sarkar, *The Śukranīti* (Allahabad, 1914), pp. 57-58.
109. Ibid., p. 59.
110. *PHAI*, p. 492.
111. Ibid., p. 493.
112. *IHQ*, XIV, p. 462.
113. Ibid., p. 473.
114. *IA*, VII, p. 161.
115. *CA*, p. 246.
116. *Ancient India*, V, p. 54.
117. V.V. Mirashi, *Corpus Inscriptionum Indicarum*, IV, pt. I, pp. 123ff.
118. Ibid., p. 132.
119. *EI*, VI, pp. 86ff.
120. *IA*, V, pp. 5ff.
121. In referring to the heir-apparent in the Rāṣṭrakūṭa kingdom, A.S. Altekar (*RT*, p. 152) observes that he 'had to attain a certain age, probably 24, before he could be formally anointed' but there is no cogent evidence in support of this contention.
122. *EI*, VI, pp. 244 and 249.
123. *Mysore Gazetteer*, II, pt. 2, p. 342; *SIP*, p. 92.
124. *SIP*, p. 96.
125. *EI*, XIII, p. 275.
126. *EI*, VI, pp. 210 and 213.
127. The meaning of the epithet *sam=adhigata-pañca-mahāśabda*, 'one who has attained the *pañca-mahāśabda*' is not clear. This expression is generally used in connection with the names of heirs-apparent and feudatories, but is seldom applied to paramount kings. Scholars (*IA*, XII, pp. 95ff) are generally of opinion that the term *pañca-mahā-śabda* denotes the sound of five musical instruments such as trumpet (*śṛṅga*), tambour (*tammaṭa*), conch-shell (*śaṅkha*), kettledrum (*bherī*) and gong (*jayaghaṇṭā*). If this interpretation is relied upon, it will follow that the epithet *sam=adhigata-pañca-mahāśabda* was an honorific title bestowed upon some important office-bearers who

could make public appearance with the playing of such five musical instruments. Some scholars point out that the *Rājataraṅgiṇī* uses the above term to mean the five *Karmasthānas* (S.C. Ray, *Early History and Culture of Kashmir*, p. 126).
128. *IA*, VII, p. 34.
129. *EI*, IX, p. 172.
130. VI.
131. *EHD*, p. 383.
132. Ibid., p. 383.
133. *EI*, II, p. 297.
134. *Vikramāṅkadevacarita*, VI.
135. *EHD*, p. 383.
136. *EI*, V, p. 38.
137. *IA*, XX, p. 103.
138. *EHD*, II, p. 485.
139. *Karnatak Historical Review*, I, p. 37.
140. *EI*, V, pp. 139ff.
141. *SIP*, p. 93.
142. *EC*, V, *Cn*-269; *SIP*, p. 90.
143. *EC*, V, *BL*. 93.
144. T.V. Mahalingam, *Administration and Social Life Under Vijayanagar* (Madras, 1940), p. 12.
145. *EHD*, II, p. 671.

4

The Royal Chaplain

I

The Priest in the Pre-Ṛgvedic Period

The frequent mention of the *Purohita*[1] in Ṛgvedic passages indubitably proves the wide popularity of the institution in the early Vedic period. The distinguished German Indologist Zimmer[2] is of opinion that this office came into vogue after the establishment of the caste system which is generally believed to have taken place in the latter part of the early Vedic period. It is needless to emphasise that the origin of priesthood goes back to much remoter days; the first indications of a priest's office may be traced back almost to the very origin of religious and magical practices But in the beginning the religious rites were very simple in character and consequently almost everybody was competent to undertake the priestly functions. 'But as ritual observances and magical practices gradually became too complicated for the average man to master, a professional priesthood became necessary.'[3] The transformation of the simple ritual and magical practices into complicated systems had already taken place in India in pre-historic times, long before the advent of the Aryans in the subcontinent. Some scholars have propounded the theory that the Brāhmaṇas were the pre-Aryan priests The acceptance of this view would give rise to the surmise that the Brāhmaṇa *Purohitas* possessed uncommon cleverness and intelligence to win the encomium of their Aryan conquerors and an enviable position in Aryan society. But while on the one hand it is unhistorical to brand the Brāhmaṇas as non-Aryans in origin, it is, on the other hand, difficult to deny the existence of the institution of priesthood in the Aryan community of pre-Ṛgvedic times.

II

The Priest in the Ṛgvedic Period

Interesting details about the *Purohita* are preserved in the *Ṛgveda* which represents him as an important personage, offering sacrifices, on behalf of kings and people, to gods. But his entire energy was not devoted to the cultivation of religious pursuits; he was an active participant in wars also. Whenever the king went to the battle-field to fight with his adversaries, the priest accompanied him and rendered help to the army by the 'spiritual force of his prayers and the mystic powers of his charms'. In this respect he compared well with the clergy of mediaeval Europe. At the time of the battle of the ten kings, Vasiṣṭha[4] joined hands with his royal patron Sudās, whereas Viśvāmitra sided with the opposite camp. The story of the battle of the ten kings shows that the priests remained in office as long as they enjoyed the confidence of their patron-kings. Notwithstanding the insecurity of their service, they succeeded in exercising tremendous influence in the contemporary royal courts, as instanced by the success of Viśvāmitra, the deposed priest of Sudās, in organising a coalition of ten kings against his erstwhile master. The importance of the office of *Purohita* in this period is further emphasised by a passage in the *Ṛgveda*[5] which says, 'That king alone in front of whom the *Brahman* walks (*pūrvam=eti*) lives well established in his house; for him there is ever abundance of food; before him the people bow of their own accord.' There is another verse[6] wherein Agni is described as the divine ministrant of the sacrifice, the *Hotṛ* priest and the greatest bestower of treasures. From this it is obvious that Agni does not hold the position of a private chaplain in the kingdom of gods, but he is the 'divine ministrant' and the 'king of all worship'. It is, therefore, evident that the vast majority of the Ṛgvedic kings needed the service of their domestic priests who functioned as chief adviser in matters, both temporal and spiritual. Even by the time of the *Ṛgveda*, the *Purohita* then raised himself to a much higher position than that of a private chaplain. A.B. Keith[7] rightly observes, 'The Vedic *Purohita* was the forerunner of the Brāhmaṇa statesmen who from time to time in India have shown conspicuous ability in the management of affairs and there is no reason to doubt that a Viśvāmitra or Vasiṣṭha was a more important element of government of the early Vedic realm.' In return for his service to the king and the state, he was entitled to rewards which were doubtlessly large. As pointed out by A.B. Keith,[8] 'the *dānastutis* of the *Ṛgveda* speak of generous gifts of patrons to the poets and we may safely assume that the largest donations were those of kings to the *purohita*'.

III

The Priest in the Later Vedic Period

The august position which the priesthood had attained in the period of the *Ṛgveda* was maintained unabated in the succeeding age when he was alternatively designated as *Brahman*. This is evidenced, in the first place, by some of the Vedic texts which include him in the list of the *Ratnins*. In the *Taittirīya Saṁhitā*,[9] *Maitrāyaṇī Saṁhitā*,[10] *Taittirīya Brāhmaṇa*[11] and *Kāṭhaka Saṁhitā*, he is assigned the first position among the *Ratnins*, whereas in the *Śatapatha Brāhmaṇa*[12] he occupies the second position. The status of the *Ratnins* was exceedingly high as they formed the king's council. The *Taittirīya Brāhmaṇa*[13] describes them in explicit terms as bestowers of the kingdom upon the king (*ete vai rāṣṭrasya pradātāraḥ*). The lofty position of the priest is further attested by the *Aitareya Brāhmaṇa*[14] which states that the *Purohita* surrounds and protects the king with his power like the sea, girdling the earth (*Purohitas=tābhiḥ rājānaṁ parigṛhya tiṣṭhati samudra eva bhūmiṁ*). We are further told that the subjects of such a king enjoy the blessings of perpetual happiness and are ever devoted to him as he is guided by a wise priest.[15] Some *Brāhmaṇa* texts like the *Taittirīya*[16] and *Pañcaviṁśa* show that his installation in the office was legalised by the performance of the *Bṛhaspatisava* sacrifice.

The observance of rituals for the royal family and the state continued to be one of the chief concerns of the *Purohita* in this age. The belief[17] that gods would not accept the oblations of the king provided they were offered through his priest gained momentum during this period. The *Aitareya Brāhmaṇa*, for instance, lays down, 'Verily gods do not eat the food offered by the king who is without a *Purohita*. Therefore let the king, who wishes to sacrifice, place a Brāhmaṇa at the head.' He was, however, not personally concerned with all the minute details of the rituals, which were entrusted to the subordinate priests, called *Ṛtviks*, but participated in the more important details. In addition to his sacrificial duty, he used to guide the king in all religious matters. In this age also we find him accompanying the king to the battle-field. The *Atharvaveda* states that by performing the various rituals, the *Purohita* not only thwarts the magical charm of the enemies, but also contributes greatly to the development of his own kingdom. It is but fitting that he was looked upon as the guardian of the realm (*rāṣṭra-gopa*).

But what were the actual functions of the *Purohita* at the sacrifice? A passage of the *Ṛgveda*[18] indicates that for performing a sacrifice was necessary a body of seven priests, comprising the *Hotṛ*, *Potṛ*, *Neṣṭṛ*, *Agnīdhra*, *Praśāstṛ*, *Adhvaryu* and *Brahman*. The chief amongst them was the *Hotṛ* who recited verses from the *Ṛgveda*. The *Adhvaryu*, with the assistance of the *Agnīdhra*, undertook the practical work of the sacrifice like preparing the altar, digging the fire-pits, cooking the oblations, etc. Macdonell and Keith[19] describe the functions of other priests as follows: 'The *Praśāstṛ*, *Upavaktṛ* or *Maitrāvaruṇa*, as he was variously called, appeared only in the greater sacrifices as giving instructions to the *Hotṛ*, and was entrusted with certain litanies. The *Potṛ*, *Neṣṭṛ* and *Brahman* belonged to the ritual of the *Soma* sacrifice, the latter being later styled *Brāhmaṇāc-chaṃsin* to distinguish him from the priest who in the later ritual acted as supervisor. Other priests referred to in the *Ṛgveda* are the singers of *Sāmans* or chants, the *Udgātṛ* and his assistant the *Prastotṛ*, while the *Pratihartṛ*, another assistant, though not mentioned, may quite well have been known. Their functions undoubtedly represent a later stage of the ritual, the development of the elaborate series of sacrificial calls on the one hand, and on the other the use of long hymns addressed to the *Soma* plant. Other priests, such as the *Achāvāka*, the *Grāvastut*, the *Unnetṛ* and the *Subrahmaṇya*, were known later in the developed ritual of the *Brāhmaṇas*, making in all sixteen priests, who were technically and artificially classed in four groups: *Hotṛ*, *Maitrāvaruṇa*, *Achāvāka*, and *Grāvastut*; *Udgātṛ*, *Prastotṛ*, *Pratihartṛ*, and *Subrahmaṇya*; *Adhvaryu*, *Pratisthātṛ*, *Neṣṭṛ*, and

Unnetṛ; *Brahman*, *Brāhmaṇācchamsin*, *Agnīdhra*, and *Potṛ*.' Geldner[20] believes that whenever the *Purohita* actually participated in a sacrifice, he played the role of the *Brahman*. Geldner has cited in support of his contention a number of passages of the *Ṛgveda* and the later literature where the *Purohita* and the *Brahman* are identified. But Oldenberg is probably more correct when he points out that 'in the earlier period this was not the case; the *Purohita* was then normally the *Hotṛ*, the singer of the most important of the songs; it was only later that the *Brahman*, who in the capacity of overseer of the rite is not known to the *Ṛgveda*, acquired the function of general supervision hitherto exercised by the *Purohita*, who was *ex officio* skilled in the use of magic and in guarding the king by spells which could also be applied to guarding the sacrifice from evil demons.'[21]

Normally, there was one *Purohita* for one kingdom. But there are instances in Vedic literature to show that sometimes they combined in themselves the office of the house-priest of a number of kingdoms simultaneously. The *Śatapatha Brāhmaṇa*,[22] for instance, mentions that Devabhāga Śrautarṣa was the priest of both the Kuru and the Sṛñjaya kingdoms. The *Śatapatha Brāhmaṇa* states, 'Devabhāga Śrautarṣa is the priest of both the Kurus and the Sṛñjayas. Now, a high position is held by him who is the priest of one state; how much greater, then, is the status of one who is the *Purohita* of two kingdoms?' The instance of a highly efficient Brāhmaṇa holding the office of the priest of even three states is, likewise, known. The *Sāṅkhāyana Śrauta Sūtra*[23] alludes to the fact that Jāla Jātukarṇya acted as the priest for the kings of Kāśī, Kosala and Videha (*Jālo Jātukarṇyaḥ . . . trayāṇāṁ rājyaṁ . . . prāpa . . . Kāśyā-Vaidehayoḥ purohito babhūva| Kauśalasya ca rājñaḥ|*). 'This fact', as J. Basu[24] rightly points out, 'proves the close connection and alliance of these three states and the extraordinary administrative ability of the Brāhmaṇa priest as well.'

In the Vedic period the *Purohita* was the kingpin among the state functionaries. This is quite in line with the spirit of the age which believed that success in the realms of peace and war was largely dependent on divine favour to be secured through priests. A well-known passage in the *Śatapatha Brāhmaṇa* tells us that the king who is weaker than his Brāhmaṇa priest is stronger than his foes. This is, however, hardly in agreement with the statement[25] of the *Vājasaneyī Brāhmaṇa Upaniṣad* that 'since there is none above the ruler, the Brāhmaṇa sits under the Kṣatriya in *Rājasūya*' (*Tasmāt kṣatrād=paraṁ n=āsti tasmād=brāhmaṇaḥ kṣatriyam=adhas=tu upāste rājasūye*). Notwithstanding the great importance that was attached to the post, its incumbent was never considered above the law of the land. 'Like any other citizen, he was punished whenever there was a departure from his *svadharma* or loyalty to the king.' The *Pañcaviṁśa Brāhmaṇa*[26] tells us that a *Purohita* might be punished with death in cases of treason. It cannot escape notice that we do not find in the Aryan kingdoms of Vedic India that strange combination of priestly functions with royal authority, instances of which are met with in ancient Europe and many an Asiatic and African country. In Egypt, for example, at the time of Menes and his immediate successors, all the religious and political functions were united in one person, the king. Thus the king became, in theory, the high priest of the state. But no king in Vedic India is known to have played the role of a king-priest.

IV

The Priest in the Dharmasūtra and Jātaka Literature

The *Dharmasūtras* and the Buddhist *Jātakas* throw a flood of light upon the position of the royal chaplain in the post-Vedic period. In referring to the office of the priest, the *Dharmasūtra* of Gautama[27] observes, 'And he shall select as his domestic priest (*Purohita*) a Brāhmaṇa who is learned in the *Vedas*, of noble family, eloquent, handsome, of a suitable age, and of a virtuous disposition, who lives righteously and who is austere. With his assistance, he shall fulfil his religious duties' (*Brāhmaṇañ=ca purodadhīta vidy=ābhijana-vāg-rūpa-vayaḥ śīla-sampannaṁ nyāyavṛttaṁ tapasvinaṁ tatprasūtaḥ karmāṇi kurvīta*). The commentator Haradatta, however, has interpreted some of the terms differently. He takes *vāksampannaḥ* to mean 'one who knows Sanskrit', *vayaḥ* to denote the prime of life when men are neither too young nor too old, and *tapasvin* to signify 'not given to sensual enjoyments'. We thus see that Gautama not only enumerates the qualifications of the *Purohita* but also urges the king to be guided by his advice in religious matters. In defining the functions of the priest, Gautama[28] says: *Śānti-puṇyāha-svastyayan-āyuṣya-maṅgala-saṁyukt=āny=ābhyudayik-āni vidveṣiṇāṁ sambalanam-abhicārad-viṣad=avyādhi-saṁyuktāni ca śālāgnau kuryād yath=oktam=Ṛtvij=onyāni.* G. Bühler[29] translates the passage thus, 'He shall perform in the fire of the hall the rites ensuring prosperity which are connected with expiations, festivals, a prosperous march, long life, and auspiciousness; as well as those that are intended to cause enmity, to subdue (enemies), to destroy (them) by incantations, and to cause their misfortune. Officiating priests shall perform the other sacrifices according to the precepts (of the Vedas).' It is therefore evident that the *Purohita* did not perform all the rites, some other priests were entrusted with the performance of other sacrifices, which, as Haradatta would have us believe, comprised the *Gṛhya* and *Śrauta* rites.

Baudhāyana,[30] likewise, enjoins the king to choose a *Purohita* who should be proficient in all transactions (*sarvato dhuraṁ*). The king should act, of course, in spiritual matters, according to his instructions. Āpastamba[31] maintains a liberal view about the qualifications of the *Purohita* and lays down that the priest need be proficient only in sacred and political knowledge. Nevertheless, the power of the *Purohita*, as depicted by Āpastamba, was enormous, he being empowered not only to protect a criminal from punishment by his intercession,[32] excepting in the case of a capital offence, but also to try cases concerning transgression of order. The *Āśvalāyana Gṛhyasūtra*[33] states that the priest has to discharge some military functions. Āśvalāyana lays down that before the king commences his journey to the battle-field, the priest stands to the west of the king's chariot, chants *mantras* from the *Ṛgveda*, arms the king with various weapons, recites *mantras* over the horse and accompanies him as the king advances to the battle-field. Vasiṣtha[34] lays down that it is obligatory on the part of the king to appoint a *Purohita* since it is the Brāhmaṇa priest who is capable of protecting the kingdom (*Vijñāyate Brāhmaṇaḥ Purohito rāṣṭraṁ dadhāt=īti*) and that the king should reward him with various gifts on different occasions (*gārhasthya-naiyamikeṣu Purohite dadyāt*). Besides, we have the following account about the priest in the *Dharmasūtra* of Vasiṣtha:[35] 'In case (a criminal) worthy of punishment is allowed to go free, the king shall fast during one (day and one) night; and his domestic priest during three days and nights. If an innocent man is punished, the domestic priest shall perform a *Karikkhra* penance.'

The Buddhist *Jātakas* afford us an interesting insight into the office of the priest. The office was generally hereditary[36] and held by the same family for generations. Once some Brāhmaṇas opposed the installation of a young son of the deceased *Purohita*. But the mother of the boy argued, 'For seven generations we have managed the elephant festivals from father to son. The old custom will pass from us, and our wealth will melt away.'[37] Sometimes, of course, new men were appointed to the post, presumably in place of the old ones. The supervision of the domestic sacrifices of the king constituted the most important function of the priest. Time and again[38] we find him acting as the preceptor of the king and instructing him in the various branches of learning in his youthful days. The *Jātakas* tell us very little about his political activities and we fully agree with the view of Fick[39] that 'the political power of the *Purohita* was purely individual and had its source wholly and solely in the personal influence which he obtained over the king through his function as sacrificer and magician.' The *Kiṁchanda* and *Dhammadhaja Jātakas* mention the *Purohita* as participating in the administration of justice and helping the rightful claimant to regain his property. It is thus evident that the *Purohita* sometimes discharged judicial functions. His connection with the royal treasury is clearly borne out by the *Bandhanamokkha Jātaka*,[40] where a priest is found saying, 'I am the officer of the king (*ahaṁ rāja-kammiko*) and have rendered him much service and I know where great treasures are hidden. The treasures of the king, I have guarded; if you don't take me to the king, much wealth will be lost.'[41] We do not know whether the *Purohita* actually went to the battle-field in this age, but the *Susīma Jātaka* tells us that he consecrated the war-horses and elephants in order to increase their efficiency. Sometimes the *Purohita* is described as a *Sabbatthaka*, which suggests that he advised the king in all matters, spiritual as well as temporal. As regards his qualifications, the *Jātakas* tell us that he was to be a master in Vedic lore[42] and other sciences.[43] The Jātaka stories sometimes bear testimony to the degradation of the priest. His greed of wealth carried him to the depth of moral degeneration which was unbecoming of such a man. But it would be wrong to disparage the whole community of priests since quite a good many of them were held in high esteem by virtue of their righteousness and wisdom. It is difficult, in the circumstances, to agree with R.N. Mehta when, in referring to the priest as depicted in the Jātaka texts, he observes, 'Wealth, and not power, seems to have been his innermost desire, and the ultimate goal.'[44]

Some of the *Jātakas* mention the term *attha-dhammānu-sāsaka-amacca* which Fick[45] translates as the 'guide of the king in worldly and spiritual matters'. This officer, if the interpretation of Fick be accepted, then took over some of the functions of the *Purohita.* It cannot be known definitely whether the post of the *Attha-dhammānusāsaka Amacca* was created in most of the kingdoms or was confined to a few states only.[46]

V

The Priest in the Kauṭilīya Arthaśāstra

The *Arthaśāstra* of Kauṭilya provides us useful information about the *Purohita* who is distinguished from the *Ṛtvij*, 'sacrificial priest', *Ācārya*, 'spiritual preceptor', *Kārttāntika*, 'interpreter of omens', *Mauhūrttika*, 'astrologer' and the like. Kauṭilya thus advocates the idea of decentralisation of priestly functions and is opposed to the concentration of all power in the hands of one man. Speaking of his qualifications, Kauṭilya[47] points out that the *Purohita* should be a man of noble descent, a man of stainless character *(udit=odita-kula-śīle)*, well-versed in the *Vedas* and the sixfold Aṅga (*Ṣaḍaṅge Vede*), skilful in reading portents, providential as well as accidental (*daive nimitte*), well-grounded in the science of government (*daṇḍanītyāñ=ca*), obedient (*abhivinītaṁ*) and capable of warding off calamities, divine or human, by performing such expiatory rites as are prescribed in the *Atharvaveda* (*Daiva-mānuṣīṇām=Atharvabhir=upāyaiś=ca pratikartāraṁ kurvīta*). It appears from the above and several other passages of the *Arthaśāstra* that the Kauṭilīya *Purohita* was entrusted with the following functions:

First, he accompanied the king at specific hours.

Second, he warded off divine and human calamities like flood, fire, epidemic, famine, wild elephants, snakes, evil spirits, etc., by employing certain means, as enumerated in the *Atharvaveda*.

Third, he encouraged the soldiers to fight against the enemies by promising them great rewards in the next world in the event of their death on the battle-field. In this respect, his work was similar to that of the poet-bards called *Pāṇar* who are mentioned in the Tamil texts of the Śaṅgam epoch as following the king to the theatre of war and infusing 'fresh spirit into the minds of the soldiers during the encounter'.

Fourth, when the chief queen was in the period of menstruation, the priest had to offer a *caru*-oblation to Indra and Bṛhaspati. He performed the sacraments for the newly-born prince.[48]

The high position of the *Purohita*[49] in the Kauṭiliyan state is indicated by the fact that he was to get 48,000 *paṇas*[50] as his emolument and was grouped in the same category of such high functionaries as the *Mantrin*, the *Senāpati*, the crown prince, the queen-mother and the queen consort. Kauṭilya[51] further states that the king should make grants of revenue-free lands to the sacrificial priest, the spiritual guide, the domestic chaplain and the learned Brāhmaṇas (*Ṛtvik=ācārya purohita-śrotriyobhyo brahmadeyāni adaṇḍakarāṇi abhirūpadāyakāni prayacchet*). The *Purohita* thus enjoyed the special privilege of mixed remuneration in both cash and kind. That the *Purohita* exerted a great influence over the king is apparent from Kauṭilya's statement[52] that 'as a student his teacher, a son his father and a servant his master, the king shall follow him' (*tam=ācāryaṁ śiṣyaḥ pitaraṁ putro bhṛtyaḥ svāminam=iva c=ānuvarteta*). Kauṭilya is at the same time aware of the evils emanating from the priestly class and recommends their imprisonment and even banishment in the case of their committing a great offence. The king is even advised to employ spies on his priest to ascertain the activities of the latter.[53] Even then Kauṭilya admits that the king cannot prosper unless he is aided by the chaplain. He[54] says, 'Kṣatriya power, made to prosper by the Brahmin (chaplain), sanctified by spells in the form of the counsel of ministers, (and) possessed of arms in the form of compliance with the science of politics), triumphs, remaining ever unconquered.'

It has to be admitted that the Kauṭiliyan *Purohita* was a shadowy figure as compared with his forerunners of the Vedic and post-Vedic periods. The functions, which in the earlier epochs were concentrated in his hands, came to be distributed among several officials. As a natural corollary of the decentralisation of his power and functions, there was a decline of his position. Even he was not entrusted with the temple administration for which a special officer called *Devatādhyakṣa*, was appointed. It may be mentioned in this connection that the latter officer was required to realise revenue for the king at a time of emergency by appropriating the wealth of temples and exploiting popular superstitions.

We are unfortunately unable to decide with certainty how far the Kauṭiliyan system was executed in practice in the Maurya period. That the post of the royal chaplain was in abeyance in the courts of most of the Maurya kings, who were staunch Buddhists, appears to be fairly certain. The *Dharma-mahāmātras* of the Aśokan edicts were in no way connected with the office of the *Purohita*.

VI
The Priest in the Epics

The two epics, the *Rāmāyaṇa* and the *Mahābhārata*, show that the *Purohita* wielded enormous influence in the kingdom during the contemporary period. The *Ayodhyākāṇḍa*[55] of the *Rāmāyaṇa* tells us how the chief priest Vasiṣṭha carried on the administration of the Ikṣvāku kingdom with the help of the council of ministers during the interregnum between the death of Daśaratha and the assumption of power by Bharata. The epics generally depict the priests as advising the king in all matters, not excluding political. In the *Śāntiparvan*[56] of the *Mahābhārata*, we have the following passage: *Ātm=āmātyaś=ca koṣāś=ca daṇḍo mitrāṇi c=aiva hi.* This means that a kingdom is an amalgam of seven elements like *Ātmā* or *Svāmī*, friends, treasury, *rāṣṭra*, fort and *daṇḍa*. Now, the commentator Nīlakaṇṭha explains the term *svāmī* as follows: *Svāmīrūpā prakṛtiḥ Ṛtvika-Purohita-nṛpa-bhedena trividhāḥ.* If this interpretation is accepted, it would follow that the priest was considered to be one of the lords of the realm. The role of the *Purohita* as a political adviser of the king did not meet with universal approval and is denounced by the *Mahābhārata*[57] in the following words: 'The place for priests is in the hall of debate; good are they as inspectors; they can oversee elephants, horses and war-cars; they are learned in detecting the faults of food; but let not the (priestly) teachers be asked for advice when emergencies arise.' We may probably be justified in assuming that some of the *Purohitas*, endowed as they were with uncommon ability and experience, guided kings in both religious and political matters, while others, who were of lesser merit, concentrated their attention on ecclesiastical matters alone.

As regards the qualities of the *Purohita*, the *Mahābhārata*[58] points out that he should be well-versed in the *Vedas* and be endowed with such noble virtues as purity, truthfulness and piety (*Vede Ṣaḍaṅge niratāḥ śucayaḥ satyavādinaḥ| Dharmātmānaḥ kṛtātmānaḥ syur=nṛpāṇāṁ purohitāḥ||*). The *Mahābhārata* elsewhere lays down that modesty, learning, noble descent, devotion, etc., are some of the virtues befitting a *Purohita.*[59]

An interesting insight into the problem whether the epic *Purohita* was immune from punishment in the eyes of law is afforded by the following passage of the *Mahābhārata*:[60] *Guror =apy=avaliptasya kāry=ākāryam=ajānataḥ| Utpatha-pratipannasya nyāyaṁ bhavati śāsanaṁ||*. A controversy has cropped up on the meaning of this passage. E.W. Hopkins[61] interprets it to mean that the advice of a sinful priest is commendable. But more convincing is the explanation of N.N. Law[62] that 'even a preceptor, if he be vain, ignorant of what should be done and what left undone, and vicious in his ways, should be chastised'. We may accordingly suggest that the priests, if proved to be guilty or unworthy of their position, were subjected to punishment by the king. The relations between the king and his priest were normally cordial, but that at times they were involved in animosity is illustrated by the disputes between Janamejaya and the Kāśyapas, and between Kutsa Aurava and his priest Upagu Sauśravasa.

In the epics there are a few passages which suggest that the priestly profession did not always occupy a prestigious position. Thus in the *Ādiparvan*[63] we find that Śarmiṣṭhā compares the position of Śukra, the royal chaplain, with that of a flatterer, extolling his master (*Āsīnañ=ca śayānañ=ca pitā te pitaraṁ mama/ Stauti band=īva c=ābhīkṣaṇaṁ nīcaiḥ sthitvā vinītavat//*). Again, there is a statement in the *Anuśāsanaparvan*[64] to the effect that one has to accept the post of the priest in consequence of the sin committed in the previous life (*Etena karma-doṣeṇa purodhās=tvam=ajāyathāḥ//*). A similar tradition is recorded in the *Adhyātma Rāmāyaṇa*[65] where Vasiṣṭha[66] says to Rāma, 'Sir, I know that priesthood is a despised profession. Still I have accepted it for the reason that I shall be your preceptor' (*Paurohityam=ahaṁ jāne vigarhyaṁ dūṣya-jīvanaṁ*).

E.W. Hopkins[67] observes that the royal chaplain was an ordinary figure in the early heroic age but he gained an extraordinary position in the latest period of the epics when he ruled his master. It is difficult to agree with the above two contentions of Hopkins. The *Purohita* had already emerged as a powerful figure in the kingdom by the early Vedic period. The early part of the *Rāmāyaṇa*, likewise, alludes to the pivotal role that Vasiṣṭha played in the administration of the Ikṣvāku kingdom. Secondly, Hopkins appears to have magnified the importance of the priest. There are, no doubt, some passages[68] in the didactic portions of the *Mahābhārata* which refer to the superiority of priests to royal personages but they are of doubtful value. The priest depended for his livelihood on the patronage of the king, who possessed vast economic resources; he failed to promote himself to the rank of the head of the priestly class by organising it into a well-knit body, and proved incapable of posing a serious threat to the king, who could call upon his militiamen for help in times of emergency, and, furthermore, no *Purohita* would have dared to risk the displeasure of his royal employer, who alone would decide his appointment and the length of his service. Placed in such adverse circumstances, he was hardly empowered to rule the master he liked. It is a truism that some of the royal chaplains triumphed over all obstacles and claimed control of the sceptre but such cases, it must be admitted, were rather the exceptions to the rule. The keynote of all the activities and policies of the royal *Purohita*, who could not afford to be indifferent to the consequences of the displeasure and favour of his master, was to keep the latter well-disposed towards him at any price.

VII
The Priest in Early and Later Dharmaśāstra Texts

The *Manusaṁhitā*[69] says, 'Let him (the king) appoint a domestic priest (*Purohita*) and choose an officiating priest (*Ṛtvig*); they shall perform his domestic rites and the (sacrifices) for which three fires are required.' We thus see that the *Purohita*, according to Manu, was concerned with the performance of the domestic and other sacrifices of the king. But this is not all. Manu[70] insists that the monarch must act in all matters, not excluding his foreign policy, in line with the instructions of the *Purohita* (*Sarveṣāṁ tu viśiṣṭena brāhmaṇena vipakṣitā/ Mantrayet =paramaṁ mantraṁ rājā ṣāḍguṇya-saṁyutam// Nityaṁ tasmin sam=āśvastaḥ sarva-kāryāṇi niḥkṣipet/ Tena sārdhaṁ viniścitya tataḥ karma sam=ārabhet//*).

In this connection, we may note the account of the qualifications and functions of the *Purohita* in the later *Dharmaśāstras* and see how far they differ from one another. A later writer like Yājñavalkya[71] lays down that the *Purohita*, besides being born of a high family, was to be well-versed in astrology, portents, propitiatory rites, different branches of learning, good acts, as prescribed in the *Śāstras*, the science of politics and economics (*Purohitañ=ca kurvīta daivajñam=udit=oditaṁ/ Daṇḍanītyāñ=ca kuśalam=Atharv=āṅgirase tathā//*). The above qualities, as enumerated by Yājñavalkya, leave no room for doubt that the *Purohita* was more than a mere religious teacher. Verse 312 of the *Rājadharmaprakaraṇaṁ* may be quoted in this context—*Sa mantriṇaḥ prakurvīta prajñān maulān sthirān śucīn/ Taiḥ sārddhaṁ cintayed=rājyaṁ vipreṇ=ātha tataḥ svayaṁ//*. The passage proves that the royal priest, though he was not included in the council of ministers, was to be consulted by the king, after his deliberation with ministers, in all secular and religious affairs.

Another later text, i.e., the *Viṣṇusaṁhitā*[72] states that only such a person as is thoroughly conversant with the *Vedas*, *Itihāsa* and *Dharmaśāstras*, is free from any physical disability and is a mendicant and high-born should be made the *Purohita* (*Ved=etihāsa-dharmaśāstr=ārthakuśalaṁ kulīnam=avyaṅgaṁ/ Tapasvinaṁ purohitañ=ca varayet//*). But unlike Yājñavalkya, Viṣṇu does not assign any worthwhile functions to the *Purohita*, and advises the king to rely more on the *Sāṁvatsara* than on the priest. The king is enjoined to be guided by the *Sāṁvatsara*,[73] or, astrologer, in all matters (*Rājā ca sarva-kāryeṣu sāṁvatsar=ādhīnaḥ syāt*). It is clear then that Yājñavalkya and Viṣṇu hold different views in regard to the constitutional position of the royal chaplain.

Kātyāyana[74] appears to be in favour of associating the *Purohita* with the administration of justice, as he enjoins the king to enter the court of justice in the company of learned Brāhmaṇas, ministers, the chief justice, the *Purohita* and other persons.

VIII

The Priest in the Gupta and Post-Gupta Period

The Gupta inscriptions do not take any notice of the *Purohita* but mention a class of officers called *Vinayasthitisthāpakas* who might have taken over some of the priestly functions. But they cannot be regarded, by any stretch of imagination, as identical with the royal chaplain. The absence of any reference to them in the Gupta inscriptions does not necessarily prove the abeyance of the post. If any credence is to be placed in the evidence of the *Kāmandakīya Nītisāra* and the *Mālavikāgnimitram* by Kālidāsa, it may be justifiably concluded that the post of the royal *Purohita* existed in the Gupta kingdom.

Kāmandaka[75] says that the *Purohita*[76] should be thoroughly conversant with the three *Vedas*, the science of politics and the Atharvan lore (*Trayyāṁ ca daṇḍanītyāṁ ca kuśalaḥ syāt Purohitaḥ*). He is required to perform the daily propitiatory ceremonies for the welfare of the state[77] (*artha-vihitaṁ nityaṁ kuryāc=chāntika-pauṣṭikaṁ*). Ramachandra Dikshitar[78] would have us believe that the Gupta *Purohita* was even empowered to influence the decision of the council of ministers. 'Whenever a decision was taken,' says he, 'it was the *Purohita* who was to certify whether such a decision fell within the bounds of the Śāstra injunctions. He would set his seal of approval before it was actually adopted by the council. He was apparently the *Buddhi-saciva*.' There is no evidence, either in inscriptions or in the *Nītisāra*, which is in agreement with this contention. Similarly untenable is his suggestion that the '*Rājaguru*, of whom so much is said in the opening pages of the *Nītisāra*, was the *Rājapurohita* also'. It seems more reasonable to suggest that the Kāmandakīya *Rājaguru*, who was to instruct the king in humility and self-control, corresponds to the Kauṭilīya *Ācārya*. Inscriptional records show that in later days the two functions were sometimes united in one person, the royal chaplain.

The office of the royal priest finds mention in the *Mālavikāgnimitram*, wherein there is an indication that the *Purohita* received a monthly salary (*dakṣiṇāṁ māsikīṁ purohitasya*). Thus, the system of making monthly payment to the *Purohita*, which was so popular in the Kauṭiliyan state, continued even in the days of Kālidāsa. In the *Abhijñānaśakuntalam*,[79] mention is made of an officer entitled *Dharmādhikārī*. The king Duṣyanta therein represents himself to Śakuntalā and her associates as an officer 'who was employed by the king, the descendant of Puru, in the *dharmādhikāra* and visited the sacred grove in order to ascertain if the religious rites of the sages were being performed without obstacles' (*Yaḥ Pauraveṇa rājñā dharmādhikāre niyuktaḥ so=ham=a-vighnakriy=opalambhāya dharm=āraṇyam=idam=āyātaḥ*). This would bear witness to the existence of the department of religious affairs over which the royal chaplain did seldom exercise any authority. But there also might have been kingdoms where this department was placed in charge of the royal priest and not under a different functionary styled *Dharmādhikārī*.[80]

In the *Daśakumāra-carita*,[81] composed by Daṇḍin, mention is made of a *Purohita* who was employed by a king to instruct his son in statecraft.[82] The same text[83] also gives us a pitiable picture of some priests, connected with the royal palace, in these words: 'During the eight and half hours, those led by the priests would approach the king and say, "The dream you dreamt just now is inauspicious. Planets are in unfortunate positions. Omens are foreboding evil. Let expiatory rites be done. Sacrificial utensils must all be made of gold. Then alone the rite will be efficacious. These Brāhmaṇas are equal to Brahmā and the auspicious rites conducted by them would become doubly auspicious. Suffering from intolerable poverty and burdened with too many children, these conductors of sacrifices are yet characterised with such firmness that till now they have never received donations. Gifts given to them promote our life, confer heavenly happiness on us, and destroy all that is inauspicious." Thus they make the king give gifts to Brāhmaṇas and through those Brāhmaṇas they swallow their share secretly.'

IX

The Priest in the Later North Indian Kingdoms

The testimony of inscriptions and literary texts implies that the *Purohita* occupied an important place in the court of the Pratīhāra kings. The Pratīhāra kingdom, as a revivalist state, witnessed the revival of so many ancient ceremonies, sacrifices and *dānas* and the *Purohita* was required to preside over such religious functions. The inscriptions of the Pratīhāra kings frequently mention the *Purohita*, *Mahāpurohita* and other allied officials like the *Daivajña*, *Daivāgārika* and *Śaṅkhadhārī*. The Partapgarh inscription,[84] which was composed by the *Purohita* Trivikramanātha, of the Pratīhāra king Mahendrapāla II, shows that he was sometimes entrusted with the 'work of composing the text of the royal charters'. The selection of the royal priest for this work does not sound strange as he was usually a scholar, while the charters were mainly religious in character.

For a detailed knowledge of the Pratīhāra *Purohita*, we turn to the testimony of the contemporary writer Somadeva Sūri, for the details supplied by inscriptions are far from adequate. The *Kathāsaritsāgara*[85] speaks of a royal priest enjoying a thousand villages and the privilege of *chattra* and *vāhana* just like a *Sāmanta* (*sāmanta tulya*). Somadeva Sūri[86] points out that the *Purohita* should be educated in the *Vedas*, sixfold Aṅga and the science of government; he should claim noble descent and character; he should be obedient and skilful in reading portents and capable of preventing calamities, providential or human. One of the principal duties of the *Purohita*, as Somadeva[87] points out, was the training of princes. This, no doubt, contributed to the augmentation of his power in the royal court. Somadeva's statement that the advice of the priest is inviolable and the chief minister and the *Purohita* are mother and father of the king (*Samau mātṛ-pitṛbhyāṁ rājño mantri-purohitau| atas=tau vāñjitār-thair=na kathañcid=vistarayet||*) testifies to the great influence that the royal priest was destined to exert in the Pratīhāra court.

The copper plate grants of the Kalacuri-Cedi kings speak of the *Mahāpurohita* as one of the state functionaries who were kept abreast of the royal order about a land-grant. It seems that the royal priest in the Kalacuri kingdom was not entrusted with the education of princes. The Jabalpur plates[88] of king Jayasiṁha, for example, distinguish the royal priest Rāghava, designated as a *Mahāpurohita*, from the royal preceptor Vimalaśiva (*śrīmad=rājaguru-Vimalaśivaḥ*). The Kumbhi plates[89] of Vijayasiṁha, likewise, refer to Vidyādeva and Yajñadhara as being the *Rājaguru* and the *Mahāpurohita*, respectively. That the royal priest was sometimes called upon to look after the department of religion is vouchsafed by the Jabalpur plates, for Rāghava is called both *Mahāpurohita* and *Dharmapradhāna*. But since in most of the Cedi records[90] the posts of the *Dharmapradhāna* and *Mahāpurohita* are said to be held by different persons, it seems that, generally speaking, the *Purohita* was not chosen to be the head of the department of religion. The Kharod inscription[91] of Ratnadeva III, dated in the Cedi year 933, refers to one *Śreṣṭhin* Ralhaṇa who was appointed to the exalted post of the *Dharma-karmādhikārī*, i.e., *Dharmapradhāna*. The evidence of the Kharod inscription may be regarded as highly important for providing us with one of the rare instances of a non-Brahmin official being preferred for the chiefship of the department of religion. The Khajuraho record of V.S. 1059 tells us that a royal priest was placed in charge of the judiciary by the Candella king Dhaṅga.[92] Notwithstanding the absence of any corroborative evidence, it is not unlikely that in the Kalacuri kingdom the royal chaplain was a member of the king's council of ministers.

The *Rājadharmakāṇḍa* of the *Kṛtyakalpataru*[93] by the statesman-poet Lakṣmīdhara enables us to get a glimpse into the office of *Purohita* in the Gāhaḍavāla kingdom. Lakṣmīdhara, who wrote his work at the command of king Govindacandra, lays down that a Brāhmaṇa coming of a good family, observing penance, well-versed in the *Vedas, Itihāsa*, *Dharmaśāstras* and astrology and skilful in performing various sacrifices and religious ceremonies, should be chosen as a priest. A study of the *Kṛtyakalpataru* would make it clear that the Gāhaḍavāla priest worked on the same lines as the Pratīhāra *Purohita*, their duties including, among other things, education of princes. That the *Purohita* discharged the duties of the royal preceptor under the

Gāhaḍavālas is further corroborated by a Gāhaḍavāla record[94] which speaks of Prahlādaśarman as being the *Mahāpurohita* and *Mahārājaguru* of king Jayacandra.

The *Purohita* finds prominent mention in the inscriptions of the Kāmboja, Varman and Sena kings of Bengal but the Pāla records hardly take any notice of him. This office could not have been popular in the Buddhist Pāla kingdom but existed in the Kāmboja, Varman and Sena kingdoms, the rulers of which were all followers of orthodox Hinduism. It is noteworthy that in the inscriptions of the Candra, Varman and the later Sena kings, we often come across the term *Mahāpurohita*. 'The prefix 'Mahā' probably indicates the great importance attached to religious and social aspects of administration during the rule of the orthodox Hindu kings.'[95] But generally speaking, during those early mediaeval days, the *Purohita* 'became associated more with the rituals of the royal household than with the details of administration; he, therefore, gradually lost his seat in the ministry, though he was honoured even more highly than a minister'.[96]

The contemporary inscriptions also speak of the following religious functionaries:

1. The *Śāntivārika*. He was the priest in charge of propitiatory rites.

2. The *Śāntyāgārika* (also called *Śāntyāgārādhikṛta*). He was the priest in charge of the room where propitiatory rites were performed.

X

The Priest in the Śukranīti

In the *Śukranīti*, the priest, or *Purodhā*, as he is called, is included in the council of ministers[97] (*Purodhā ca Pratinidhiḥ Pradhāna-Sacivas=tathā/ Mantrī ca Prāḍvivākaś=ca Paṇḍitaś=ca Sumantrakaḥ/ Amātyo Dūta ity=etā rājñaḥ prakṛtayo daśa//*). But of all the ministers, the priest is the foremost and the mainstay of the king and the kingdom[98] (*Purodhāḥ prathamaṁ śreṣṭhaḥ sarvebhyo rāja-rāṣṭrabhṛt*). He is entitled to the highest emoluments, getting one-tenth greater than the *Pratinidhi*.[99] The *Purohita* is, however, not allowed to discharge the functions of the king during the latter's illness or absence from the capital. That function devolves upon the *Pratinidhi*. In referring to his qualifications, Śukra[100] says, 'One who is versed in *mantras* and rituals, master of the three sciences, skilful at work, conqueror of the senses, subduer of anger, devoid of greed and passions, equipped with the knowledge of six *Aṅgas* (*Vedāṅgas*) and of the science of archery with all its branches, one who knows the science of moral as well as religious interests, one fearing whose anger even the king takes to virtuous ways of life, one who is well up in *Nīti Śāstra* and master of military implements and tactics is the priest.' We thus see that apart from the ethical and physical training, the priestly curriculum, according to Śukra, includes the study of economics, theology, sociology and military science.

Śukra does not specifically mention the functions of the *Purohita* and it seems that his functions and responsibilities do not extend beyond the fringe of sacrificial ceremonies.[101] He is not authorised to advise the king in matters relating to religion and morality which become the prerogative of the *Paṇḍita*. It is the *Paṇḍita* who 'has to study the rules of moral life obtaining in society in ancient and modern times, which have been maintained in the codes, which are now opposed, and which militate against the customs of the folk, and to advise the king by those which are efficacious both for his life and hereafter'.[102] Yet it is interesting to note that Śukra invests the royal chaplain with the power to remove a tyrant. 'If the king is an enemy of virtue, morality and strength,' says he, 'people should desert him as the ruiner of the state. In his place for the maintenance of the state, the priest with the consent of the *Prakṛti*, i.e., ministers, should install one who belongs to his family and is qualified.'[103] Śukra enjoins the king to take at the time of coronation the following oath at the hands of the consecrating priest: 'From the night of my birth to that of my death, for the space between these two, my sacrifice and my gifts, my place and good deeds, my life, and my offspring mayest thou take if I play thee false.' Since this coronation oath was administered by the priest, it has been suggested that the priest was authorised to remove an unrighteous monarch from the throne. But the competence of the priest to punish the king with the removal of his position has been questioned on valid grounds. Indeed, it is difficult to ascertain how far the picture of the *Purohita*, as portrayed by Śukra, is realistic.

XI

The Priest in the South Indian Kingdoms

V.R. Ramachandra Dikshitar[104] observes that the institution of the *Purohita* was not alien to Dravidian polity. The commentator of the *Śilappadhikāram*, a classic of the period of the Tamil Śaṅgam, includes the *Purohita* in the list of ministers, the other members being the commander-in-chief, the ambassador and the Director of Public Information. Similar references to the *Purohita* occur in other ancient Tamil treatises.

As we come to the time of the Pallava kings, we meet with one Brahma Śrīrāja, who combined in himself the offices of chief minister and royal priest. He is described in one of the Pallava grants[105] as both the *Potra* and the *Mukhyamantri* of king Nandivarman II.

We hardly get any account about the *Purohita* in the Rāṣṭrakūṭa inscriptions. But it is not improbable that in the Rāṣṭrakūṭa kingdom 'he may have been an officer of the royal household rather than a member of the ministry'.[106] It is worth noting that the Mangallu plates[107] of the Eastern Cālukya king Amma II Vijayāditya VI (A.D. 945-A.D. 970) include the *Purohita* in the list of the eighteen *tīrthas*.

The inscriptions of the Cālukya kings of Kalyāṇī mention a number of *Rājagurus* who were mostly Śaiva in their religious persuasion. But we are at present unable to decide whether they were appointed to the office of the *Purohita* or were merely the preceptors of kings. Someśvara[108] has referred to the office of the royal priest in his work entitled *Mānasollāsa* and pointed out that such persons as were well-grounded in the threefold *Veda*, politics, expiatory rites and Atharvavedic lore should be selected for the post (*Trayyāṁ ca daṇḍanītyāṁ ca śānti-karmaṇi pauṣṭike| Ātharvaṇe ca kuśalaḥ sa syād rāja-purohitaḥ*). The priest is regarded as the principal guardian of the kingdom, being superior to the *Pratinidhi* and the *Pradhāna*[109] (*Purodhāḥ prathamaḥ śreṣṭhaḥ sarvebhyo rāja-rāṣṭrabhṛt| Tad=anu syāt=pratinidhiḥ pradhānas=tad=anantaram||*).

XII

Some Observations on the Institution of Priesthood

Every living institution, worth the name, must undergo a process of evolution; it must pass through the stages of rise and decadence. There seems to be little room for doubt that from the 'comparatively modest position of a private chaplain who had to attend to the sacrificial obligations to his master, he appears to have gradually raised himself to the dignity of so to say a minister of public worship and confidential adviser of the king'.[110] The influence of the royal chaplain was again on the wane in the Gupta and post-Gupta periods when he was mostly a mere ministrant to the personal spiritual needs of his master. But V.R. Ramachandra Dikshitar[111] maintains that 'from the earliest known literature, the *Ṛg Veda Saṁhitā*, down to the later treatises on the *Arthaśāstra*, the *purohita* maintained one and the same position in the state, at least in every Kṣatriya-ruled state'. Indian literature, which is generally the product of the priestly class and sacerdotal in character, does not help us at all in tracing the evolution of the institution of the *Purohita* as its account is more exaggerated than real. It is not unoften that the later writers have copied their predecessors of earlier epochs. When we speak of the priest of Ṛgvedic times, we always think of him as he is painted in the *Ṛgveda* and not of an actual figure in a real Ṛgvedic state. Kauṭilya attaches a high degree of importance to the office of the priest but it is difficult to believe that the Maurya kings like Aśoka and his successors, who were Buddhists, and Candragupta, especially in his later days after his conversion to Jainism, would have held this sacerdotal order in the same esteem as the writer of the *Arthaśāstra*. The discovery of archaeological material can only dispel the pall of dense darkness that enshrouds the problem.

References and Notes

1. The term *purohita* literally means 'placed in front', 'appointed' (*puro dhīyate=sau*).
2. *Altindisches Leben*, pp. 195ff.
3. *Encyclopaedia of Religion and Ethics*, X (New York, 1955), p. 280.
4. *Ṛgveda*, VII.18. Vasiṣṭha claims that his prayer alone brought about the victory for Sudās (*Ṛgveda*, VII.83). *Aitareya Brāhmaṇa* (VII.34),

likewise, states that it was a peculiar mode of the *Soma* sacrifice by Vasiṣṭha that contributed to the success of the Bharata king.

5. IV.50.8.
6. I.1.
7. *CHA*, I, p. 85.
8. Ibid.
9. I.8.9.
10. II.6.5; IV.3.
11. I.7.3.
12. V.3.1.
13. I.7.3.
14. *IAB*, p. 25.
15. VIII.40.2,
16. II.7.1.2.
17. *Aitareya Brāhmaṇa*, VIII.24.25.
18. II.1.2.
19. *VI*, I, pp. 112-113.
20. Ibid., p. 113.
21. Ibid., p. 114.
22. II.4.4.5.
23. XVI.29.5.
24. *IAB*, p. 27.
25. K.P. Jayaswal, *Hindu Polity*, II, p. 31.
26. XIV.6.8. H.C. Raychaudhuri (*PHAI*, p. 359) observes that the life of a Brāhmaṇa was not so sacrosanct in ancient as in medieval and modern India. The evidence of literature would, however, lead to a contrary proposition.
27. XI.12-13.
28. XI.17-18.
29. *SLAI*, II, p. 233.
30. I.10.7.
31. II.5.11.14.
32. II.5.10.20. According to Haradatta, the intercession is to take place as follows: that mutilation is commuted to a fine, a fine to a flogging, a flogging to a reprimand.
33. III.12.
34. XIX.2-6.
35. XIX.40-42; *SLA*, II, p. 96.
36. I.437; II.47; III.392, 455; IV.200.
37. II.47.
38. *SONEI*, p. 169.
39. Ibid., p. 175.
40. I.439.
41. *SONEI*, pp. 173-74.
42. II.243; IV.245-46.
43. II.46, 243; VI.475.
44. *Pre-Buddhist India*, p. 134.

45. Ibid., p. 144.
46. R.N. Mehta (*Pre-Buddhist India*, p. 131) identifies the *Attha-dhammānusāsaka* with the *Purohita* for the reasons that, first, a *Jātaka* begins with the statement—*Sucīrato nāma Brāhmaṇo Purohito Attha-dhamm=ānu-sāsako ahosi* and secondly, one of the *Jātakas* (III.400) contains the passage—*Purohitakula nibbattitvā . . . purohita-ṭṭhānaṁ labhitvā rañño attha-dhamm=ānu-sāsako ahosi.*
47. I.9.10.
48. I.17.24-27.
49. V.R. Ramachandra Dikshitar is of opinion that the Kauṭilīya phrase *mantri purohita-sakhaḥ* suggests that the *Purohita* was one among the council of advisers to the king.
50. A heated controversy centres round the salaries prescribed for the different categories of officers in the *Arthaśāstra* (V.3). K.P. Jayaswal (*HP*, II, p. 136) holds the view that the salaries were annual and the *paṇas* were made of silver. K.V.R. Aiyangar (*Ancient Indian Polity*, pp. 44-45) opines that the salaries, which were paid in gold *paṇas*, were monthly. Dikshitar (*MP*, p. 151) points out that the salaries were monthly. But in his *Hindu Administrative Institutions* (p. 125), he refers to the salary, as fixed by Kauṭilya, as being the one per annum. P.V. Kane (*HD*, III, p. 123) has adduced good grounds for believing that the salaries, as envisaged in the *Arthaśāstra*, were in copper *paṇas* and were monthly. Indeed, a monthly salary is more practical than a yearly one. Śaṅkhalikhita (*Rājanītiprakāśa*, p. 252) who flourished at a much later date, advocates the monthly salary of two *suvarṇas* for each soldier.
51. II.1.46.
52. I.9.10.
53. I.12.6.
54. I.9.11; *KA*, II, p. 20.
55. II.67.
56. 69.64.
57. IV.47.25.
58. *Ādiparvan*, 170.75.
59. *Sabhāparvan*, 5.41.
60. I.140.54.
61. *JAOS*, XIII, p. 153.
62. *AAIP*, p. 28.
63. 78.9.
64. 10.56.
65. *Ayodhyākāṇḍa*, 2.28.
66. The Ikṣvāku kings invariably speak of Vasiṣṭha as their priest. Orthodox tradition asserts that the same Vasiṣṭha, who lived for thousands of years on account of his great penance, served all these monarchs. This would only indicate that 'there must have been a number of hereditary *Purohitas* each called after the far-famed ancestor Vasiṣṭha, taking a legitimate pride in their birth in such a

distinguished line'. The custom to adopt the surnames or hereditary titles of famous forefathers is still in vogue in India.

67. *The Social And Military Position Of The Ruling Caste In Ancient India* (Varanasi, 1972), p. 106.
68. To quote one such passage, 'Thou shouldst worship those Brāhmaṇas that are devoted to their duties, possessed of learning, regular in worshipping the gods, observant of high virtues, and employ them in officiating in thy sacrifices. With thy priest, accompanying thee, thou shouldst rise up when they approach and touch and worship their feet, and do every other act that is necessary' (P.C. Roy, *The Mahabharata*, VII.LXXI, pp. 167-68).
69. VII.78.
70. VII.58-59.
71. I.313.
72. III.41.
73. The importance of the *Sāṁvatsara* is also alluded to in the *Bṛhatsaṁhitā* (II.9) which states that a king, without a *Sāṁvatsara*, errs like a blind man.
74. *HD*, III, p. 123.
75. IV.31.
76. In commenting on verses 30 and 31 of Chapter IV of the *Kāmandakīya Nītisāra* Śaṅkarārya characterises the *Purohita* as a special minister (*viśeṣa-amātya*) who is appointed to look after matters, visible and unseen (*Pur=odhīyate niyujyate dṛṣṭ=ādṛṣṭeṣu iti purohitaḥ*).
77. IV.31.
78. *GP*, p. 148.
79. II.64.
80. The *Matsya Purāṇa* (I.27.10) does not include the *Purohita* in its list of royal officials but it elsewhere refers to Śarmiṣṭhā, the daughter of the Asura king Bṛṣaparva, as reproving Devayānī, the daughter of the royal chaplain Śukra by the following words, 'Your father, seated below, flatters my father in humility time and again even when he lies prostrate or is seated. Whereas you are the daughter of a beggar, panegyrist and recipient, I am the daughter of a donor and not of an acceptor, a person who is himself flattered (*Āsīnañ=ca śayānañ=ca pitā te pitaraṁ mama| Stauti pṛcchati c=ābhikṣaṇaṁ nīcastathaḥ suvinītavat|| Yācatas=tvaṁ=ca duhitā stavataḥ pratigṛhṇataḥ| Sutā=haṁ stūyamānasya dadato na tu gṛhṇataḥ||*).
81. The date of Daṇḍin has long been a matter of keen controversy. Some have placed him in the sixth century A.D., others in the ninth, and some others in the eleventh century A.D. V.V. Mirashi (*Nagpur University Journal*, XI (December, 1945), p. 21) opines that Daṇḍin must have flourished not long after A.D. 550 as his 'narrative faithfully reflects the actual political situation in the Deccan in the beginning of the sixth century A.D.'
82. *Ucchvāsa* VIII.

83. V. Satakopan, *Daśakumāra-carita* (1963), pp. 141-42.
84. *EI*, XIV, pp. 182-88.
85. III.8.124-26.
86. *PHNI*, p. 351.
87. *Nītivākyāmṛta*, pp. 160-61.
88. *CII*, IV, pp. 324ff.
89. Ibid., pp. 645ff.
90. The Kumbhi plates (*CII*, IV, p. 652) of Vijayasiṁha mention Yajñadhara as the *Mahāpurohita* and Kīkī as the *Dharmapradhāna*.
91. *EI*, XXI, pp. 159ff.
92. Ibid., I, pp. 140ff.
93. P. 164.
94. *EI*, IV, p. 121.
95. R.C. Majumdar, *History of Ancient Bengal* (Calcutta, 1971), p. 327.
96. *PIA*, p. 93.
97. II.69-70.
98. II.74.
99. II.71.
100. B.K. Sarkar, *The Śukranīti* (1914), p. 69.
101. In the *Śukranīti*, we have the statement that the priest is also the *Ācārya* and he is competent both to curse and to bless (B.K. Sarkar, *op. cit*., p. 69). This would imply that the *Purohita* was entrusted with the education of princes.
102. B.K. Sarkar, *op. cit*., p. 73.
103. Ibid., p. 89.
104. *Hindu Administrative Institutions*, p. 123.
105. *ASLUP*, p. 54.
106. *RT*, p. 169.
107. *EHD*, II, p. 673.
108. *Mānasollāsa*, II.2.60.
109. Ibid., 64.
110. Eggeling as quoted by Ramachandra Dikshitar in *Hindu Administrative Institutions*, p. 119.
111. *Hindu Administrative Institutions*, p. 121.

5

The Minister

I

The Importance of Ministers

As in modern times, in early days also, ministers constituted an important wheel of the administrative machinery of the state; they played a decisive role in the formulation as well as in the implementation of the policy of the government and not unoften enjoyed a position of extraordinary importance and influence. The works and responsibilities of the state being manifold and diverse, it was wellnigh impossible for the king to perform them single-handed; he required the services of ministers and other functionaries for their successful accomplishment.

The importance of ministers for the proper upkeep of the state was never lost sight of in ancient India. In emphasising the importance of ministers, Kauṭilya[1] observes, 'Sovereignty is possible only with assistance. A single wheel can never move. Hence he shall employ ministers and hear their opinion' (*Sahāya-sādhyam rājatvaṁ cakram=ekaṁ na vartate/ kurvīta sacivāṁs=tasmāt teṣāṁ ca śruṇuyān=matam*). There arise occasions with respect to affairs of state, when a king has to perceive the unknown, to corroborate the known, to clear dubious issues, to guess the whole from the knowledge of a part (*Pratyakṣa-parokṣ=ānumeyā hi rāja vṛttiḥ*) but all these are only possible with external assistance from able and accomplished advisers and assistants (*ity=Amātya-karma*). Kauṭilya[2] elsewhere compares the king without his ministers with a bird deprived of its feathers (*chinna-pakṣasya=eva rājñaś=ceṣṭā-nāśaś=ca*), for, as he further emphasises, a minister is the mainstay of the security of the king's life. The

Śāntiparvan,[3] likewise, points out that it is physically impracticable for a king to perform all the affairs of state single-handed; he cannot run the administrative machinery for three days even without the assistance of ministers. The *Ādiparvan*[4] lays down that the king is entirely dependent upon ministers as animals upon clouds, the Brāhmaṇas upon the *Vedas* and women upon their husbands. Manu[5] echoes a similar sentiment when he says, 'Even a single piece of work appears difficult if one is to do it unaided; why is then the attempt to rule over a prosperous kingdom without the assistance of ministers?' Bhāravi,[6] who flourished in the sixth century A.D., observes, "That servant is a bad counsellor who does not give salutary advice to his sovereign, and that sovereign is a bad master who does not pay heed to the advice of a well-wisher. For, all kinds of prosperity delight to live there where the king and his ministers act in concert' (*Sa kiṁsakhā sādhu na śāsti y=o'dhipaṁ| hitān=na yaḥ saṁ-śṛṇute sa kiṁprabhuḥ|| Sad=ānukūleṣu hi kurvate ratiṁ| nṛpeṣv=amātyeṣu ca sarva-sampadaḥ||*). Kāmandaka,[7] likewise, has recognised the importance of ministers. He describes them as the hands or eyes of the king and compares the king, without his ministers, to a wingless bird. 'A king,' says Somadeva[8] in highlighting the importance of ministers, 'who is assisted by his ministers, *Purohita* and *Senāpati*, is generally victorious and successful' (*Mantri-Purohita-Senāpatināṁ ye yuktaṁ muktaṁ karoti sa ahāryabuddhiḥ*). All these references in early Indian texts of different ages and regions would indubitably point to the great importance that was attached to ministerial posts in ancient India.

II

The Interpretation of Mantrī, Amātya and Saciva

The terms that were generally employed in Indian literature in the sense of a minister are *mantrī*, *amātyah* and *sacivaḥ*. Etymologically speaking, the word *mantrin* means one who is concerned with *mantra*, secret counsel. The term *amātyaḥ*, which is based on *amā*, meaning near, close to, etc., denotes a companion or follower of the king. *Sacivaḥ*, likewise, means a friend, companion, etc. The commentator Kullūka has taken the term in the sense of a helper, *sahāya* (*Nityam=eva rājñaḥ pārśva-vartino bhaveyuḥ)*.[9] Notwithstanding this marked difference in meaning, these three terms are often used in Indian literature as synonyms. Thus, the *Rāmāyaṇa*, for instance, refers to Sumantra as an *Amātya* in one place[10] and a *Mantrin* in another,[11] implying thereby the interchangeability of the two words. The *Āraṇyakaparvan*,[12] likewise, applies the designations *Saciva* and *Mantrin* to the same ministers of an Orissan king and the titles *Amātya* and *Mantrin* to one and the same minister of a ruler,[13] indicating the synonymity of the terms *amātya*, *saciva* and *mantrin*. The testimony of the epics in regard to the identification of the three terms receives confirmation from the Kautala inscription of Arjunadeva wherein one Sāmantasiṁha is described as a *Saciva* in verse nine and called a *Mantrin* in the verse, following, as well as from a Kākatīya epigraph[14] which applies the designations *amātya*, *saciva* and *mantrī* to Vaija, the minister of king Beṭa, at different places. Manu[15] seems to have used the words *saciva* and *mantrī* as synonyms.

It cannot escape notice that these terms are sometimes treated as quite distinct from each other. In the *Rāmāyaṇa* a distinction is made between a *Mantrin* and a *Saciva*. As is evident from the facts noted below, the *Arthaśāstra*, too, distinguishes the *Mantrin* from the *Amātya*:

1. The *Arthaśāstra*[16] states, 'Having divided the spheres of their powers and having taken into consideration the time, place and the work to be accomplished, such persons shall be employed as *Amātyas* but not as *Mantrins*' (*Vibhajya=Amātya-vibhavaṁ deśa-kālau ca karma ca/ amātyāḥ sarva ev=aite kāryāḥ syur=na tu mantriṇaḥ//*). The distinction between *Mantrins* and *Amātyas* is amply brought to light by this statement of Kauṭilya.

2. A *Mantrin*, according to Kauṭilya, had a salary of 48,000 *paṇas* per annum, while an *Amātya* was entitled to an emolument of 12,000 *paṇas*.

3. The *Arthaśāstra* lays down that a king should appoint three or four *Mantrins* but as many *Amātyas* as he deemed necessary.

4. Kauṭilya says that those who were found honest after one of the four tests of *dharma*, *artha*, *kāma* and *bhaya*, were employed as *Amātyas*, whereas *Mantrins* were appointed after they had proved their integrity and loyalty by successfully

undergoing the fourfold test (*sarv=opadhā-śuddhān mantriṇaḥ kuryāt*).

5. Kauṭilya observes that *Mantrins* and the *Mantri-pariṣad* were summoned for consultation on grave occasions (*ātyayika-kārya*). The passage *Mantri-pariṣadaṁ dvādaś=āmātyān kurvīta* would imply that the council of ministers used to be recruited from *Amātyas*. The separate mention of *Mantrins* and *Amātyas* (though the reference to the latter is an indirect one) in one and the same passage is a clear indication of distinction in the denotation of the two terms.

The distinction between the terms *mantrin* and *amātya* is also maintained by Kāmandaka who, however, seems to have used the words *saciva* and *amātya* as synonyms. This is evident first from his comparison of *Mantrins* and *Amātyas* with the eyes and arms of the king, respectively, as well as from his statement that the king should think of the welfare of his kingdom along with his *Mantrins* and *Amātyas*. A Saindhava grant[17] of the time of Agguka II of the Gupta year 513 from Ghumli in Kathiawar includes the *Mantrin* and *Amātya* in its list of royal officers, indicating their separate identity. The terms *amātya*, *saciva* and *mantrin* are employed in the *Agni Purāṇa* in diverse senses. The *Agni Purāṇa*[18] observes that the king gives audience to *Amātyas* and *Mantrins* in the royal court. The separate use of the two terms clearly emphasises the difference between the two groups of functionaries. Again, we are told that after the coronation ceremony, the Pratīhāra comes along with *Amātyas* and *Sacivas* to introduce them to the newly consecrated king.[19] The simultaneous use of these words shows their difference which is further brought to light by the separate mention of the limitations and qualifications of *Amātyas* and *Sacivas* which we meet with in the *Agni Purāṇa*. In the *Abhilaṣitārtha-cintāmaṇi*,[20] a work of the twelfth century A.D., *Mantrins*, *Amātyas* and *Sacivas* are represented as distinct functionaries. The *Mantrins*, *Amātyas* and *Sacivas* are asked to take their respective seats in the court and to occupy their respective residences in different quarters of the city. The difference in the denotation of these three terms is further brought to light by another passage of the text which urges the king to patronise the angry and disillusioned *Mantrins*, *Amātyas* and *Sacivas* of the enemy-kingdom.

The reason why there has been so much controversy amongst early Indian writers over the use of these three terms is, however, difficult to explain and whatever suggestion may be offered in this regard will always be regarded as tentative. Ministerial functions in ancient India seem to have comprised the formulation and implementation of governmental policies and programmes. Whereas in some kingdoms there were two separate bodies for these two different kinds of works, in other kingdoms one and the same body was concerned with both. The ministers entrusted with the implementation of state policies were generally known as *Amātyas* or *Sacivas*, while those, in charge of counsels, were called *Mantrins*. When the Junagadh rock inscription speaks of *Matisacivas* and *Karmasacivas*, it merely refers to the existence of two separate bodies of ministers in charge of the formulation and execution of governmental policies. The commentator Rāmavarman[21] speaks of *Mantrins* as policy-makers or counsellors and of *Amātyas* as executive officers (*Amātyā deś=ādi kārya-nirvāhakā mantriṇo vyavahāra-draṣṭāra iti bhedaḥ*/). The *Amarakośa* states that the *Amātya* who is a *Dhīsaciva* is called a *Mantrin*, while other *Amātyas* are known as *Karmasacivas* (*Mantrī dhī-sacivo='mātyo='nye karma-sacivās=tataḥ*/). Therefore, when a literary text or an inscription speaks of the identity of *Mantrins*, *Amātyas* and *Sacivas*, it only implies that these ministers had combined in themselves the functions of the formulation and implementation of state policies and programmes. That a *Mantrin* was not always a mere counsellor but was sometimes charged with the function of execution is borne out by the evidence of the *Mahābhārata* and other texts.

III

The Ministers in the Vedic Period

In Vedic literature,[22] barring, of course, the *Aitareya Brāhmaṇa*, we do not come across such terms as *amātya*, *saciva* and *mantrin* but meet with the word *ratnin* which means a jewel. The *Ratnins* were in fact some high functionaries, including the *Mahiṣī*, crowned queen, *Vāvātā*, favourite queen, *Yuvarāja*, heir-apparent, *Purohita*, royal chaplain, *Senānī*, commander-in-chief, *Sūta*, commander of the chariot corps of the royal army,

Grāmaṇī, village-headman, *Saṁgrahītā*, treasurer, *Bhāgadugha*, tax-collector, *Kṣattā*, royal chamberlain, *Akṣavāpa*, the keeper of dice and *Pālagala*, king's bosom companion. Sometimes the *Govikartana*, officer in charge of the royal store of cattle, *Takṣā*, carpenter and *Rathakāra*, chariot-maker are also found included in the list of the *Ratnins*. That they were not inconsequential persons becomes clear from the fact that they are described as bestowers of the kingdom upon the king[23] (*Ete vai rāṣṭrasya pradātāraḥ*) and they, in all probability, discharged the functions of the *Mantrins* and *Amātyas* of later days.

IV

The Ministers in the Post-Vedic Period

The Buddhist texts refer to *Mahāmattas* and *Amaccas* who have usually been identified with chief ministers and ministers, respectively. But since there are references to several *Mahāmattas*, holding responsible positions in the different departments of administration under a king, it seems that the term *mahāmatta*, as used in these texts, denotes a senior minister as opposed to the word *amacca* which, in all probability, means a junior member. Such a contention is further supported by the etymology of the terms, for, the word *mahāmatta* is formed of the components *mahān* and *amatya* or *amātya*. the latter being comparable to *amacca*. The close correspondence between their designations would tend to suggest that *Mahāmattas* and *Amaccas* belonged to two different tiers of the same hierarchy of officers.

The senior ministers, referred to in the Buddhist texts, were of the following types:

1. The *Sabbatthaka Mahāmatta.*[24] He was the minister in charge of the general affairs of the kingdom.

2. The *Vohārika Mahāmatta*. He was the minister of law. The *Mahāvagga*[25] mentions them as being consulted by king Bimbisāra in connection with the award of punishment to those who initiated hired soldiers into religious order. In the *Cullavagga*[6] they are the subject of a discussion between Anāthapiṇḍika and prince Jeta.

3. The *Senānāyaka Mahāmatta*. He was the minister of defence.

The senior ministers enjoyed an enormously high position in administration. The *Pādañjali Jātaka*[27] recognises their right of accession to the throne in the event of absence of a suitable heir of the deceased king, while in another *Jātaka*[28] they are represented as selecting a suitable successor from amongst the relations of a previous ruler. The *Mahāvaṁsa*[29] refers to some Ceylonese ministers who took over administration in their own hands consequent upon the death of king Vijaya but transferred power subsequently to the king's nephew when he returned from India after one year. There are also other references to ministers exercising sovereign power.[30] Two senior ministers of the Magadhan king Ajātaśatru were Sunīdha and Vassakāra, who built, at the command of their king, a fort at Pāṭaligrāma to repel the Vṛjis. Vassakāra was a Brāhmaṇa.

Of the junior ministers, as enumerated in the Buddhist texts, mention may be made of the following:

1. The *Vinicchayāmacca*. This minister, who finds mention in several *Jātakas*, is identified by Fick with the minister of justice. The *Rathalaṭṭhi Jātaka*[31] tells us how a *Vinicchayāmacca* had once induced king Brahmadatta to revise an unjust judgement which was made without proper investigation. Such an incident, however, should not be interpreted to mean that this minister was empowered to pronounce an opinion upon the king's judgement but may be taken to imply that he 'advised the king and in some cases, had some influence upon his judgement'.[32] It is not possible to draw a line between cases which the king alone decided and those which were judged by these ministers. It is conceivable that the legal life of the people generally passed into the hands of these ministers and the king as the highest authority intervened only in those cases where appeals were made to him against the judgement of these officers. The *Kurudhamma Jātaka*[33] records how a prostitute, on receiving 1,000 gold pieces from a youth, promised not to receive the least thing from any person but having waited in vain for three years for his return and being relegated to extreme poverty, she went to the court and was advised by the *Vinicchayāmaccas* to return to her former profession. This story would clearly indicate that the *Vinicchayāmaccas* not only discharged judicial functions but also advised the people on matters of law and morality.

2. The *Rajjugāhaka-amacca* He was connected with land revenue and, if the view of R.S. Sharma[34] be accepted, he might have been primarily an assessor of taxes rather than a collector. Bühler compares him with the Land Revenue Settlement Officer of British India, and suggests that the measurement was made for the purpose of assessing ground rent. Bühler's identification[35] of this officer with the *Rājuka* or *Lajuka*, mentioned in Aśokan edicts, does not receive any countenance. The way this officer worked can best be described in the words of Fick,[36] 'He fastens a rope to a stick, and whilst he gives one end of the rope to the owner of the land, he himself holds the other end (and wants to put the stick on the ground). In this way the stick got into the hole of a crab. He reflects, 'If I push the stick into the hole, the crab will perish; if I place the stick in front, the king will suffer loss; if I place it behind, the farmer will be injured; what is then to be done?' It is evident from the above citation that the *Rajjugāhaka-amacca* himself measured fields whereas some other Pāli texts[37] imply that measurement was actually made by his assistants.

3. The *Attha-dhammānusāsaka-amacca*. The minister, who is repeatedly mentioned in the *Jātakas*, is identified by Fick[38] with the guide of the king in worldly and spiritual matters. It is rather unfortunate that our sources do not provide us with any worthwhile information about his work or position.[39]

The Buddhist texts do not throw any light on the system of remuneration of ministers, although we hear of bad ministers who were either dismissed or degraded and of good ones who were promoted for their services.

V

The Ministers in the Maurya Period

An elaborate account of ministers of ancient India, particularly of the Maurya period, is met with in the *Kauṭilīya Arthaśāstra* which divides them into two principal classes—*Mantrins*, Counsellors and *Amātyas*, executive ministers. The *Mantrins*, who were superior in rank to *Amātyas*,[40] were not large in number inasmuch as Kauṭilya fears that the constitution of a large body of *Mantrins* would lead to the disclosure of state secrets and indecision in the formulation of policies and programmes. He would recommend the appointment of three or four *Mantrins*[41] only (*Mantribhis=tribhiś=caturbhir=vā sa mantrayet*). He is of opinion that in complicated state affairs, consultation with a single *Mantrin* may not lead to any definite conclusion[42] (*Mantrayamāṇo hy=eken=ārtha-kṛcchreṣu niścayaṁ n=ādhi-gacchet/*) as the minister may prove to be an autocrat[43] (*Ekaś=ca mantrī yath=eṣṭam-anavagrahaś=carati*). In the case of the king having two *Mantrins*, they may both join hands with each other to overpower the sovereign or may differ, thus bringing about a deadlock or even ruin to the state[44] (*Dvābhyāṁ mantrayamāṇo dvābhyāṁ saṁhatābhyām=avagṛhyate vigṛhītābhyāṁ vināśyate*). According to the exigencies of time, place and the nature of the work to be done, the king could exercise his option of consulting one or two *Mantrins* or of overlooking them altogether[45] (*Deśa-kāla-kārya-vaśena tv=ekena saha dvābhyām =eko vā yathā-sāmarthaṁ mantrayet*).

What were the functions of a *Mantrin*? In Chapter XV of Book I of the *Arthaśāstra* we have the statement, *Mantra-pūrvāḥ sarv=ārambhāḥ*, which R. Shamasastry[46] translates thus, 'All kinds of administrative measures are preceded by deliberations in a well-formed council.' This translation, unfortunately, is not a happy one, and the real implication of the passage would be that all kinds of administrative measures were preceded by deliberations with *Mantrins*, who alone were connected with counsels, *mantra*. If our interpretation be accepted, *Mantrins* advised the king on all matters, concerning administration, no doubt, at the instance of the king himself. Secondly, *Mantrins* along with the royal chaplain helped the king in examining the character of *Amātyas* who were in charge of different departments of the government[47] (*Mantri-purohitasakhaḥ sāmānyeṣ= adhikaraṇeṣu sthāpayitv=āmātyān=upadhābhiḥ śodhayet*). Another function of these ministers was to accompany the king to the battle-field and give encouragement to the troops.

In referring to the executive ministers, *Amātyas*, Kauṭilya observes that they should be natives of the king's own kingdom (*jānapada*), born of a high family (*abhijātaḥ*), influential[48] (*svavagrahaḥ*), well-versed in all arts (*kṛtaśilpa*), possessed of foresight (*cakṣuṣmān*), wise (*prājño*), possessed of a retentive memory (*dhārayiṣṇur*), quick in action (*dakṣo*), eloquent (*vāgmī*), skilful (*pragalbhaḥ*), intelligent (*pratipattimān*), possessed of enthusiasm, dignity and endurance (*utsāha-prabhāva-yuktaḥ kleśasahaḥ*), pure in character (*śuciḥ*), affable (*maitro*), firm in loyal devotion (*dṛḍhabhaktiḥ*), endowed with excellent conduct, strength, health and bravery (*śīla-bal=ārogya-sattva-saṁyuktaḥ*), free from procrastination and fickleness (*stambha-cāpala-hīnaḥ*), affectionate (*saṁpriyo*), and free from such qualities as excite hatred and enmity (*vairāṇām=akarttā*). Thus high birth and theoretical knowledge were not the sole basis for the appointment of *Amātyas*; their practical efficiency and personal merits were also taken into consideration. The qualifications of *Amātyas* (*amātya-sampat*) are to be ascertained by the king directly from personal experience, indirectly from the report of reliable persons and also inferentially from the course of conduct adopted by them.

Besides being possessed of the qualifications noted above, the *Amātyas* had to undergo successfully any of the four allurements (*upadhā*) of *Dharma*, *Artha*, *Kāma* and *Bhaya*. Of these tried persons, those whose character had been tested under religious allurements were employed in *Dharmasthīya* and *Kaṇṭakaśodhana* courts (*Tatra dharm=opadhā-śuddhān dharmasthīya-kaṇṭakaśodhaneṣu karmasu sthāpayet*); those whose purity had been verified under monetary allurements were employed in the department of revenue (*arth=opadhā-śuddhān Samāhartṛ-Sannidhātṛ-nicayakarmasu*); those who had been tried under love allurements were appointed as superintendents of pleasure grounds (*kām=opadhā-śuddhān bāhy=ābhyantara-vihāra-rakṣāsu*) and those who had been tested by allurements under fear were appointed to immediate services (*bhay=opadhā-śuddhān āsanna-kāryeṣu rājñaḥ*).

The *Amātyas*, to judge from the nature of their work, as enumerated by Kauṭilya, may be classified into the following groups:

1. Those who were the members of the council, *Mantri-pariṣad*.

2. Those who were employed as judges in *Dharmasthīya* and *Kaṇṭakaśodhana* courts and were styled *Dharmasthas* and *Pradeṣṭṛs*.

3. Those who were appointed as superintendents of departments, including the collector-general of revenue (*Samāhartā*), chamberlain (*Sannidhātā*), superintendent of store-house

(*Koṣṭh=āgār=adhyakṣa*), superintendent of commerce (*Paṇy=ādhyakṣa*), superintendent of forest produce (*Kupyādhyakṣa*) and the like.

4. Those who were employed to look after immediate matters (*āsanna-kāryeṣu*), the exact nature of which is not explained by Kauṭilya.

Besides the aforesaid fourfold category of *Amātyas*, there were also others who were in charge of the colonization and improvement of wild tracts of land, recruitment of the army (*daṇḍa-praṇayaṇam*), installation of the heir-apparent (*Kumāra-rakṣaṇam=abhiṣekañ-ca*) and protection of princes[49] (*Kumārā-ṇām=āyattvam=amātyeṣu*).

Kauṭilya also refers to a council of ministers, called *Mantri-pariṣad*. From the different views that he quotes on the composition of the council, we come to learn that the Mānava, Bārhaspatya and Auśanasa schools were in favour of a council of 12[50] (*Mantri-pariṣadaṁ dvādaś=āmātyān kurvīta iti Mānavāḥ*), 16[51] (*Ṣoḍaśa iti Bārhaspatyāḥ*) and 20[52] (*viṁśatim ity=auśana-sāḥ*). Kauṭilya, on the other hand, maintains that the council should consist of as many members as the need of the business of administration demands[53] (*yathā-sāmarthyam=iti Kauṭilyaḥ*). It cannot escape notice that Kauṭilya's *Mantri-pariṣad* was composed of those who were not *Mantrins* but *Amātyas*, and as such a designation like *Amātya-pariṣad* would have been a more suitable description of the council. R.G. Basak[54] observes that the council of *Amātyas* was not a deliberative body but an executive one, forming as it were, an outer council of executive ministers.

In referring to the functions of the *Mantri-pariṣad*, Kauṭilya says, 'In works of emergency (*ātyayike kārye*), he (the king) shall call both his *Mantrins* and the council of ministers (*mantriṇo mantri-pariṣadaṁ ca*) and tell them of the same ((*āhūya bruyāt*). The king shall accept what is settled by the majority (*Tatra yad bhūyiṣṭhā bruyuḥ . . . tat kuryāt*) or do what appears to him to be beneficial to the state' (*kārya-siddhikaraṁ vā*). The second alternative, *kārya-siddhikaraṁ vā*, as stated by Kauṭilya, appears to imply that the king was empowered to accept the opinion of the minority in the interest of the state. It is further clear that the *Pariṣad* was not consulted on all occasions but was summoned when the works of emergency had to be transacted. The other function of the *Pariṣad* was to attend on the king at the time of the reception of envoys.

Kauṭilya says that while holding consultations with the *Mantrins* or members of the *Mantri-pariṣad*, the king should take sufficient precautionary measures against the disclosure of counsels. 'The subject matter of a council,' says Kauṭilya,[55] 'shall be entirely secret, and deliberations in it shall be so carried on that even birds cannot see them; for it is said that the secrecy of counsels was divulged by parrots, minas, dogs and other low creatures of mean birth. Hence without providing himself with sufficient safeguards against disclosure, he shall never enter into deliberations in a council.' This account of Kauṭilya may be an exaggeration but still it demonstrates the extreme need of secrecy in the council.

It cannot escape notice that the *Mantrins* and *Amātyas*, of which Kauṭilya speaks so much, do not figure at all in the edicts of Aśoka or in any Maurya inscription. But the Pāli text *Divyāvadāna*, which is, no doubt, a work of a much later date, refers to the *Amātyas* as being employed by Maurya kings and princes. The *Divyāvadāna*[56] states that it was the ministerial oppression that had goaded the people of Taxila to rise in revolt (*api tu duṣṭ=āmātyā asmākaṁ paribhavaṁ kurvanti*). The same text further states that Taxila again revolted during the reign of Aśoka and the cause was once more the tyranny of ministers[57] (*duṣṭa=rātmano='mātyā āgaty=āsmākam=apamānaṁ kurvanti*). Here we possibly get an allusion to illegal methods adopted by corrupt ministers to amass a fortune, leading to enormous hardships to the people.

The important role played by a *Mantrin* in the Maurya court, as testified by the *Arthaśāstra*, stands corroborated by the *Mudrārākṣasa*[58] of Viśākhadatta, where king Candragupta is depicted as a mere puppet in the hands of minister Cāṇakya. The king does not take any measures without the advice of Cāṇakya; whenever the two meet, Candragupta greets Cāṇakya by touching the latter's feet. The following passage,[59] quoted from the *Mudrārākṣasa*, admirably reflects their position:

Rājā—(āsanād=utthāya) Ārya, Candraguptaḥ praṇamati (iti pādayoḥ patati)

Cāṇakya—(pāṇau gṛhītvā) uttiṣṭh=ottiṣṭha vatsa.

In the absence of any corroborative evidence, it is difficult to determine the authenticity of the account.

The *Mantrins* of the *Arthaśāstra* may be identified with the members of the seventh caste, as mentioned by the Greek writers. They observe, 'The seventh caste consists of the councillors of state who advise the king or the magistrates of self-governed cities, in the management of public affairs. In point of numbers, this is a small class, but it is distinguished by superior wisdom and justice (and hence enjoys the prerogative of choosing governors), chiefs of provinces, deputy governors, superintendents of the treasury, (generals of the army, admirals of the navy, controllers) and commissioners who superintend agriculture.'[60] The functions of the councillors, as described by the Greek writers, are exactly those of the *Mantrins* in a Kauṭilīya state.

Rock Edicts III and VI refer to a *Palisā*. The term *palisā* in Prākṛt corresponds to Sanskrit *Pariṣad*. D.R. Bhandarkar has identified the *Pariṣad* of Aśokan edicts with the *Mantri-pariṣad* of the *Arthaśāstra*, although R.G. Basak[61] would interpret the *Pariṣad* in the sense of an assembly of Buddhists or the audience. It is, however, difficult to believe that the audience or the assembly of religious devotees functioned as an intermediate administrative body between the king and the *Mahāmātras*. If the view of D.R. Bhandarkar, equating the *Palisā* with the *Mantri pariṣad* of the *Arthaśāstra*, be accepted, the existence of a ministerial council, as known from the *Arthaśāstra*, under the Mauryas, stands corroborated by the epigraphic source.[62] The functions of the *Pariṣad*, as outlined in the edicts, were the following:

First, to scrutinise any oral orders, issued by the king;

Second, to meet and discuss whenever any emergent matter devolved upon a *Mahāmātra*;

Third, to direct the *Yuktas* to calculate the expenses of the touring officials.

It appears that the king did not always preside over the deliberations in the council and that occasions were not few and far between when its members were divided in their judgement. It is equally clear that the king was very keen to keep himself abreast of deliberations in the council with the help of spies called *Prativedakas*.

VI

The Ministers in the Epics

It is rather unfortunate that the observation of the *Mahābhārata* on the composition of the ministry is varied and contradictory. The *Śāntiparvan*[63] states that the *Mantrins* should be eight in number (*Aṣṭānāṁ mantriṇāṁ madhye mantraṁ rāj=opadhārayet*), comprising four Brāhmaṇas, three loyal, disciplined and obedient Śūdras and one *Sūta*. It is worth observing that this list of eight *Mantrins* includes three Śūdras but passes over the claim of the Kṣatriyas in silence. It is difficult to ascertain how far this list is realistic. There are reasons to believe that in actual practice the Śūdras were not appointed as ministers and the field was dominated by the Brāhmaṇas and Kṣatriyas. The recommendation of the *Śāntiparvan* about the formation of a body of eight *Mantrins* is fortunately corroborated by the *Bālakāṇḍa*[64] of the *Rāmāyaṇa* which, likewise, refers to eight ministers of king Daśaratha. But the *Śāntiparvan*[65] elsewhere lays down that the *Mantrins* should not be less than three in number. With this may be compared the statement[66] of Rāma, entreating Bharata to consult three or four *Mantrins* in connection with the fixation of his policy. There is, likewise, a verse in the *Śāntiparvan*[67] which may be quoted here:

Parīkṣya ca guṇān=nityaṁ prauḍhabhāvān dhurandharān/
Pañc=opadhā-vyatītāṁś=ca kuryād=rāj=ārthakāriṇaḥ//

In commenting on this verse, the *Bhārata-Kaumudī* observes: *Upadhā-vyatītān chalarahitān, pañca arthakāriṇaḥ mantriṇ=ādi-kārya-kārakān mantriṇaḥ kuryāt.* Now, if the expression *pañca* be treated as being applied to *arthakāriṇaḥ*, as is done by the commentator, it will legitimately follow that the verse, in question, recommends a ministry of five members only.

The *Śāntiparvan*[68] also speaks of a larger ministry of thirty-eight members. But these ministers, who are called *Amātyas*, were, in all probability, junior ones, corresponding to their namesakes of the *Arthaśāstra*. Of these thirty-eight junior ministers, four were learned Brāhmaṇas, eight brave Kṣatriyas, twenty-one prosperous Vaiśyas, three Śūdras, one *Sūta* and one Paurāṇika. If the word *paurāṇikaṁ* of the original passage be taken as a descriptive epithet of the term *sūtam*, the number of junior ministers would be reduced to 37. This passage, which gives weightage to the Vaiśyas, no doubt, in consonance with the great influence of the community, does not occur in the Poona critical edition of the *Mahābhārata*.

In referring to the qualifications of ministers, the *Śāntiparvan*[69] states: 'Those who are of good birth and good behaviour, who can read all signs and gestures, who are destitute of cruelty, who know the requirements of place and time, and who always seek the good of their master in all acts, should be appointed as ministers by the king in all his affairs' (*Kulīnān śīla-sampannān=iṅgitajñān=a - niṣṭhurān| deśa-kāla-vidhānajñān bhartṛ-kārya-hitaiṣiṇaḥ|| Nityam=artheṣu sarveṣu rājā kurvīta mantriṇaḥ||*). Another passage of the *Śāntiparvan*[70] points out that the king 'should have for ministers persons, connected with his trusted friends, possessed of high birth, born in his own kingdom, incapable of being corrupted, unstained by adultery and similar vices, well-tested, belonging to good families, possessed of learning, sprung from sires and grandsires that held similar offices and adorned with humility'. There is striking disagreement between the above two passages of the *Śāntiparvan* on ministerial qualifications, for, whereas according to the latter, descent from a family of ministers and birth in the same kingdom are two essential qualifications of a minister, the former does not take any notice of them. The *Śāntiparvan*[71] further says that ministers should possess eight cardinal virtues but be free from sevenfold vice (*Varjitañ=c=aiva vyasanaiḥ sughoraiḥ saptabhir=vṛśam aṣṭābhiś=ca guṇair=yuktaṁ*). The virtues include (i) fifty years of age (*pañcāśad=varṣa-vayasaṁ*), (ii) sense of dignity (*pragalbhaṁ*), (iii) absence of envy (*anasūyakaṁ*), (iv) knowledge of the *Śrutis* and *Smṛtis* (*Śruti-Smṛti-samāyuktaṁ*), (v) modesty (*vinītaṁ*), (vi) impartiality (*samadarśinaṁ*), (vii) competence to decide readily in the midst of disputants urging different courses of action (*kārye vivadamānānāṁ śaktaṁ*) and (viii) uncovetousness[72] (*artheṣu alolupam*).

Similar details of ministerial qualifications are also furnished by the *Rāmāyaṇa*. The *Bālakāṇḍa*[73] refers to the ministers of king Daśaratha as virtuous, scorning to do wrong, benevolent, versed in moral law, of wide experience, disinterested, magnanimous, acquainted with the spirit of scriptures, forbearing, patient, loyal, truthful, cheerful, free from avarice and well-acquainted with the affairs of their subjects and with those of the subjects of other monarchs. They were efficient, firm in friendship and they even passed judgement on their own sons, if they transgressed the law. In the *Ayodhyākāṇḍa*,[74] Rāma calls upon Bharata who meets him in his exile to employ ministers who are of pure heart, full of integrity and of a noble disposition and whose ancestors have served the crown in positions of authority. We thus see that heredity is upheld in the epics as an essential qualification of a minister; the reason was to eliminate the possibility of an inexperienced man being appointed as a minister.

The *Mahābhārata* refers to the practice of the trial of ministers by means of *upadhās* but, unlike the *Arthaśāstra* it does not specify them. The *Ayodhyākāṇḍa*[75] of the *Rāmāyaṇa* refers to similar tests which ministers were required to undergo before they were appointed to their posts. There are indications in the *Śāntiparvan*[76] that ministers at large were corrupt and irreligious (*Kevalāt punar=ānāt karmaṇo n=opapadyate| Parāmarśo viśeṣāṇām=aśrutasya=eha durmateḥ||*); they were guided by self-interest and formed cliques. The ministers of the Kosalan monarch Kṣemadarśin, for instance, were divided into several groups. If a minister proved to be a traitor, he was either removed from his office[77] (*svāmī sthānāc=c=aiv=āpakarṣati*) or was punished[78] (*paścād=daṇḍaṁ*). The occurrence of such terms as *pradhānāmātya*[79] and *mantri-mukhya*[80] may prove the existence of the post of the chief minister in the cabinet.

Some of the important functions of ministers, as gleaned from the epics, may be stated below:

1. The most essential duty of a minister was to advise the king in regard to the formulation of the state's policies and programmes[81] (*mantragūḍho hi rājyasya mantriṇo ye maṇīṣiṇaḥ*).

2. They acted as checks upon the autocracy of kings. The ministers of king Nala warned him against playing dice but the unfortunate king did not pay any head to their advice. Vidura had advised the Kauravas to follow the just path by offering to the Pāṇḍavas their due share. The *Mahābhārata* expressly demonstrates that it was not obligatory on the king to accept the advice of his ministers.

3. They participated in military operations and helped the king in the task of defence. Duryodhana is known to have

invaded the Trigartas in the company of his ministers; Jayadratha[82] is found to have consulted his ministers in the battle-field of Kurukṣetra; Vṛṣavarmā,[83] the *Saciva* of Dhṛtarāṣṭra, lost his life while fighting with the Pāṇḍavas. The *Śāntiparvan*[84] refers to the appointment of ministers as in charge of military affairs.

4. Ministers were sometimes employed as governors of territories. The *Sabhāparvan* refers to some such ministers who had oppressed the subjects by their tyranny (*rāṣṭraṁ tav=ānuśāsanti mantriṇo*).

5. They sometimes acted as the guardians of the royal family with a high sense of loyalty. After the sudden death of Parīkṣit, his ministers held the reins of government, enthroned the infant prince Janamejaya and looked after his proper education.[85] The ministers of king Nala during the period of his exile protected his son and daughter by sending them to the abode of their maternal grandfather.[86]

6. Occasions were not altogether rare when ministers carried on the administrative affairs of the kingdom. Thus the ministers of Bhagīratha and Yuvanāśva looked after the administration of the kingdom. Parīkṣit, while going on a hunting expedition, had entrusted the affairs of state to his ministers. King Saṁbaraṇa had urged his ministers to look after the state during his absence. Mahākarṇi, the minister of the Magadhan king Ambuvic, was in charge of the kingdom for a long time.

7. They were expected to supervise watchfully the activities and mutual relations of district and provincial officers[87] (*Dharmajñaḥ sacivaḥ kaś=cit=tath=āpaśyed=atandritaḥ*).

VII

The Ministers in the Post-Maurya Period

As we approach the post-Maurya period, we find ministers being prominently mentioned in Chapter VII of the *Manusaṁhitā*,[88] wherein the king is advised to consult his ministers on such matters as those pertaining to peace and war, *sthāna* (army, treasury, capital and the country), sources of revenue, protection (of himself and of the country) and the disbursement of wealth (*Taiḥ sārdhaṁ cintayen=nityaṁ sāmānyaṁ sandhi-vigrahaṃ| Sthānaṁ samudayaṁ guptiṁ labdha-praśamanāni ca||*).

In defining the sphere of the jurisdiction of a minister, Manu is evidently as specific as Kauṭilya. He[89] further points out that ministers are to look after the affairs of the kingdom at the time of the illness of the king—a prerogative which a Kauṭilīya minister could hardly enjoy. Again, when Manu[90] says, 'Having first ascertained the opinion of each minister separately and then the views of all [of them] together, let him do what is most beneficial in his affairs,' he may be said to have departed from Kauṭilya who is loath to recognise the importance of individual consultation. Both of them, however, concur in granting the king the power to annul the decisions of his ministers. Manu[91] holds that the ministry should consist of seven or eight members (*Sacivān sapta c=āṣṭau vā prakurvīta parīkṣitān*). Referring to the qualifications of these ministers, Manu says that they must be those whose ancestors have been loyal servants (*maulān*), who are versed in the sciences (*śāstravidaḥ*), heroes (*śūrān*), skilled in the use of weapons[92] (*labdha-lakṣān*), descendants of noble families (*kul=odgatān*) and who have been tried[93] (*parīkṣitān*). It appears from the narrative of Manu[94] that one Brahmin minister was superior in status to all other ministers; it was he who guided the king in external affairs as well as in all other official business (*sarva-kāryāṇi*).

Manu[95] also refers to junior ministers, described as *Amātyas*, who were to be honest (*śucīn*), wise (*prājñān*), firm (*avasthitān*), able to collect revenue (*samyag=artha-samāhartṛn*) and well-tried (*suparīkṣitān*). Kullūka regards them as executive ministers (*karma-sacivaḥ*). Manu does not delimit their number but points out that it should be in consonance with the requirements of the state. They were employed in the offices for the collection of revenue[96] (*arthe*) as well as in the interior of the palace (*antar=niveśane*).

A wealth of information about ministers is, likewise, provided by other contemporary or near contemporary works. The *Milindapañho*[97] describes them as royal employees who were exempted from taxation. Kātyāyana[98] refers to the *Amātyas* as belonging to the Brāhmaṇa caste and says that the king should not decide even a law-suit without their assistance. The *Mālavikāgnimitraṁ*[99] informs us that the crown prince Agnimitra, who was appointed as governor of Malwa by his father Puṣyamitra, had a council of ministers. The council would discuss the decisions of the king and communicate its opinion to the latter through its president or chief minister.

Tiruvalluvar in his Tirukkural discusses at length the qualifications and functions of a minister, called an *Amaiccar*. 'The first essential quality in a minister is an ability to judge aright ways and means of achieving great things, timeliness of action and enterprise and initiative. Along with these the minister must have resolution, interest in the welfare of the people, constant study and drive to get things done. The affairs of the State are not simple things fit only for philosophers as many difficult situations have to be faced. Tiruvalluvar says that he is an able minister who possesses the capacity to disunite allies, cherish and keep friendship and bring back people who have (been) estranged. This is paying attention to both *sandhi* and *vigraha* aspects in relations within the State and outside. The minister should not waver in his advice and must possess penetrating insight and comprehension and clearheadedness in decision and action.'[100] He points out that 'the minister should dare to speak out and give correct advice even if the king is unwise and might throw away his advice. Duty must be performed at all costs and not burked to retain his position or the king's favour.'[101] Tiruvalluvar further lays down that both learning and eloquence are necessary for a minister. 'The importance of persuasion and of public communications, now so much valued in modern governments, is also valued by Tiruvalluvar.'[102] Decision should be reached only after a thorough deliberation and in the execution of such decisions, there should be no delay.[103] In dealing with a matter, five things should be taken into consideration, viz., the resources at disposal, instruments, time, nature of the action and the proper place for its execution.[104]

What is known of ministers from literature is fortunately corroborated and supplemented by archaeological evidence. The inscriptions of the Śātavāhanas speak of *Amātyas* who were not counsellors, *Mantrins*, but were executive ministers, being employed as district officers and as heads of departments. The *Amātyas* Viṣṇupālita, Śyāmaka and Śivaskandadatta successively governed the district of Govardhana, identified with Nasik, at the time of Gautamīputra Śātakarṇi and Pulumāyi. The *Āhāra* of Māmala, located in Poona district, was under an

Amātya whose name ended in-gupta. It is not clear whether all the districts of the Śātavāhana kingdom were placed under charge of the *Amātyas* or they were entrusted with the administration of those districts that lay close to the Kṣatrapa dominions, although the latter suggestion appears to be more reasonable. The royal donor of the gift of a tank and monastery at Banabasi had entrusted the work of the execution of her project to *Amātya* Khadasati, described in the record as head of the department of works (*Karmmāntika*). It seems that in the Śātavāhana kingdom important districts and departments were placed in charge of executive ministers, styled *Amātyas*, who maintained close contact with the central government. Such an assumption does not appear to be unlikely as there are numerous references to ministers in charge of territorial units in inscriptional and literary records, both earlier and later.

References to the *Amātyas* are found in a few seals of the Kuṣāṇa period. A seal[105] in the Bharat Kala Bhavan bears in Kuṣāṇa characters the legend, *Amaca Hatthikasa*. A seal[106] from Basarh in Muzaffarpur district, Bihar, bears in Brāhmī script the legend, *Amātya Bhadrika-putrasya Amātya Hastabalasya*, 'a seal of *Amātya* Hastabala, son of *Amātya* Bhadrika'. A seal[107] from Bhita bears the legend, *Amātya Nāgadāma* in characters of the second or third century A.D. A seal[108] from Sirkap contains the legend, *Sihasa(madri)na-putasa Vīrabāhusa*, 'a seal of Vīrabāhu, son of *Mantrin* Siṁha'. As one studies critically the above seals, mentioning *Amātyas*, one finds with dismay the dearth of information about the nature and importance of the work they discharged in these records. The seals guaranteed in the names of these persons the genuineness of some documents which must have carried royal orders, contracts between parties or their own instructions. This may indicate that they were either heads of departments or placed in charge of territorial units. That the *Amātyas* were generally connected with the administration of territorial units is confirmed by the Junagadh rock inscription of Rudradāman which speaks of the *Amātyas* Kulaipa and Suviśākha as governors of provinces under the *Mahākṣatrapa*. An interesting glimpse into the qualities of head and heart of the *Amātyas* is also provided by the Junagadh inscription which describes Suviśākha as being endowed with ability, patience, resoluteness, uprightness, incorruptibility and modesty. A seal of the Kuṣāṇa period, mentioning *Amātya* Hastabala, son of *Amātya* Bhadrika, probably attests the hereditary character of that office, a fact that stands supported by literary evidence as well.

The division of ministers into two broad classes, comprising counsellors (*Matisacivas*) and executive ministers (*Karmasacivas*), as found in literature, is maintained in the Junagadh rock inscription which helps us to ascertain the power and responsibility of these ministers and their relations with the king. The Sudarśana lake sustained a very huge breach in its dam by a rain storm and caused a high flood in the neighbouring rivers. The *Matisacivas* and *Karmasacivas* all vetoed the undertaking of repairs as they thought that such a measure would involve the wastage of a great deal of public money and time. But the king set aside their advice and without raising any money either in the shape of new taxes or benevolences, sanctioned a huge sum of money from the royal treasury and undertook the work of repairs, to the great relief of the people. The record illustrates how the will of the king triumphed over the unanimous decision of the *Matisacivas* and *Karmasacivas* and is thus in tune with the evidence of literature, investing the king with the right to annul the decisions of ministers.

VIII

The Ministers in the Gupta and Contemporary Periods

As we arrive at the Gupta period, we find ministers being classified into three broad divisions—*Mantrins*, *Sacivas* and *Amātyas*—in the *Kāmandakīya Nītisāra*. Whereas the *Mantrins*[109] and *Amātyas* were primarily concerned with the sixfold policy and with the charge of territorial units and revenue, respectively, the *Sacivas* were placed in charge of the military department. In referring to the qualifications of the *Sacivas*, Kāmandaka[110] lays down that they should possess high birth (*kulīnāḥ*), purity (*śucayaḥ*), prowess (*śūrāḥ*), learning (*śrutavanto*), loyalty (*anurāgiṇaḥ*) and training in practical politics (*daṇḍanīteḥ prayoktāraḥ*). A *Mantrin*, according to Kāmandaka,[111] is required to possess a retentive memory (*smṛtiḥ*), application of the mind to works undertaken (*tatparat=ārtheṣu*), capacity for a thorough discussion (*vitarko*), power to arrive at a proper decision (*jñāna-niścayaḥ*), steadiness in work (*dṛḍhatā*) and preservation of state secrets (*mantraguptiś=ca*). Kāmandaka attaches great importance to the advice of the *Mantrins* but he, at the same time, does not undermine the importance of the king's authority. It is he with whom rests the final decision.

The *Nītisāra* refers to a minister, called *Narmasaciva*. The word *narma* is used in the *Mahābhārata* in the sense of jokes and Monier-Williams translates it to mean 'pastimes and amusements'. The *Narmasaciva* was, in all likelihood, the private secretary of the king whose work included, among others, cutting jokes and jesting. This minister, on account of the closeness of his association with the king, proved to be very powerful and might have influenced the latter's decisions. The *Nītisāra* would, however, create the impression that he was sometimes treated with scorn by royal servants.

The *Yājñavalkya-Smṛti*,[112] which was also a product of the Gupta age, urges the king to appoint wise, righteous, noble and resolute persons as ministers and entreats him to consult them collectively (*Sa mantriṇaḥ prakurvīta prājñān maulān sthrirān śucīn| Taiḥ sārdhaṁ cintayed=rājyaṁ vipreṇ=ātha tataḥ svayam||*). The work further states that whatever the *Mantrins* decide has to be approved by the priest, thus implying that the advice of ministers without the approval of the royal chaplain would be ineffective. The commentator Vijñāneśvara,[113] however, includes the *Purohita* in the list of ministers. If this was the case, it may be presumed that the royal chaplain enjoyed a special position as compared to other ministers. Yājñavalkya recommends the appointment of Brāhmaṇas[114] as *Mantrins* who should be hereditary and of noble descent.[115] The *Matsya Purāṇa*,[116] likewise, alludes to the importance of the advice of the *Mantrins*.

Leaving aside the literary source, we may now turn to archaeological evidence and see how far the account of literature is corroborated by the testimony of archaeology. The existence of the *Amātyas* during this period, as alluded to by Kāmandaka, is proved beyond doubt by the discovery of a large number of seals, assignable to this period. A terracotta seal[117] of about the fourth or fifth century A.D. from Bhita bears the legend, *Amātya=Eśvaracandrasya*, 'seal of *Amātya* Īśvaracandra'. Another contemporary seal[118] from the same site contains the legend, *Amāty=Eśvarānana*, 'seal of *Amātya* Īśvarānana'. Another Bhita seal[119] of the Gupta period reads *Amātya-Dharmadevasya*, 'seal of *Amātya* Dharmadeva'. A seal[120] from Basarh reads *Amātya-Bhadrika-putrasya Amātya-Hastabalasya*, 'seal of *Amātya* Hastabala, son of *Amātya* Bhadrika'. The Mathura Museum preserves a seal[121] of *Amātya* Upalihama (*Amātyasya Upalihamasya*). A large number of Rajghat seals[122] of about the time of Samudragupta bear the name of *Amātya* Janārdana. Another seal[123] from Rajghat, now preserved in the Bharat Kala Bhavan, reads *Amātya-putra Kalabhakasya* in early Gupta characters. Two other seals from the same place bear the legends, *Amātya-Kapilakasya*[124] and *Amātya-Āryaśarmā*, respectively, also in early Gupta characters.

It is rather unfortunate that although the seals, mentioned above, contain numerous references to *Amātyas*, they hardly provide us with any positive information in regard to the nature of the work they discharged. K.K. Thaplyal[125] observes that the *Amātyas* of these seals constituted a general class of officers, who were assigned numerous duties and offices. But Amarasiṁha, the famous Buddhist lexicographer of the Gupta age, mentions the *Mantrins* and *Amātyas* as belonging to the same class of officers, the only difference between them is that while the *Mantrins* were counselling *Amātyas*, the latter were executive *Amātyas*. This would imply that the *Amātyas* of the Gupta period were superior in rank to the general class of officers, thus lending support to our interpretation of the term *amātya* in the sense of an executive minister.

Although seals leave us in the dark about the precise nature of the functions of ministers, the inscriptions of the contemporary period have proved to be very useful in this regard. Vīrasena, also known as Śāba, a foreign minister under Candragupta II Vikramāditya, is said in the Udayagiri cave inscription to have accompanied the king in the course of the latter's campaign of conquests in Malwa and Gujarat (*kṛtsna-pṛthvī-jay=ārthena rājñ=aiv=eha sah=āgataḥ*). This would imply that ministers, especially the foreign ministers, were required to perform military functions according to the exigency of circumstances. That military leadership was one of the important qualifications of a minister is also probably corroborated by the Allahabad pillar inscription which describes Hariṣeṇa, who was a foreign minister under Samudragupta, as a *Mahābalādhikṛta*, a term that has often been interpreted to mean a military general.

Inscriptions also afford us an interesting glimpse into the qualifications of these ministers. Śāba is expressly described as well-grounded in the science of politics and poetics (*śabd=ārtha-nyāya-nītijñaḥ kavi Pāṭaliputrakaḥ*). Hariṣeṇa has, likewise, demonstrated his skill in penmanship.

Inscriptions further bring to light the hereditary character of ministership. The Allahabad pillar inscription shows that Hariṣeṇa was a *Mahādaṇḍanāyaka* which post was also held by his father Dhruvabhūti. The Udayagiri cave inscription speaks of Śāba as having acquired the post of a minister by hereditary descent (*anvaya-prāpta-sācivyo*). The Karamdanda inscription of Kumāragupta I states that both Pṛthvīṣeṇa and his father Śikharasvāmin served as *Mantrins* under Kumāragupta I and Candragupta II, respectively. Sūryadatta was a foreign minister under the Parivrājakas in A.D. 482 and his son Vibhudatta was appointed to the post in A.D. 510.[126] Under the Ucchakalpas, Gallu was a foreign minister in A.D. 496, while his brother Manoratha held the post in A.D. 512. We have, however, no means to ascertain whether the transmission of office in the same family was occasional or permanent. If it was occasional, it was doubtless to the advantage of the government but if it was made a permanent affair, it often proved to be a liability, for, learning and ability do not descend for long in any family in an undiminished quality and quantity. It is equally uncertain whether all heads of departments under Gupta administration were ministers. Attention may be invited in this connection to the passage, occurring in the Karamdanda inscription, *Pṛthvīṣeṇo mahārāj=ādhirāja-śrī-Kumāraguptasya mantrī Kumārāmāty=onantarañ=ca mahā-balādhikṛtaḥ*, which means that Pṛthvīṣeṇa was first a minister but was afterwards made a general of the army. This may imply that Pṛthvīṣeṇa was promoted to the rank of a general which was superior to that of a minister. Or, it may have been simply a changeover from one department to another of an officer, without affecting his rank or status. If the latter interpretation be accepted, it would follow that the *Mahābalādhikṛta*, like the *Sāndhivigrahika*, enjoyed the status of a minister.

Ministers enjoyed a prominent position in the contemporary Kadamba kingdom of Banabase in South India. Ministers were so powerful that without their approval even a king would not make any grant of land. King Śivavitta,[127] for instance, is said to have made a grant with the consent of his ministers, including the chief amongst them. Again, when the same king agreed to found an *agrahāra* at the behest of his queen Kamalādevī, all the ministers, headed by the *Purohita* Śrī-Vindhyavāsi-Bhaṭṭopādhyāya, discussed the matter afresh and notified their consent for the execution of the grant.[128] This incident suggests that the priest was an important member of the ministry, a conclusion which receives confirmation from Yājñavalkya.

IX

The Ministers in the Post-Gupta Period

The *Kādambarī*, composed by Bāṇa, affords us interesting glimpses into the office of a minister in the post-Gupta period. It speaks of a minister called Kumārapālita[129] who served under king Śūdraka of Ujjain. In the royal court the minister, who was aged, of noble birth, wise and well-grounded in politics, used to occupy a golden throne close to the king. Mention is also made in the *Kādambarī* of a Brahmin minister of king Tārāpīḍa, named Śukanāsa, 'the castle of constancy, the station of steadfastness, the bridge of bright truth, the guide to all goodness, the conductor in conduct, the ordainer of all ordered life'.[130] He was thoroughly conversant with arts, *Vedas*, *Vedāṅgas* and other *Śāstras*, loyal to the king and skilled in the precepts of the political science. As Bāṇa[131] would make us believe, the quarters of Śukanāsa were frequented by a multitude of tributary kings at all times.

We learn from the *Harṣacarita*, another work of Bāṇa, that in times of emergency, ministers often decided the question of succession to the throne. Thus ministers chose Harṣa as the king of Thanesar on the death of Prabhākaravardhana. A similar role was played by the Maukhari ministers when they offered the crown to Harṣa since king Grahavarman died without leaving any male heir to the throne. A special meeting was held for the purpose at which the chief minister first proposed the name of Harṣa for the throne and other ministers were asked to give their opinion. When an agreement was reached, Harṣa was offered the crown. This would indicate that ministers wielded considerable power and authority in administration in some of the kingdoms during the first half of the seventh century A.D., especially when there was an interregnum. Hiuen Tsang refers to a minister of king Vikramāditya of Śrāvastī who had objected to the king's order to distribute daily five lacs of gold coins as that would lead to the drainage of the resources of the state. In the account of Hiuen Tsang, mention is made of a minister of Aśoka who had declined to comply with the king's desire to give away all his possessions in charity. The cause of the ministers' refusal to endorse the order of the kings in these cases might be that they felt a sense of moral responsibility to the people or more probably they were acting in the interest of the kings, as a depleted treasury would have adversely affected their position. That the interest of the king and of the royal family was the main concern of a minister is further illustrated by a story in the *Harṣacarita* where ministers are represented as blaming themselves for the treacherous murder of Rājyavardhana at the hands of Śaśāṅka. In contemporary Tamil literature, ministers are called *Amaiccas*. The *Periyapurāṇam*[132] speaks of the *Amaiccas* of the Pallava king Guṇabhara.

But when we turn to contemporary inscriptional records, we find scanty information about ministers in them. The evidence of the Nalanda stone inscription[133] of the reign of Yaśovarman is worth considering here, for it mentions a *Mantrin*, who is therein described as a *Mārgapati, Udīcīpati* and *Pratīta-Tikina.* The term *mārgapati* literally means the guardian of roads but here it probably means the guardian of the passes or frontier. The expression *udīcīpati*, which etymologically means the lord of the north, signifies the chief guardian of the passes of the north. The application of the designations *Mārgapati* and *Udīcīpati* to a *Mantrin* presupposes his skill in the art of warfare. The term *tikina*, which is equivalent to Turkish *tigin*, *tegin* or *tāgin*, means a prince and *pratīta* denotes 'distinguished'. The applicability of the designation *Pratīta-Tikina* to a minister would show that the princes of the royal family were sometimes appointed to the ministerial post. The appointment of a prince to the post of a minister was, of course, very rare in ancient India. References to ministers are found in the Pallava inscriptions as well. The

Hirahadagalli plates of Śivaskandavarman mention an *Amātya* along with other dignitaries who were informed of the grant of a piece of land that the king had made from his capital. The Vaikuntha Perumal temple inscription of Nandivarman refers to the *Mantri-maṇḍala*, council of ministers, of the king. The Kasakudi plates[134] bring to light the qualities of Brahmaśrīrāja, the chief minister of Nandivarman. We learn that friendliness, virtue, modesty, learning, firmness, valour and refinement were some of the qualities with which he was endowed. He is moreover described as the eldest priest.

X

The Ministers in the Pratīhāra-Pāla-Rāṣṭrakūṭa Period

When we turn to the period of the Gurjara-Pratīhāra, Pāla, Rāṣṭrakūṭa and other contemporary kings, we find abundant material about ministers in the contemporary literary documents. The *Śiśupālavadha*,[135] which was composed by Māgha in the eighth century A.D., refers to ministers and points out that the king should seek their opinion on all important matters. The king cannot correctly adopt the line of action without the assistance of ministers.

Medhātithi[136] favours the appointment of seven or eight *Mantrins* and is opposed to a very large or a very small body of ministers. He says that it is sometimes difficult for a large body to arrive at unanimous decisions; furthermore, such a body is liable to be torn into pieces on account of mutual jealousies of its members. On the contrary, a single minister may turn to be an autocrat, and if there are two, they may form an alliance to harm the interest of the state. Medhātithi also refers to the tests of virtue, wealth, love and fear which ministers were required to undergo before their appointment.

In his *Nītivākyāmṛta*,[137] Somadeva Sūri recommends the appointment of three, seven or eight *Mantrins*[138] (*Trayayaḥ pañca sapta vā mantriṇaḥ kāryāḥ*). He further tells us that if one *Mantrin* is eminently suitable for carrying on properly the burden of the kingdom, more *Mantrins* need not be appointed. It is reasonable to presume that such a suggestion is hardly realistic for a big kingdom. Somadeva[139] lays down that ministers should be recruited from the Brāhmaṇa, Kṣatriya and Vaiśya communities. Regarding the qualifications of the *Mantrins*, he points out that they should be endowed with real character, noble descent, resourcefulness, courage and continence. Somadeva[140] attaches great importance to the counsels of the *Mantrins* and expressly states that the king would cease to be king if he violated the dictates of his ministers (*Mantra-pūrvaḥ sav=opy-ārambhaḥ kṣitipatīnām/ Sa khalu no rājā yo mantriṇ=otikramya varteta/*). Somadeva[141] also refers to executive ministers, *Amātyas*, who were chiefly concerned with income, expenditure, royal safety and maintenance of order (*Āya-vyayaḥ svāmi-rakṣa-mantra-poṣaṇaṁ c=āmātyānām=adhikāraḥ*). Somadeva[142] says that those who are quarrelsome, allies of a strong party, passionate, characterless, born of humble origin, disloyal, spendthrifts, foreigners and misers, should not be selected for the post of an *Amātya* (*Tikṣṇaṁ balavad pakṣaṁ aśuciṁ avyasaninam=aśuddh=ābhijanam=aśakya-pratyāvartanam = ativyaya-śīlam=anya-deś=āyatam=aticikkaṇaṁ c=āmātyaṁ na kurvīta*). The *Kathāsaritsāgara*, another literary work, composed by Somadeva, refers to some ministers as playing a key role in administration. It speaks of Yaugandharāyaṇa, the *Mantrin* of king Udayana of Vatsa, as being constantly consulted by the king on every matter, including his marriage to Vāsavadattā and Padmāvatī. He was often entrusted with the sole administration of the kingdom and the king was a mere passive figure. The *Kathāsaritsāgara* elsewhere refers to king Vikramaśakti who was offered the throne by the ministers of his father. Phalabhūti was, likewise, offered the crown by the ministers of king Ādityaprabha. But it is difficult to deduce any conclusion on the basis of these stories the historicity of which is not beyond dispute.

We meet with a thorough treatment of ministers, both counsellors and executive ministers, in the *Agni Purāṇa* It does not suggest the actual number of *Mantrins* but informs us that Daśaratha[143] had eight *Mantrins* and Rāvaṇa[144] seven. It appears from the *Agni Purāṇa*[145] that ministers were recruited not only from the Brāhmaṇa community but also from the Kṣatriyas. The king is urged to seek the advice of the *Mantrins* separately.[146] Joint deliberation with ministers is discouraged to eliminate the possibility of any concerted ministerial opposition. Prescribing the qualifications of the *Mantrins*, the *Agni Purāṇa* points out that they should be noble in descent, eloquent, modest, honest, sons of the soil, well-grounded in *daṇḍa-nīti*, arts, crafts and other *Śāstras*, able to negotiate war and peace, well acquainted with secret counsels and preparations being made in neighbouring countries and should be free from vices like anger, greed, fear and falsehood. The accounts of the *Agni Purāṇa* in regard to the functions and qualifications of executive ministers, *Amātyas* and *Sacivas*, are almost exactly those that we find in the *Nītivākyāmṛta*. Like the *Kāmandakīya Nītisāra*, the *Agni Purāṇa*[147] refers to the *Narmasaciva* who, as has already been observed, was a minister in charge of the king's pastimes (*śṛṅgāre narma-sacivaḥ*).

The evidence of literary documents on the importance of ministers is in agreement with the testimony of the epigraphic records of the period. The Badal pillar inscription of the reign of Nārāyaṇapāla attests the great power and influence that a Brahmin family of ministers exercised in the administration of the Pāla kingdom for several generations. This record speaks of Garga, the minister of king Dharmapāla, as being superior in knowledge to Bṛhaspati. His son Darbhapāṇi, who was well-grounded in the fourfold knowledge, served as a minister under Devapāla and helped the latter through his diplomacy to exact tributes from the whole of North India from the Himalayas to the Vindhya mountains and from the eastern to the western seas (*nītyā yasya bhuvaṁ cakāra karadāṁ śrī-Devapālo nṛpaḥ*). Darbhapāṇi's son Someśvara, who was very liberal and served under Devapāla as a minister, compared well with Dhanañjaya in point of prowess. His son Kedāramiśra, who was a great donor and an erudite scholar, helped Devapāla to enjoy the sea-girt earth after having eradicated the race of the Utkalas, humbled the pride of the Hūṇas and destroyed the conceit of the Draviḍa and Gurjara kings. His son was Gauravamiśra who was a minister under Nārāyaṇapāla and endowed with oratory and a thorough knowledge of the *Āgamas*, *Vedas* and astrology. The following facts emerge from the above account:

1. Ministers took a leading part in the formulation of the foreign policy of the state.
2. Under the Pālas, the hereditary principle was followed in the appointment of ministers.

3. The question of creed did not crop up at the time of the appointment of ministers. The Brahmanical family of Garga served under four successive Pāla kings who were Buddhists.

The Badal pillar inscription, however, does not clearly indicate whether Darbhapāṇi or Kedāramiśra had actually participated in wars or were endowed with military qualities but that ministers often led the royal army to quell an uprising or to repel foreign invasions is amply borne out by the Kamauli plate of Vaidyadeva. Vaidyadeva is described in his own record as the sharp-rayed sun into the lotuses of the assembly of *Sacivas* (*Saciva samāja-saroja-tigma-bhānuḥ*) of the *Gauḍeśvara* Kumārapāla who flourished at about the end of the twelfth century A.D. He won a victory in a naval battle in South Bengal and, being ordered by his master, put down the rebellion of Tiṁgyadeva in the east (*tam=avanipatiṁ jitvā yuddhe*). Vaidyadeva was afterwards appointed governor of Prāgjyotiṣa-*bhukti* and Kāmarūpa-*maṇḍala* in place of Tiṁgyadeva. Some more facts about ministers under the Pālas and their contemporaries may be gleaned from other inscriptions of the period. The Bangarh inscription[148] of Mahīpāla refers to *Mantrī* Bhaṭṭa Vāmana as the *Dūta* of the grant. The Amagachi grant[149] of Vigrahapāla III also refers to a *Mantrī* who acted as the messenger of the grant. The mention of a minister called Ādideva is made in the Bhubaneswar *praśasti* of Bhaṭṭa Bhavadeva where he is described as a *Viśrāma-saciva*. That Ādideva was a minister of no mean importance is clear from the fact that the inscription shows that he used to discuss with the king matters of statecraft in complete privacy. The Bhubaneswar *praśasti*, likewise, refers to a minister named Bhaṭṭa Bhavadeva who is described as a *Mantraśakti-saciva*. The term *mantraśakti* may mean policy of war and peace; the *Mantraśakti-saciva* might have been a foreign minister, so intimately associated with war and peace. It is evident that the hereditary principle in the appointment of ministers was also followed by the Varman kings of East Bengal.

Inscriptions testify to the importance of ministers in the Kalacuri-Cedi administration. A senior minister is called *Mahāpradhāna*, *Mahāmantrin* and *Mahāmātya* in the Kalacuri-

Cedi inscriptions where the terms *pradhāna*, *mantrin* and *amātya* are used as synonyms. The Karitalai[150] inscription mentions a senior minister named Bhākamiśra and states that the kingdom of king Yuvarāja prospered immensely during his ministership. He was a Brāhmaṇa by caste, well-versed in the sacred lores and a great poet. Bhākamiśra's son Someśvara[151] acted as a senior minister during the reign of Lakṣmaṇarāja (*Mantri-tilaka*). That the hereditary principle was followed in the appointment of ministers in the Cedi kingdom is not only proved by the instances of Bhākamiśra and Someśvara but also by the fact that the Kāyastha or Śūdra family of Gollāka[152] supplied ministers to the Kalacuri kings of Tripurī for several generations. Gaṅgādhara,[153] the minister of the Cedi king Ratnadeva III, was a highly qualified person who was brave, courageous, kind, intelligent, upright and well-grounded in the science of polity and law. It was he who by dint of his wonderful ability made the kingdom of Ratnadeva III free from all foes and restored peace and prosperity. This statement, which is found in a Cedi record, is no doubt general in nature and exaggerated in import but it probably points to the importance of the role played by Gaṅgādhara in internal and external affairs of the Cedi kingdom during the reign of Ratnadeva III. The Jabalpur copper plate of the Cedi king Yaśaḥkarṇadeva implies that ministers sometimes played the role of king-makers, for we are told that Kokalla II was placed on the throne by a minister (*amātya-mukhya*) of Yuvarāja II.[154]

Like the Kalacuri-Cedi inscriptions, the Rāṣṭrakūṭa records also emphasise that ministers were expected to be vastly learned. In extolling the role of ministers in administration, a contemporary inscription says, 'When Caṅgadeva was the good premier, the nation flourished, subjects and allies were content, religion (i.e., virtue) increased, all aims were attained, the wise were happy and prosperity was visible everywhere.'[155] The Salotgi inscription[156] mentions Nārāyaṇa, the foreign minister under king Kṛṣṇa III, and compares him with the king's right hand. The high status of ministers is further borne out by the fact that they were sometimes honoured with feudatory titles and entitled to the use of the *Pañcamahāśabdas*. Dalla,[157] who was a foreign minister under king Dhruva, was invested with the title of *Sāmanta* and empowered to use the five great musical instruments (*Sam=adhi-gata pañca-mahā-śabda-mahā-sandhi-vigrah=ādhi-kṛta-sāmanta-śrīmān=Dallen=eti*). The Pathari inscription[158] of Prabala suggests that some of the feudatories under the Rāṣṭrakūṭas enjoyed the service of ministers.

XI

The Ministers in the Post-Pāla-Pratīhāra Period

As we approach the age following, we find, to judge from the combined study of the contemporary literary and archaeological evidence, ministers constituting a very important limb of the government. The *Rājataraṅgiṇī*[159] takes note of ministers who were sometimes recruited from the members of the royal family. The selection of princes for ministerial offices was, however, rare in ancient India, and is not in tune with the recommendations of early Indian political thinkers King Harṣa[160] is represented in the *Rājataraṅgiṇī* as consulting his ministers jointly, whereas king Jayasiṁha[161] is seen deliberating with only a few ministers. The system of joint consultation with ministers was in vogue but its rigid or modified application, no doubt, depended on the king himself. The *Rājataraṅgiṇī* alludes to an effective role of ministers in the selection of a successor to the throne. Queen Sugandhā[162] was forced to accept Pārtha as her successor in place of her own nominee Sūryavarman whose candidature was set aside by ministers. Kalhaṇa also records a few cases of kings overruling their ministers and acting according to their own discretion. Such was the case with king Bijjā[163] who disobeyed his ministers and with king Pratāpāditya II[164] whose ministers merely carried out the policy laid down by him.

Lakṣmīdhara in the section entitled *Rājadharmakāṇḍa* of the *Kṛtyakalpataru*, which he had composed at the command of the Gāhaḍavāla monarch Govindacandra, gives a graphic description of the ministerial qualifications which included, according to him, heroism, success, noble descent, coolness of mind and knowledge of the *Śāstras*, *Nītis* and *Mantras*. Lakṣmīdhara tells us that in the selection of ministers preference is to be given to the Brāhmaṇas and to those whose ancestors had served as ministers.[165] The author of the *Yuktikalpataru* is more liberal than Lakṣmīdhara as he recommends the appointment of people of low status for ministership in times of distress. The hereditary principle in the appointment of ministers is also upheld in the *Rājanītiprakāśa*.[166]

The *Mānasollāsa*,[167] which was composed in A.D. 1129 by king Someśvara III of the Western Cālukya dynasty, recommends the appointment of seven or eight ministers (*Sacivān sapta c=āṣṭau vā kurvīta mnatimān nṛpaḥ*) who should be versed in the *Nītiśāstras*, courageous, born of a high family, clever and free from diseases. It is worth mentioning in this connection that Śivājī, the founder of the Maratha empire, had a council of eight ministers, called *Ashṭa-Pradhānas*. The *Mānasollāsa* also refers to dishonest ministers who used to take recourse to repressive measures against the people and urges the king to protect them on such occasions. The *Viṣṇudharmottara Purāṇa*, likewise, refers to ministers who should be endowed with noble birth, modesty, honesty, loyalty, indigenous origin and knowledge of the *Daṇḍanīti*, arts, crafts and *Śāstras*. A minister is further said to be free from such vices as anger, greed, fear and untruthfulness. The *Dvyāśraya*, which was composed in the reign of the Caulukya kings of Gujarat, brings out the importance of ministers in the Caulukya kingdom. Ministers were consulted on important occasions but the king was free to follow any course of action according to his own discretion. The *Dvyāśraya*[168] speaks of a minister of king Arṇorāja who had advised the king not to wage war with Kumārapāla but the latter set aside his minister's counsel. The *Hammīra Mahākāvya*[169] of Nayacandrasūri, likewise, speaks of the Cāhamāna king Vīra Nārāyaṇa, as setting aside his ministers' advice and concluding a treaty with Alāuddīn which brought about his end. That the king was authorised to annul the decision of his ministers is further corroborated by the *Prabandhacintāmaṇi*[170] which refers to the Paramāra king Muñja, also called Vākpatirāja II, as having launched an expedition against the Cālukya king Tailapa II of Kalyāṇa in the teeth of opposition of his minister Rudrāditya. A passage of the *Prabandhacintāmaṇi*,[171] which gives us an insight into the functions of ministers, is worth noticing here:

> "That man is really a minister and full of wisdom, who
> without taxation accumulates treasure,

Without killing defends the kingdom, and extends its territory without war."

The enrichment of the treasury, internal security and territorial expansion were thus three important functions of ministers. The *Vasantavilāsa*[172] refers to one of Vīradhavala Baghela's minister, called Tejaḥpāla who is known to have installed Vīsaladeva Baghela on the throne and earned the title of *Rāja-sthāpan=ācārya.*

The *Saciva*, *Mantrī* and *Amātya* figure in the *Śukranīti*[173] as three distinct office-bearers, being included in the ministry of ten members, comprising such other functionaries as the *Purohita* (priest), *Yuvarāja* (crown prince), *Pradhāna* (premier), *Prāḍvivāka* (judge), *Paṇḍita* (scholar), *Sumantraka* (finance minister) and *Dūta* (ambassador). That the *Saciva*, *Mantrī* and *Amātya*, as well as other members of the ministry, do not claim the same rank and position is evident from Śukra's statement that the 'Priest, who is the mainstay of the king and kingdom, is superior to all. The *Yuvarāja* comes next, being followed in succession by the Premier, *Saciva*, *Mantrī*, Justice, Scholar, *Sumantra*, *Amātya* and lastly the *Dūta*; all these officers are successively meritorious in order.'[174]

Śukra points out that the *Saciva* 'has to study the elephants, horses, chariots, foot-soldiers, camels, oxen, bandsmen, ensign-bearers, men who practise battle-arrays, men who are sent out eastward and westward (on missions), bearers of royal emblems, arms and weapons, attendants of superior, ordinary and inferior grades, and the various classes of ammunitions; he has to find out the groups that are complete in all their parts, how many of these are in active condition, how many are old and how many new, how many are unfit for work, how many troops are well equipped with arms, ordnance and gunpowder, and what is the amount of commissariat and other contingencies. Then he has to communicate the result of his studies to the king.'[175] These are, no doubt, the functions and responsibilities of a war minister. The *Mantrī* 'has to study when, how and to whom the policies of Peace, Purchase, Partition and Penalty have to be adopted and the various effects of each, whether great, moderate or small; and having decided on the course of action to communicate that to the king'.[176] The *Mantrī* thus appears to be in charge of external affairs. While referring to the duties discharged by the *Amātya*, Śukra observes, 'How many cities, villages and forests are there, the amount of land cultivated, who is the receiver of the rent, the amount of revenue realised, who receives the remainder after paying off the rent, how much land remains uncultivated, the amount of revenue realised through taxes and fines. The amount realised without cultivation (i.e., Nature's gifts), how much accrues from forests, the amount realised through mines and jewels. How much is collected as unowned or unclaimed by anybody, got back from the thief, and the amount stored up—knowing these things the *Amātya* should inform the king.'[177] The *Amātya* was thus connected with various sources of revenue like rent from land (*bhāga*), duties (*śulka*), fines (*daṇḍa*), nature's contribution (*akṛṣṭapacyā*), income from forests (*araṇya-saṁbhava*), mineral wealth (*ākara*), deposits as in a bank (*nidhi-prāpta*), unowned property (*asvāmika*) and articles recovered from thieves (*taskar=āhṛta*). The *Amātya* would thus favourably compare with the revenue minister of modern times. That the *Amātya* was in some way connected with the administration of justice is evident from Śukra's statement that 'the king should alternatively look after law-suits (*vyavahāra*) by freeing himself from anger and greed according to the dictates of *Dharma Śāstras*,—in the company of the Chief Justice, *Amātya* Brāhmaṇa and Priest'.[178] No person was allowed to hold the post of a *Mantrī*, *Amātya* or *Saciva* permanently, for Śukra clearly states that the king should never assign office for ever to anybody and everybody but is to appoint the *Prakṛtis* to each post by rotation.[179]

References to ministers and their importance in Indian kingdoms are found in the contemporary inscriptions as well. The mention of ministers is to be met almost invariably in the records[180] of the Gāhaḍavāla kings. The minister Vidyādhara is said to have been respected and propitiated by king Madana who was in all probability a Gāhaḍavāla feudatory.[181] The fact that Vidyādhara's grandfather Vilvaśiva was a minister under Madana's father Gopāla illustrates that the practice of appointing hereditary ministers was in vogue in the Gāhaḍavāla kingdom.

The inscriptions of the Caulukya kings of Gurajat provide us with important information in regard to the functions of ministers who were generally known as *Mantrins* and *Mahāmātyas*. The term *mahāmātya*, as employed in the Caulukya inscriptions, should not be understood in the sense of the chief minister, for a finance minister is also called a *Mahāmātya*. It seems that under the Caulukyas ministers were often made governors of provinces. Thus the minister Udayana was placed in charge of Cambay during the reigns of Siddharāja, Jayasiṁha and Kumārapāla, whereas another minister named Sāmanta was entrusted with the administration of Bālapadrapāṭaka in the reign of Kumārapāla. The drawing up of documents seems to have been another function of ministers. This is clear from the evidence of the Veraval inscription[182] of king Arjuna which describes the *Mahāmātya* Māladeva as conducting all the business of the seal, including the marking of *śrī śrī* at the beginning of the document (*śrī-śrī-karaṇ=ādisamasta-mudrā-vyāpārān=paripanthayati*). In another inscription[183] Māladeva is called *Mantri-mukhya* of king Arjunadeva.

The Paramāra inscriptions[184] refer to *Mahāmantrins* and *Mahāpradhānas* but the exact difference between them is far from being known at present. The two terms, *mahāmantrin* and *mahāpradhāna* do not appear to have been used as synonyms for one Puruṣottamadeva is described as a *Mahāmantrin* and *Mahāpradhāna* of king Yaśovarman in a Paramāra inscription. The Godarpura inscription[185] describes Ajayadeva, a minister under king Jayavarman II, as a Rājā. But it is difficult to suggest from this designation alone that ministers were often invested with a feudatory status. Whatever may have been the exact status of a minister in the Paramāra court, there is hardly any doubt that he was a highly qualified person. Rudrarāja, the minister of king Naravarman, was well grounded in the *Śāstras*; Lālārka, the minister under king Jagaddeva, was brave, truthful and pure-souled. A perusal of inscriptions would tend to suggest that the ministers of the Candella kingdom were not less qualified. Prabhāsa,[186] who served as a minister under kings Dhaṅga and Gaṇḍa, possessed excellent qualities and was an expert in the science of politics. Ananta, the Brahmin minister under kings Kīrtivarman and Sallakṣaṇavarman, was adorned with sacred knowledge, bravery, efficiency, intelligence, eloquence, resoluteness, compassion, uprightness and practical knowledge of administration. Ananta[187] was furthermore endowed with military skill as he is said to have been an expert in controlling elephants, horses and chariots, besides being a skilled archer. The minister Gadādhara[188] who served under kings Pṛthvīvarman and Madanavarman, is stated to have surpassed Bṛhaspati in the power of understanding; Lāhaḍa,[189] the minister of king Madanavarman, was well grounded in sacred texts and different arts; Gadādhara,[190] the minister of peace and war of king Paramardi, was an excellent poet; Vatsarāja,[191] the minister of king Kīrtivarman, was equal to Vācaspati in both counsel and action; Śivanāga,[192] the minister of king Vidyādhara, was an expert in sacred knowledge and military art and Mahīpāla,[193] the minister of king Vijayapāla, was truthful, intelligent and pious.

The system of appointing hereditary ministers was prevalent in the Candella kingdom. The Mau[194] inscription of the time of king Madanavarman speaks of five generations of one family, represented by Prabhāsa, Śivanāga, Mahīpāla, Ananta and Gadādhara, serving as ministers under nine generations of the Candella dynasty, including Dhaṅga, Gaṇḍa, Vidyādhara, Vijayapāla, Devavarman, Kīrtivarman, Sallakṣaṇavarman, Pṛthvīvarman and Jayavarman. Again, Lāhaḍa was a minister under Madanavarman and his descendants Sallakṣaṇa and Puruṣottama served under king Paramardideva.[195] Of the functions of the ministers in the Candella kingdom, it may be stated that one of the chief concerns of some of these ministers was to guide the foreign policy of the state. This is clear from the fact that the minister Śivanāga is said to have secured for king Vidyādhara a paramount position in the circle of kings by means of his clever policy.[196] They are also found to have played the role of military leaders. Thus the minister Jayasiṁha[197] assisted his king Jājalla in his fight with adversaries; Vatsarāja[198] is credited with the conquest of a territory by his counsel and valour. There are reasons to believe that there were occasions when ministers exercised great influence upon kings and functioned as guides. Kings Dhaṅga and Gaṇḍa obtained the threefold object of life, comprising *Dharma*, *Artha* and *Kāma*, by following the advice of the minister Prabhāsa. The Baghari stone inscription[199] tells us how king Paramardideva became, as it were, the lord of the earth with three eyes through the advice of his minister Sallakṣaṇa. The inscription would create the impression that Sallakṣaṇa constituted the third eye of the king.

References to ministers are few and far between in the Cāhamāna records. A reference to a minister is found in a Cāhamāna inscription[200] where the *Mantrin* Śrīdhara is said to have been consulted by king Vigraharāja on the course of conduct in connection with an impending struggle. The designation *Mahāpradhāna* was applied to a minister in the Yajvapāla kingdom. The Buddha pillar inscription[201] of king Gaṇapati mentions the *Mahāpradhāna* Dei or Deuva who was stationed at Kīrtidurga, probably as the governor of the area. A *Mahāpradhāna* named Dejai, Deje or Dejā under king Gopāla is mentioned in the Bangla inscription[202] where he is probably represented as the governor of the region around the Narwar fort. The inscription further tells us that the minister conducted all the business of the seal (*gadani*[*-madani*] *vyāpāra*). It is worth noting here that the practice of appointing ministers as governors of provinces was also followed by Sultan Muhammad whose Kalyan inscription[203] speaks of a minister as governing Mahārāṣṭra-*maṇḍala* in the Śaka year 1248. The India Office plate inscription[204] of Lakṣmaṇasena refers to hundred ministers in the Sena kingdom in Bengal. During this period ministers were generally designated as *Pātras* and *Mahāpātras* in Orissa. The *Tārīkh-i-Fīrūz Shāhī* of Shams-i-Sirāj tells us that in the country of Jajnagar (i.e., Orissa), the Mahtas (i.e., *Mantrins*) were called *Pātars* (i.e., *Pātras*), and the Gaṅga king Bhānudeva III (A.D. 1352-A.D. 1378) had a body of twenty such functionaries under whose advice he conducted the affairs of the kingdom.[205] *Pātra* and *Mahāpātra* are still popular surnames in Orissa.

The inscriptions of the Śīlāhāra kings of South India are specially important for the reason that they throw welcome light on the numerical strength of ministers. An inscription[206] speaks of a ministry of five members, including the *Sarvādhikārin* (either the chief minister or the minister in charge of all affairs), *Sandhivigrahin* (minister for peace and war), *Sandhivigrahin* in Kanara and *Śrīkaraṇa* (chief secretary). The list of ministers, as found in this inscription is, however, somewhat different from that found in another inscription[207] where king Anantadeva is said to have had a ministry of four members, consisting of the *Mahāmātya*, *Mahāsandhivigrahin* (the great minister of peace and war), *Mahāpradhāna* who was in charge of the treasury and *Pradhāna* who was also connected with the treasury. The following facts emerge from the above account:

First, the numerical strength of the council of ministers varied from time to time.

Second, the council of ministers was not composed of all heads of departments and sometimes the heads of important departments like the treasury were left out.

Third, there was hardly any uniformity in the designations of the heads of different departments in the same kingdom at different times.

The Western Cālukya king Someśvara I had a council of seven members,[208] comprising the *Maneverggade* (steward of the household), two *Tantrapālas*, *Pradhāna*, *Aliya* (probably the son-in-law of the king), *Aḍapa* (steward of the betel bag) and *Tasutrada-senabova* (secretary). Kālidāsa, the minister of king Jagadekamalla[209] was entitled to the use of the *Pañcamahāśabdas*. An inscription[210] of A.D. 1024 speaks of a minister who had the title *Mahāpracaṇḍadaṇḍanāyaka*, proving thereby that the ministers under the Cālukyas were also good generals. It seems that under the Cālukyas a minister would sometimes hold two or more portfolios, as was the case with the *Mahāpradhāna* Brahmadevayya who served under king Bhūlokamalla as the *Senādhipati* and *Sandhivigrahin* and with Mahādevayya[211] who was the *Maneverggade* and *Kannada Sandhivigrahin* under king Vikramāditya VI.

The ministers of the Kākatīya kingdom may broadly be divided into two categories, *Mahāpradhānas* and *Pradhānas*, the former being superior in rank to the latter. The *Mahāpradhānas* were either guides in the formulation and execution of the policy of the state or were in charge of provinces. The *Mahāpradhānas* Vepeṭi Kammayyaṅgāru, Gaṅgideva and Indulūri Gannaya guided the policy of the state; the *Mahāpradhāna* Muppiḍi Nāyaka governed Nellore-*rājya* which extended from Addaṅki in Guntur district to Kanchipuram in the south; Juttaya-leṅka Reḍḍi governed several districts including Muliki-*nāḍu*, Sakili, Pottapi-*nāḍu* and Gaṇḍikoṭa, whereas the *Mahāpradhāna* Kolani Rudradeva was in charge of Veṅgī with its headquarters at Kolanu, modern Ellore in West Godavari district. The exact functions of the *Pradhānas* are not precisely known but one such minister named Kāmaneni Boppaningāru was in charge of revenue. The view that the *Pradhānas* were mere administrative officers, as advanced by S. Sarma and N. Venkataramanayya,[212] does not appear to be correct for one such *Pradhāna* is expressly described in an epigraph at Daksharaman as a *Saciva* and *Mantri-cūḍāmaṇi*. The prominence of ministers in the Yādava kingdom is proved by a record of king Kṛṣṇa which states that the minister was the very tongue and right hand of the king himself. Jaitrapāla,[213] the chief minister of king Billama V, was a great general and statesman. The minister Nāgarasa[214] was, likewise, a prominent general and scholar.

XII

Epilogue

As is evident from the foregoing discussion, ministers constituted an important limb of the government in ancient Indian kingdoms. Ministers were selected on merit, although the question of heredity was also seriously considered at the time of appointment. In those days the social institutions of castes and families were based on essential social functions being expected to be carried on, generation to generation, by men coming from specific families and castes. Individuals developed hereditarily meaningful traits and attributes. This explains why heredity came to be regarded as a principal factor in appointment to government offices. The people had no role to play in the selection of ministers which was exclusively a royal prerogative. In no sense did they appear to be the people's representatives but were, in reality, royal servants (*bhṛtya*) who had always to work under threat of dismissal. The result was that they could seldom exercise any effective curb on the despotism of the king who had the power to annul the decision of his ministers and adopt any course of action according to his own discretion. Notwithstanding these limitations, some ministers, aided by their uncommon wisdom and strong personality, were destined to play a commanding role in the affairs of the kingdom but the number of such ministers was, no doubt, meagre.

Secondly, for appointment to ministerial posts, the candidates in ancient India were required to undergo some kind of test. The system was, however, different in ancient China where ministerial appointments were made by holding competitive examinations.

Thirdly, in ancient India ministers were generally known as *Mantrins*, *Amātyas*, *Sacivas*, *Pradhānas*, etc., although there were special designations for special ministers, as was the case with the foreign minister who was known as *Sandhivigrahin* or *Mahāsandhivigrahika*.

Fourthly, there was no uniform rule in regard to the numerical strength of ministers in ancient Indian kingdoms, the number was determined by the requirements of the state and the will of the king.

Fifthly, the system of appointing ministers as governors of administrative units was fairly popular in ancient India.

Finally, the institution of ministers, so important an organ of administration in early Indian kingdoms, did not find favour with the kings of some well-known dynasties of the ancient world like the Achaemenids and Seleucids. But the institution gained its popularity in Persia under the Sassanians when ministers were commonly known as *Divans*. The functions of ministers included 'the office of the chancellery, and dispatches, appointments and honours, justice, war and finance'.[215] At the head of the ministerial pyramid stood the grand *vizier* or prime minister who often deputized for the king during his absence, signed treaties and conventions and was given the high command of the army in the field.

References and Notes

1. I.7.9.
2. VIII.1.
3. *Śāntiparvan*, 81.1. *Na rājyam=anamātyena śakyaṁ śāstum=api trayam* (106.11-12).
4. *Ādiparvan*, 5, 37.
5. *Manusaṁhitā*, VII.55.
6. I.5.
7. XIII, 25.
8. *Nītivākyāmṛta*, Chapter X.
9. On Manu VII.54.
10. I.7.3.
11. I.8.4.
12. 110.27-29.
13. 127.8-10.

14. *EI*, IX, p. 263.
15. VII.54 and 146.
16. I.8.29.
17. *EI*, XXVI, p. 202.
18. 226.11; 235.8.
19. 218.31.
20. This work, which was also known as *Mānasollāsa*, was composed by the Western Cālukya king Someśvara III (*Cālukya-vaṁśa-tilakaḥ śrī-Someśvara-bhūpatiḥ| Kurute Mānasollāsaṁ śāstraṁ viśv=opakārakam|| Anukramaṇikā*, verse 9).
21. On the *Rāmāyaṇa*, I.7.4.
22. The *Ratnins* find mention in the *Saṁhitās of the Yajurveda* and the Brāhmaṇa literature.
23. *Taittirīya Brāhmaṇa*, I.7.3.
24. *Jātaka*, II, p. 59.
25. I.40.3.
26. VI.4.9.
27. *Jātaka*, II, p. 264.
28. *Jātaka*, I, p. 470; V, p. 187.
29. Chapter IX.
30. *Jātaka*, II, p. 2; III, p. 170.
31. *Jātaka*, III, p. 104.
32. *SONEIBT*, p. 111.
33. *Jātaka*, II, p. 380.
34. *APIIAI*, p. 136.
35. *ZDMG*, vol. 47 (1893), p. 466.
36. *SONEIBT*, pp. 150-51.
37. *Jātaka*, IV, p. 169.
38. *SONEIBT*, p. 144.
39. From the use of the epithet *sabbatthaka*, as applied to him in one of the *Jātakas* (*Atīte Vārāṇasiyaṁ Brahmadatte rajjaṁ kārento Bodhisatto tassa sabbatthako atthadhammānusāsaka-amacco ahosi| Jātaka*, II, p. 30), it is sometimes suggested that the *Attha-dhammānusāsaka-amacca* was the chief minister, *Amātya-mukhya*. This is wrong.
40. R.S. Sharma (*APIIAI*, p. 16) observes that in the *Arthaśāstra*, 'the *Amātyas* constitute a regular cadre of service from which all high officers such as the chief priest, ministers, collectors, treasurers, officers employed in civil and criminal administration, officers in charge of harem, envoys and superintendents of various departments' were recruited.
41. 1.15.34.
42. 1.15.35.
43. 1.15.36.
44. 1.15.37.
45. 1.15.41.
46. *Kauṭilya's Arthaśāstra*, p. 26.
47. 1.10.1.

48. The term *sva-vagraha*, as applied to an *Amātya*, may also mean that he must himself be easily controllable and manageable.
49. VIII.1.
50. 1.15.47.
51. 1.15.48.
52. 1.15.49.
53. 1.15.50.
54. *IHQ*, I, p. 524.
55. R. Shamasastry, *Kauṭilya's Arthaśāstra* (Mysore, 1960), p. 26.
56. Page 371.
57. Page 407.
58. M.R. Kale, *The Mudrārākṣasa* (Delhi, 1965).
59. Ibid., p. 164.
60. J.W. McCrindle, *Ancient India As Described By Magasthenes And Arrian* (Calcutta, 1960), p. 218.
61. *Aśokan Edicts* (Calcutta, 1959), pp. 13-14.
62. It is interesting to note that Patañjali in his *Mahābhāṣya* refers to Candragupta's council as *Candragupta-sabhā*. The existence of a council of ministers under the Mauryas is thus proved by the combined evidence of the *Arthaśāstra*, *Mahābhāṣya*, Aśokan edicts and *Divyāvadāna* which refers to a council of 500 members (*mantripariṣad*) under king Bindusāra. The last-named text refers to his minister Khallātaka who espoused the cause of Aśoka in his alleged contest for the throne.
63. 85, 11.
64. 7, 2.
65. The expression *trayavaraḥ* which is used in this connection is explained by Nīlakaṇṭha as 'not less than three'.
66. The *Ayodhyākāṇḍa*, 100, 74.
67. 81, 21.
68. 83, 7-10.
69. 81, 8-9.
70. P.C. Roy, *The Mahābhārata*, VII, p. 194.
71. 83, 11.
72. The *Mahābhārata* does not mention the *vyasanas*, which, however, included, as is known from other sources, hunting, dicing, indulgence in sexual enjoyment, wine, cheating, abusing and destroying things of others.
73. *The Rāmāyaṇa of Vālmīki*, translated by H.P. Sastri (London, 1952), I, p. 21.
74. Ibid., p. 370.
75. 100, 26.
76. 81, 20.
77. 81, 32.
78. 80, 64.
79. The *Āraṇyakaparvan*, 190, 21.
80. The *Sabhāparvan*, 51, 20.

81. The *Śāntiparvan*, 81, 50.
82. The *Droṇaparvan*, 67, 32.
83. The *Karṇaparvan*, 3, 51.
84. 89, 29.
85. The *Ādiparvan*, 4, 5-7.
86. The *Āraṇyakaparvan*, 57, 19-20.
87. The *Śāntiparvan*, 85, 10.
88. VII, 56.
89. VII, 226.
90. VII, 57.
91. VII, 54. It is interesting to note that the Mānava school, as cited by Kauṭilya, is in favour of twelve ministers (I, 14).
92. The expression *labdha-lakṣān* has been interpreted by Medhātithi, Govindarāja and Rucidatta as 'those who do not fail in their undertakings'.
93. A variant reading suggests *parīkṣakān* in place of *parīkṣitān*. The term would mean 'who examine the state affairs'.
94. VII, 59.
95. VII, 60.
96. VII, 62.
97. Page 146.
98. Chapter II.
99. Chapter V.
100. *TSELT*, p. 594.
101. Ibid.
102. Ibid., p. 598.
103. Ibid., p. 600.
104. Ibid.
105. D.C. Sircar, *Early Indian Political And Administrative Systems* (Calcutta, 1972), p. 77.
106. *ASI*, *AR* (1913-14), p. 134.
107. D.C. Sircar, *op. cit.*, p. 76.
108. Marshall, *Taxila*, II, p. 681, No. 27.
109. *Ṣāḍ-guṇya-niścitam-atiguhyaṁ gūḍha-pracāravān/ Mantrayet=eha mantrajño mantrajñaiḥ saha mantribhiḥ//* XII, 1.
110. IV, 24.
111. IV, 30.
112. I, 312.
113. On Yājñavalkya, I, 353.
114. I, 310.
115. I, 312.
116. 215, 2.
117. *ASI*, *AR* (1911-12), p. 53, No. 36, Pl. XIX.
118. Ibid., p. 54, No. 41.
119. Ibid., p. 53, No. 37A, Pl. XIX.
120. *ASI*, *AR* (1913-14), p. 134, No. 210, Pl. XLVII.

121. D.C. Sircar, *Early Indian Political And Administrative Systems* (Calcutta, 1972), pp. 76-77.
122. Allahabad Museum—Nos. 14, 30, 69, 73, 80, 103, 128, 131-32, 162 and 178.
123. No. 6371.
124. D.C. Sircar, *op. cit.*, p. 77.
125. Ibid., p. 80.
126. *CII*, III, pp. 104 and 108.
127. *JBBRAS*, IX, p. 284.
128. *SIP*, p. 275.
129. *The Kādambarī of Bāṇa*, translated by C.M. Ridding (1896), p. 11.
130. Ibid., pp. 49-50.
131. Ibid., p. 217.
132. Vv. 90-92.
133. *EI*, XX, pp. 37ff.
134. *SII*, II, pt. III, pp. 350-51.
135. II, 12.
136. Medhātithi on Manu VII, 54.
137. Chapter X.
138. In his *Yaśastilaka* Somadeva recommends the appointment of five *Mantrins*.
139. Chapter XXV. Elsewhere Somadeva decries the appointment of Kṣatriyas as ministers for, those who live on arms, press for the adoption of their own views by force (X, 101-103).
140. *The Nitivākyāmṛta*, p. 114.
141. Ibid., p. 185.
142. Ibid., p. 180.
143. 6.3.
144. 9.7.
145. 239.12.
146. 225.19; 225.18.
147. 339.39.
148. *EI*, XIV, p. 325.
149. Ibid., XV, p. 298.
150. *EI*, II, p. 174.
151. Ibid.
152. *CII*, IV, Introduction, p. cxi.
153. *EI*, XXI, p. 164.
154. Ibid., XII, pp. 207 and 210.
155. *IA*, VIII, p. 41.
156. *EI*, IV, p. 60.
157. Ibid., X, p. 89.
158. Ibid., IX, p. 254.
159. VII, 1043, 1145; VIII, 874, 3082-83.
160. VII. 1043, 1145.
161. VIII, 3082-83.
162. V, 253-55.

163. VII, 555.
164. IV, 51.
165. Lakṣmīdhara uses the term *maulān* and explains it as *pitṛ-paitāmahān.*
166. P. 176.
167. *Cālukya-vaṁśa-tilakaḥ śrī-Someśvara-bhūpatiḥ| Kurute Mānasollāsaṁ śāstraṁ viśv=opakārakam|| Anukramaṇikā*, v. 9.
168. XVIII, 15-37.
169. Introduction, p. 9.
170. *The Prabandhacintāmaṇi*, translated by C.H. Tawney (Calcutta, 1901), p. 33.
171. Ibid., p. 156.
172. III, 69.
173. *Purodhā ca pratinidhiḥ pradhānaḥ sacivas=tathā|| Mantrī ca prāḍvivākaś=ca paṇḍitaś=ca sumantrakaḥ| Amātyo dūta ity=etā rājñaḥ prakṛtayo daśa|| Śukranīti*, II, vv. 69-70.
174. B.K. Sarkar, *The Śukranīti*, pp. 68-69.
175. Ibid., p. 72.
176. Ibid., p. 72.
177. Ibid., Chapter II, lines 207-14.
178. Ibid., p. 183.
179. Ibid., p. 74.
180. *EI*, XXIV, p. 291.
181. *IA*, XVIII, pp. 62-64.
182. *EI*, XXXIV, pp. 141ff.
183. *IA*, VI, p. 191.
184. *EI*, XX, p. 79.
185. Ibid.
186. Ibid., I, p. 199.
187. Ibid., pp. 200 and 205.
188. Ibid., p. 206.
189. Ibid., p. 210.
190. Ibid., p. 211.
191. Ibid., p. 203.
192. Ibid., pp. 195-97.
193. Ibid., p. 195.
194. Ibid., p. 199.
195. Ibid., pp. 208-11.
196. Ibid., p. 199.
197. *IA*, XVII, p. 35.
198. *DHNI*, II, p. 700.
199. *EI*, I, pp. 207-14.
200. *IA*, XX, p. 211.
201. *EI*, XXX, pp. 111-13.
202. Ibid., XXXI, p. 331. D.C. Sircar (ibid., p. 164) is of opinion that the expression *gadani(-madani) vyāpāra* is equivalent to *mudrā-vyāpāra.*
203. *EI*, XXXII, p. 165.
204. Ibid., XXVI, p. 12.

205. Ibid., XXVIII, p. 65.
206. *IA*, V, p. 278.
207. Ibid., IX, pp. 35 and 38.
208. *EI*, XV, pp. 78-79.
209. *IA*, VI, p. 140.
210. Ibid., XIV, p. 26.
211. *EI*, XIII, p. 57.
212. *EHD*, Pts. VII-XI, p. 662.
213. *EI*, III, p. 219.
214. *IA*, XIV, p. 76.
215. R. Ghirshman, *Iran* (1965), p. 311.

6

The Sandhivigrahika

I

Definition of Ṣāḍguṇyam

The *Sandhivigrahika*, also known as *Sāndhivigrahika, Sandhivigrahādhikṛta, Sandhivigrahādhikaraṇādhikṛta* and *Sandhivigrahin* was a high-ranking officer of the state to whom were entrusted the important problems of peace (*sandhi*), war (*vigraha*), neutrality (*āsana*), marching (*yāna*), seeking refuge (*śaṁśraya*) and dual policy (*dvaidhībhāvaḥ*). In order to appreciate properly the duties and responsibilities which this officer was called upon to discharge, it is imperative to know beforehand the true implications of this sixfold measure, technically called *ṣāḍguṇyam* by Indian writers on polity.

In defining *sandhi*, Kauṭilya observes, 'Among them, entering into a treaty is peace'[1] (*tatra paṇabandhaḥ sandhiḥ*). He further points out that 'Peace, treaty, hostage, these are one and the same thing. The creation of confidence among kings is (the purpose of) peace, treaty or hostage'[2] (*Śamaḥ sandhiḥ samādhir=ity=ek=orthaḥ| rājñāṁ viśvās=opagamaḥ śamaḥ sandhiḥ samādhir=iti||*).[3] It follows from the above definition that the treaty was an agreement concluded between two kings for mutual confidence. The commentator Kullūka defines a treaty as an agreement between two kings for mutual surrender or exchange of elephants. horses, troops and money[4] (*tatr=obhay=ānugrahārthaṁ hasty=aśva-ratha-hiraṇy=ādi-nivandhanen=āvābhyām=anyonyasy=opakartavyam=iti*). The obligations connected with such a treaty were generally considered immutable but 'when conditions and circumstances changed requiring a ruler to repudiate a treaty, repudiation was permissible, and probably advisable too'.[5] Kauṭilya has enumerated five kinds of alliances comprising the *Mitra-sandhi*, pact for acquisition of an ally,[6] *Hiraṇya-sandhi*, treaty for money,[7] *Bhūmi-sandhi*, alliance for acquisition of lands,[8] *Anavasita-sandhi*, agreement for planting a colony in unsettled lands,[9] and *Karma-sandhi*, alliance for an undertaking.[10] The king is advised to conclude peace in view of the following circumstances:[11]

To ruin the enemy's undertakings by those of his own, bearing abundant fruits;

To enjoy the fruits of his own productive works or of those of his enemy;

To utilise the confidence derived from the treaty to ruin the enemy's undertakings by the employment of secret remedies and occult practices;

To seduce the enemy's skilled workers by offering them facilities or favours, exemptions and a higher remuneration;

To induce the enemy, in alliance with an extremely strong king, to ruin his own undertakings;

To prolong the enemy's war with a king under whose pressure the enemy has made peace with himself;

To induce the enemy to harass another hostile king;

To annex the enemy's territory, laid waste by his enemy;

To ensure the security of the kingdom from any possible attack from the enemy;

To achieve advancement in his own undertakings;

To detach the enemy from his circle of kings and win over the latter to his side; and lastly,

To create between the enemy and his circle hostility, culminating in the former's destruction.

While defining *vigraha*, Kauṭilya observes: 'Doing injury is war'[12] (*apakāro vigrahaḥ*). According to Śukra,[13] 'That is said to be *vigraha* or war by which the enemy is oppressed and subjugated.' It would, therefore, follow that mere outbreak of hostilities could not make war unless it was backed by a desire to do harm. Kauṭilya advises the king to wage war in the following circumstances:[14]

When his kingdom is rich in troops or is guarded by forts with one way of exit and is thus capable of warding off the enemy's attack;

When he is able to ruin the enemy's undertakings by taking shelter in an impregnable fort on the border of his kingdom;

When the enemy, being depressed by a calamity, has reached a time when his undertakings face ruin; and

When the enemy is fighting elsewhere.

Kauṭilya defines *āsana* as follows: 'Remaining indifferent is staying quiet'[15] (*upekṣaṇam=āsanam*). The commentator Kullūka[16] has used the word *nirapekṣya*, impartiality, to explain the term *āsana*. Kṣīrasvāmī has interpreted *āsana* to mean abstention from war (*āsanaṁ vigrah=ādi-nivṛttiḥ*). Śukra[17] points out that 'An *āsana* is said to be that from which one's self can be protected and the enemy is destroyed.' An *āsana* may accordingly be interpreted as an opportunistic neutrality which would prove beneficial to the king but ruinous for the enemy. The king is urged to adopt neutrality in the following circumstances:[18]

When the king feels that neither he nor his enemy is capable of ruining the work of the other; and

When their mutual conflict would be like that of the hound and the boar.

In defining *yāna*, Kauṭilya points out that 'Augmentation (of power) is marching'[19] (*abhyuccayo yānam*). *Yāna* has been interpreted by Kullūka[20] to mean an offensive march against the enemy (*yānaṁ śatruṁ pratigamanam*). Śukra[21] has used the term to mean an expedition for the furtherance of one's own objects and destruction of the enemy's interests. The king is advised to launch an attack against the enemy when he realises that the enemy's work can be ruined only thereby and that the defence of his own works has been safeguarded.[22]

Kauṭilya has defined *śaṁśraya* to mean 'submitting to another'[23] (*par=ārpaṇaṁ śaṁśrayaḥ*). Kullūka[24] points out that seeking shelter means to take refuge with a stronger king when oppressed by the enemy (*śatru-pīḍitasya pravalatara-rāj=āntar =āśrayanaṁ śaṁśrayaḥ*). Manu[25] points out that *śaṁśraya* is of two kinds (*dvividhaḥ śaṁśrayaḥ*); a king, being oppressed by the enemy, may seek the protection of another, and secondly, a king, anticipating similar troubles in future, may seek the protection of another king. The king is advised to seek refuge when he feels that he is incapable of ruining the enemy's undertakings nor is he able to avert the ruin of his own works.[26]

In explaining *dvaidhībhāva* Kauṭilya[27] points out that 'Resorting to peace (with one) and war (with another) is dual policy' (*sandhi-vigrah=opādānaṁ dvaidhībhāvaḥ*). A similar interpretation has also been advanced by Kullūka[28] (*kenacit sandhiṁ kencid=vigraham=ity=ādikam*). The king is advised to pursue this policy when he feels that he can promote his own undertakings by making a treaty with one king and ruin the enemy's works by making war with him.[29]

While evaluating the aforesaid six measures of foreign policy, Kauṭilya[30] observes: 'If there is equal advancement in peace or war, he should resort to peace. For, in war there are losses, expenses, marches away from home and hindrances. By that is explained (preference for) staying quiet, as between staying quiet and marching. As between dual policy and seeking shelter, he should resort to dual policy. For, he who resorts to the dual policy, giving prominence to his own undertakings, serves only his own interests, while he who takes shelter (with another) serves the interests of the other, not his own.' 'This extract,' writes U.N. Ghosal,[31] 'involves the principle that while progress should be the fundamental objective of all types of foreign policy, the selection of the particular type should be made so as to ensure for the king his maximum advantage.' But this arduous task could hardly be successfully discharged by the king unless he was aided by his wise counsellors. A special class of officers, called the *Sandhivigrahikas*, was accordingly created to advise the monarch on inter-state relations.

II

Evidence of the Manu-Saṁhitā

Since early days, India was usually studded with a large number of states which had been maintaining intercourse among themselves in times of peace and war. But it is rather strange that we do not hear of any foreign minister in Indian kingdoms till we come to the age of Manu[32] who urges the king to consult his Brāhmaṇa minister on matters relating to the sixfold measure of foreign policy (*Sarveṣāṁ tu viśiṣṭena brāhmaṇena vipaścitā| mantrayet paramaṁ mantraṁ rājā ṣāḍguṇya-saṁyutam||*). It seems that in the earlier period inter-state relations were the joint responsibility of the ministry and that no special minister was appointed to deal with them.

III

The Sandhivigrahika in Gupta and Other Contemporary Kingdoms

The earliest mention of the *Sāndhivigrahika* seems to occur in the famous Allahabad *praśasti* where Hariṣeṇa is said to have been holding the same office during the reign of the emperor Samudragupta[33] (*Sāndhivigrahika-kumārāmātya-mahādaṇḍanāyaka-Hariṣeṇasya*). The Udayagiri cave inscription of G.E. 82 speaks of Vīrasena Śāba as the incumbent of the same post under Candragupta II[34] (*anvaya-prāpta-sācivyo vyāpṛta-sandhi-vigrahaḥ*). It seems that military leadership was considered one of the essential qualifications expected of a foreign minister. Hariṣeṇa is described as a *Mahādaṇḍanāyaka*, military general, although the use of the term *daṇḍa* in the sense of 'fine' and 'rod' (of chastisement) is not unknown. Śāba is also known to have joined hands with the emperor in his campaign against the Śakas of Western India[35] (*kṛtsna-pṛthvī-jayārthena rājñ=aiv=eha sah=āgataḥ*). He is further described as being well grounded in the science of politics and poetics[36] (*śabd=ārtha-nyāya-nītijñaḥ kavi pāṭaliputrakaḥ*). It is, therefore, evident that besides being proficient in the military art, the *Sāndhivigrahika* was expected to be well-versed in the cultivation of political science as well. As the cases of Hariṣeṇa and Śāba would demonstrate, the *Sāndhivigrahikas* were generally recruited from amongst the members of those families which were holding the ministerial posts for more than one generation. It cannot escape notice that the *Sāndhivigrahika* must have been the busiest minister in the Gupta kingdom when Samudragupta and Candragupta II were planning their campaigns in different parts of India. It was the prerogative of his department to decide which kingdoms were to be annexed, which were to be allowed to remain as vassal states and which were to be left undisturbed.

That the good service of the *Sandhivigrahika* was often utilised by several other states of contemporary India is conclusively proved by a large number of inscriptional records discovered from different parts of the country. The Khoh copper plate grant of *Mahārāja* Hastin of the year 163 mentions Sūryadatta as serving in the capacity of a foreign minister in the Parivrājaka kingdom. It was he who composed the charter[37] (*likhitañ=ca . . . bhogika Ravidatta putreṇa mahāsāndhivigrahika-Sūryadattena*). Sūryadatta's son Vibhudatta occupied the office of the *Mahāsāndhivigrahika* under the same *Mahārāja* Hastin twenty-eight years later and was the writer of the Majhgawan copper plate inscription of the year 191[38] (*likhitañ=ca Sūryadatta-putreṇa mahāsāndhivigrahika-Vibhudatten=eti*). Gallu was the *Sandhivigrahika* under the Ucchakalpas in A.D. 496[39] (*bhogika-Phālgudatt=āmātya-naptā bhogika-Varāhadinna-puttra sāndhi-vigrahika-Gallunā*) to be followed in the office by his younger brother Manoratha who is reputed to have composed the Khoh copper plate inscription in A.D. 512[40] (*likhitaṁ saṁvatsara-śate tri-navaty=uttare caitra-māsa-divase daśame bhogika-Phālgudatt=āmātya-naptā bhogika-Varāhadinna putreṇa mahā-sāndhivigrahika-Manorathena*). The title *Mahāsāndhivigrahika*, as applied to some royal officials in these records, would suggest that in the department of external affairs in those kingdoms, there were a few *Sandhivigrahikas* who worked as subordinate officers under the supreme officer of the department. As in the Gupta kingdom, in other states also we often find a tendency for the ministerial office to become hereditary, as is demonstrated by the cases of Sūryadatta and Gallu both of whom were succeeded to their office by their kinsmen.

IV

The Sandhivigrahika in the Post-Gupta Period

The references to the *Sandhivigrahikas* are not less numerous in the inscriptions of the post-Gupta period. The Palitana copper plates[41] of Dharasena II, dated Gupta year 252, speak of a *Sandhivigrahādhikṛta*, named Skandabhaṭa who is known to have composed the edict[42] (*likhitaṁ sandhivigrahādhikṛta-Skandabhaṭena*). It is of interest to note that Skandabhaṭa served both Dharasena II[43] and his father and predecessor Guhasena.[44] A Central Indian epigraph[45] of A.D. 592 records that the *Dūtaka* of the document was Bhaḍḍaka who was the officer in charge of the department of peace and war[46] (*dūtako=tra-sandhivigrahādhikaraṇādhikṛta-Bhaḍḍakaḥ*). The Sarsabani copper plate grant of the Kalacuri monarch Buddharāja, issued in A.D. 609-10, mentions a *Mahāsandhivigrahādhikṛta* named Śivarāja as the writer of the charter[47] (*likhitam=idam mahāsandhivigrahādhikaraṇādhikṛta Śivarājen=eti*). The Mallasarul copper plates[48] mention a *Sāndhivigrahika* named Bhogacandra as having drafted the grant (*likhitaṁ sāndhivigrahika-Bhogacandreṇa*). The Jayrampur copper plate grant[49] of the same monarch Gopacandra, however, does not take any notice of any *Sandhivigrahika* and the task of composing the charter, as we are told in the inscription, was entrusted to a Kāyastha named Mānadatta[50] (*likhitaṁ kāyastha-Mānadatten eti*). The Chandeswar copper plates[51] of the Śailodbhava king Mānabhīta Dharmarāja mention the *Sāndhivigrahika Bhogin* Sāmanta as the writer of the charter (*likhitaṁ sāndhivigrahika-bhogi-sāmantena*). Thus while the *Sandhivigrahikas* generally figure in these inscriptions as writers of charters, a few of them are known to have acted as conveyors of the royal approval regarding land-grants. The load of these duties, which could have been successfully borne by some minor officers as well, must have adversely affected the energy and resourcefulness of a foreign minister whose main responsibility was to safeguard the security of the kingdom by a cautious handling of matters relating to peace and war.

Useful information about the office of the foreign minister during the post-Gupta period may further be obtained from contemporary literature as well. The office of the *Mahāsandhivigrahādhikṛta* was not unknown to Bāṇa[52] who refers to Avanti as the incumbent of this post under king Harṣavardhana. He sat near the king in the assembly, and was dictated by the Puṣyabhūti king his proclamation of *dig-vijaya*. In making his decision of conquests, Harṣa hardly felt the need of consulting his supreme minister of peace and war but asked him to act in consonance with his instructions. Kalhaṇa's *Rājataraṅgiṇī*,[53] which was, however, composed at a much later date, speaks of Mitraśarman, the *Sāndhivigrahika* of Lalitāditya, king of Kashmir, as being present at the time of drafting the treaty between Lalitāditya and king Yaśovarman of Kanauj and as objecting to recording the latter's name first in the treaty.

V

The Sandhivigrahika in Early Mediaeval Indian Kingdoms

Welcome light on the status and position of the *Sandhivigrahikas* in different early mediaeval Indian kingdoms is thrown by the inscriptions of the contemporary period. The *Sandhivigrahika* Mahindaka was the writer of the Haddala grant[54] of the Gurjara Pratīhāra monarch Mahīpāla. A foreign minister named Ṭhakkura Puruṣottama is mentioned in the Jubbalpore Kotwali copper plates of the Kalacuri king Jayasiṁhadeva, while another officer of the same department, Cāhīla, is known to have acted as the *Dūtaka* of the Sunaka plate of Karṇadeva.[55] The Mandhata plates[56] of the Paramāra king Devapāla speak of the *Mahāsāndhivigrahika* Bilhaṇa with whose approbation the grant was recorded by the king's preceptor Madana[57] (*racitam=idaṁ=mahāsāndhivigrahika-paṇḍita-śrī-Bilhaṇa - saṁmatena rāja-guruṇā Madanena*). He is applauded as being blessed with learning. Bilhaṇa is likewise known from Arjunavarman's grant[58] where he is described as the minister of peace and war. The poet Āṣāḍha in his *Dharmāmṛta*[59] refers to the 'learned Bilhaṇa, the lord of poets' as the '*Mahāsāndhivigrahika* of the glorious Vindhya' (*Vindhyabhūpati*). Since this king Vindhya has usually been identified with Arjunavarman's grandfather Vindhyavarman, it may be reasonably held that Bilhaṇa enjoyed the confidence of no less than four successive kings of Mālava from Vindhyavarman to Devapāla. The description of the qualities of Bilhaṇa would remind us of a similar one of those of Vīrasena Śāba, as found in the Udaygiri cave inscription of the Gupta period. Gadādhara, the minister of peace and war of the Candella king Paramardi, is expressly described as an excellent poet.[60] The *Sandhivigrahika* Khelāditya drafted the grant, as recorded in the Kiradu stone pillar inscription[61] of the Caulukya king Kumārapāla. The *Dūtaka* of the Radhanpur plate[62] of king Bhīma of the same dynasty was the *Sandhivigrahika* Candraśarman.

The *Mahāsandhivigrahin* finds frequent mention in the inscriptions of the Somavaṁśī kings of Orissa and Madhya Pradesh. It is known from the Sonpur copper plates[63] and the Nagpur Museum plates[64] of Mahābhavagupta II Janamejaya that a *Mahākṣapaṭalin* named Alava was connected with (*prati-*

baddha) the *Mahāsandhivigrahin*. The testimony of these inscriptions suggests that the minister of peace and war was entitled to some sort of control over the department of accounts.[65] One of the foreign ministers under the Somavaṁśīs was Malladatta who appears to have served in the same capacity for a long time, for he figures both in the Patna plates[66] and the Cuttack grants[67] of the 6th and the 31st years, respectively, of the reign of Mahābhavagupta II Janamejaya. The Daspalla grant[68] of the year 184 mentions the *Sandhivigrahin* Yaśodatta as having received the grant of a village at the hands of king Devānanda II. He is further described as belonging to the Kāyastha caste. The Orissa plates[69] of Vidyādharabhañja mention that the grant, recorded in those plates, was written by Arkadeva (*likhitañ=ca sāndhivigrahika-Arka devena*) who is described as the minister of peace and war. The Musunika grant[70] of the Gaṅga king Devendravarman III mentions the *Mahāsāndhivigrahika* Sarvacandra as the scribe of the record. It is interesting to note that Sarvacandra is mentioned in the Chicacole plates, issued two years later, as a *Sāmanta* and in the Tekkali plates, which were issued at a still subsequent date, as a *Rahasya*, private secretary, of the king. It seems that the Gaṅgas hardly allowed their officers to remain associated with a particular office for long but transferred them, quite frequently, from one office to another.

The *Sandhivigrahikas* are prominently mentioned in the inscriptions from Bengal also. The Belwa copper plates[71] of Mahīpāla I and those[72] of Vigrahapāla III mention the *Mahāsāndhivigrahika* in the list of officials who were requested by the king to protect their grant. The Manahali grant of Madanapāla mentions a *Mahāsāndhivigrahika* in the list of officials, being entrusted with the protection of the grant and a *Sāndhivigrahika*, named Bhīmadeva, who was appointed the messenger.[73] The Bhubaneswar *Praśasti*[74] of Bhaṭṭa Bhavadeva gives the account of a Brāhmaṇa family which produced some successive generations of the *Sāndhivigrahikas*. The earliest of them was Ādideva who served as foreign minister under a Candra king, described in the inscription as ruler of Vaṅga. 'He enjoyed the greatest confidence of his master,' writes B.C. Sen,[75] commenting on the position of Ādideva in the government, 'as he was allowed, not in his private capacity, but as a *Saciva*, to enjoy the company of the king when he was free from all preoccupations; that is to say, matters of statecraft used to be discussed in complete privacy between these two persons.' An outstanding personality, Bhaṭṭa Bhavadeva, who flourished in a subsequent period, serving under Harivarmadeva, is described as being well acquainted with the *Vedas*, the *Āgamas*, the *Arthaśāstra*, the science of medicine, the science relating to the use of arms, *Siddhānta, Tantra, Gaṇita* and the *Phalasaṁhitā*. As B.C. Sen[76] points out, 'There seems to be no doubt that his functions were the same as those of his ancestor Ādideva; he was a *Mantrī* and *Saciva* like him, his principal authority being associated with *Mantra-śakti* which means the policy of war and peace.' Harighoṣa served as a *Sāndhivigrahika* under Vallālasena and performed the duties of a *Dūtaka* in connection with the grant recorded in the Naihati copper plates.[77] Lakṣmaṇasena's *Sandhivigrahika* was entrusted with the work of a messenger in connection with his Tarpandighi,[78] Govindapur[79] and Anulia[80] grants. The *Sāndhivigrahika* Nāñisiṁha, who served under the later Sena monarch Viśvarūpasena, carried out similar functions in respect of the Sahitya Parisad grant.[81] In the Madanpada grant[82] of Viśvarūpasena mention is made of a *Gauḍa-Sāndhivigrahika*. B.C. Sen[83] is of opinion that he was so called because he was serving under a Gauḍa king. It is not unlikely that this foreign minister was appointed to look after the affairs of Gauḍa which formed a part of his master's dominions. The Madanpur plate[84] of Śrīcandra mentions that the record was officially approved by the *Mahāsāndhivigrahika*, proving thereby that the minister of peace and war was intimately connected with land grants also.

The frequent mention of the *Mahāsandhivigrahika* and the *Sandhivigrahika* in the Rāṣṭrakūṭa records would tend to suggest that several ministers were associated with the department of peace and war. The *Mahāsandhivigrahika* was the superior officer of the department, having under him several ordinary *Sandhivigrahikas* to assist him in his work. This inference, suggested by the formation of the two words, *mahān* and *sandhivigrahika*, is further confirmed by the Bhandup plates[85] of the Śilāhāra king Cittarājadeva which speak of Sīhapeya and śrī-Kapardin as the principal *Sandhivigrahika* and the *Karṇāṭa-Sandhivigrahika*, respectively. It seems that under the Rāṣṭrakūṭas even feudatory kings were empowered to appoint foreign ministers for their own kingdoms. Karkarāja Suvarṇavarṣa, who was ruling over Southern Gujarat as a feudatory of his uncle, the Rāṣṭrakūṭa emperor Govinda III, had under him a foreign minister (*Mahāsandhivigrahādhipati*) named Nārāyaṇa who is reputed to have drafted the Surat plates.[86] Nārāyaṇa happened to be the son of Durgabhaṭṭa who is also known to have held the important post of chief foreign minister. It may accordingly be suggested that succession to this important office was occasionally hereditary.

The importance of these foreign ministers in the Rāṣṭrakūṭa administration is revealed by an inscription[87] which describes Nārāyaṇa, a foreign minister under Kṛṣṇa III, as another hand (*pratihasta*) of the king. The high position of these officers is further borne out by the fact that the status of a *Sāmanta* and the *Pañcamahāśabdas* were conferred upon them not unoften. It may be noted in this connection that the meaning of the expression *sam=adhigata-pañca-mahāśabda* was different for different parts of India. In most of North Indian records, the five titles appear as the five official designations, beginning with the word *mahā*,[88] viz., the *Mahāpratīhāra*, superintendent of the king's chamber or of the gate and guards of the palace or capital city, the *Mahāsandhivigrahika*, the *Mahāśvaśālādhikṛta*, superintendent of stables, the *Mahābhāṇḍāgārika*, treasurer, and the *Mahāsādhanika*, commander of the forces. The expression seems to have been used in some West Indian records[89] to mean the five titles, including the *Mahārāja*, *Mahāsāmanta*, *Mahākārtākṛtika*, *Mahādaṇḍanāyaka* and *Mahāpartīhāra*. In South India,[90] however, the tittle seems to refer to the privilege granted by the overlord to enjoy the sounds of five kinds of musical instruments, comprising the trumpet, tambour, conch-shell used as a horn, kettledrum and gong.

The *Mahāsandhivigrahika* is generally represented in the Rāṣṭrakūṭa records as being entrusted with the drafting of the copper plate charters. The connection of the office of the *Sandhivigrahika* with the drafting of land grants is likewise established by Smṛti literature. While commenting on a passage of Yājñavalkya, Vijñāneśvara quotes the following anonymous verse:[91]

sandhivigrahakārī tu bhavedyas=tasya lekhakaḥ|
svayaṁ rājñā sam=ādiṣṭaḥ sa likhed=rāja-śāsanam||

'The drafter (of the copper plate charter) should be the person who is the foreign minister; he should draft the charter as instructed by the king himself.' Vijñāneśvara further says that the charter should be caused to be drafted by the foreign minister and by no one else (*Sandhivigrahakāriṇā śāsanaṁ kārayet n=ānyena kenacit*). But the reasons why the right of drafting all the copper plate grants was vested in the *Sandhivigrahika*, instead of the revenue minister, are not precisely known. A land-grant, as a rule, contains an account of the genealogy of the donor as well as the details about the grantee and the village, to be granted. A.S. Altekar[92] holds that the *Sandhivigrahika* drafted all such land-charters because in the archives of the foreign office were preserved the most reliable and up-to-date materials on the exploits of the donor, to be incorporated in the grants. But it is difficult to agree that none but the foreign minister had access to the materials preserved in the state archive. R.S. Sharma[93] has advanced a new theory on this issue; he says, 'Since peacetime relations with the vassals consisted in stipulating tributes levied on grants of land or in confirming the jurisdiction of the vassal over the fiefs, he (i.e., the *Sandhivigrahika*) drafted all secular charters and even those relating to land grants to Brāhmaṇas and temples.' But the main defect of this theory lies in its assertion that no royal grant would be made without involving a feudal lord. It is not unlikely that the *Sandhivigrahika* was preferred to the rest as the writer of the royal charter because of his superior skill in penmanship, to which most of the early mediaeval Indian writers on polity would bear witness. This suggestion, it must be admitted, should only be regarded as one belonging to the realm of probability.

By the time of the Cālukya kings of Kalyāṇī, the foreign ministry, on the ground of its efficient functioning, came to be divided into two or three broad divisions, each being spearheaded by a separate minister. Epigraphs speak of the following foreign ministers of the Western Cālukya kingdom:

1. *Kannaḍa-Sāndhivigrahika.*[94] He was in charge of the

Karṇāṭaka division which formed the southern half of the Cālukya kingdom.

2. *Lāta-Sāndhivigrahika.*[95] He was entrusted with the affairs of the northern part of the kingdom which was styled Lāṭa or Lāta.

3. *Heri Sāndhivigrahika.*[96] It is sometimes argued[97] that *Heri-Sāndhivigrahika* was a minister in charge of the secret intelligence department of the foreign ministry. Such a hypothesis does not find favour with K.A. Nilkanta Sastri,[98] who points out that the term *heri* 'merely implies the seniority of the particular officer above others doing similar work under him'. If this view be accepted, '*Heri-sāndhivigrahika* may indeed well have been the Kannaḍa form of the expression *Mahā sāndhivigrahika* which occurs in a record of A D. 1066.'[99]

It is of interest to note that the *Kannaḍa-Sāndhivigrahika* and the *Lāta Sāndhivigrahika*, as is suggested by the etymology of the two words, were in charge of the two divisions of the Cālukya kingdom, and it is not clear how far they were connected with the maintenance of the relations of the state with foreign powers. It appears to be fairly certain that their duties were primarily connected with the relation of the suzerain power to the quasi-independent vassal chiefs within their respective jurisdictions. These feudal chiefs, as K.A. Nilkanta Sastri[100] rightly points out, 'belonged to ancient ruling families, cherished memories of past glory and hopes of future independence, and maintained private armies of their own; their relation with the suzerain power must have always given rise to a number of delicate problems which could be handled successfully only by the employment of diplomatic methods.'

The Sanskrit text *Mānasollāsa*,[101] which was composed during this period, while bringing to light some of the notable qualifications of a *Sandhivigrahika*, lays down that he should be intelligent as well as efficient, be thoroughly conversant with numerous languages and scripts, skilful in summoning and dismissing and in installing the various categories of feudatories like the *Maṇḍaleśas*, *Sāmantas* and *Mānyakas*, adept in the sixfold policy and an expert in finance.

The information about the office of the minister of peace and war, as gleaned from epigraphic evidence, is corroborated and supplemented by literary documents. The *Agni Purāṇa*,[102] for instance, insists on the appointment of a foreign minister who should be well grounded in the sixfold policy of the state (*sāndhivigrahiko kāryo ṣāḍguṇy=ādi-viśāradaḥ*). The *Matsya Purāṇa*[103] points out that proficiency in the sixfold policy, sound knowledge of languages and countries and diplomacy were some of the qualities of an efficient *Sāndhivigrahika* (*Ṣāḍguṇya-vidhi-tatvajño deśa-bhāṣā viśāradaḥ| sāndhivigrahikaḥ kāryo rājñā naya-viśāradaḥ||*). A similar interesting account of the *Sāndhivigrahika* is provided by the *Viṣṇudharmottara Purāṇa*[104] which lays down that the foreign minister should be endowed with the knowledge of countries and their languages, statesmanship, beauty, youth, intelligence, firm loyalty and noble birth. He should keep himself abreast of the know-how of income and expenditure and be able to find out the loyalty and disaffection of the royal servants and capable of defending the country.

The evidence of the *Yaśastilaka-campū*, composed by Somadeva, in regard to the office of the *Sāndhivigrahika* is of no mean importance. It is laid down that the foreign minister should be well-versed in grammar, logic, scripts, language, caste regulations, the laws (*vyavahāra*) and usages (*sthiti*). Endowed with great presence of mind, he should be able not only to analyse things but also to read and write fluently (*Vācayati likhati kavate gamayati sarvālipiś=ca bhāṣāś=ca| ātma-para-sthiti-kuśalaḥ sapratibhaḥ sāndhivigrahī kāryaḥ||*. The *Nītivākyāmṛta*[105] tells us that the *Sāndhivigrahika* should possess the knowledge of grammar, logic, power of fluent talking, wisdom, discretionary power, be conversant with most of the languages and alphabet and be well-grounded in the knowledge of time, place and *varṇāśrama*. The requisite intelligence in rapid reading and writing was another essential quality, expected of this minister. Equally important is the testimony of the *Kathākośa* of Jineśvara which speaks of a *Sandhivigrahika* as being sent by a king to one of his rebellious feudatories with the instruction that he should act as circumstances demanded. His duties in this case compare favourably with those of the *Nisṛṣṭārtha*, as mentioned by Kauṭilya and other writers on polity.

The *Sāndhivigrahika* finds mention in the *Rājadharmakāṇḍa* section of the *Kṛtyakalpataru* where we find some interesting details of the qualifications expected of him. It is laid down that he should be an adept in the sixfold policy, a judge of opportunity and a diplomat[106] (*Ṣāḍguṇyavidhi-tatvajño deśa-kāla-viśāradaḥ| sāndhi-vigrahikaḥ kāryo rājñā naya-viśāradaḥ||*). It is worth remembering that this description of the qualifications of a foreign minister has been provided by a man who himself was appointed to the high office of the *Sāndhivigrahika* during the reign of the Gāhaḍavāla king Govindacandra[107] (*śrīmad=Govindacandra-mahārāja-sandhivigrahika-śrī-Lakṣmīdharabhaṭṭa*). It may be noted that Lakṣmīdhara[108] refers to himself as a *Mantrīśvara*, chief minister as well. This would prove that there were occasions when the two offices were combined in one person.

The foreign minister is called the *Mantrī* in the *Śukranīti* and not the *Sandhivigrahika*, as he was more popularly known in contemporary India. It was the duty of the *Mantrī* to study when, how and to whom (*keṣu kadā kattaṁ*) the fourfold policy of *sāma*, *dāma*, *daṇḍa* and *bheda*[110] was to be adopted (*sāma-dāmañ=ca bhedaś=ca daṁḍaḥ*) and the various effects of each of the policies whatsoever great, moderate or small they were[111] (*kartavyaḥ kiṁ phalaṁ tebhyo bahu madhyaṁ tath=ālpakam*). He decided on the course of action first and subsequently communicated the same to the king for approval[112] (*etat=saṁcintya niścitya mantrī sarvaṁ nivedayet*). Śukra elsewhere[113] points out that the *Mantrī* was one who was adept in diplomacy (*Mantrī tu nīti-kuśalaḥ*). The account of Śukra is interesting for two reasons. First, he had no control over military affairs which passed into the hands of the *Saciva*, war minister, and second, no decision of the *Mantrī*, unless it was approved by the king, would be reckoned as final. Even then the status of the *Mantrī* was of no mean significance; for, he was included, along with the *Purodhā*, *Pratinidhi*, *Pradhāna*, *Saciva*, *Prāḍvivāka*, *Paṇḍita*, *Sumantra*, *Amātya* and *Dūta*, in the list of the ten principal officers (*prakṛtayo daśa*) of the kingdom.[114]

The Jaina work *Prabandhacintāmaṇi*[115] refers to a *Sāndhivigrahika* as being sent by king Bhoja of Malava to the court of the Caulukya king Bhīma of Gujarat. Occasions were then not infrequent when these officers acted as emissaries to foreign courts to cement friendship between the two kings or to iron out differences that were likely to jeopardise their relations.

VI

Functions of the Mahāsāmantādhipati

In some of the inscriptions of later times, reference is made to an officer called *Mahāsāmantādhipati* who was very probably the minister in charge of the department dealing with feudal vassals. T.V. Mahalingam[116] is of opinion that he took the place of the *Sandhivigrahika* of earlier times.

References and Notes

1. VII, 6.
2. *KA*, p. 434.
3. VII, 17, 1-2.
4. Kullūka on Manu VII, 160.
5. *IRAI*, p. 68.
6. VII, 9.
7. VII, 9.
8. VII, 10.
9. VII, 11.
10. VII, 12.
11. VII, 1, 32.
12. VII, 1, 7.
13. B.K. Sarkar, *op. cit.*, IV, 7, 468-69.
14. VII, 1, 33.
15. VII, 1, 8.
16. Kullūka on Manu VII, 161.
17. B.K. Sarkar, *op. cit.*, IV, 7, 471.
18. *Arthaśāstra* VII, 1, 34.
19. VII, 1, 9.
20. Kullūka on Manu VII, 160.
21. B.K. Sarkar, *op. cit.*, IV, 7, 470.
22. *Arthaśāstra* VII, 1, 35.
23. VII, 1, 10.
24. Kullūka on Manu VII, 160.
25. VII, 168.
26. *Arthaśāstra* VII, 1, 36.
27. VII, 1, 11.
28. Kullūka on Manu VII, 161.
29. *Arthaśāstra* VII, 1, 37.
30. *KA*, p. 376; VII, 2, 1-5.
31. *HIPI*.
32. VII, 58.
33. *SI*, p. 268.
34. Ibid., p. 280.

35. Ibid.
36. Ibid.
37. *CII*, III, p. 104.
38. Ibid., p. 108.
39. Ibid., p. 123.
40. *SI*, p. 393.
41. *EI*, XI, pp. 80ff.
42. Ibid., p. 84.
43. *CII*, III, p. 167.
44. *IA*, IV, p. 175; ibid., V, p. 207.
45. *EI*, XXX, pp. 163ff.
46. Ibid., p. 181.
47. Ibid., VI, p. 299.
48. *SI*, p. 377.
49. Ibid., pp. 530ff.
50. Ibid., p. 531.
51. *EI*, XXX, pp. 269ff.
52. *The Harṣacarita of Bāṇa*. Translated by E.B. Cowell and F.W. Thomas, Delhi, 1961, p. 187.
53. IV, 137-38.
54. *IA*, XII, pp. 190-95.
55. *EI*, I, p. 317.
56. *EI*, IX, pp. 103ff.
57. Ibid., p. 113.
58. Ibid., p. 107.
59. See Bhandarkar's *Report on the search for Sanskrit MSS. during 1883-84*, p. 391.
60. *PIA*, p. 86.
61. *EI*, IX, pp. 63-65.
62. *IA*, VI, p. 193.
63. *EI*, XXIII, pp. 248ff.
64. Ibid., VIII, pp. 143ff.
65. The term *akṣapaṭala* has been variously rendered as 'record office', 'court of rolls', 'court of justice', 'archive' and 'Accountant General's Office'.
66. *Bhandarkar's List*, No. 15558.
67. Ibid , Nos. 1562-64.
68. *EI*, XXIX, p. 186.
69. *EI*, IX, p. 272.
70. Ibid., XXX, pp. 23ff.
71. *EI*, XXIX, pp. 1ff.
72. Ibid., pp. 9ff.
73. *JASB*, LXIX, pp. 68ff; A.K. Maitreya, *Gauḍa-lekhamālā*, pp. 147ff.
74. *PIHC*, Calcutta, 1939, pp. 313ff.
75. *SHAIB*, p. 545.
76. *SHAIB*, p. 546.
77. *EI*, XIV, pp. 156ff.

78. Ibid., XII, pp. 6ff.
79. *IB*, pp. 92ff.
80. Ibid., pp. 81ff.
81. *IHQ*, II, p. 77; *IB*, pp. 140ff.
82. *EI*, XXXIII, p. 315.
83. *SHAIB*, p. 553.
84. *EI*, XXVIII, pp. 51ff.
85. *RT*, p. 167.
86. *EI*, XXI, pp. 146ff.
87. Ibid., IV, p. 60.
88. *IE*, p. 342.
89. Ibid.
90. Ibid.
91. The *Mitākṣarā* on Yājñavalkya I, 319-20.
92. *RT*, p. 166. A similar view has been advanced by V.V. Mirashi (*CII*, IV, pp. cxiii-iv) who observes: 'The Department of Peace and War was most likely to have an accurate information about the conquests of the king and his ancestors which were generally described in the initial part of such charters.' P.B. Udgaonkar (*PIA*, p. 98) holds the same view.
93. *IF*, p. 103.
94. *SII*, IX(i), 223.
95. *SII*, IX(i), 240.
96. *EI*, XVI, p. 45.
97. Ibid.
98. *EHD*, p. 389.
99. Ibid.
100. Ibid.
101. S.S. Mishra, *Mānasollāsa—Ek Sāṁskṛtik Adhyayan*, Banaras, 1966, pp. 160-61.
102. 220, 3.
103. 215, 16. The expression *naya-viśāradaḥ* has been explained as *naye nītau viśārado vijñaḥ/ nīti-śāstrajñaḥ*.
104. II, 24, 16-17.
105. *Nītivākyāmṛta*, p. 379.
106. *Kṛtyakalpataru* of Bhaṭṭa Lakṣmīdhara, XI, *Rājadharmakāṇḍa*, Gaekwad's Oriental Series, Baroda, 1943, p. 26.
107. Ibid., p. 212.
108. Ibid., p. 50.
109. II, 89, II, 95. In Śivājī's cabinet, the foreign minister was called *Mantrī*.
110. In the vast majority of Indian texts, the four political expedients are referred to as conciliation, bribery, creating dissension and force. Kāmandaka and Bṛhaspati have added to these four primary expedients a supplementary list, comprising deceit (*māyā*), indifference (*upekṣā*) and creating illusion (*indrajāla*). In evaluating these expedients, Manu (VII, 109) observes that conciliation and fight are

superior to the rest (*Śām=ādīnām=upāyānāṁ caturṇām=api paṇḍi-tāḥ/ sāma-daṇḍau praśaṁsanti nityaṁ rāṣṭr=ābhivṛddhaye//*). While commenting on the above passage of Manu, Kullūka points out that conciliation is advantageous for the reason that it does not involve any physical effort or loss of money and army, whereas, notwithstanding the drainage of men and money, force is still praised for the length of success it leads to (*sāmni prayāsa dhana-vyaya-sainyakṣay=ādi-doṣ=ābhāvāt, daṇḍe tu tatsadbhāve=pi kāryaṣiddhy=atiśayāt//*). This view does not find favour with the author of the *Mānasollāsa* as 'Conciliation,' he says, 'is the best in bringing success without injury to others and loss of substance, creating dissensions is middling as partaking of suspicion of those evil men who are thus divided from their master, bribery is an evil as involving present loss with success dependent upon destiny, and force is the worst as victory, the kingdom and life itself are brought into jeopardy by war. Conciliation should first be applied towards those who are high-born, grateful, kind-hearted and good, and who seek some advantage for themselves; the policy of dissension should be applied against those enemies who in the intoxication of their pride cannot be won over by conciliation; the king should apply the policy of bribery against those ministers who are disaffected against their master for various reasons and those who are the enemy's support in war and in counsel, as well as his own ministers and others who have no attachment for himself; what cannot be accomplished by means of dissension can be accomplished by bribery; when the king is strong, he should apply force against the enemy who cannot be reduced by means of the three expedients' (U.N. Ghosal, *A History of Indian Political Ideas*, Bombay, 1959, p. 453).

111. II, 94-95.
112. II, 95.
113. II, 89.
114. II, 70.
115. P. 41.
116. *SIP*, p. 120.

7

The Ambassador

I

Importance of the Office of Ambassador

A large volume of evidence, both literary and archaeological, Indian as well as foreign, would indubitably disclose the prevalence of the office of ambassador in the early Indian kingdoms. But it is almost equally certain that such an office was far from being a permanent one, being created for a specific purpose. 'The system,' observes T.V. Mahalingam,[1] 'of accrediting ambassadors permanently from one court to another is of modern origin and was not known in medieval India.' Even then, the Indian ambassadors of those days wielded enormous power and shouldered no mean responsibilities. It is they on whom depended, in no small measure, the maintenance of friendly relations between kings, the outbreak of hostilities between kingdoms and the conclusion of peace between warring parties.

II

Ambassadors in Vedic Literature

The term *dūta* in the sense of an envoy occurs in the *Ṛgveda*[2] as a qualifying epithet of the god Agni who was urged to bring the gods to the sacrifice. The word is also once used in the *Ṛgveda*[3] in its feminine form as an epithet of Sarama who was deputed by Indra to discover the treasure of the Panis. The later Vedic texts like the *Atharvaveda*[4] and the *Kauṣītaki Upaniṣad*[5] likewise use the term *dūta* in the sense of a messenger or envoy. But the information that the Vedic literature supplies in regard to these envoys or messengers is unfortunately meagre.

This would probably imply that the science of diplomacy was in its infancy in those days.

III

Ambassadors in Early Buddhist and Jaina Sources

We seldom come across any detailed information about *Dūtas* in the early Buddhist and Jaina sources. The *Bhaddasala Jātaka*[6] refers to an envoy, being sent by the Kosalan monarch Prasenajit to the Śākyas who were urged to offer him one of their daughters in marriage. To provide the envoys from abroad with accommodation (*tirojanapadehi āgatānaṁ dūtanaṁ nivesanatthānādīni*) was a matter of great concern with a king desirous of winning popularity at home.[7] In the *Tevijja Sutta*[8] of the *Dīgha Nikāya*, some of the *Śrotrīya* Brāhmaṇas are represented as discharging the functions of *Dūtas*. This and similar other Buddhist texts would create the impression that *Dūtas* were occasionally recruited from amongst the *Śrotrīya* class of the Brāhmaṇas.[9]

The *Dūtas* are almost passed over in silence in *Dharmasūtra* literature. They are once referred to in the *Gautama Dharmasūtra*[10] which advocates the inviolability of their person.

IV

Ambassadors in Classical Accounts

The accounts of Classical authors like Pliny, Arrian and Curtius throw positive light on the position of ambassadors in the pre-Mauryan epoch. Pliny's *Anabasis of Alexander IV*, for example, shows that ambassadors were an important part of the government in Indian kingdoms in the fourth century B.C. When the Macedonian conqueror, in the course of his campaigns, reached Nysa, that lay at a distance of four to five miles west from Jalalabad, the Nysians sent out to him their president named Akouphis and thirty deputies as ambassadors, to 'entreat him to spare the city for the sake of the God'. They duly reached the camp of Alexander and their leader Akouphis urged the invader to spare Nysa. The mission bore fruit. The city was left unmolested.[11] It is learnt from the narrative of Arrian that Abisarus, king of Taxila, also despatched envoys to

Alexander with enormous presents. Another Indian king, the less consequential Porus, is believed to have tendered his submission to Alexander through the agency of envoys. Curtius[12] speaks of the tribal ambassadors of the Mālavas and the Kṣudrakas, who met Alexander, consequent upon the defeat of their tribes at the hands of the foreign invader, as men of uncommon stature and dignified bearing, and as being clad in purple and gold. 'From a close study,' observes H.L. Chatterjee,[13] 'of the services rendered by them and judging by their results, one can only conclude that these persons were saddled with responsibilities of a very delicate nature, fulfilment of which called for a good deal of statesmanship and foresight on the part of the persons performing them.'

V

Ambassadors in the Maurya Period

In the section entitled *Dūta-praṇidhiḥ* of the *Arthaśāstra*, Kauṭilya[14] has elaborately discussed the problem of *Dūtas* who are divided into the following three groups:

1. The *Nisṛṣṭārthas*, Plenipotentiaries. The word *nisṛṣṭārtha* literally means 'to whom the matter has been entrusted (with full powers of negotiation)'.[15] These officers who were endowed with ministerial qualifications[16] (*amātya-sampad=opeta*) enjoyed full discretion to negotiate with the foreign ruler.

2. The *Parimitārthas*, Charges d'Affaires. To this group belonged officers who were deficient in respect of a quarter of the qualities expected of those belonging to the first group. They were granted limited freedom in making any negotiations with the foreign power (*pāda-guṇa-hīnaḥ parimitārthaḥ*).[17]

3. The *Śāsanaharas*, Conveyers of royal writs. They possessed only half the qualifications of the officers of the first group and were, as the etymology seems to signify, the bearers of a message (*ardha-guṇa-hīnaḥ śāsanaharaḥ*).[18]

Kauṭilya describes at length how an ambassador should start on his mission, enter the enemy's capital, deliver his master's message and observe the formalities of behaviour and conduct in a foreign state. An envoy[19] would start only when there were excellent arrangements for carriage (*yāna*), conveyance (*vāhana*), servants (*puruṣa*) and subsistence[20] (*parivāpa*).

He had to study carefully beforehand the message of his master and think over the replies to the possible queries of the enemy-king.[21] As he moved through the enemy-kingdom, he would make friends with officers there such as those in charge of wild tracts, boundaries, cities and rural areas, assess the military resources and the vulnerable as well as the unassailable points of the enemy.[22] Having obtained permission, he would enter the enemy's capital, report the object of his mission as exactly as entrusted to him, even at the risk of his own life.[23]

While defining the functions of a *Dūta*, Kauṭilya[24] observes:

Preṣaṇaṁ sandhi-pālatvaṁ pratāpo mitra-saṁgrahaḥ|
upajāpaḥ suhṛd=bhedo gūḍha-daṇḍ=ātisāraṇam||
Bandhu-ratn=āpaharaṇaṁ cāra-jñānaṁ parākramaḥ|
samādhi mokṣo dūtasya karma yogasya c=āśrayaḥ||
Sva-dūtaiḥ kārayed=etad=para-dūtāṁś=ca rakṣayet|
prati-dūt=āpasarpābhyāṁ dṛśy=ādṛśyaiś=ca rakṣibhiḥ||

R. Shamasastry[25] translates the above verse as follows: 'Transmission of missions, maintenance of treaties, issue of ultimatum (*pratāpa*),[26] gaining of friends, intrigue, sowing dissension among friends, fetching secret force; carrying away by stealth relatives and gems, gathering information about the movements of spies, bravery, breaking of treaties of peace, winning over the favour of the envoy and government officers of the enemy—these are the duties of an envoy (*dūta*). The king shall employ his own envoys to carry on works of the above description, and guard himself against (the mischief of) foreign envoys by employing counter envoys, spies and visible and invisible watchmen.'

As is evident from the above verses of the *Arthaśāstra*, the duties of a diplomatic envoy comprised the following:

(i) Transmission of the message of his own master to the head of the foreign state he was deputed to;
(ii) Safeguarding the terms of a treaty for the maintenance of cordial relations between states;
(iii) Delivery of an ultimatum to the head of the foreign country;
(iv) Winning of friends;

(v) Carrying on intrigues in the enemy's territory;
(vi) Sowing of dissension among the friends of the enemy;
(vii) Carrying away by stealth relatives and gems;
(viii) Expulsion of the enemy's secret agents and armymen;
(ix) Exhibiting the strength of his own master; and
(x) Kidnapping of the enemy's kinsmen and treasures.

Referring to the other duties and responsibilities that a *Dūta* was expected to discharge, Kauṭilya[27] observes: 'He should find out (about) the instigation of seducible parties, the employment of secret agents against non-seducible parties, the loyalty or disaffection (of the enemy's subjects) towards their master and the weak points in the constituent elements (of the enemy's realm) through spies appearing as ascetics or traders, or through their disciples or assistants or through agents in the pay of both appearing as physicians or heretics. In case conversation with them is not possible, he should find out secret information from the utterances of beggars, drunken persons, insane persons or persons in sleep, or, from pictures, writings or signs in holy places or temples of gods. When (such information is) found out, he should make use of instigation.' The following facts emerge:

First, the *Dūta* was empowered to employ spies for eliciting secret information about the enemy's strong and weak points. Second, he was expected to travel widely in the enemy's territory to derive necessary information from the conversation of men from various walks of life as well as from paintings and secret writings.

A sharp controversy exists among Indologists on the question of Kauṭilya's view on diplomatic privileges and immunities. Scholars like B.A. Saletore[28] are of opinion that Kauṭilya did not acknowledge the inviolability of the person of ambassadors. But such an opinion cannot be upheld as Kauṭilya[29] explicitly states: 'Kings indeed have envoys as their mouthpieces, you no less than others. Therefore, envoys speak out as they are told even when weapons are raised (against them). Of them even the lowest born are immune from killing; what to speak of Brahmins? These are the words of another. This is the duty of an envoy' (*Dūta-mukhā hi rājānaḥ tvaṁ c=ānye ca/ tasmād= udyateṣv=api śastreṣu yath=oktaṁ vaktāro dūtāḥ/ teṣām=ant=*

āvasāyin=opy=avadhyāḥ kim=aṅga punar=brāhmaṇāḥ| parasy =aitad vākyaṁ| eṣa dūta-dharmaḥ iti|).[30] But there are in the *Arthaśāstra* some statements[31] which imply that its author was aware of ambassadors being subjected to discourteous treatment and capital punishment at the hands of foreign kings.

It seems that Kauṭilya was not in favour of assigning any fixed salary to *Dūtas*. He says, 'The average envoy should receive ten *paṇas* per *yojana*, a double wage beyond ten (*yojanas*) up to one hundred *yojanas*'[32] (*daśa paṇiko yojane dūto madhyamaḥ, daś=ottare dviguṇa-vetana ā-yojana śatād= iti*).[33] S.C. Banerji[34] argues that as *Dūtas* were not entitled to any fixed salary, there was no independent post of *Dūtas* as such and that officers of different ranks were employed, as occasions arose, to perform the duties of envoys. This suggestion may not be correct. It is not unlikely that the real motive behind mileage being considered the sole determinant of their emolument was to make *Dūtas* feel sufficiently enthused to put in that extra bit of effort which would make all the difference between an indifferent official and a brilliant one. R.P. Kangle,[35] on the other hand, thinks that the *Dūta* was entitled to his regular salary, and the rates given in the passage cited would cover his travelling expenses.

Furthermore, *Dūtas* were granted lands[36] which were not transferable through sale or mortgage and they were also exempted from paying tolls while crossing rivers.[37]

The meagre information hardly allows us to ascertain how far the Kauṭiliyan system of envoys was in actual operation in the kingdom of Candragupta Maurya in whose reign the *Arthaśāstra* was, in all probability, composed. But if the validity of the Greek accounts is indisputable, the illustrious Megasthenes, who was originally an officer in Arachosia, must have resided at the court of the Maurya emperor, in the capacity of an ambassador of Seleucus some time after the conclusion of a treaty between the Indian and Greek kings by c. B.C. 302.[38] The actual object of this mission is unfortunately shrouded in obscurity. It might have been that Seleucus, on the strength of his diplomatic relations with Candragupta, secured help in the shape of mercenary troops in his encounter with his formidable antagonist Antigonus, but of this we do not possess any definite evidence. It is also likely that the furtherance of commercial interests[39] with India—a definite incentive for the Seleucid king—was the principal motive behind this Greek embassage. Equally imperfect is our knowledge about the duration of Megasthenes' stay at the Maurya court, although V.A. Smith[40] is inclined to hold that it was a prolonged one.

The diplomatic relations with the Maurya court were maintained by the next Seleucid king Antiochus Soter, evidently with the help of ambassadors. The Greek historian Athenaisus informs us that once Bindusāra requested Antiochus to buy and send him sweet wine, dried figs and a sophist when the latter replied: 'We shall send you the figs and the wine, but in Greece the laws forbid a sophist to be sold.'[41] It is evidently natural to presume, although the details are lacking, that there were occasional exchanges of embassies between the Seleucid and the Maurya kings.

It is known from Rock Edict XIII that Aśoka maintained *Dūtas* in frontier states like those of the Yonas, Kāmbojas, Gāndhāras, Nābhakas, Ṛṣṭikas, Bhojas, Andhras and the Pārinda Pāradas, and in the courts of such foreign kings as Antiochus, Ptolemy, Antigonus, Megas and Alexander, as well as in the five independent territories of the Colas, Pāṇḍyas, Satiyaputras, Keralaputras and the Tāmraparṇyas. Aśoka's *Dūtas* were primarily concerned with *Dharma-vijaya*, the conquest of the law of piety, interpreted by D.R. Bhandarkar[42] to mean the spread of Buddhism, and the carrying out a programme of medical treatment in those territories. As pointed out by B.M. Barua,[43] some of the *Dharma-Mahāmātras* were probably deputed as emissaries by Aśoka. Rhys Davids[44] had challenged long ago Aśoka's claim to have sent emissaries to distant countries, but the veracity of the inscriptional evidence remains irrefutable.

Foreign sources also attest the friendly intercourse and exchange of embassies between the Maurya and foreign kings during the reign of Aśoka. The Ceylonese chronicle *Mahāvaṁsa*[45] expressly states that Aśoka despatched an embassy, composed of his nephew Mahāariṭṭha, his Brahmin chaplain or councillor and a Vaiśya Treasurer, with coronation presents and happy wishes to his Ceylonese contemporary Tissa. It is further learnt from the narrative of Pliny that king Ptolemy Philadesphos of Egypt sent an envoy named Dionysius to the court of Pāṭaliputra either during the reign of Aśoka or at the time of his father Bindusāra.[46]

VI

Ambassadors in the Post-Maurya Period

It is in the post-Maurya period that one comes across the earliest epigraphic reference to ambassadors. The Besnagar Garuḍa Pillar inscription,[47] assignable to the last quarter of the second century B.C., speaks of a Greek ambassador (*yonadūta*) named Heliodorus who visited the court of king Bhāgabhadra at Vidiśā in his fourteenth regnal year as a representative of Mahārāja Aṁtalikita, identified with Antialcidas of the coins. Bhāgabhadra has been identified with Bhadraka,[48] the fifth Śuṅga king, as mentioned in the *Bhāgavata Purāṇa*. It may be presumed that the Bactrian Greeks cultivated friendly relations with their Śuṅga counterparts with the help of envoys. Although no reason is shown in the inscription for the visit of Heliodorus, it is not improbable that Antialcidas sought the friendship of the Indian king in his struggle for existence against the Euthydemian monarch Menander.[49]

We may now turn to the evidence of the *Rāmāyaṇa* and the *Mahābhārata* which reflects the condition of India during the period between the fourth century B.C. and the fourth century A.D. when the epics, in all probability, were finally composed. The *Rāmāyaṇa* speaks of *Dūtas* as being sent out on important occasions to the enemy-kingdom for delivering their master's message to others and reporting back their reaction or as carrying out a certain mission, as was the case with Hanumān who was sent by Sugrīva to find out Sītā who was leading a prisoner's life in Rāvaṇa's kingdom. The *Ayodhyākāṇḍa*[50] insists on the employment of such ambassadors as were citizens of the kingdom, capable of guessing the motive of others,[51] possessed of sound judgement, eloquent and able to overcome their opponents in debate[52] (*Kaccij=jānapado vidvān=dakṣiṇaḥ pratibhānavān/ yath=oktavādī dūtas=te kṛto Bharata paṇḍitaḥ//*). In the *Yuddhakāṇḍa*[53] mention is made of the threefold category of envoys; those who accomplished an undesirable and arduous task with devotion and love were the best among men; those who performed their mission but were not guided by approbation and affection were middling persons; and those who failed to discharge their duty satisfactorily were the lowest amongst men (*Yo hi bhṛtyo niyuktaḥ san=bhartā karmaṇi duṣkare/ kuryāt=tad=anurāgena tam=āhuḥ puruṣ=ottamam// Yo niyuktaḥ paraṁ kāryaṁ na kuryān=nṛpateḥ priyaṁ/ bhṛtyo yuktaḥ samarthaś=ca tam=āhur-madhyamaṁ naram// Niyukto nṛpateḥ kāryaṁ na kuryādyaḥ samāhitaḥ/ bhṛtyo yuktaḥ samarthaś=ca tam=āhuḥ puruṣ=ādhamam//*). This division of envoys, as envisaged in the *Rāmāyaṇa*, is in no way similar to the one referred to in the *Arthaśāstra*. There is, however, perfect agreement between the *Rāmāyaṇa* and Kauṭilya's work in regard to the inviolability of the ambassador's person. When Hanumān courted arrest and was ordered to be killed by Rāvaṇa, Vibhīṣaṇa saved the life of the envoy by reminding his brother of the Śāstric injunction[54] with regard to the treatment of an ambassador. But in certain cases, specially in the event of any gross misbehaviour on their part, envoys were subjected to torture, as was done to Māruti by Rāvaṇa.[55]

The *Mahābhārata* seems to imply that there were no permanent ambassadors in the contemporary period; persons of eminence were temporarily called upon by the king to carry his message or to conduct negotiations, on his behalf with a foreign king. Dhaumya, Kṛṣṇa and Sañjaya were all urged to discharge their duty as ambassadors only on important occasions. As regards the qualifications of an envoy, the *Śāntiparvan*[56] lays down that 'he should be high-born, of a good family, eloquent, clever, sweet-speeched, faithful in delivering the message with which he is charged, and endowed with a good memory'[57] (*Kulīnaḥ kula-sampanno vāgmī dakṣaḥ priyaṁvadaḥ/ yath=okta-vādī smṛtimān dūtaḥ syāt saptabhir=guṇaiḥ//*). The *Udyogaparvan*[58] mentions that a *Dūta* would be courageous, swift in action, kind, amiable, free from diseases and endowed with a fine mode of speech; he would neither be stiff-necked, nor liable to be won over by others (*Astavdham=aklīvam=adīrghasūtraṁ sānukrośaṁ ślakṣṇam = ahāryam = anyaiḥ/ aroga jātīyam = udāra-vākyaṁ dūtaṁ vadanty=aṣṭa-guṇ=opapannam//*). The *Udyogaparvan*[59] elsewhere states that the *Dūta* could speak only what he had been ordered by his king to speak, and if he would transcend his jurisdiction, he was liable to be killed. But this injunction would apply only to ordinary ambassadors who were the mere conveyers of messages, as was the case with Ulūka, while there were others who enjoyed a greater degree of freedom, comparing favourably with the *Nisṛṣṭārthas* of the *Arthaśāstra*. On the eve of the great battle at Kurukṣetra, Kṛṣṇa was sent to the Kaurava court as an ambassador of the Pāṇḍava brothers to do such things as he considered proper and fruitful. The person of the *Dūta* was sacred. 'A king,' as the *Śāntiparvan*[60] says, 'should never slay an envoy under any circumstances. That king who slays an envoy sinks into hell with all his ministers'[61] (*Na tu hanyān=nṛpo jātu dūtaṁ kasyañcid=āpadi| dūtasya hantā nirayam=āviśet sacivaiḥ saha||*). Hopkins[62] is of opinion that the ambassadors mentioned in the epics were recruited from amongst the priestly and the military communities.

Manu, whose writings appear to reflect the condition of the country during the early centuries of the Christian era, is aware of the importance of the institution of ambassadors, for, as he rightly points out, it is they who bring about alliance or war (*dūte sandhi-viparyayau*).[63] The government was accordingly very careful to select eminently suitable persons for these posts. These ambassadors were versed in all sciences, skilled in reading hints and expressions of the face and gestures, honest, intelligent, high-born, loyal, possessed of good memory, endowed with the knowledge of place and time, handsome, dauntless and eloquent[64] (*Dūtañ=c=aiva prakurvīta sarva-śāstra-viśāradaṁ| iṅgit=ākāra ceṣṭajñaṁ śuciṁ dakṣaṁ kul=odgataṁ| Anuraktaḥ śucir=dakṣaḥ smṛtimān deśa-kāla-vid| vapusmān vītabhīr=vāgmī dūto rājñaḥ praśasyate||*). It was they who united the disunited (*dūta eva hi saṁdhatte*), and created divisions among the united[65] (*bhinatty=eva ca saṁhatān*), no doubt, in consonance with the interest of their employers. They ascertained correctly the motives of other kings and kept their masters well-informed beforehand of their intentions, so that they might not be threatened with any trouble.[66] Manu does not tell us whether these officers were permanently stationed in a foreign country or were deputed to foreign courts as occasion arose. Similarly, it is far from being known for certain whether there were at the time of Manu different gradations of ambassadors which his predecessor Kauṭilya bears witness to.

Bhāsa's *Pratimānāṭakam* testifies to the envoys being generally received in a foreign court with honour and courtesy. King

Udayana is said to have respectfully received an envoy of king Mahāsena Pradyota.

The Tamil classics called *Toḷkāppiyam* and the *Kural* preserve interesting information about ambassadors. Unfortunately, there is wide divergence of opinion among scholars on the chronology of these works but there is every likelihood that they reflect the condition of the Tamil countries in the early centuries of the Christian era. It appears from the testimony of the former text that Brāhmaṇas were generally appointed *Dūtas*. But for fuller details about ambassadors, we may turn to the *Kural* where we have the following interesting account: 'The characteristics of an ambassador (*tūtu*) are lovability, noble birth and other qualities which evoke the monarch's respect. Love, wisdom, ability to talk with full knowledge are the three indispensable qualities of an ambassador. A skilful ambassador who wishes to gain his mission among other monarchs wielding the spear must be more learned than the learned. Only those who have wisdom, personality, and mature scholarship must be sent on a mission. A good ambassador is he who can talk cogently and sweetly, and who is not offensive even in saying (things) that are disagreeable. The envoy must be learned, fearless, persuasive and expedient. The qualifications of a true envoy are morality, loyalty to his monarch and courage. He who does not falter even when faced with personal danger is fit to deliver the king's message. A true envoy delivers his message even at the risk of death.'[67] The above account of the *Kural* as regards the nature, qualifications and duties of ambassadors agrees so remarkably with that in the *Arthaśāstra* as to create the impression of its being probably modelled on Kauṭilya's description. It is evident from the above account of the *Kural* that an ambassador often ran the risk of losing his life in discharging his duty. While distinguishing an ambassador from a spy, the *Kural* observes: 'An ambassador may be a spy in some circumstances, but a spy cannot be an ambassador who must be of high birth, good manners and loving nature.'[68]

As is evident from the contemporary indigenous sources, the institution of ambassadors was widely popular in the Indian kingdoms during the early centuries of the Christian era. A close study of foreign sources would lead to a similar conclusion. The Roman historians record the exchange of embassies time and again between the Roman empire and the Indian kingdoms during this period. Pliny[69] speaks of an embassy being sent to emperor Claudius from the kingdom of Taprobane which has been identified by some scholars with Ceylon, and located in South India by others. Again, the Roman emperor Trajan is said to have received an Indian embassy about A.D. 103[70] and, if the opinion of Warmington[71] is to be trusted, the embassy was sent out by the Kuṣāṇa king Kaṇiṣka I to seek help against the Indians or the Chinese. The suggestion of B.A. Saletore[72] and V.A. Smith that the Indian embassy was sent by Kadphises II is beset with chronological difficulty. Emperor Hardian likewise received an embassy from an Indian king, although neither its date nor the identification of the Indian ruler by whom it was despatched is at present known. B.A. Saletore[73] identifies him with Kaṇiṣka I but this is not in agreement with the generally accepted chronology of the Kuṣāṇa monarch. It would not be far from truth to surmise that these Indian embassies to the Roman court were like the modern missions of good will, offering presents to the heads of the governments concerned, and claiming some commercial concessions.

VII

Ambassadors in the Gupta Period

We now come to the age of the Guptas. It is interesting to note that the great poet Kālidāsa does not mention ambassadors at all in any of his works. This has given rise to the speculation that 'Probably the work of these costly and comparatively useless and ornamental figureheads was more efficiently done by clever spies who were deputed to watch the activities of enemies in foreign territories.'[74] No argument can at present be advanced to explain satisfactorily why Kālidāsa, who has provided us with such rich information about the government of his times, has passed over ambassadors in silence. The *Dūtas* are mentioned only once in the Yājñavalkya *Dharmaśāstra*[75] where the king is urged to consult his ministers on the issue of despatching his ambassadors (*dūtān prerayen=mantrisaṁyutaḥ*). The Chinese author Wang Hiuen-tse tells us that the king of Ceylon named Chi-mi-kia-po-mo, i.e., Śrī Meghavarṇa, sent an embassy with presents to the Gupta emperor Samudragupta to secure his permission for the building at Bodh Gaya of a monastery for the use of Ceylonese pilgrims. The permission was at once granted.[76]

Notwithstanding the uncertainty about its chronology, the evidence of the *Kāmandakīya Nītisāra* is often utilised as reconstructing the history of the Gupta period. In the *Dūtapracāraprakaraṇam* section of this work *Dūtas* appear as top-ranking officers of the state, being recruited from amongst those few ministers who were noted for their astuteness in the sixfold policy of alliance, war, etc.[77] (*Kṛtamantraḥ sumantrajño mantrinaṁ mantriśammatam| yātavyāyaprahiṇuyāt dūtaṁ duty=ābhimāninam||*). Intelligence (*pragalbhaḥ*), strong memory (*smṛtimān*), eloquence (*vāgmī*), skill in wielding arms (*śāstre*), learning (*śāstre ca niṣṭhitaḥ*), and dexterity (*abhyasta-karmā*) were some of the requisite qualifications that characterised a *Dūta*.[78] Following in the footsteps of his illustrious predecessor Kauṭilya, Kāmandaka has classified them into three divisions, namely, the *Nisṛṣṭārthas*, the *Mitārthas* and the *Śāsanahārakas*. In order to strengthen their master's position, they maintained cordial relations with frontier-guards and foresters[79] (*antapālaṁś=ca kurvīta mitrāny=āṭavikāṁs=tathā*). They visited the capital and the court of the enemy at opportune moments and gathered all sort of information in regard to the strength and equipment of forts, official secrets, vulnerable points and financial as well as military resources[80] (*Sāravattāṁ ca rāṣṭrasya durgaṁ tad=guptim=eva ca| chidraṁ ca śatror=jānīyāt kośa-mitra-balāni ca||*). They were never reluctant to deliver their master's message to the enemy even when such an act might involve a threat to their life[81] (*udyateṣv=api śastreṣu yath=oktaṁ śāsanaṁ vadet*). In order to guard themselves effectively against the unwilling revelation of secrets, they used to sleep alone and avoid women and drinks[82] (*Bhāvam=antargataṁ vyaktaṁ supto mattaś=ca bhāṣate| tasmād=ekaḥ svapen-nityaṁ striyaḥ pānaṁ ca varjayet||*) They applauded the prowess of their master in the presence of enemies with a view to striking terror in his enemies whose aggressive designs might thus be curbed.[83] They sowed seeds of dissension among friends and relations of the enemy (*ripoḥ śatru-paricchedaḥ suhṛd=bandhu-vibhedanaṁ*), traced out the routes of escape for the army in an exigency[84] (*yuddh=āpasāra-bhū-*

jñānaṁ-dūta-karm=eti kīrtitaṁ), and kept their master alive to the machinations of a foreign envoy[85] (*svapakṣe ca vijānīyāt para-dūta-viceṣṭitam*). In short, Kāmandaka's account of ambassadors strikingly agrees with that furnished by Kauṭilya centuries earlier.

It is from about this period onwards that we find the word *dūtaka* being used time and again in both north and south Indian epigraphs. The term, which literally means 'a messenger', is a technical title of an officer who was employed in connection with formal grants. These *Dūtakas*, who carried not the actual charter itself but the king's sanction and order to the local officials, whose duty it was to have the charter drawn up and delivered in favour of the recipients of land grants,[86] were evidently different from *Dūtas* or envoys.

VIII

Ambassadors in the Post-Gupta Period

As we approach the seventh century A.D., we come across evidence which would testify to ambassadors being employed by Indian kings to cultivate diplomatic ties with foreign powers. Thus king Harṣavardhana of Thanesar is known to have sent a Brāhmaṇa envoy to Tai-Tsung, the Tang emperor of China, in A.D. 641,[87] whereupon the latter reciprocated by sending a mission, carrying his reply to Harṣa's dispatch. If V.A. Smith[88] is right, the mission remained in India for a considerable period till A.D. 645. Again, in the early part of A.D. 648, the Chinese emperor sent an ambassador named Wang-heuen-tse to Harṣa, who had, however, passed away before the envoy arrived in India.[89]

Besides Harṣavardhana, some other Indian kings of the seventh century A.D. are known to have maintained diplomatic relations with foreign powers. The Arab historian Ṭabari tells us that Khusrū II (Khusrū Parvīz), king of Persia, received an embassy from an Indian king in the thirty-sixth year of his reign, i.e., A.D. 625-26. Ṭabari gives the name of the Indian ruler as Prmesha, i.e., Parameśa or Parameśvara which is known from epigraphic evidence to have been a second name of the illustrious Cālukya monarch Pulakeśin II (cf. *parameśvar=āparanāmadheya*). Some scholars surmise that a painting in one of the Ajanta caves depicts the Persian embassy presenting Khusrū's reply to Pulakeśin II but this is far from being certain.[90] Later in A.D. 692 an embassy was sent to China from the Cālukya court at Badami.[91]

Among other Indian rulers to have maintained friendly relations with foreign courts, mention may be made of the Pallava king Narasiṁhavarman II who is known to have sent an embassy to the Chinese court. T.V. Mahalingam observes: 'The Chinese Emperor received the Ambassador with all kindness and issued instructions to his officers that they must look after him with greatest care till his departure and act in such a way that his hopes might be fulfilled. When he left China, the Ambassador was given a robe of flowered silk, a golden girdle, a purse with an emblem in the form of a fish and the seven objects (?).'[92]

Dūtas were further employed by Indian kings to establish friendly relations among themselves. The *Harṣacarita* records that Bhāskaravarman, king of Kāmarūpa, dispatched an envoy to Harṣavardhana in order to conclude an alliance, presumably against Śaśāṅka, their common enemy and king of Bengal.[93] Bāṇa's narrative[94] would indicate that ambassadors visited foreign courts with presents, were honourably treated and they delivered their commission in confidence.

In A.D. 731, as Chinese authorities would have us believe, a king of central India named I-cha-fon-mo dispatched the envoy Seng-po-ta to China. The central Indian ruler has been identified with Yaśovarman[95] of Kanauj. The identification of the Indian ruler may not be incorrect but it is not possible in the present state of our knowledge to trace the circumstances in which the embassy was sent.

Inscriptions from Bengal of about the ninth and tenth centuries A.D. seem to prove the prevalence of the office of ambassadors in the Pāla kingdom, although the view, as held by B.B. Mishra,[96] that they were permanent officers in the Pāla government, may be considered too exaggerative. These officers find mention in several epigraphs like the Pandukeswar copper plates[97] of the ninth century A.D. and the Irda inscription of the Kamboja dynasty. As pointed out by B.C. Sen,[98] the latter record probably indicates that the *Dūtas* were helped in their work by a number of secret agents. The Nalanda copper plate grant[99] states that the Śailendra monarch Bālaputradeva, ruling in Java, Sumatra and the Malay Peninsula (*Yavabhūmipālaḥ*) sent an ambassador to the Pāla king Devapāla. The object of this embassy was to secure a grant of five villages with which the Śailendra king proposed to endow a monastery he had built at Nalanda. A great patron of Buddhism, Devapāla granted the request of the Śailendra king.

An officer called *Dūtapraiṣaṇika* is mentioned in a large number of contemporary inscriptions, mostly from Bengal. The term literally means 'one who sends out an envoy' (*dūtaṁ preṣayati iti*). If the interpretation of the expression, as suggested above, be endorsed, it would follow that the *Dūtapraiṣaṇika* was a top-ranking officer who was authorised to supervise the work of envoys.

Similarly, a cloud of uncertainty hangs over the identification of a class of officers called *Gamāgamika* in epigraphic documents. *Gamāgamika* literally means 'one who comes and goes'. The commentator Utpala[100] has taken the term in the sense of an envoy. They might have been the officers 'carrying out functions of an urgent character in connection with the diplomatic department of the state, requiring frequent visits to the neighbouring kingdoms or to the dominions of vassals'.[101]

The *Agni Purāṇa*, which appears to have been composed at about the same period, repeats the age-old classification of ambassadors into three categories, viz., the *Nisṛṣṭārthas*, the *Mitārthas* and the *Śāsanahārakas*, each succeeding type being one fourth less in qualities than the preceding one.[102] It is laid down that intelligence, retentive memory, ingenuity, proficiency in the art of war and scriptural knowledge and eloquence of speech were the essential qualifications that were expected of an ambassador.[103] He had to be very careful in the execution of his duties. He would not enter the enemy's house or seek an interview with him without proper verification. He had to wait patiently for the opportune moment to operate his action against the enemy. He was also required to know the loopholes, the financial resources and the strength of the army and allies of the enemies, as well as their personal likings and dislikings.[104] The *Agni Purāṇa* further points out that ambassadors were open spies.[105] This statement is a definite reflection on the secret nature of their duties which were evidently carried on with the help of secret agents. But the *Agni Purāṇa* does not explain the status of these ambassadors or the caste barriers, if there were any, in the case of their appointment.

The *Nītiśāstra*-writers of about the same and the succeeding periods have made important observations on ambassadors who have been almost passed over in silence in the contemporary official documents. An outstanding author in this category is Somadeva who composed the *Nītivākyāmṛta* during the reign of the Rāṣṭrakūṭa king Kṛṣṇa III (c. A.D. 940-968). We are told in the *Nītivākyāmṛta* that an ambassador was expected to be loyal to the king, pure in character, wise, talented, able to read facial expressions and signs, honest, born of a high family, free from vices, endowed with the gift of the gab, compassionate and familiar with other people's thoughts.[106] Following in the footsteps of such early writers as Kauṭilya and Kāmandaka, Somadeva lays down: 'An ambassador should not be put to death, even if he is a Caṇḍāla, not to speak of a Brāhmaṇa.'[107] This statement would show that although ambassadors were mostly recruited from among the Brāhmaṇa community, Caṇḍāla envoys were not altogether unknown. Somadeva[108] further testifies to the employment of lady messengers in dealing with women (*strīṇāṁ dautyaṁ striya eva kuryuḥ*). These ambassadors studied the ins and outs of the enemy's kingdom and ascertained how far the officers in the enemy-state were devoted to the cause of their master.[109] It was an offence on their part to accept any grant or tribute from the enemy.[110]

It is difficult at present to decide how far the recommendations of Somadeva and other *Nītiśāstra*-writers were accepted by the government in those days. There are, however, indications that the service of ambassadors was in great demand for maintaining friendly relations with foreign powers. The Cola king Rājarāja the great sent to China just before his death an embassy which reached there in A.D. 1015.[111] Rājarāja cultivated cordial relations with Cūlāmaṇi Varma, the Śrī Vijaya king of the Malay Peninsula, who commenced, apparently with the approval of his Indian counterpart, the construction of a Buddhist *vihāra* at Nāgapaṭṭinam in Tanjavur district. Cūlāmaṇi died soon after, leaving the *vihāra* to be completed by his son Śrī Māravijayottuṅgavarman who named it after his departed father. King Rājarāja made a grant of the village of

Ānaimaṅgalam for the upkeep of this monastery in A.D. 1006.[112] The construction of this monastery by these foreign kings in the dominions of an Indian ruler must have been preceded by the exchange of embassies between the two courts. Rājarāja's son and successor Rājendra Cola sent an embassy to China in A.D. 1033.[113] Kulottuṅga I is, likewise, known to have sent an embassy to China in A.D. 1077. 'The embassy consisted of seventy-two men who carried with them as tributes glass, camphor, brocades, rhinoceros' horns, ivory, incense, rose water, borax, cloves, etc., each of the value of a dollar.'[114]

The *Dūtas* find mention in the *Rājadharmakāṇḍa* section of the *Kṛtyakalpataru*, composed by Lakṣmīdhara who is known to have served the Gāhaḍavāla king Govindacandra as his minister of peace and war in the second quarter of the twelfth century A.D. In dealing with these officers Lakṣmīdhara does not make his own observation but merely cites a few well known quotations from Manu and the two epics. His citation from the *Rāmāyaṇa* shows that *Dūtas* could not be slain but, if caught in unfriendly acts, might be chastised or disfigured[115] (*dūtasya daṇḍo hi vadho na dṛṣṭaḥ*).

The *Śukranīti*, which in its present form cannot probably be placed later than the fourteenth century A.D., includes the *Dūta* in the list of the ten principal officers of the king[116] (*Amātyo dūta ity=etā rājñaḥ prakṛtayo daśa*). The reading of emotions and gestures, a good memory, a sound knowledge of time and space,[117] oratory, courage and proficiency in the six-fold means of peace (*sandhi*), war (*vigraha*), march (*yānaṁ*), neutrality (*āsanaṁ*), dual policy (*dvaidhībhāvaṁ*) and seeking refuge (*saṁśraya*) were some of the prerequisites of a *Dūta*[118] (*Iṅgit=ākāra-ceṣṭajñaḥ smṛtimān deśa-kāla-vid| ṣāḍguṇya-mantra-vid=vāgmī vītabhīr=dūta iṣyate||*). It is evident from Śukra's account[119] that he was generally a Brāhmaṇa by caste, but sometimes a Kṣatriya or even a Vaiśya would have been tipped for the post.

The exchange of embassies between the South Indian and the Chinese courts gained momentum with the emergence of the Pāṇḍyas as the dominant power in the South in the thirteenth century A.D. T.V. Mahalingam[120] briefly describes them as follows: 'After the decline of the Cola power, the Pāṇḍya rulers maintained contact with the Chinese court.'

Kulaśekhara Pāṇḍya, easily the greatest among the rulers of the second Pāṇḍya Empire, sent one Jamāl'ud-dīn to the Chinese Emperor in 1280 with valuable articles as tribute to him and sought his help against his enemies. The Chinese Emperor, who was himself anxious to induce the Pāṇḍya king to accept his overlordship, was very happy to receive the embassy. He sent his envoy Yang Ting-pi to Ma'bar. He stayed in South India for some time and returned to China in 1282. The king of Ma'bar sent two missions to China in 1283 and 1284 with presents which included pearls, rare jewels and light silks. In 1285 the Emperor sent a mission to Ma'bar which was followed by a return embassy to the Chinese court from the states in South India, namely, Ma'bar, Mangalore, Cranganore, Manifattan (a port on the Coromandel coast), Nellore, etc. Thereafter missions from Ma'bar to China became almost a regular annual feature. The Emperor was anxious to have products from South India as also South Indians learned in Sciences, interpreters of different languages, jugglers, etc. Missions were sent from South India in 1288, 1289 and 1290, while return missions were received from China in 1290, 1291, 1296 and 1297. Even in 1314 when there was political confusion in Ma'bar, a mission was sent to China.'

A fourteenth-century writer on polity named Caṇḍeśvara points out in the *Rājanītiratnākara* that the *Dūta* was required to be well-versed in all *Śāstras*, capable of understanding delicate situations, facial expressions and signs, pure in character, painstaking, born of a noble lineage, loyal to the king, possessed of a retentive memory, able to understand the proper time and place of delivering the king's message, fearless, handsome and endowed with excellent expression. He would further need to have the capacity to unite the kings who had been separated and create divisions among the allied. He collected information about the activity of others, including the royal servants and other kings. A staunch advocate of the inviolability of the person of the *Dūta*, Caṇḍeśvara lays down that even a Mleccha *Dūta* should not be killed, because he was merely a spokesman of his royal master[121] (*Dūto mlecch=opy=avadhyaḥ syād=rājā dūta-mukho yataḥ| udyateṣv=api śastreṣu dūto vadati n=ānyathā||*).

The *Dūtas* are mentioned in several other texts. It would

appear from the *Vasanta-vilāsa* that the *Dūtas* of the opposite camp were treated with honour. Vastupāla did not humiliate the envoy of Śaṅkha who spoke bitterly.[122] The immunity of ambassadors from capital punishment is emphasised by the writer of the *Nītiprakāśa* who observes:[123] 'Even if an ambassador is guilty of a grievous wrong, he cannot be put to death.' The Jaina work *Prabandhacintāmaṇi*, composed by Merutuṅga at the beginning of the fifteenth century A.D., highlights the functions of diplomatic agents who were clever in speech and skilled in penetrating others' minds. One such officer was Ḍāmara who was sent by the Caulukya king Bhīma I to the court of king Bhoja Paramāra with a view to dissuading him from launching an attack against Gujarat.[124] The *Prabandha-cintāmaṇi* speaks of the three classes of ambassadors being sent in order, according as the foreign court was considered to be of low, medium or high rank.[125] Sometimes the *Sāndhivigrahikas* were called upon to act as ambassadors.[126]

IX

Epilogue

The above discussion would then indubitably establish that ambassadors constituted one of the main organs of the government of the early Indian kingdoms, and the post carried with it enormous power as well as a high degree of prestige. These officers were generally recruited from amongst those persons who were possessed of uncommon intelligence and diplomatic wisdom. These ambassadors were admittedly the heroes of diplomatic battles.

References and Notes

1. *SIP*, p. 304.
2. III, 3, 2; VI, 8, 4; VII, 3, 3; X, 14, 12.
3. X, 108, 2-4.
4. VIII, 8, 10, etc.
5. II, I, etc.
6. *Jātaka*, IV, p. 145; No. 465.
7. Ibid , p. 132; *JDL*, XX, p. 54.
8. *AI*, p. 185.
9. *IDETBJ*, p. 155; *APIIAI*, p. 190.

10. *Adhyāya* X.
11. *IDRW*, pp. 83-84.
12. 9, 8.
13. *ILISRAI*, pp. 50-51.
14. *Arthaśāstra*, 1, 16.
15. *KA*, p. 41.
16. *Arthaśāstra*, 1, 16, 2.
17. Ibid., 1, 16, 3.
18. Ibid., 1, 16, 4.
19. Ibid., 1, 16, 5.
20. R.P. Kangle (*KA*, p. 41) interprets the word *parivāpa* in the sense of a retinue of servants.
21. *Arthaśāstra*, 1, 16, 6.
22. Ibid., 1, 16, 7-9.
23. Ibid., 1, 16, 10.
24. Ibid., 1, 16, 33-35.
25. *KA*, pp. 31-32.
26. R.G. Basak takes *pratāpa* to mean prowess (*Kauṭilīya Arthaśāstra*, Part I, Calcutta, 1950, p. 36), whereas Meyer understands by it 'majesty, dignity', i.e., the maintenance of his master's prestige at the foreign court (R.P. Kangle, *op. cit.*, p. 43).
27. *KA*, p. 42; *Arthaśāstra*, 1, 16, 24-26.
28. *IDRW*.
29. *KA*, p. 42.
30. *Arthaśāstra*, 1, 16, 13-17.
31. Ibid., 1, 16, 10.
32. R.P. Kangle, *op. cit.*, p. 351.
33. *Arthaśāstra*, V, 3, 19.
34. *AAILFSS*, p. 68.
35. R.P. Kangle, *op. cit.*, pp. 351-52.
36. R. Shamasastry, *Arthaśāstra*, Book II, p. 46.
37. Ibid., p. 143.
38. *IDRW*, p. 133.
39. Ibid., p. 132.
40. *EHI*, p. 120.
41. *IDRW*, p. 134.
42. *CHI*, II.
43. *AI*, p. 185.
44. Ibid., pp. 327ff.
45. *Mahāvaṁsa*, XI, 20-26.
46. *EHI*, p. 148.
47. *SI*, pp. 88ff.
48. Ibid., p. 88.
49. *AIU*, p. 116.
50. *Ayodhyākāṇḍa*, 100, 36.
51. The word *vidvān* is interpreted as *par=ābhiprāyajñaḥ*.
52. The expression *paṇḍitaḥ* is taken by the commentator as *paricchettā. Paricchedo hi pāṇḍityam ity=uktaḥ*.

53. *Yuddhakāṇḍa*, I, 7-9.
54. *Dūtāḥ na vadhyāḥ*.
55. Attention may be drawn to the following passage in the *Rāmāyaṇa*: 'One does not assault an ambassador, O Kakutstha, therefore, send away these monkeys. He who withholds the message of his master and gives voice to that which he has not been authorized to utter, merits death' (H.P. Shastri, *The Rāmāyaṇa of Vālmīki*, London, 1959, *Yuddha Kāṇḍa*, p. 47).
56. 85, 28.
57. P.C. Roy, *Mahābhārata*, *Śāntiparva*, Section LXXXV, p. 199.
58. *Udyogaparvan*, 37, 27.
59. Ibid., 72, 7.
60. *Śāntiparvan*, 83, 26.
61. P.C. Roy, *op. cit.*, p. 198.
62. *JAOS*, XIII, 1889, p. 95.
63. VII, 65.
64. VII, 63-64.
65. VII, 66.
66. VII, 67-68.
67. Dikshitar, *The Kural of Tiruvalluvar*, Madras, 1949, pp. 140-41.
68. *TSELT*, p. 599.
69. B.A. Saletore, *op. cit.*, pp. 228ff.
70. *The Cambridge Ancient History*, Vol. XI, p. 238.
71. *Commerce between the Roman Empire and India*, Cambridge, 1928, p. 95.
72. B.A. Saletore, *op. cit.*, p. 243.
73. B.A. Saletore, *op. cit.*, p. 246.
74. S.A. Sabnis, *Kālidāsa, His Style and His Times*, Bombay, 1966.
75. I, 328. Jolly has assigned this work to the fourth century A.D., while P.V. Kane has fixed its date as A.D. 100-A.D. 300.
76. *JA*, 1900, pp. 316ff.
77. 13, 1.
78. 13, 2.
79. 13, 5.
80. 13 7.
81. 13, 9.
82. 13, 16.
83. 13, 15.
84. 13, 24.
85. 13, 25.
86. *CII*, III, p. 100.
87. V.A. Smith, *op. cit.*, p. 352.
88. Ibid., p. 352.
89. *HK*, p. 188.
90. *CA*, p. 240.
91. *SIP*, p. 306.
92. Ibid., p. 306.

93. R.C. Majumdar, *History of Ancient Bengal*, Calcutta, 1971, p. 52.
94. *The Harṣacarita of Bāṇa.* Translated by E.B. Cowell and F.W. Thomas, Delhi, 1961, p. 212.
95. R.S. Tripathi, *op. cit.*, p. 196.
96. *Polity In The Agni Purāṇa*, Calcutta, 1965, p. 118.
97. *EI*, XXXI, p. 277.
98. *SHAIB*, p. 539.
99. *EI*, XVII, pp. 310ff.
100. Utpala on *Bṛhatsaṁhitā* 85, 34.
101. *PIA*, p. 120.
102. *Adhyāya* 241, 8.
103. *Adhyāya* 241, 7.
104. *Adhyāya* 241, 9-10.
105. *Adhyāya* 241, 11.
106. *Nītivākyāmṛta* 13, 1-2.
107. Ibid., 13, 19.
108. 13, 22.
109. 13, 17.
110. 13, 15.
111. *SIP*, p. 306.
112. Ibid., p. 308.
113. Ibid., p. 307.
114. Ibid., p. 307.
115. K.V. Rangaswami Aiyangar, *Kṛtyakalpataru*, XI, *Rājadharmakāṇḍa*, Introduction, p. 49; Text, p. 34.
116. II, 141-43.
117. While explaining the reason why a sound knowledge of space and time was expected of a *Dūta*, B.K. Sarkar (*The Śukranīti*, Allahabad, 1914, p. 71) observes: 'For unless he is well-grounded in the actual conditions of time and place and the special characteristics of the relations between persons he has to deal with, he is likely to misunderstand or misrepresent facts and thus bungle the state's affairs.'
118. II, 859-61.
119. Kṣemarāja Śrī Kṛṣṇadāsa, *Śukranīti*, p. 38, v. 86.
120. *SIP*, p. 307.
121. *Rājanītiratnākara*, Chapter XI, pp. 46-47. Edited by K.P. Jayaswal.
122. *GOS*, VII, pp. 22ff.
123. VII, 64.
124. *The Prabandhacintāmaṇi*, translated by C.H. Tawney, Calcutta, 1901, p. 44.
125. Ibid., p. 44.
126. Ibid., p. 11.

8

The Judge

I

Introduction

Early Indian literature portrays the king as the fountain-head of justice and highest judge in civil and criminal matters. But it was well-nigh impossible for him to hear and decide single-handed all the cases in his kingdom.[1] There was accordingly a special body of officers devoted to the administration of justice. An attempt has been made in the following pages to present, on the basis of the sources at our disposal, a critical account of these officers who may be called judges.

II

The Judge in Vedic Literature

The *Vedas* provide us with meagre information about these officers. The *Yajurveda*[2] speaks of an officer called *Grāmyavādin* who appears to have been a village judge. His *Sabhā*, court, is mentioned in the *Maitrāyaṇī Saṁhitā*.[3] In referring to the administration of justice, as prevalent in the Vedic period, Macdonell and Keith[4] observe, 'There is no trace of organised criminal justice vested either in the king or in the people . . . there was some sort of judicial procedure in vogue in the later Vedic period.'

III

The Judge in Buddhist Literature

The judicial officers, however, find prominent mention in Jātaka literature. In the *Jātakas*, mention is made of an officer called *Vinicchayāmacca* who, to judge from the etymology of the word as well as from the nature of his work, as envisaged in the *Jātakas*, may be identified, with a great deal of exactitude, with a judge. That he was an officer of the ministerial rank is evident from the expression *amacca* which is often applied to him. The *Rathalaṭṭhi Jātaka*[5] narrates a story about how king Brahmadatta originally pronounced a wrongful decision but was subsequently persuaded by the *Vinicchayāmacca* to reverse his erroneous judgement. But this solitary instance would hardly justify us in deducing the conclusion that the *Vinicchayāmacca* was authorised to annul the king's judgement. It may reasonably be suggested that he 'took part in the administration of justice, advised the king and in some cases had some influence upon his judgement'.[6]

The evidence of the *Kurudhamma Jātaka* would show that the *Vinicchayāmaccas* not only discharged judicial functions, they were also empowered to advise the people on matters of morality. Once a young man gave away 1,000 gold coins to a prostitute and on assuring her of paying a visit to her house in the near future, he parted from her. The latter who promised that she would not receive the least farthing from any other persons, waited in vain for three years for him and was reduced to extreme poverty. She went to the court of the *Vinicchayāmacca* to seek his advice, whereupon she was permitted to return to her original profession.[7]

Though not in the *Jātakas* proper, another class of judges finds mention in the *Mahāvagga*,[8] a commentary on the *Mahāparinibbāna Sutta* and the *Cullavagga*.[9] They are the *Vohārikamahāmattas*. The *Mahāvagga* states that Bimbisāra approached these officers to know what punishment he deserved who initiated a hired soldier into a religious order. The *Vohārikas* were evidently judicial officers of ministerial rank.

What was the number of judges in a kingdom? That there were more than one justice can be surmised from the expression *vinicchayāmahāmattā*, occurring in some of the *Jātakas*. One *Jātaka*[10] gives the number as five (*Tassa paṇa rañño pañca amaccā . . . vinicchaye niyuttā*). It is reasonable to presume that the number of judges varied according to the dimension and need of a state.

Some remarkable light on the daily routine of a judge is

thrown by one of the *Jātakas* which represents a king as advising a judge in the following words: 'It will be to the advantage of the people if you decide cases: henceforth you are to sit in judgement . . . you need not judge the whole day, but . . . go at early dawn to the place of judgement and decide four cases; then return . . . and partaking of food, decide four more cases.'[11] If this account is relied upon, it would follow that a judge was required to decide only eight cases per day and that the court sat in the morning and in the afternoon with a break for lunch at noon. R.N. Mehta[12] observes that the court usually sat for the whole day from morning to sunset after which all business was to stop. In referring to the judicial system, as depicted in the Buddhist texts, R.N. Mehta[13] observes, 'In the instances of cases that we noticed before, we nowhere see anything like legal proceedings, lawyers defending their clients and raising points against the opposite party. Nevertheless it does not seem proper to hold that there were absolutely no lawyers who could place and defend the cases of their clients before the court, and earn their livelihood from that profession. For there are some references to '*Vohāra*' which, if consistent and correct in their application, would go to prove that some sort of legal practice was followed . . . Though we have no details of hearing suits, the instances . . . at least show that the complainant stated his case, and the accused made his statement in return, probably on oath. The court was attended by others than the parties to a suit, and applause was not suppressed, but on the contrary, considered with respect and due weight by the king. Witnesses (*Sakhī*) may be produced, though there is no clear indication for this.'

IV

The Judge in Dharmasūtra Literature

A judge is called *Prāḍvivāka* in the *Dharmasūtra*[14] of Gautama. The term itself speaks of the duty of a judge. It consists of two parts, viz., *prāḍ* and *vivāka*. *Prāḍ* is derived from the root *pracch* and means 'one who puts questions (*pṛcchati*) to the parties and the witnesses in a dispute'. *Vivāka*, which originates from the verb *vac*, denotes 'one who speaks out or analyses the truth'. We then see that the functions of the judge were twofold: he examined suitors and ascertained the truth.

Gautama says that a judge should not take up a case unless it is brought to his notice by the litigant. This, however, does not mean that the state did not consider itself injured by individual acts of crimes. It cannot escape notice that if the state takes the formal prosecution in its own hand, it would have to depend largely on the injured party for the successful conduct of the case. 'If in such a case there is a collusion between the offender and the injured, the state is generally helpless and there is every possibility that the former would evade punishment.'[15] As to the period of time that a judge required to wind up the trial, Gautama observes, 'If (the defendant) is unable to answer (the plaint) at once, (the judge) may wait for a year. But (in an action) concerning kine, draught-oxen, women, or procreation (of offspring), the defendant (shall answer) immediately, likewise in a case that will suffer by delay.'[16] Gautama evidently does not fix the same time-limit for rounding off the trial of all cases. Sometimes the trial was to be concluded without delay and occasions were not rare when it continued for several months. As regards the sources of law, Gautama points out that the administration of justice should be regulated by the *Vedas*, *Dharmaśāstras*, *Aṅgas*, *Upavedas* and *Purāṇas*. The customs of countries, castes and families should also be regarded as authoritative[17] (*Tasya ca vyavahāro Vedo Dharmaśāstrāṇ=Aṅgāny=Upavedāḥ Purāṇaṁ| deśa-jāti-kula-dharmaś=c=āmnair=avirud-dhāḥ pramāṇaṁ||*). The disputes among the cultivators, merchants and foresters should be settled in accordance with the age-old customs of such people[18] (*karṣaka-vaṇika-paśu-pāla-kusīdakā-ravaḥ sve sve varge pramāṇaṁ*). Gautama lays down that in order to arrive at a decision a judge may seek the advice of those who are learned in the three *Vedas*.[19]

As regards the qualifications of a judge, Āpastamba[20] points out that he should be learned, aged, clever in reasoning, careful in fulfilling the duties of castes and orders and born of a good family. While trying a case he should ascertain the truth by inference, ordeals, cross-examinations, etc.[21] This brief account of Āpastamba about judges may be regarded as supplementary to the information furnished to us by Gautama in two respects. First, Āpastamba lays down the qualifications of a judge and furthermore he recommends ordeals as one of the approved means of ascertaining the truth.

Baudhāyana says that a judge should always guard himself against pronouncing any unjust decision, otherwise he will incur sin. He says, 'Of injustice (in decisions) one quarter falls on the party in the cause, one quarter on his witnesses, one quarter on all the judges, and one quarter on the king. But where he who deserves condemnation is condemned, the king is guiltless and the judges free from blame; the guilt falls on the offender (alone).'[22]

V

The Judge in the Kauṭilīya Arthaśāstra

When we come to the Maurya period, we have abundant material on the judge. Kauṭilya mentions two kinds of judges, called *Dharmasthas* and *Pradeṣṭṛs*. These judges[23] are described as *Amātyas* (*Dharmasthās=trayas=tray=omātyā*) and were evidently top-ranking officers. The meaning of the expression *tray=omātyāḥ* in the passage *Dharmasthās=trayas=tray=omātyāḥ*, however, is not clear. Some scholars have taken it to mean 'three ministers in addition to three judges'. But the expression should better be taken to mean that judges should possess the qualifications or status of an *Amātya*. A passage in Book II[24] implies that judges were generally recruited from the Brāhmaṇas. The persons who proved loyal by the test of piety were appointed to such posts (*Tatra dharm=opadhā-śuddhān Dharmasthīya-kaṇṭakaśodhaneṣu sthāpayet*). Kauṭilya explains the test of piety in the following words: 'The king should (seemingly) discard the chaplain on the ground that he showed resentment when appointed to officiate at the sacrifice of a person not entitled to the privilege of a sacrifice or to teach (such a person). He should (then) get each minister individually instigated, through secret agents, under oath (in this manner): 'The king is impious: well let us set up another pious (king), either a claimant from his own family or a prince in disfavour or a member of the (royal) family or a person who is the one support of the kingdom or a neighbouring prince or a forest chieftain or a person suddenly risen to power; this is approved by all; what about you?' If he repulses (the suggestion), he is loyal. This is the test of piety.'[25] The above passage from the *Arthaśāstra* would clearly indicate that judges were required to tender their allegiance to the king even under adverse circumstances.

That the *Dharmastha* judges presided over the courts which were established in the frontier towns and posts (*janapada-sandhi*) and the chief cities of the *Saṁgrahaṇas* (units of ten villages), *Droṇamukhas* (units of four hundred villages) and *Sthānīyas* (units of eight hundred villages) is evident from the passage,[26] *Dharmasthās=trayas=tray=omātyā janapada-sandhi-saṁgrahaṇa-droṇamukha-sthānīyeṣu vyavahārikān=arthān kur-yuḥ.* The repeated use of the word *trayaḥ* in the passage would show that three *Dharmasthas* were to sit in each court. The passage, however, leaves us in the dark on many important issues. For example, we are not told anything as to whether there were different grades among judges in small and large towns, what steps were taken in the case of disagreement among judges or whether there were any provisions for making appeals from one court to another. The *Dharmastha* judges tried cases relating to the law of marriage, violation of women's property, supersession of a wife as a result of a second marriage, marital duty, maintenance, cruelty, disaffection, misconduct, leaving home, going away with a man, short or prolonged absence from the husband's home, order of inheritance, disputes regarding immovable property, non-observance of conventions, non-payment of debts, deposits, rules and regulations about slaves and labourers, non-conveyance of gifts, sale without ownership, forcible seizure, verbal injury, physical injury, gambling, betting and miscellaneous matters.

Book IV of the *Arthaśāstra*, which furnishes us with invaluable information regarding the *Pradeṣṭṛs*, begins with the statement, 'Three *Pradeṣṭṛs*, (all) three (of the rank of) minis-ters, shall carry out the supervision of criminals.'[27] The *Dharmasthas* and the *Pradeṣṭṛs* thus appear to have belonged to the same rank. But what were the functions of the *Pradeṣṭṛs*? The artisan's failure to keep his contract with his employer and *vice versa*, corruption on the part of the heads of depart-ments and their subordinates, violation of maidens, use of fraud in the standard of weights and measures, treasonable conspiracy against the king, search for thieves, the death of a patient in consequence of incompetence of a medical practitioner—all these and similar other items came under the purview of these judges. In a word, the *Pradeṣṭṛs* were employed by the king to safeguard society against the anti-social activities of officers, private individuals and corporate bodies. They were authorised to employ spies to detect crimes and to torture the offenders to extort confessions.

How the functions of the *Dharmasthas* differed from those of the *Pradeṣṭṛs* cannot be definitely known. Kane suggests that while the former tried cases brought before them by the parties themselves, the latter took up only such cases as were brought to their notice by the executive. But there is hardly any evidence in the *Arthaśāstra* which would warrant this contention. It has been held, on the other hand, that these two kinds of judges presided over the civil and criminal courts, respectively. But it may be pointed out that even a cursory glance at the heads of laws coming under the purview of these judges would show that the *Dharmasthas* also dealt with some of the criminal cases, while the *Pradeṣṭṛs* disposed of civil suits also. It seems that in the days of Kauṭilya law-suits were haphazardly divided into two categories and the *Dharmasthas* were charged with the disposal of one, the *Pradeṣṭṛs* with the other. The *Pradeṣṭṛs* were moreover entrusted with some revenue functions. In Book II, Kauṭilya states, 'In the headquarters of the revenue and divisional officers, the *Pradeṣṭṛs* should carry out their duties and secure the recovery of dues.' The *Dharmasthas*, however, had no such duty to perform. It is evident from the *Arthaśāstra*[28] that the *Pradeṣṭṛs* were placed under the supervision of the *Samāhartṛ* but the *Dharmasthas* do not appear to have been subordinate to any such officer.

That judges were not themselves above punishment is evident from the following observations of Kauṭilya, 'If the judge threatens, upbraids, drives away or browbeats a litigant, he shall impose the lowest fine for violence on him, double that in case of verbal injury. If he does not question one who ought to be questioned, questions one who ought not to be questioned, or after questioning dismisses (the statement), or instructs, reminds or prompts him, he shall impose the middle fine for violence on him. If he does not ask for evidence which ought to be submitted, asks for evidence that ought not to be submitted, proceeds with the case without evidence, dismisses it under a pretext, carries away one tired with delays, throws out of context a statement which is in proper order, gives to witnesses help in their statements (or) takes up once again a case which is completed and in which judgement is pronounced, he shall impose the highest fine for violence on him. In case the offence is repeated, double (the fine) and removal from office (shall be the punishment).'[29] 'If the judge or the magistrate imposes a money fine on one not deserving to be fined,' says Kauṭilya, 'he shall impose on him double the fine imposed, or eight times the shortfall or excess (over the prescribed fine). If he imposes corporal punishment (wrongly), he shall himself suffer corporal punishment or pay double the (normal) redemption amount. Or, he shall pay eight times the just claim which he disallows or unjust claim which he allows.'[30]

VI

The Judge in Aśokan Edicts

The *Dharmasthas* and the *Pradeṣṭṛs*[31] of Kauṭilya do not find mention in the edicts of Aśoka. On the other hand, the functions of the *Rājūkas*, as detailed in the edicts, would leave the impression that the executive officers carried on the administration of justice, in addition to their other works.[32] The First Separate Kaliṅga Rock Edict, however, mentions the *Nagalaviyohālakas*. The root *vyavahṛ* in Sanskrit means 'to carry on commerce, to trade, to deal in, and to conduct any judicial procedure, to judge'.[33] Accordingly, we may be justified in identifying them with the city administrators of justice and, as suggested by Luders and H.C. Raychaudhuri, comparing them with the *Paura-vyavahārikas* of the *Arthaśāstra* who were paid 12,000 *paṇas*. Shamasastry takes *Paura* and *Vyavahārika* as two separate designations and treats the first to signify 'the officer in charge of the town' and the second to mean 'the superintendent of law and commerce'. But this is hardly in agreement with the text where *Paura-vyavahārika* is employed in the singular and not in the dual form. As B.M. Barua[34] observes, 'The Aśokan use of the designation *Nāgaraka* as a variant of *Nagara-vyavahārika* sets at rest all doubts as to *Paura-vyavahārika* being the same designation as *Nāgaraka*. To be more precise, the *Vyavahārika* is a general designation, while the designation of *Paura-vyavahārika* is applicable only to a *Nāgaraka* in charge of the capital city.' The First Separate Rock Edict tells us that the *Nāgarakas* were sometimes found guilty of taking recourse to high-handed and rash actions, sudden arrest, coercion and imprisonment. But the Maurya emperor took steps to stop them and threatened the officers with sending forth a *Mahāmātra* every five years to see that all his injunctions for the proper administration of justice were carried out. In the edicts of Aśoka, we then come across, in no uncertain manner, witness to the miscarriage of justice, perpetrated by the judiciary.

VII

The Judge in the Rāmāyaṇa

In the *Rāmāyaṇa*, the judges are called *Dharmapālakas* who were chosen for their knowledge of law (*Vyavahāra-jñāna*) and politics. They were expected to be impartial and not to take bribes. The *Rāmāyaṇa* further brings to light that Rāma's court of justice, which was presided over by Rāma himself, was composed of Vasiṣṭha, Brāhmaṇa sages, ministers, Kṣatriya counsellors, *Nitijña-Sabhyas*, leading merchants and royal princes. P.C. Dharma[35] points out the following noticeable points in the judicial system of Rāma:

'1. The ease with which justice could be had without any expenditure.
2. The absence of professional lawyers and stamp fees and a complicated machinery.
3. The personal administration of justice by the king.
4. The accessibility of the king.
5. Speedy trial and impartial judgement.
6. The small amount of litigation, as the people were terribly afraid of a stern impartial king administering speedy justice.
7. The care with which the king selected his colleagues for their profound learning in various branches of law.'

VIII

The Judge in Dharmaśāstra Literature

For our knowledge about judges during the post-Maurya and pre-Gupta periods, we may turn to the accounts of Manu. Manu[36] states that learned Brāhmaṇas should be appointed to investigate suits. Manu[37] elsewhere observes, 'Even an ordinary Brāhmaṇa may at the king's pleasure interpret the law to him, but never a Śūdra.' This passage forbids the employment of a Śūdra as a judge but approves the appointment of the Kṣatriyas and Vaiśyas as judges in case of necessity. A judge is enjoined to discharge his duty properly. 'One quarter of (the guilt) of an unjust (decision),' as Manu[38] says, 'falls on him who committed (the crime), one quarter on the (false) witness, one quarter on all the judges, one quarter on the king.' If a judge acts improperly in the discharge of his duty, then the king should reverse his decision and fine him, according to the nature of the case, 1000 *paṇas* being the lowest punishment,[39] and in some cases their property is liable to be confiscated. How great is the insistence on the impartial administration of justice is evidenced by the following statements of Manu: 'Where justice, wounded by injustice, approaches and the judges do not extract the dart, there (they also) are wounded (by that dart of injustice). Where justice is destroyed by injustice, or truth by falsehood, while the judges look on, there they shall also be destroyed. Justice, being violated, destroys; justice, being preserved, preserves; therefore, justice must not be violated, lest violated justice should destroy us.'[40]

Manu classifies the cases under the following eighteen titles[41] of law: (i) non-payment of debts, (ii) deposit and pledge, (iii) sale without ownership, (iv) concerns among partners, (v) resumption of gifts, (vi) non-payment of wages, (vii) non-performance of agreements, (viii) rescission of sale and purchase, (ix) disputes between the owner of cattle and his servants, (x) disputes regarding boundaries, (xi) assault, (xii) defamation, (xiii) theft, (xiv) robbery and violence, (xv) adultery, (xvi) duties of man and wife, (xvii) partition of inheritance, and (xviii) gambling and betting. Manu[42] holds that the *Vedas*, the *Smṛtis*, the customs of holy men and one's own inclination[43] are the four sources of law (*Ved=okhilo dharma-mūlaṁ Smṛti-śīle ca tad=vidāṁ| Ācāraś=c=aiva sādhūnām=ātmanas=tuṣṭir=eva ca||*). He further points out that in the case of any conflict, the *Śruti* prevails over the *Smṛti* and that these are of superior validity as compared with the last two. He further maintains that the judge will try a suit with the help of three[44] assessors, who are to be appointed by the king, and should be endowed with knowledge, both religious and secular, law and truthfulness.

We may now pause here for a while to see what the other jurists, though some of them belonged to a much later date, have said about the judges and their courts. According to Yājñavalkya[45] a judge, called *Prāḍvivāka*, should preferably be a learned Brāhmaṇa (*Apaśyatā kāry=āvasād vyavahārān nṛpeṇa tu| Sabhyaiḥ saha niyoktavyo Brāhmaṇaḥ sarva-dharmavid||*). While trying a case, he should act in co-operation with the jurors who are to be not only impartial, but also well-versed in the law[46] (*Śruty=adhyayana-sampannā dharmajñāḥ satyavādinaḥ| Rājñā sabhāsadaḥ kāryā ripau mitre ca ye samāḥ||*). Emphasising the rightful discharge of his duties, Yājñavalkya says, 'If the members of the judicial assembly pronounce any decision which is opposed to the *Smṛtis* and usage through affection, greed or fear, each of them will be fined twice the amount to be paid by the defeated party'[47] (*Rāgāl=lobhād=bhayād=api Smṛty=apet=ādi-kāriṇaḥ| Sabhyāḥ pṛthak pṛthak daṇḍyā vivādād dviguṇaṁ damaṁ||*).

In referring to the sources of law, Yājñavalkya makes mention of the *Smṛtis*, the principles of equity as determined by popular usage, the *Dharmaśāstras* and the *Arthaśāstras*. The *Smṛtis* are given the foremost place. But if there is any conflict between the *Smṛtis*, the principles of equity are to prevail and in the case of any disparity between the *Dharmaśāstras* and the *Arthaśāstras*, the evidence of the former is to be upheld[48] (*Smṛtyor=virodhe nyāyas=tu balavān vyavahārataḥ| Arthaśāstrāt =tu balavad=Dharmaśāstram=iti sthitiḥ||*). Yājñavalkya[49] describes systematically the judicial procedure. He mentions the four stages of *Vyavahāra* but does not refer to them by name (*catuṣpād-vyavahār=oyaṁ*). The plaint along with particulars about the year, the month, the day, the name, etc., of the parties has to be written first in the presence of the defendant. The reply of the defendant is to be put down in writing in the plaintiff's presence. The evidence offered by the plaintiff is to be written down immediately afterwards. After the parties have submitted their plaint and answer, evidence has to be presented before the court. And finally, the judge has to arrive at the truth with the help of the recognised kinds of proofs like documents, witnesses, possession and ordeal.[50]

Kātyāyana says that a judge should be self-controlled, born of a noble family, not repellant, steady, afraid of the world hereafter, religious, assiduous and free from temper (*Dāntaṁ kulīnaṁ madhyastham=anudvegakaraṁ sthiraṁ/ Paratrabhaktiṁ dharmiṣṭham=udyuktaṁ krodhavarjitaṁ//*). Kātyāyana[51] further says that judges should ordinarily be recruited from the Brāhmaṇa community, but in the absence of suitable Brāhmaṇas, Kṣatriyas and Vaiśyas, who are thoroughly conversant with the *Dharmaśāstras*, may be appointed to such posts. The *Sabhyas* should help the judges in carrying out their duties. But neither the judge nor the *Sabhya* should hold any conversation in private with any of the litigants, when the suit is pending, and if he does so, he is liable to be fined.[52] If a party suffers any loss through the negligence of the *Sabhyas*, the latter would make good the loss, but their decision would stand.

Kātyāyana says that *vyavahāra* has four stages, comprising *purvāpakṣa* (plaint), *uttara* (reply), *pratyākalita* (deliberation as to the burden of proof) and *kriyāpada*[53] (adducing proof). The plaintiff has to write down his plaint first on the ground or on a board and finally on a leaf or on paper. If the judge considers that the cause is reasonable, he either makes over the court-seal to the plaintiff, or sends a court official for summoning the defendant. The defendant then has to submit his reply which may be of one of these four forms, admission (*satya*), denial (*mithy=ottara*), a special plea (*praty=avaskandana*), and a plea of former judgement[51] (*pūrva-nyāyavidhi*). When both the parties have submitted their evidence, the court is to deliberate and deliver its judgement. Dealing with the means of proof, Kātyāyana points out that these are of five kinds, including documents (*likhita*), witnesses (*sākṣī*), possession (*bhukti*), reasoning (*yukti*) and ordeals[55] (*divyas*).

Bṛhaspati[56] observes that a court of justice may be of four kinds, viz., the *Pratiṣṭhitā*, the court established in a fixed place, *Apratiṣṭhitā*, the roving court, *Mudritā*, the court of a judge who is authorised to use the royal seal and *Śāsitā* (or *Śāstritā*), the court over which the king himself presides. We thus see that while some judges presided over fixed courts, others had to move from place to place in order to discharge their duties. It is also evident from the foregoing accounts that there were different gradations among judges and those empowered to use the royal seal, no doubt, were of a higher category. Bṛhaspati also refers to the *Sabhyas* and states that they may be seven, five or three. As in the case of the *Prāḍvivākas*, the *Sabhyas* should preferably be Brāhmaṇas, but they may be recruited from the Kṣatriyas and Vaiśyas also in accordance with the exigency of circumstances.

Bṛhaspati further states that the proper functioning of a court depends in no small measure on the efficiency of some minor officials, connected with the court. One such minor court official is the *Sādhyapāla* or bailiff whose duty is to 'summon the witnesses, the plaintiff and the defendant, and to look after them'.[57] This post was generally reserved for the Śūdras. The other court officials, according to Bṛhaspati, were the *Gaṇakas*, i.e., accountants, *Lekhakas*, i.e., scribes and *Smṛtis*, i.e., proclaimers. The *Gaṇakas* were to be proficient in grammar, lexicography, accountancy, mathematics, astronomy, astrology and several alphabets and were to be men of pure character. They were to compute the wealth or contents of the claims. The *Lekhakas* were to write down the pleadings, depositions and decisions and they were conversant with grammar and endowed with truthfulness and even temper. The *Smṛti* or herald would proclaim the judgement of the court.

Nārada points out that a judge should have a thorough knowledge of the eighteen titles of law and their 8000 sub-heads and that they should be well-versed in the *Vedas*, *Smṛtis* and *Ānvīkṣikī*. Just as a physician takes out from the body an iron dart by making a surgical operation, so a judge should extricate from a law-suit the deceit, underlying it. Nārada[58] insists on the unanimity of opinion by judges and jurors, for, according to him, a unanimous decision leaves no grievances (*Yatra sabhyo janaḥ sarva sādhv=etad=iti manyate| Sa niḥśalyo vivādaḥ syāt saśalyaḥ syād=at=onyathā||*). If their decisions are opposed to the *Smṛtis* and usage, they are liable to be punished. Nārada[59] observes that the transaction of legal business has four different stages, viz., receiving information from the party, classification of the information into different sections of law, consideration of the pleadings of the parties and the evidence, furnished by them, and finally arriving at a decision (*Āgamaḥ prathamaṁ kāryo vyavahārapadaṁ tataḥ/ Cikitsā nirṇayaś=c=aiva darśanaṁ syāś=catur-vidhaṁ//*).

IX

The Judge in the Gupta Records

Inscriptions of the Gupta period mention some officers who were, in all probability, connected with the judicial department. A few of them may be noted below:

1. *Pramātṛ*. Bühler[60] is of opinion that the term means a spiritual councillor. The term has also been taken by some scholars, including R.C. Majumdar, to denote an officer in charge of land survey.[61] But none of these suggestions appears to be conclusive, for, as Vogel has shown, on the authority of the chronicler Śrīvara, this officer was entrusted with the administration of justice. But the passage, quoted by Vogel, would imply that the *Pramātṛ* was primarily connected with civil suits only.[62] The term *pramātṛ* is probably derived from the root *mā* which means to perceive or judge.

2. *Daṇḍanāyaka* (*Mahādaṇḍanāyaka*). There has been a great amount of speculation about the exact meaning of the term *daṇḍanāyaka*[63] which occurs not only in Gupta inscriptions but also in the Kuṣāṇa, Ikṣvāku and some of the later epigraphs. The term has been variously translated as a 'trying magistrate'[64] (Prinsep), 'the great leader of forces'[65] (Fleet), 'prefect of police'[66] (Vogel), 'commissioner of police' (R.S. Pandit), 'chief officer of police'[67] (Marshall), 'feudatory chief' (B.N. Puri), 'chief minister', and so on. Such a wide divergence of opinion among scholars on the meaning of *daṇḍanāyaka* is not unlikely when it is remembered that the term *daṇḍa* etymologically means the army, the rod of punishment, fine, punishment, etc. Most of the lexicons, including the *Abhidhāna-cintāmaṇi*[68] and the *Kalpadrukośa*[69] take *daṇḍanāyaka* in the sense of commander of the army. In the *Kāmandakīya Nītisāra*[70] the title *Daṇḍamukhya*, no doubt the same as *Daṇḍanāyaka*, is used to signify a general. The two terms, *senāpati* and *daṇḍa-nāyaka*, are found bracketed together in the *Bṛhatsaṁhitā*. In

the *Tilakamañjarī*, a work of a much later period, one and the same officer is called *Daṇḍādhipati*, *Mahādaṇḍādhipati* and *Vāhinīpati*. The references from the *Tilakamañjarī* leave no doubt that the *Daṇḍanāyaka* was primarily a military officer, though very often 'he was put in charge of newly-conquered territories and discharged not only military but also civil functions'.[71] We also hear of an officer called *Daṇḍādhyakṣa*. According to A.S. Altekar,[72] he was a judge of a criminal court.

3. *Pañca-maṇḍalī*. The Sanchi stone inscription[73] of Candragupta II refers to *Pañca-maṇḍalī* which is evidently the same as the Panchayat of modern times, 'the village jury of five (or more) persons, convened to settle a dispute by arbitration, to witness and sanction any act of importance'.[74]

X

The Judge in the Post-Gupta Period

The *Daśakumāracarita*[75] speaks of a court of justice called *Adhikaraṇa*, whereas judges, called *Dharmādhikaraṇas*, are referred to in the *Pañcatantra*.[76]

Useful information about the judge is preserved in the *Agni Purāṇa* which describes him as a *Dharmādhikaraṇa*. The *Agni Purāṇa* states that a judge should be impartial to friends and enemies alike, well-versed in the *Dharmaśāstras* and should be a Brāhmaṇa of noble descent (*Samaḥ śatrau ca mitre ca dharma-śāstra-viśāradaḥ/ Vipra-mukhyaḥ kulīnaś=ca Dharmādhikaraṇo bhavet//*). We find in the *Agni Purāṇa*[77] a systematic division of the law-suits into eighteen groups in accordance with the main causes of their occurrence which are debt, breach of trust, partnership, resumption of gifts, non-rendition of services, non-payment of wages, sale of a commodity by one who is not the rightful owner, non-delivery of sold goods, purchase, regulations of religious sects and corporations, land, adultery, partition, criminal acts, blasphemy, assault, gambling and prize-fighting and miscellaneous matters. These titles of litigation have further been divided into a hundred sub-branches,[78] 'caused by the difference in the nature and behaviour of the people'.[79]

The famous trial scene in Act IX of the *Mṛcchakaṭika*,[80] which was composed some time after Bāṇa, gives us a very clear insight into the office of judge. The judges are called *Adhikaraṇabhojakas* or simply *Adhikaraṇikas.* They owed their appointment to the king and remained in office as long as they enjoyed the confidence of the latter. This is evident from the statement of Śakāra, the king's brother-in-law, who, on being refused to be heard about his complaint, threatened the judge with the following words, 'How, my cause cannot be tried! If it is not tried, then I shall apply to king Pālaka, my sister's husband and inform both my sister and mother of this and have the judge removed and another appointed in his place.'[81] This would imply that when a despot was on the throne, the judge's position was precarious. We are further told that the judge was assisted by the *Śreṣṭhin* who was a prominent merchant or banker and a *Kāyastha* who owed his appointment to the crown. It seems that a litigant, demanding justice in any suit, had to wait outside and a court-official would lead him inside the court-room (*vahir=niṣkramya jñāyatāṁ kaḥ kaḥ kāry=ārthī*). The complainant then appeared in person before the judge and made a statement on his plaint. The defendant was next summoned by the judge to appear in the court to defend himself against the charge. According to the *Mṛcchakaṭika*, a model judge should be 'learned in law, expert in tracing frauds, eloquent, not ireful, impartial towards friends, strangers and relatives, delivering his judgement after carefully consulting the prevailing traditions or customs, a protector to the weak, a terror to the rogues, righteous, not greedy even when bribes are offered to him, always intent on finding out the sought-for truth, and able to pacify the king's wrath' (probably, if he be displeased by the judge sometimes deciding against his wish).[82] We further learn from the play that the judge only decided whether the accused was guilty or innocent but he was seldom the final authority in the award of punishment. Thus when Cārudatta's alleged murder of Vasantasenā was established by circumstantial evidence, the judge declared in the court-room thus, 'The business of proof it was ours to effect, the rest (i.e., the sentence) rests with the king'[83] (*Ārya Cārudatta! nirṇaye vayaṁ pramāṇaṁ śeṣe tu rājā*). That judges were merely a recommending authority is further proved by the *Vyavahāramuyūkha* which states that 'the king is the authority to deliver the judgement of capital punishment as the highest judicial authority and the other judges are only the investigators of the case'.[84]

The trial of Cārudatta, as recorded in the *Mṛcchakaṭika*, bears ample testimony to the fact that miscarriage of justice was not unknown in ancient India. Judges were sometimes lukewarm and did not penetrate beyond the surface of so-called facts, thus indulging in the maladministration of justice. Cārudatta admitted that it was sometimes futile to speak the truth, for the judge was incapable of discerning the truth (*Durbalaṁ nṛpateś=cakṣur=n=aitad tattvaṁ nirīkṣate*). Such misguided judges could even believe that a crow was white, and they caused ruin to thousands of victims[85] (*Idṛśaiḥ śveta-kākīaiḥ rājñaḥ śāsana-duṣakaiḥ| Apāpānāṁ sahasrāṇi hanyante ca hatāni ca||*).

The Nidhanpur copper plates of Bhāskaravarman speak of the *Nyāyakaraṇika* Janārdanasvāmin. As maintained by P. Bhattacharya,[86] he was probably the adjudicator who had to settle all cases of boundary disputes. Some scholars are, however, inclined to take him to be an officer of the department of land and revenue.

XI

The Judge in the Pallava and Rāṣṭrakūṭa Kingdoms

Our knowledge[87] about the judges in the Pallava kingdom is unfortunately fragmentary. The *Mattavilāsa Prahasana* shows that the courts in the districts were known as *adhikaraṇas*. The Kasakudi plates imply that these judicial courts were presided over by officers called *Adhikaraṇas*.[88] The *Mattavilāsa* further indicates that judges were not free from corruption and pre-judices. This is clear from what Devasomā had said when she was asked to appear in the court, 'Why, this man has heaps of riches drawn from the revenues of many monasteries; and with it he can stuff the mouths of the court officials at pleasure. But I am the maid of a poor *Kapālin* whose only wealth is a snake's skin and sacred ash and what riches have I here that I should go into the court?'[89] In the Pallava records mention is made of another court called *dharmāsana* which appears to have been an 'organised judicial body or law court which controlled the village administrative body and dealt with cases concerning temple affairs'.[90] Like the *adhikaraṇas*, the *dharmāsanas* were likewise controlled by the central government. We, however, hardly get any account about the judges who presided over these courts.

The judges likewise find mention in the Rāṣṭrakūṭa records. One such officer is mentioned in the Sanjan plates of Amoghavarṣa I as the drafter of the grant. A.S. Altekar[91] is of opinion that the chief justice was a member of the ministry in the Rāṣṭrakūṭa kingdom.

XII

The Judge in the Pāla and Sena Records

The inscriptions of the Pāla and Sena kings prove the existence of at least the following state functionaries who were associated with the department of justice:

1. The *Dāṇḍika*. He is probably the same official who is mentioned as *Daṇḍaśakti* in the Khalimpur inscription, *Dāṇḍapāṇika* in the Ramganj grant of Īśvaraghoṣa and *Daṇḍin* and *Daṇḍapāṇi* in the inscriptions of Chamba. The *Dāṇḍika*, to judge from the etymology of the term, was an officer, entrusted with criminal justice. The word *dāṇḍapāṇika* literally means 'one who holds the rod'.

2. The *Daṇḍapāśika*. He is mentioned in the Khalimpur and Nalanda plates of Dharmapāla and was probably identical with the *Daṇḍavāśika* who appears in other inscriptions. The *Daṇḍapāśika* also finds mention in the Rampal and Kedarpur copper plates of Śrīcandra, Barrackpur plates of Vijayasena and Calcutta Sahitya Parisad plates of Viśvarūpasena. This officer is mentioned even in much earlier records like the Palitana[92] and Valabhi[93] plates of Dharasena II, both being dated in the Gupta year 252. The expression is derived from *daṇḍa* and *pāśa*, i.e., rod and rope, and it literally means 'one who holds the rod and rope'. He was in all probability an officer in charge of punishment of criminals.[94] Vogel[95] observes that the form *Daṇḍavāśika* is due to vernacular influence.

3. The *Daśāparādhika*. He was the judge who tried cases of ten specific offences. But what actually these ten offences were we cannot definitely ascertain. J.F. Fleet[96] points out that the ten sins were (i) the appropriation of things that are not

given, (ii) killing in a manner that is not in accordance with precept, (iii) the pursuit of the wives of other men, (iv) harshness of language, (v) untruthfulness, (vi) slandering in all directions, (vii) incoherent conversation, (viii) coveting the property of others, (ix) thinking with the mind about things which are wrong and (x) tenacity of that which is not true. B.C. Mazumdar[97] quotes the opinion of some elders to the effect that these ten offences included 'adultery, assault, defamation, and offences relating to village roads and water reservoirs'. We agree with P.V. Kane[98] in his view that these are 'disobeying the king's order, murder of a woman, confusion of *varṇas*, adultery, theft, pregnancy from one not the husband, abuse and defamation, obscenity, assault and abortion'. A.S. Altekar[99] is of opinion that the *Daśāparādhika* was in charge of the collection of fines in the case of crimes tried in the state courts. Such is also the view of R.C. Majumdar.[100]

XIII

The Judge in the Pratīhāra Records

All the above-mentioned judicial officers appear in the inscriptions of contemporary Pratīhāra kings. Some useful information about judges in the Pratīhāra kingdom and of the contemporary period is preserved in the *Nītivākyāmṛta* and the *Yaśastilakacampū*. The *Nītivākyāmṛta* testifies to the continuity of the practice of appointing *Sabhyas*, the jury. The court, says Somadeva,[101] resembles a desolate forest if it does not consist of learned jurors (*Sā sabhā araṇyāṇi yasyāṁ na santi vidvāṁsaḥ*). Somadeva, however, does not give the number of jurors. Somadeva says that the king should carefully select the *Sabhyas* who should never indulge in greed or favouritism. The *Yaśastilakacampū*[102] speaks of a class of judges called *Dharmasthas* who are described as '*sakala-vidyā-vyavahāra-vedī*', '*dṛṣṭa-śrut=ānek=ācira-vicāra*' and '*yath=ārtha-darśanastha*'. In the Barah plate[103] of Bhojadeva mention is made of a *Vyavahārin* through whose incapacity the stipulations of the grant could not be implemented. He was probably a judicial officer whose duty was to look after such matters. In the Cedi and Candella inscriptions[104] mention is made of a class of officers called *Dharmalekhins*. It cannot be known with certainty whether they were judicial officers who wrote the judgements or pleaders who wrote the complaints. P.B. Udgaonkar[105] thinks that since they are sometimes seen as drafting the copper plate charters, they were, in all probability, state judicial officers.

XIV

The Judge in the Rājataraṅgiṇī

The testimony of the *Rājataraṅgiṇī*[106] would bear witness to the fact that in the Lohara kingdom in Kashmir the chief justice was called the *Rājasthānīya* or *Rājasthānādhikāra.* It cannot escape notice that the *Rājasthānīya* appears as a subordinate ruler in the *Subodhikā* commentary on the *Kalpasūtra.* The evidence of the *Subodhikā* stands corroborated by the Mandasore inscription[107] of Yaśodharman and Viṣṇuvardhana wherein a viceroy is described as a *Rājasthānīya.* It would thus appear that the officer, bearing the title of *Rājasthānīya*, was entrusted with different responsibilities in different regions and ages.[108]

In the *Rājataraṅgiṇī*[109] mention is made of an officer called *Tantrapati* who might have been associated with the administration of justice in the ancient kingdom of Kashmir. Although the *Rājataraṅgiṇī* does not expressly define his functions, that he was a judge in Kashmir is amply proved by the combined testimony of two early writers named Maṅkha and Jonarāja. Maṅkha in his *Śrīkaṇṭhacarita*[110] says that his brother was offered 'the garland of the office of the *Bṛhattantrapati*' by Sussala, king of Kashmir. Jonarāja in his commentary on the above verse explains *Bṛhattantrapati* as a *Dharmādhikārin*, a term which has been interpreted by some scholars as a judge, and as an official in the department of religion by others. It may be noted that in South Indian records[111] the term *tantrapati* is often employed in the sense of a military officer.

XV

The Judge in the Śukranīti

The *Śukranīti* mentions different categories of judges among whom the *Prāḍvivāka* occupies the highest rank. In explaining the term *prāḍvivāka*, Śukra[112] says, 'The *Prāḍvivāka* is so called because he asks questions (and is therefore *Prāḍ*) and analyses cases, judges disputes or states what should be done and what not (and is therefore *Vivāka*).' As regards his qualifications, it is mentioned that he should be well-versed in the knowledge of men, *Śāstras* and morality. He presides over the highest court of justice in the absence of the king and is a member of the ministry. The chief justice, however, cannot discharge his duty unaided, but is to be helped by a body of *Sabhyas*. He should reach the inevitable decision by the application of reasoning, direct observations, inference, analogy as well as local customs.[113]

In referring to the *Sabhyas*, Śukra points out that the king or the chief justice should be assisted by a panel of three, five or seven jurors[114] (*Loka-vedajña-dharmajña sapta pañca tray=opi vā| Yatr=opaviṣṭā viprāḥ syuḥ sā yajña-sadṛśī sabhā||*). If necessary, the jurors should be fearless to express their opinion freely even in opposition to the view of the king. They should keep a vigilant watch upon the king so that the latter may not go astray[115] (*Adharmataḥ pravṛtaṁ taṁ n=opekṣeran sabhā-sadaḥ| Upekṣamānāḥ sa-nṛpā narakaṁ yānty=adhomukhāḥ||*). 'Śukra (IV.5.63-64) prescribes the punishment of a thief for a *lekhaka* (a scribe) taking down a different deposition from the one actually given or for a *sabhya* making use of such a deposition knowingly; IV.5.93 prescribes fine and removal from office if a *sabhya* gives a wrong decision through greed, etc. and IV.5.282 prescribes a fine of 1000 *paṇas* against a judge giving a corrupt decision. There must have been a few cases of judges taking bribes in ancient India as in modern times.'[116] As regards the caste of the *Sabhyas* Śukra observes that they should be recruited from all castes[117] (*Rājñā niyojitavyās=te sabhyāḥ sarvāsu jātiṣu||*). 'He further points out that the foresters are to be tried with the help of foresters, merchants with the help of merchants, soldiers with the help of soldiers, making it clear that jurors were selected from all the castes.'[118] It may be mentioned, as indicated earlier, that centuries ago Yājñavalkya denounced the appointment of non-Brāhmaṇas as *Sabhyas*. It is worth mentioning in this connection that some of the *Dharmaśāstra*-writers recommended that 'the cases should be tried with the help of jurors selected from the castes or professions of the parties themselves'.[119] It cannot escape notice that centuries later in the Vijayanagar kingdom, the jurors were Brāhmaṇas in cases where complicated law points were involved; otherwise they were merchants and agriculturists.

Besides the *Prāḍvivāka*, there were other judges, though of subordinate rank, who were generally Brāhmaṇas. They should be 'versed in the *Vedas*, self-controlled, high-born, impartial, unagitated and calm, and who fear next life, are religious-minded, active and devoid of anger'.[120] But in the absence of properly qualified Brāhmaṇas, persons from other castes, excepting the Śūdras, could be selected for these posts. These judges are expected to be conversant with actions, character and attributes of people and impartial to both enemies and friends. Furthermore, they should be truthful and possess a sound knowledge of the duties of men.[121]

A close scrutiny of the *Śukranīti* would disclose certain fundamental principles of Hindu jurisprudence which may be noted below:

Judgement was to be in harmony with the rules as enumerated in the *Dharmaśāstras*. In order to eliminate the miscarriage of justice, cases were tried without any delay. Evidence was to be recorded in the presence of both the parties. Cases were decided after taking into consideration all the available evidence, oral, documentary and circumstantial. In taking up a case, the order of priority was generally followed but the gravity or importance of the case was also not set aside. Amendment in the plaint was possible before the statement of the opponent was recorded but after the filing of the statement no amendment was entertained. Retrial was possible only after depositing a double stamp (?) duty (*dvi-guṇaṁ daṇḍaṁ*). The judges were to act with ideal decency, avoiding any private talk or communications with the parties during the pendency of a suit.

XVI

The Evidence of the Vyavahāramātṛkā

Jīmūtavāhana, who flourished in Bengal in the twelfth century A.D., in his *Vyavahāramātṛkā* deals, at great length, with the constitution of the court of justice, the grades of courts, the four stages of judicial proceedings, the role of agents, the order of hearing of suitors, the time allowed for filing the plaint, the four kinds of reply and the different kinds of proof. He enjoins that judicial proceedings will be conducted in accordance with the instructions of the *Dharmaśāstras* and the *Arthaśāstras*. While evaluating the sources of law he points out that in the case of any discrepancy between the *Dharmaśāstras* and the *Arthaśāstras*, the former texts are to be preferred to the latter and that where the *Dharmaśāstras* themselves are in disagreement, popular usage is to be followed. The *Sabhyas*, who are guilty of pronouncing any wrongful decision, of taking bribes and so forth, are liable to be banished. Similarly, a judge or a *Sabhya*, speaking secretly to a plaintiff or a defendant on a case under trial, deserves to be punished. Jīmūtavāhana further emphasises that among the kinds of proof, viz., possession, documents, witnesses and inference, each preceding one is superior to the one immediately following, and that where even inference is not possible, recourse may be taken to ordeal.[122]

References and Notes

1. G.N. Jha (*Hindu Law In Its Sources*, I (1930), p. 51) points out that some of our ancient jurists lay down that even when the king is trying the suits himself, he shall have the judge to advise him. In such cases, however, the role of the judge is purely advisory.
2. VI, I, p. 248.
3. Ibid.
4. *JOI*, II, p. 154.
5. III.104.
6. *SONEI*, p. 111.
7. II.380.
8. I.40.3.
9. VI.4.9.
10. V.228.
11. *PBI*, pp. 152-53.
12. Ibid., p. 153.
13. Ibid., pp. 156-57.
14. XIII.26-27.
15. R.P. Das Gupta, *Crime And Punishment In Ancient India* (Calcutta, 1930), p. 11.
16. XIII.28-30.
17. XI.21-22.
18. Ibid., 23.
19. X.25.
20. II.11.29.5.
21. II.11.29.6.

22. I.10.19.8.
23. *Arthaśāstra* III.1.1.
24. 10.2.
25. *KA*, II, pp. 20-21.
26. IV.1.
27. *KA*, II, p. 294.
28. IV.4.1; IV.5.13; II.35.7.
29. *KA*, II, pp. 322-23.
30. Ibid., p. 323. R.P. Das Gupta (*Crime And Punishment In Ancient India*, p. 17) observes that in the Hindu theory of punishment four ideas were involved, viz., deterrent, preventive, corrective and purificatory.
31. In the edicts of Aśoka, mention is made of a class of officers called *Prādesika*. R.G. Basak (*AI*, p. xxiii) agrees that the word *prādesika* is derived from the root *diś* which means to ordain, indicate, direct, decide, determine or order. If this be accepted, the *Prādesika* was an officer who pronounced judgement after decision of a legal case, thus corresponding to the *Pradeṣṭṛ* of the *Arthaśāstra*. Some scholars are inclined to connect the term *prādesika* with *pradeśa*, meaning a region, province or district.
32. It is difficult for us to agree with R.K. Choudhury (*JOI*, II, p. 160) when he says, 'The judiciary was separate from the executive, generally independent in form and ever independent in spirit.'
33. *AI*, p. 121.
34. *AAHI*, pp. 203-04.
35. *The Rāmāyaṇa Polity* (Madras, 1941), p. 62.
36. VIII.9. Medhātithi, while commenting on the passage of Manu, adds that the judge should know the science of morality also which will save him from undue influences.
37. VIII.20.
38. VIII.18.
39. IX.234.
40. *AIU*, p. 341; Manu, VIII.12; 14-15.
41. VIII.3-7.
42. II.6.
43. Kullūka points out that 'self-satisfaction' is authoritative only in regard to the choice of alternatives. Nandana holds that *ātmanas=tuṣṭi* is to be taken along with *sādhūnāṁ* to mean that the self-satisfaction of righteous men is trustworthy.
44. This number, according to Medhātithi, is the minimum.
45. II.3.
46. II.2.
47. II.4.
48. II.21.
49. II.8.
50. Yājñavalkya mentions nine kinds of ordeals, including those by balance, fire, water, poison, sacred libation, etc.

51. 67.
52. 74-78.
53. 31.
54. *CA*, p. 358.
55. II.22.
56. *Pratiṣṭhit=āpratiṣṭhitā mudritā śāsitā tathā| Catur-vidhā sabhā proktā sabhyāś=c=aiva tathā-vidhāḥ|| Pratiṣṭhitā pure grāme calāmām=āpratiṣṭhitā| Mudrit=ādhyakṣa-saṁyuktā rāja-yuktāś=ca śāsitā||* (*SBE*, XXXIII, p. 277). Another text of Bṛhaspati, cited by the *Mayūkha* says, 'For forest dwellers the court (*karaṇa*) shall be in the forest, for soldiers in the army, and in the market for merchants' (*Ye c=āraṇya-carās=teṣām=araṇye karaṇaṁ bhavet| Senāyāṁ sainikānāṁ tu sārthe tu vaṇijas=tathā||* Gaekwad ed., p. 2).
57. *LGAI*, p. 140.
58. III.17. Jaimini (XII.2.22) points out that in the case of any dispute the opinion of the majority of the *Sabhyas* should prevail.
59. I.36.
60. *EI*, I, p. 118.
61. *HK*, p. 140; *HB*, p. 286.
62. *SHAIB*, pp. 547-48.
63. The earliest reference to the term is found in an inscription of the time of Kaṇiṣka I (*EI*, XXXIV, pp. 9ff). The word also occurs in the Prākṛt inscriptions from Nagarjunakonda.
64. *EI*, XIII, p. 43; N.G. Majumdar, *Inscriptions of Bengal*, III, p. 185.
65. *CII*, III, p. 10; *EI*, IX, p. 242; ibid., XXIV, p. 206.
66. *Antiquities of Chamba*, I, p. 23.
67. *ASI* (1911-12), p. 54.
68. II.9.
69. I.6; V.17.
70. XVIII.49.
71. *RTA*, p. 331. U.N. Ghosal (*The Beginnings of Indian Historiography and Other Essays* (Calcutta, 1944, p. 179) is of opinion that the term *mahādaṇḍanāyaka* is employed in the Kuṣāṇa, Andhra, Ikṣvāku and Gupta inscriptions to mean the commander-in-chief.
72. *SGAI*, p. 196.
73. *CII*, III, pp. 29ff.
74. Ibid., p. 32.
75. In the *Daśakumāracarita* mention is made of the *Madhyasthas* who 'mediated between the disputing parties and got remuneration from both' and of the corrupt legal officers who misguided the king deliberately for serving their own interests. Referring to the administration of justice, as depicted in the *Daśakumāracarita*, D.K. Gupta (*Society And Culture In The Time Of Daṇḍin* (Delhi, 1972), pp. 165-66) points out: 'The offence of a culprit and also the punishment meted out to him were announced in public with the beating of drum. The convict with his arms bound behind his back was taken to the place of execution by the *rakṣins* or the *caṇḍālas* who thrice made

the proclamation of the offence and the punishment awarded. The punishments were generally severe. Capital punishment was awarded for treason, murder, theft, robbery and for criminally assaulting a virgin. Carrying [away] of a maiden was punishable with confiscation of property (*sarvasva-haraṇa*). For offences such as abetment of crime, the offender was banished from the state or was put into prison with his property confiscated. A prisoner's hands or feet or both were generally fettered with iron girdles. In awarding punishment, caste and class considerations mattered much.'

76. Jolly, *Recht Und Sitte*, p. 134.
77. 253.13-30.
78. 253.31.
79. *PAP*, p. 128.
80. *PHAI*, p. 562. P.V. Kane (*History of Dharmaśāstra*, III, p. 279) is of opinion that the drama is as old as the fourth or fifth century A.D.
81. *IHQ*, V, p. 319.
82. *IHQ*, V, p. 320. *Śāstrajñaḥ kapaṭ=ānusāra-kuśalo vaktā na ca krodhanas=tulyo mitra-parasvakeṣu caritaṁ dṛṣṭ=aiva datt=ottaraḥ | Klīvān pālayitā śaṭhān vyathayitā dharmo na lobh=ānvito dvārbhāve paratattva-vaddha-hṛdayo rājñaś=ca kopāpahaḥ ||* IX.5.
83. *IHQ*, V, p. 320.
84. Ibid., *Vadh=ādhyakṣo nṛpaḥ śāstā sabhyāḥ kārya-parīkṣakaḥ |*
85. IX.41.
86. *EI*, XII, p. 79.
87. There are very few references to judicial officers in the inscriptions of the Vākāṭakas. The Kalachhala plate separately mentions the *Daṇḍapāśika* and the *Dāṇḍika*. V.V. Mirashi (*CII*, IV, p. cxlii) points out that whereas the former was a police officer, the latter was a magistrate.
88. This suggestion has been put forward by C. Minakshi (*ASLUP*, p. 58). Hultzsch's explanation of the term as ministers is wide of the mark.
89. This passage is quoted in *ASLUP*, p. 58.
90. *ASLUP*, p. 59.
91. *RT*, p. 167.
92. *EI*, XI, p. 83.
93. *IA*, XV, p. 187.
94. *IB*, p. 129.
95. P.C. Chaudhury (*HA*, p. 306) points out that the *Dāṇḍika* was the magistrate who pronounced verdict in the court and the *Daṇḍapāśika* carried out the order. R.S. Tripathi (*History of Kanauj*, p. 343) suggests that the *Daṇḍapāśika* might have been a hangman or executioner.
96. *CII*, III, p. 189.
97. *JBORS*, 1916, p. 53.
98. *HD*, III, p. 214.
99. *SGAI*, p. 196.
100. *HB*, p. 285.

101. *Nītivākyāmṛta*, p. 110.
102. Pp. 372-73; *RTA*, p. 321.
103. *EI*, XIX, pp. 17ff.
104. *IA*, XVI, p. 208; *EI*, IV, p. 160; *EI*, X, pp. 47ff. The Dhureti copper plate grant uses the expression *arthalekhin* evidently as a synonym of *dharmalekhin*.
105. *PIA*, p. 128.
106. VII.601; VIII.181, 1046, 1982, 2618, 2624.
107. *SI*, p. 390.
108. *IE*, p. 367. The *Lokaprakāśa* (IV) explains the term as follows—*Prajā-pālan=ārtham=udbahati rakṣayati ca sa rājasthānīyaḥ|* It means that he who carries out the object of protecting subjects and shelters them is called a *Rājasthānīya* (*IA*, V, p. 207).
109. VIII.2422.
110. III.50.
111. *IE*, p. 373.
112. B.K. Sarkar, *The Śukranīti*, p. 189. *Prāḍ* is derived from the root *pracch* and *vivāka* is based on the root *vac*.
113. Ibid., p. 72.
114. *Śukranīti*, IV.26.
115. Ibid., 5.275.
116. *HD*, III, p. 273.
117. *Śukranīti*, IV.5.17.
118. *PIA*, pp. 206-07.
119. Ibid., p. 206.
120. B.K. Sarkar, *The Śukranīti*, p. 184.
121. Ibid., p. 184.
122. *SE*, pp. 287ff.

9

The Chief District Officer

I

The Chief District Officer in the Maurya Kingdom

For the period before the advent of the Mauryas on the political chessboard, we hardly possess any reliable account of the officers who were in charge of the smaller divisions of a province. In the inscriptions of Aśoka mention is made of the *Rājūkas* who possibly carried on the government of such small administrative units. Thus Pillar Edict IV furnishes us with the following information:

First, they were placed in charge of a hundred thousand men (*Lajūkā me bahusu pāna-sata-sahasesu janasi āyatā*).

Second, they enjoyed sole control in awarding rewards and inflicting punishment upon the people (*tesaṁ ye abhihāle vā daṁḍe vā atapatiye me kaṭe*), but were not allowed to be prejudiced and partial in the dispensation of justice (*viyohāla-samatā ca siya daṁḍa-samatā ca*).

Third, like a nurse securing the welfare of the children placed in her charge, they were to look after, with maternal care, the well-being and happiness of the country people and grant favours to them (*Athā hi paja viyatāye dhātiye nisijitu asvathe hoti viyata dhāti cadhati me pajaṁ sukhaṁ palihatave hevaṁ mamā Lajūkā kaṭā jānapadasa hita-sukhāye*). They are further enjoined to work for the *sukhiyana* of the people. According to D.R. Bhandarkar,[1] the expression *sukhiyana* should be taken in the context of Pillar Edict VII as denoting 'the works of public utility, the digging of wells on roads and such other charities' as he has specified in that edict.

Rock Edict III likewise throws welcome light into the functions of these officers. It tells us that in addition to their usual administrative functions, the *Rājūkas* were to undertake the quinquennial tours of inspection in order to propagate certain instructions[2] of piety.

The above details would show how not merely judicial but executive functions too were assigned to the *Rājūkas* and this, when it is considered in the context of the fact that these officers were placed in charge of a hundred thousand men, may lead us, not without sufficient reason, to suggest that they were the chief officers of a kind of administrative division. Since we cannot associate them with the provincial government, with which the *Prādeśikas*[3] were possibly connected, they may be identified with the chief officers of the next smaller divisions, viz., districts.[4]

Pillar Edict IV implies a close liaison between the emperor and the *Rājūkas*. Hultzsch[5] seems to suggest that the *Rājūkas* were placed under the supervision of the *Puruṣas*, as he translates a few passages of Pillar Edict IV in the following words, 'The *Lajūkas* also must obey me. They will also obey the agents (*pulisā*) who know (my) wishes.' Such a suggestion is not borne out by a critical study of the text itself, and D.R. Bhandarkar[6] translates it rightly thus, '*Rājūkas* are eager to obey me. And just because *Rājūkas* desire to obey me, *Purushas* also will obey my wishes and orders.' D.R. Bhandarkar[7] has equated the *Puruṣas* with the sub-divisional officers, in contradiction to the view of Hultzsch, identifying them with the highly placed 'intelligence officers' who were posted all over the empire for supplying the king with secret information and carrying to the local officers the instructions of the emperor. If we accept the interpretation of D.R. Bhandarkar, the above passage would then indicate that in the Maurya kingdom the chief district officers exercised little control over the sub-divisional officers who were directly accountable to the king himself.

The Aśokan inscriptions do not help us even in the least in tracing the terms by which the districts or the units over which the *Rājūkas* ruled were designated in those days. His Sarnath Pillar Edict,[8] no doubt, mentions an *āhāra* and a *Koṭṭaviṣaya* (a *viṣaya* around a fortress or a *koṭṭa* and a *viṣaya*) but there is no evidence to suggest that they were placed under the charge of the *Rājūkas*.

Having surveyed epigraphic evidence, we may now turn to the literature of the contemporary period to get a glimpse into the office of the chief district officer. Literature is expected to give us much more information, for it reflects the condition of the contemporary period with such richness of detail as is not expected of inscriptions.

Kauṭilya[9] states that a group of ten villages formed a *saṁgrahaṇa*, two hundred villages a *khārvaṭika*,[10] four hundred villages, a *droṇamukha* and eight hundred villages, a *sthānīya* (*Aṣṭa-śata-grāmyā madhye sthānīyaṁ, catuḥśata-grāmyā droṇamukhaṁ, dvi-śata-grāmyāḥ khārvaṭikaṁ, daśagrāmī saṁgraheṇa saṁgrahaṇaṅ sthāpayet*). In another place,[11] while dealing with judicial administration, Kauṭilya refers to three divisions only, viz., the *saṁgrahaṇa*, *droṇamukha* and *sthānīya*. It is interesting to note that the division of the *khārvaṭika* is omitted here. Can we infer that the *khārvaṭikas* refer only to the frontier divisions? Now, the *sthānīya*, which was the highest administrative unit in the Kauṭiliyan state, probably corresponds to a province and the *droṇamukha*, being next to the former in extent, a district. It cannot, however, be ascertained, in the absence of any positive evidence, whether the districts of the Maurya kingdom were called *droṇamukhas* or were differently designated.

But who were the officers in charge of the *droṇamukhas*? It is unfortunate that Kauṭilya is silent on this point. But that they were not charged with any functions other than executive appears to be fairly certain. They were not given judicial functions which came to be exercised by the *Dharmasthas* or judges, as may be inferred from his statement that 'Three judges, (all) three (of the rank of) ministers, should try cases arising cut of transactions at frontier posts, in the *saṁgrahaṇas*, *droṇamukhas* and *sthānīyas*.'[12] Similarly, they had no control over the revenue administration which was carried on by officers like the *Samāhartās*, *Gopas* and *Sthānīyas*.

II

The Chief District Officer in the Mahābhārata

The *Śāntiparvan*[13] of the *Mahābhārata* mentions a number of officers who were in charge of different kinds of administrative units like those of one village, ten villages, twenty villages, one hundred villages and one thousand villages The lord of one thousand villages of the *Mahābhārata*, who was charged with the administration of the biggest unit, may be compared with a provincial governor and the lord of one hundred villages with the chief officer of a district. It appears from the *Mahābhārata* that first, the lord of one hundred villages bore the designation of *Śatapāla*; second, he was directly appointed by the crown (*Grāmasy=ādhipatiḥ kāryo daśa grāmyās=tathā paraḥ| Dviguṇāyāḥ śatasy=aivam sahasrasya ca kārayet||*);[14] third, he was entrusted with the preservation of law and order in his district and he had to inform his superior officer of the crimes committed which he could not satisfactorily tackle; and fourth, he received as his emolument the revenue of a prosperous village (*Grāmaṁ grāma-śat=ādhyakṣo bhoktum=arhati satkṛtaḥ| Mahāntaṁ Bhārata-śreṣṭha! susphītaṁ jana-saṁkulam||*).[15]

III

The Chief District Officer in the Manu-saṁhitā

Manu similarly mentions a number of officers, who were in charge of different kinds of administrative units, like the lord of ten villages, lord of twenty villages, lord of one hundred villages and lord of one thousand villages. The *Śateśa* or the lord of one hundred villages mentioned by Manu may aptly be compared with the *Śatapāla* of the *Mahābhārata*. Manu gives the following information:

1. The lord of one hundred villages owed his appointment to the king himself (*Grāmasy=ādhipatiṁ kuryād daśa-grāma-patiṁ tathā| Viṁśatīśaṁ śateśañ=ca sahasra patim=eva ca||*).[16]

2. He did not interfere with the day-to-day administration of the villages within his jurisdiction, but intervened only in case of incompetence on the part of his subordinate officers to detect crimes and took the help of his superior officers in times of need (*Viṁśatīśas=tu tad sarvaṁ śateśāya nivedated| Śaṁsed grāma-śateśas=tu sahasrapataye svayam||*).[17]

3. He was not entrusted with the defence of the country, which was assigned to the military officers stationed in different parts of the kingdom (*Dvayos=trayāṇāṁ pañcānāṁ madhye*

gulmam=adhiṣṭhitaṁ| Tathā grāmaśatānāñ=ca kuryād=rāṣṭra-sya saṁgrahaṁ||).[18] The *Mahābhārata*, however, does not clearly state whether the defence of the country was one of the concerns of the *Śatapāla* or it was under the jurisdiction of a separate official.

4. And finally, he was entitled to enjoy the revenue of a village in return for his services (*grāmaṁ grāmaśat=ādhyakṣaḥ sahasr=ādhipatiḥ puraṁ||*).[19]

We would then see that the deficiency of the epigraphic records in furnishing us with adequate information about the chief district officer is considerably made up by contemporary literary evidence. It may not be here irrelevant to make, in brief, a comparative study among the *Rājūkas* of Aśoka, the *Śatapālas* of the *Mahābhārata* and the *Śateśas* of Manu. First, all of them were directly appointed by the king, but while the *Rājūkas* wielded unrestricted authority in the discharge of their duties, the *Śatapālas* and the *Śateśas* were denied such unfettered power. Second, while the *Rājūkas* administered justice in their own areas, it is not clear whether the *Śatapālas* or *Śateśas* discharged similar functions. Third, the *Rājūkas* were entrusted with, besides executive and judicial, the execution of works of public utility. Neither the *Mahābhārata* nor Manu assigns any such function to the *Śatapālas* or *Śateśas*. And last, the *Śatapālas* and the *Śateśas* were remunerated in kind, but if the accounts of Kauṭilya are applicable to the Maurya period, the officers under Candragupta and his grandson Aśoka were paid in cash.

IV

The Chief District Officer in the Kingdoms of Foreign Rulers

Inscriptions do not give us useful information about the district officer during the rule of the Greek, Scythian, Parthian and Kuṣāṇa kings. Nor do they furnish us with the name of a solitary administrative division which may properly be termed as a district. It seems that in some parts of the Greek and Scythian kingdoms the district officer was called *Meridarch*.[20] A Kharoṣṭhī inscription of about the later period of Greek rule, discovered from the Swat valley, mentions *Meridarkha* Theudora, while a Kharoṣṭhī inscription from Taxila refers to another such officer, an Indian, unlike the former who was a Greek, as flourishing in the early Śaka epoch. Unfortunately, we are unable to form any idea about the functions and position of these *Meridarchs* as no details about these officers, save their pious acts of establishing Buddhist relics and sanctuaries, are recorded in inscriptions. W.W. Tarn[21] maintains that *Meridarchs* refer to 'governors of fractions' and opines that the expression is of a vague and uncertain connotation.

V

The Chief District Officer in the Gupta Period

When he comes to the Gupta period, the historian need hardly lament for the paucity of materials. In the Gupta inscriptions we meet with various terms which are indicative of the various administrative divisions. While speaking of the grant of a plot of land they often refer to the village, in which the land was situated, as forming a part of a particular *viṣaya*, which is further said to have been included within a *bhukti*. We may accordingly conclude that in the Gupta inscriptions, the terms *bhukti* and *viṣaya* are used in the sense of province and district, respectively.

In the early period of Gupta supremacy, the officers in charge of *viṣayas*, particularly those of North Bengal, were generally designated either as *Kumārāmātyas* or *Āyuktakas*. In the Dhanaidaha copper plates[22] of Kumāragupta I, the officer, who was administering the Khāda(ṭa)pāra-*viṣaya*, is called an *Āyuktaka*; the first two Damodarpur plates[23] of the reign of the same Gupta monarch apply the designation *Kumārāmātya*[24] to Vetravarman, the district officer of Koṭivarṣa, while Saṇḍaka, the administrator of the Koṭivarṣa-*viṣaya*, is found bearing the title of *Āyuktaka* in a third grant from Damodarpur. The use of the titles *Kumārāmātya* and *Āyuktaka* as designations of a district officer appears to have soon fallen into disuse, and the title of *Viṣayapati* to signify the head of a district came to be popularised in their place.

Some idea about the appointment of the *Viṣayapatis* and their relations with the central and provincial governments may be obtained with the help of the contemporary inscriptions. The first two Damodarpur copper plates state that Vetravarman who was in charge of the Koṭivarṣa-*viṣaya* from G.E. 124 to G.E. 128 was appointed to the post by the *Uparika* Cirātadatta (*Koṭivarṣa-viṣaye tan=niyuktaka-Kumārāmātya*).[25] This shows that the district officers as a rule were appointed to their posts by the provincial governors. The Baigram inscription[26] of A.D. 448-9, however, implies that in the matter of appointment of the district officers a different system was sometimes adopted. The inscription contains the passage, *Pañcanagaryyā bhaṭṭāraka-pād=ānudhyātaḥ Kumārāmātya-Kulavṛddhir=etad viṣay=ādhikaraṇaṁ* meaning that the *Kumārāmātya* Kulavṛddhi of Pañcanagarī was devoted to the feet of the Bhaṭṭāraka. The word *bhaṭṭāraka*, which literally means 'one who is entitled to reverence or homage' is a technical title usually applicable to a sovereign ruler. There is in reality no difficulty in taking the Bhaṭṭāraka as referring to the ruling Gupta emperor Kumāragupta I. If this suggestion is valid, Kulavṛddhi owed his appointment to the Gupta suzerain to whom he was accountable. R.S. Sharma,[27] who objects to this interpretation on the ground that Kumāragupta I is referred to as a *Paramabhaṭṭāraka* in all the inscriptions from Bengal, is of opinion that the Bhaṭṭāraka of the Baigram inscription has to be identified with the administrative head of the Puṇḍravardhana-*bhukti*. But this argument loses much of its strength when it is remembered that in the first place, the title *Bhaṭṭāraka* has never been applied to any *Uparika* of the Gupta dominions, and in the second, even paramount monarchs, adopting the high-sounding titles of *Mahārājādhirāja* and *Parameśvara*, prided themselves on being called *Bhaṭṭāraka*. D.N. Jha[28] maintains that since Pañcanagarī and Koṭivarṣa were two adjoining districts in North Bengal, it is highly improbable that 'two different methods could have been adopted at the same time and almost in the same region with regard to the appointment of officer in charge of a *viṣaya*'. He has accordingly taken the Baigram inscription to mean that 'the selection of the official was obviously made by the governor of the *bhukti*, though his appointment was formalised by the emperor himself'. Such a theory, it must be admitted, was propounded long ago by R.G. Basak.[29] Unfortunately we are unable to accept this view. The discrepancy in the accounts with reference to the appointment of the *Viṣayapati* between the Damodarpur and Baigram plates seems to allude definitely to different modes of selection in the areas to which they refer. The Baigram inscription thus proves that the district officers in some cases owed their appointment to the Gupta monarchs and were directly responsible to them.

Inscriptions suggest that the *Viṣayapati*, as the head of the district administration, was intimately connected with the land transaction of his area. The Dhanaidaha plates state that an applicant for a piece of state land approached the *Āyuktaka* who was informed of the details of the land required. On receiving full information from the applicant this officer placed the whole matter before the *adhiṣṭhānādhikaraṇa* which, after having investigated the case, granted the prayer. It is again stated in the Paharpur inscription[30] dated A.D. 479 that Nāthaśarman and his wife Rāmī appealed to the district officer and the *adhiṣṭhānādhikaraṇa* for the grant of a plot of land to be used for religious purposes in return for the payment of three *dīnāras*. It is clear from the above two records that the transaction of land formed one of the most important functions of the *Viṣayapatis* and the *adhiṣṭhānādhikaraṇa*, and that no state-owned land could be sold without their approval. It is quite likely that the *Viṣayapatis* also collected the revenue of their respective areas, no doubt, with the help of several minor officers stationed at the headquarters and different places of their districts.

The mention of the *adhiṣṭhānādhikaraṇa* along with *Viṣayapati* in the records in connection with the grant of land reveals that both acted in close co-operation. The term *adhiṣṭhānādhikaraṇa* has been variously interpreted by scholars. R.G. Basak[31] and R.C. Majumdar take it to mean 'an administrative board of the district' and 'the royal tribunal in a city', respectively, while it is taken by some other scholars to mean 'the office and probably the court of a district officer', 'a secretariat and advisory council', 'the office of the district headquarters' and so on. We are, however, inclined to interpret the expression as meaning a council which seems to have worked like a *Pañcāyat* board of the district. D.C. Sircar[32] suggests that the *adhikaraṇa* conducted the non-military administration of a city and often a wider area under the jurisdiction of the city, in question, being comparable with the *Chauthia* or council of four members, including the *Nagarseth*, the *Patel* and *Patwari*, as is prevalent in Rajasthan and described by Tod, and with the *Pañcakula*,[33] mentioned in the early medieval epigraphic and literary records of Western India.

An answer to the question as to who were the members of the *adhikaraṇa* may be found in the passage of the Damodarpur inscription of the year 124, reading *adhiṣṭhānādhikaraṇañ=ca nagaraśreṣṭhi-Dhṛtipāla-sārthavāha-Vasumitra-prathama - kulika-Dhṛtimitra-prathamakāyastha-Śāmbapāla - puroge saṁvyavaha-rati.*[34] The district council was then composed of at least the following members:

1. The *Nagaraśreṣṭhin.* He was the president, to judge from the etymology of the term, either of the various guilds or banking corporations of the district headquarters.[35] The *Nagaraśreṣṭhin* was probably the chairman of the board. The *Nagarśeṭh* (i.e., *Nagaraśreṣṭhin)* heading the *Pañcāyat* is known from the history of Rajasthan.

2. The *Prathamasārthavāha.* He was the leading merchant who represented the different mercantile associations of the district.[36]

3. The *Prathamakulika.* He was the chief artisan and representative of the various craft guilds of the *viṣaya.*

4. The *Prathamakāyastha.* The *Prathamakāyastha*, who was the chief scribe, either 'represented the Kāyasthas as a class' or acted 'as a state official in the capacity of a secretary of modern days'.

The membership of the district *adhikaraṇa* was not solely confined to the above-mentioned persons, but it was a larger body. It is far from certain whether the *Nagaraśreṣṭhin, Prathamasārthavāha, Prathamakulika*, etc. were elected by their respective constituencies or nominated by the government to their posts in the council. The discovery by Bloch[37] of a large number of seals at Basarh in North Bihar, bearing the legend *śreṣṭhi-sārthavāha-kulika-nigama*, has proved the existence of trade, industrial and banking corporations in North Bihar during the contemporary epoch. It seems that the presidents of such corporate bodies were automatically favoured with a seat in the district *adhikaraṇa.* But here again, as R.G. Basak[38] has observed, 'Whether the presidents were elected by the associations or nominated by the king, we have no definite means to determine.' If, however, the testimony of some *Dharmaśāstra-*

writers is considered trustworthy, the presidents of such associations were then elected by their colleagues. As regards the remaining members, it may be observed that those persons who commanded a great respect and confidence in their districts for their age, experience and character, were offered by a general consensus seats in the *adhiṣṭhānādhikaraṇa*.

The question which may now arise relates to the relations in which the members of the council stood to the *Viṣayapati*. It is suggested by some scholars that the members of the *adhikaraṇa* did not wield any direct authority in the district administration, but the *Viṣayapati* carried on the administrative and other functions in their presence. This theory is criticised by others who think them as forming a 'Board of Advisers'. According to R.G. Basak,[39] the members of the *adhikaraṇa* were not mere advisers of the *Viṣayapatis* but 'held concurrent authority with the district officers in the general administration or at least in certain specified branches of it'. The last suggestion appears to be more reasonable and we are inclined to think that the members of the *adhikaraṇa* possessed rights and prerogatives beyond those of mere advisers.

The functions of the *adhikaraṇa* were not limited to the transaction of land alone, but it seems that, although corroborative evidence is lacking, it, along with the *Viṣayapati*, was responsible for the discharge of executive and other functions of the *viṣaya*.

A.S. Altekar[40] is not sure about the territorial limits over which the authority of the *adhikaraṇa* prevailed. He says, 'Whether the council looked after the administration of the headquarters of the district alone or of all the territories included in the district is not known.' Inscriptions, however, do not leave us in the dark on this point. Since the *adhikaraṇa* is invariably mentioned in connection with the sale of land, situated in villages, outside the limits of district towns, the conclusion is inevitable that it held its authority over the whole district.

What we have so long said about the *Viṣayapatis* is applicable to the eastern part of the Gupta dominions. Our knowledge about those in the remaining parts of the Gupta kingdom is unfortunately fragmentary, but the little that we learn about them is in agreement with the testimony of the Damodarpur copper plate grants. The Indore copper plate grant[41] of

Skandagupta of G.E. 146 mentions the *Viṣayapati* Sarvanāga as governing the Antarvedī region or the country lying between the Ganga and the Jamuna. He is said to have been selected for his post by Skandagupta (*śrī-Skandaguptasya . . . tat-pāda-parigṛhītasya-viṣayapati-Sarvanāgasy=Āntarvvedyāṁ*). We thus see that some of the *Viṣayapatis* of Western India owed their appointment to the Gupta suzerain.

We have already seen how the *Viṣayapatis* of North Bengal discharged their functions in consultation with the members of the district *adhikaraṇa*. That such a system prevailed in other parts is proved beyond doubt by the Nandapur copper plates[42] of G.E. 169. We learn from this record that the *Viṣayapati* Chatramaha, on being desirous of purchasing four *Kulyavāpas* of fallow land in the village of Jaṅgoyikā, presented himself before the council and informed it of his willingness to pay the price for the land in accordance with the system of sale prevailing in that district. The *adhikaraṇa* appointed two *Pustapālas* who were asked to investigate and report on the case. The two *Pustapālas*, Pradyotasiṁha and Bandhudāsa, submitted their report showing that, first, the statement of the district officer with regard to the system of sale in that district was correct; second, the land yielding no revenue to the state, 'there could be no loss of income to the crown in such sale of revenue-free fallow lands'; and finally, the land could be granted. This shows that the members of the *adhikaraṇa* were not silent spectators of the activities carried on in the district, but formed an integral part of the administrative set-up.

Now, before we proceed to the next age, we may pause for a while to take notice of the changes that have crept into the office of the chief district officer by the time of the Guptas. Thus while the Maurya *Rājūka* and Manu's *Śateśa* were appointed directly by the kings, the Gupta *Viṣayapatis*, with the exception of a few among them, owed their appointment to the provincial governors. Secondly, the district officers, as mentioned in the Aśokan inscriptions and the Mānava *Dharmaśāstra*, possessed almost unrestricted authority, whereas some popular representatives as members of the *Viṣayādhikaraṇa* advised and guided the Gupta *Viṣayapatis*. Thirdly, we do not know whether the *Rājūkas* and *Śateśas* were in any way connected with the revenue function but that the Gupta *Viṣayapatis* were responsible for the collection of the king's revenue in the areas under their jurisdiction admits of no doubt. And lastly, although we have some idea about the way in which the district officers under the Mauryas and those as envisaged by Manu were remunerated, it cannot be determined how the Gupta *Viṣayapatis* were rewarded in return for their services.

VI

The Chief District Officer in the Post-Gupta Period

The *Viṣayapatis* who served as heads of districts in the Gupta kingdom find mention in the Maitraka inscriptions. It seems that the divisions of a province of the Maitraka kingdom were called *viṣayas*. Curiously enough in the Alina copper plates[43] of Dharasena II of the year 270 we meet with the expression *Kheṭak=āhāra-viṣaya*. This would lead us to suggest that the districts of the Maitraka kingdom were sometimes designated as *āhāras*. But the power of the *Viṣayapatis* was somewhat limited in the Maitraka dominions for they were not connected with the 'collection of the royal share of the produce in grain' which was entrusted to the *Dhruvādhikaraṇikas*.

The Gupta system of district administration was introduced in East Bengal by its independent kings like Gopacandra, Dharmāditya and Samācāradeva. The Faridpur copper plate grants[44] show that in this region the *Viṣayapatis* were appointed by the chiefs of the bigger units. Jajāva, for example, was put in charge of the Vāraka-*maṇḍalaviṣaya* by Sthāṇudatta who was the governor of Navyāvakāśika (*Mahārāj=ādhirāja-śrī-Dharmāditya-rājye tad - prasāda - labdhāspada - Mahārāja-Sthāṇudattasy=ādhyāsana - kāle tad - viniyuktaka - Vārakamaṇḍale viṣayapati Jajāvasyāyoge*). In an undated Faridpur grant of the same Dharmāditya, Gopālasvāmī, the officer of the Vāraka-*maṇḍalaviṣaya* is described as a *Vyāpārakāraṇḍya*. Pargiter[45] takes the word to mean 'one who has to regulate trade', while according to D.C. Sircar[16] the expression means 'one in charge of the box of documents relating to administration'. D.C. Sircar's interpretation would make one believe that the *Viṣayapatis* of the Faridpur copper plates took special care for preserving confidential and important state documents, a task which was carried on by the *Pustapālas* in the Gupta period.

The existence of a district council in this age is proved by one of the Faridpur grants which shows what a vital role was played in administration by the *Viṣayamahattaras*, who were evidently the members of such councils. We come to learn from this record that the *Viṣayādhikaraṇa* was a large body, claiming as many as twenty members, some of whom like Kulasvāmin and Śubhadeva probably belonged to the Brahmin caste and some others like Ghoracandra and Guṇacandra were non-Brahmins. There is no evidence to suggest that the functions of these *Viṣayapatis* and the district council were different from those of their Gupta counterparts.

The *Agni Purāṇa*[47] mentions the *viṣaya* and its head, called *Viṣayeśvara*. The chief district officer was appointed by the king and he was to send to the latter the taxes collected from the people on the basis of a careful assessment of their property. Each district seems to have been divided into several units of one hundred villages the heads of which were to submit a report to the officer in charge of the district in the event of emergency. Regarding the payment of wages to these officers, the *Agni Purāṇa* says that they were to be provided with 'a share in the daily offerings of revenue (*bhoga*) made by the villagers'.[48]

VII

The Viṣayapati in the Pāla Kingdom

The Pāla inscriptions refer to the *Viṣayapatis*. The passage *Jyeṣṭhakāyastha - mahāmahattara - mahattara - dāśagrāmik=ādi viṣaya-vyavahāriṇaḥ sa-karaṇān*, which is found in the Khalimpur plates[49] of Dharmapāla shows that the *Viṣayapati* discharged his functions with the help of the officers like the *Jyeṣṭhakāyastha*,[50] *Mahāmahattara*, *Mahattara*[51] and *Dāśagrāmikas*. The manner in which they are mentioned in the above record indicates that the *Jyeṣṭhakāyastha* who was either the chief scribe or the representative of the scribal class was the most prominent among all the subordinate officers of the *viṣaya*. The Khalimpur inscription further shows that for purposes of efficient administration each *viṣaya* was divided into a number of units of ten villages.

But what were the functions of the *Viṣayapatis* in the Pāla kingdom? It is unfortunate that no Damodarpur copper plate grants come to our rescue. In the Khalimpur inscription mention is made, after the *Viṣayapati*, of such officers like the *Ṣaṣṭhādhikṛta*, *Daṇḍaśakti*, *Daṇḍapāśika*, *Cauroddharaṇika*, *Dauḥsādhasādhanika*, etc. This may imply that they were all connected with districts and placed under the supervision of the *Viṣayapati*. In the Manahali plate[52] of Madanapāla, who was one of the last rulers of the Pāla dynasty, the *Viṣayapati* occupies a very low rank in the list of officers and is inferior to the *Cauroddharaṇika*, *Dāṇḍika*, *Daṇḍapāśika*, etc. Practically the same thing is repeated in the Madhainagar plate[53] of Lakṣmaṇasena. This may prove that from about the latter half of the Pāla period, all the important functions of the *Viṣayapati* were then taken over by the central government as a result of which he came to be relegated to the position of a titular head of the district. It is also not unlikely that the officers are mentioned in the list in the later Pāla and Sena inscriptions not according to their order of importance but rather arbitrarily.

VIII

The Viṣayapati in Other North Indian Kingdoms

The inscriptions of many other North Indian dynasties mention the *Viṣayapatis* but they speak very little about the functions of such officers. In the copper plates[54] of Padmaṭa, assignable to the middle of the tenth century A.D., both the *Viṣayapati* and the *Viṣayavyāpṛtaka* are mentioned. It seems that the latter was a subordinate district officer, placed under the supervision of the former. We find the *Viṣayapati* being mentioned in the Bhauma-Kara inscriptions, in the list of officers to whom the royal order relating to the grant of land was addressed. The *Viṣayapati* appears to have been very powerful in the Kalacuri kingdom as may be gleaned from the fact that the Chhoti Deori stone[55] inscription of the reign of Śaṅkaragaṇa I was issued by Cuṭu Nāgaka who was in charge of the *viṣaya* of Kakandakuṭu. The Gāhaḍavāla inscriptions[56] mention the *Viṣay=ādhikāri puruṣas* who were placed in charge of districts.

IX

The Viṣayapati in the Śātavāhana Period

Having analysed the position of the *Viṣayapati* in different kingdoms and ages in North India, we now turn to the South Indian inscriptions to get a glimpse into his position as reflected in them. We shall start with the Śātavāhana records. In the Myakadoni rock inscription,[57] dated in the eighth regnal year of Pulumāyi, we have the passage *Mahāsenāpatisa Khaṁdanākasa janapade Śatavāhaṇihāre grāmikasa Kumāradattasa grāme Vepuraka*, Sanskritised by D.C. Sircar thus, *Mahāsenāpateḥ Skandanāgasya janapade Śātavāhanīyahāre grāmikasya Kumāra-dattasya grāme Vepurake*. This passage seems to suggest that the provinces of the Śātavāhana kingdom were called *janapadas* and the districts *āhāras*. The *āhāras* were generally called after the names of their headquarters, as in the case of the Govardhana and Māmala *āhāras*. The *āhāras* were usually placed under officers who bore the designation of *Amaca*, corresponding to Sanskrit *Amātya*. Ancient Indian tradition regards the *Amātyas* as ministers or *Mantrins*, but their appointment as governors of provinces and districts does not sound astonishing when we take into account the fact that the commentator Rāmavarman assigns to them the duty of running the government in the various parts of the kingdom (*Amātya deś=ādi-kārya-nirvāhakā mantriṇo vyavahāra-draṣṭāra iti bhedaḥ*). It appears from a careful scrutiny of the Śātavāhana inscriptions that first, the post of the district officer in the Śātavāhana realm was not hereditary, being subjected to 'periodical transfers';[58] second, the invariable mention of this officer in connection with the grant of land would tend to show that he had a vital role to play in the land administration; and furthermore, since the royal orders were directly communicated to him and to no other officers, high or low, as mentioned in the copper plate grants, as in the case of a royal order regarding the grant of land in the eighteenth year of Gautamīputra Śātakarṇi's reign (*Gotami-puto Siri-Sadakaṇi ānapayati Govadhane amaca Viṇhupālitam*), it would legitimately follow that he had direct dealings with the king.

X

The Chief District Officer in the Post-Śātavāhana Period

The Ikṣvāku kingdom was divided into several parts called *rāṣṭras*, which may be said to have approached the dimensions of districts, but the title and details of the officers who were placed in charge of these divisions are not known. The kingdom of the Bṛhatphalāyanas, like that of the Śātavāhanas, was too parcelled out for administrative purposes into a number of districts called *āhāras* which were governed by officers bearing the designation of *Vyāpṛta*. An inscription[59] of king Jayavarman of this family shows how the order of the king relating to the grant of land was conveyed to the *Vyāpṛta* for necessary action. This reveals that the district officer of the Bṛhatphalāyana kingdom was more concerned with land transaction than with any other function. The charter of Jayavarman implies that the military officers bearing the title of *Daṇḍanāyaka* were stationed in the different places of the kingdom and they dealt with, besides defence, the problem of law and order.

The position of the district officer in the Bṛhatphalāyana kingdom may be compared with that of his brethren in the Śātavāhana dominions. In both the kingdoms, the districts were called *āhāras*, but the officers in charge of them were differently designated. The officers in both the kingdoms enjoyed the privilege of having direct dealings with the king. It, however, seems that in the Bṛhatphalāyana kingdom, some of the functions of the *Vyāpṛtakas* were taken over by the *Daṇḍanāyakas*, whereas in the Śātavāhana districts, there was probably no such division of power between the *Amātyas* and other officers.

XI

The Chief District Officer in the Vākāṭaka-Pallava Kingdoms

Rāṣṭra, *rājya* and *bhukti* are the different terms which are to be met with in Vākāṭaka inscriptions. The extent of these cannot be precisely determined. But since the Vākāṭaka inscriptions do not mention any other divisions between them and the villages which were situated in them, we may reasonably conclude that these different terms are used in the Vākāṭaka epigraphs to denote one and the same kind of administrative unit, which was probably equal in size to the present districts. These administrative units were usually placed under charge of officers who bore the designation of *Santaka*.[60] The functions of these officers, as evidenced by inscriptions, consisted of the collection of land revenue and the maintenance of law and order in their respective areas. They were, however, not granted unbridled authority and the central government maintained a strict police surveillance through its inspecting staff. All this would prove that the Vākāṭaka *Santakas*, notwithstanding the similitude of their functions, were not given such concessions of power as were granted to the Śātavāhana *Amātyas*, a few centuries ago.

The inscriptions of the Pallava kings suggest that a large number of villages formed a *nāḍu* which was a smaller administrative unit than the *koṭṭam* or province, proving thereby that the *nāḍus* of the Pallava kingdom correspond to the *āhāras* under the Śātavāhana kings. The *nāḍus* were generally placed under officers who were called *Āyuktakas* and *Adhyakṣas* in the early period of Pallava ascendancy and *Nāṭṭuviyavan* in later days. The Hirahadagalli copper plate grant[61] shows that the *Āyuktakas* and the *Adhyakṣas* were directly placed under the control of the central government, but whether this practice was in vogue in the later ages we do not know. It is unfortunate that we do not possess sufficient details either about these officers or the functions they discharged. Inscriptions reveal that under the Pallavas all the villages within the districts were carefully surveyed and the registers showing 'land rights including schedules of tax-free lands and alteration and transference of ownership' were maintained. Against this background, it may be surmised that the district officers were directly concerned with all these functions. The king willing to grant a piece of land to a donee generally ordered the district officers to carry out the transaction. In such cases they did the necessary work, measured the endowed lands and fixed their boundaries. The *Nāṭṭuviyavan*, however, was not connected with the administration of justice, which was discharged, if the view of C. Minakshi[62] has any validity, by the magistrates called *Adhikāras*. In the Kasakudi plates, mention is made of the term *nāṭṭuvagai*. K.V.S. Aiyar[63] has interpreted it in the sense of 'settlement duties', but this, as it stands, is a vague explanation. Since the Tamil term *vagai* means 'a part' or 'portion', *nāṭṭuvagai* may accordingly be interpreted to mean that portion of the share from the village due to the *nāḍu* which had the right of demand as an administrative authority. We may, therefore, conclude that the *Nāṭṭuviyavan* was entrusted with the collection of this tax.

The inscriptions of the Pallavas mention the *Nāṭṭārs* or the members of the district council as playing, like the *Nāṭṭuviyavan*, a significant role in the land administration. C. Minakshi[64] points out that in the Kasakudi inscription, 'we have a royal order directly addressed to the men of the *Nāḍu* (*Konolai*) "*Urrukkāṭṭukoṭṭattu Nāṭṭārum kāṇka*". The *Nāṭṭārs* were ordered to transfer a particular village named Koḍukolli as a *Brahmadeya* to a certain Brāhmaṇa. The *Nāṭṭārs*, after seeing the king's order, 'removed the former owners of the village, excluded (previous) grants to temples and to Brāhmaṇas, excluded the houses (of the ryots), walked along the boundaries which the headman of the *Nāḍu* pointed out, circumambulating the village from right to left; planted stones and milk bush around'. Occasions were not rare when the district council acted in close co operation with other corporate bodies. An inscription[65] of Nandivarman Pallava Malla alludes to one such occasion when the *Nāṭṭār*, *Ūrār* and *Alvār* by a consensus granted certain *kalañjus* of gold to the god Subrahmaṇya.

It is evident from what has been observed above that we get scant notices of the office of the chief district officer in the Pallava kingdom. That he exercised revenue functions admits of no doubt, but his judicial functions were taken over by the *Adhikāras*. And again, how much he was concerned with the executive duties, we have no means to ascertain. The existence of a district council hardly allowed the district officer to become an autocrat even in the limited sphere of his activity.

XII

The Viṣayapati in the Rāṣṭrakūṭa Kingdom

The inscriptions of the Rāṣṭrakūṭa kings imply that the *rāṣṭra* was the largest administrative unit in their kingdom and the *viṣaya* was its sub-division. If the *rāṣṭras*[66] were provinces, the *viṣayas* would correspond to districts. The *viṣayas* of the

Rāṣṭrakūṭa kingdom were placed under the supervision of the *Viṣayapatis*. Some of the districts like Puṇaka, it is learnt from the Rāṣṭrakūṭa records, were composed of 1,000 villages, whereas there were others which were big enough to include as many as 4,000 villages. The district of Karhāṭaka, for instance, comprised 4,000 villages. The Rāṣṭrakūṭa *Viṣayapatis* were usually appointed by the king himself. Persons who had demonstrated their skill and talents in the realm of administration or in battle-fields were usually chosen as district officers. Under these circumstances, the posts were not hereditary. It is at the same time reasonable to suppose that if the son of a *Viṣayapati* matched the valour and wisdom of his father, he was allowed to succeed his father on the latter's death.

The inscriptions of the Rāṣṭrakūṭa dynasty refer to some *Viṣayapatis* as having enjoyed the status of a feudatory. Kundamarāja, who was administering the Kuntala-*viṣaya* in A D. 1019, for example, was elevated to such an exalted position, as may be guessed from the titles, *Mahāmaṇḍaleśvara* and *Samadhigata-pañcamahāśabda*, applied to him.[67] It seems that this status was claimed not by all the *Viṣayapatis* but by a select few. A.S. Altekar[68] points out that some of the district officers were originally independent kings who were subsequently subdued by the Rāṣṭrakūṭa rulers but were reinstated in their former kingdoms as officers of the imperial government. We agree with the view of A.S. Altekar[69] that most of the *Viṣayapatis* claiming feudatory rank belonged to this category.

The uprising of subordinate officers was not a rare phenomenon in the Rāṣṭrakūṭa dominions. Even small *tahsil* or *taluka* officers rose in revolt and withdrew their allegiance to the central government. This leads us to surmise that all these officers, including the *Viṣayapatis*, were at the command of the military forces stationed at their headquarters.

As regards the functions of the *Viṣayapatis*, it may be noted that they invariably figure in inscriptions in the list of officers who were informed of the grant of land by the king. The expression *yathāsaṁbaddhamānakān* in the phrase *sarvvān=eva yathāsaṁbaddhamānakān rāṣṭra - viṣayapati - grāmakūṭ = āyuktaka-niyuktak=ādhikārika - mahattar=ādin sam=ādhiśaty = astu*, occurring in the Konnur inscription[70] of Amoghavarṣa, indubitably indicates that they were intimately connected with the land transactions of their districts. So much involvement in land transactions on their part may further imply that it is they who were mainly responsible for the collection of the district revenue and transmitting the same to the higher authorities. The Kunimellihalli inscription[71] of Śaka 818 refers to the *Viṣayapati* Dindeśvarada Oṅkāra-Śiva-bhaṭāra, governing the Palasūr district, as conceding the prayer of a certain individual for the remission of taxation of the village of Dantavūra (*Asagaṇṇaṁ Dantavūraṁ biḍisidoṁ Oṅkāra-Śiva - bhaṭār - biṭṭar = idaṁ kadoṅge*). It is not known whether this particular officer, while remitting taxes, obtained the prior approval of his higher authorities, or exercised this right according to his own discretion. It is similarly far from being known whether the right of granting remission was enjoyed by all or by a few among them.

The mention of the *Viṣayamahattaras* in the Kapadwanj grant[72] of Kṛṣṇa II proves the existence of a popular body in some of the districts of the Rāṣṭrakūṭa dominions. The lone mention of such a body in only one record of the family would tend to suggest that it existed in very restricted areas. Even in those regions where such a council was in vogue, we have no positive evidence to ascertain whether its members were selected by the crown or elected by the people, how frequently they used to meet, what their duties were and how they discharged them. As the country in those days lacked in well-organised systems of communications, it is natural to presume that this body could hardly meet regularly, with the result that it failed to mould the administration of the district in such an effective manner as the members of the village council succeeded in influencing the destiny of their respective localities.

XIII

The Chief District Officer in the Western Cālukya Kingdom

The *rāṣṭra* was the largest administrative unit in the kingdom of the Cālukya kings of Kalyāṇī. Each *rāṣṭra* comprised a number of *nāḍus* or *viṣayas* which thus appear to be equal to the modern districts. Each *nāḍu* was placed in charge of an officer called *Nāḍasa*, also known as *Nāl-prabhu*, who was helped in the task of administration by his subordinate officer, *Nālgāvuṇḍa*, while the *viṣayas* were governed by the *Viṣayapatis*.

Some welcome light on the duties and functions of the chief district officer is thrown by an inscription of A.D. 1045 from Morigeri.[73] It records that certain donations were made in favour of a local temple and the district officer was entrusted with the maintenance of the sanctity of the temple. The officer was granted the right of removing, if the situation demanded it, any of its occupants who would prove to be obnoxious to the institution and of installing better persons as their successors. That the district officer continued to be connected with land administration in the Cālukya kingdom is further borne out by the passage, *sarvān=eva yathā-saṁbaddhamānakān=rāṣṭrapati-viṣayapati-grāmakūṭaka-āyuktaka-niyuktak=ādhikārika-mahattar =ādīn sam=ādiśaty=astu vaḥ saṁviditam*, occurring in the Nilgunda plates[74] of Vikramāditya VI. Although adequate information on the duties and functions of and the mutual relations among the different categories of officers, connected with *viṣayas* is lacking, it seems that the *Viṣayapati* or the *Nāḍasa* was entrusted with the general administration of the district, while his subordinate, the *Nālgāvuṇḍa*, was mainly concerned with the collection of revenue, particularly land revenue.

It will not be out of context, if we make a comparative study of the position of the chief district officer in the Rāṣṭrakūṭa and Western Cālukya kingdoms. First, in the Rāṣṭrakūṭa kingdom this officer was called *Viṣayapati*. But in the latter kingdom he was not uniformly designated; in some parts he bore the title of *Nāḍasa* while in other parts he was known as *Viṣayapati*. Second, in both the kingdoms they were entrusted with the general administration of their respective districts, but it appears to be fairly certain that the Rāṣṭrakūṭa *Viṣayapatis* enjoyed a greater freedom. Third, while some of the Rāṣṭrakūṭa *viṣayas* had district councils, there is no positive evidence of the existence of such councils in the Western Cālukya dominions.

References and Notes

1. *Aśoka*, p. 53, *CA*, II, p. 29.
2. The instructions are as follows: 'Meritorious is obedience to mother and father. Liberality to friends, acquaintances and relatives, to Brāhmaṇas and Śramaṇas is meritorious. Abstention from killing

animals is meritorious. Moderation in expenditure (and) moderation in possession are meritorious.' (*CII*, I, p. 5).

3. Rock Edict III mentions the *Prādeśikas.* The term must be derived from the word *pradeśa* which means a province. B.M. Barua (*AAHI*, p. 194) thinks that the word *pradeśa* may mean 'a smaller administrative area under any jurisdiction'. K.P. Jayaswal regards them as provincial ministers. Some scholars (*AAHI*, p. 194) are inclined to identify them with reporters on the ground that the word *pradeśa* is used in the *Arthaśāstra* in the sense of report. R.G. Basak (*AI*, p. 12) thinks that the *Prādeśikas* were the magistrates who tried criminal cases (*pra+ā+diś*). But the term *pradeśa* should better be understood as a territorial term. Rock Edict III mentions the *Yuktas*, *Rājūkas* and *Prādeśikas* in an ascending order of importance. This would mean that the *Prādeśikas* were in charge of bigger administrative units than districts. In Kalhaṇa's *Rājataraṅgiṇī* (IV.126) the term *prādeśikeśvara* is used in the sense of a provincial chief. Kern (*JRAS*, 1880. p. 393) identifies the *Prādeśikas* with the provincial governors.
4. There is a good deal of confusion among scholars about the status of the *Rājūkas* (the variant forms of the term being *rajuka*, *lajuka*, *lajūka*, etc.) in the Maurya administrative machinery. R.K. Mookherji (*Aśoka*, pp. 53, 56) derives the term from the word *rājā* and interprets it to mean provincial governors. B.M. Barua (*AAHI*, pp. 192-96) holds practically the same view as he identifies them with governors or imperial commissioners. But these theories do not carry much conviction because the etymological connection of the word *rājūka* with *rājan* is extremely doubtful. K.P. Jayaswal (*JBORS*, 1918, pp. 41-2; *HP*, pp. 129-30) takes the *Rājūkas* to mean imperial high ministers, but he does not advance cogent arguments in support of his view. Bühler (*ZDMG*, 1893, p. 466) identifies, on the basis of sound philological grounds, the *Rājūkas* with the *Rajjugāhaka amacca* (literally, the rope-holding officer) as mentioned in the *Kurudhamma Jātaka.* But it should be noted that the *Rajjugāhaka amacca* was entrusted with the task of measuring the lands of the tax-paying people, 'either to determine the amount of rent payable by them to the king, or to determine from the extent of land the average produce to be brought to the king's storeroom' (*SONEI*, p. 149). But the Aśokan *Rājūka* was not a mere revenue or settlement officer. The *Rājūkas* are seldom referred to in later inscriptions and literature. Some inscriptions of the Śātavāhana period mention the *Rājūkas*, but they do not give us any clue as to their rank and functions (*EI*, II, p. 326; *Luders' List*, No. 1195). The Indore copper plate inscription of the Vākāṭaka king Pravarasena II mentions the *Rājūka* Koṭṭadeva as its writer (*EI*, XXIV, pp. 52ff). It seems that one of the duties of the *Rājūkas* in the Vākāṭaka kingdom was to record the deeds of transfer of land. Evidently by the time of Pravarasena II, they were relegated to the rank of petty officers.
5. *CII*, I, p. 124.

6. *Aśoka*, p. 309.
7. *Aśoka*, 57.
8. *AI*, p. 146.
9. 2.1.1.
10. The term *khārvaṭika* is sometimes read as *kārvaṭika* (*KA*, I, p. 32).
11. III.1.1.
12. *KA*, II, p. 219.
13. 85.3-7.
14. *Śāntiparvan*, 85.3.
15. *Śāntiparvan*, 85.7. The *Bhārata-Kaumudī* explains the term *susphītaṁ* thus: *susphītaṁ dhana-dhāny=ādibhiḥ susamṛddham*.
16. VII.115.
17. VII.117. G. Bühler (*Laws of Manu*, 1967, p. 234) translates the corresponding passages of Manu in the following words, 'The lord of one village himself shall inform the lord of ten villages of the crimes committed in his village, and the ruler of ten (shall make his report) to the ruler of twenty. But the ruler of twenty shall report all such (matters) to the lord of a hundred, and the lord of a hundred shall himself give information to the lord of a thousand.' This interpretation would make us believe that the officers, mentioned in the above passages, had to inform their superiors of all the crimes committed in the areas of their respective jurisdiction, but such meaning is opposed to the comments of Medhātithi and Kullūka. The latter commentator, for instance, explicitly states *grām=ādhipatiś-caurādi-doṣān grāme saṁjātān ātmanā pratikarttum=akṣamaḥ svayaṁ daśa-grām=ādhipataye kathayet*.
18. VII.114.
19. VII.119.
20. *EI*, XVII, p. 345.
21. *EI*, XV, pp. 129ff; ibid. XVII, p. 193.
22. *PHAI*, p. 515.
23. *GBI*, p. 242.
24. Various suggestions have been made on the interpretation of the term *kumārāmātya* which occurs so frequently in the inscriptions of the Gupta and post-Gupta period. *Kumāra* denotes a youth or a prince. *Kumārāmātya* may accordingly mean a junior minister or a minister of a prince, as distinguished from that of a king, or a minister in charge of a prince. *Kumārāmātya* may also mean one who has been a minister since the days of his youth (*Kumārād ārabhya amātyaḥ*).
25. *SI*, p. 291.
26. *EI*, XXI, pp. 78ff.
27. *APIIAI*, pp. 209-10.
28. *RSMGT*, p. 174.
29. *EI*, XXI, p. 80.
30. *EI*, XX, pp. 61ff.
31. *HB*, pp. 264ff.
32. *Journal of the University of Gauhati*, VI, pp. 83-85.

33. A grant of Arjunadatta (*IA*, XI, p. 242) of Anahillapāṭaka of the Vikrama year 1320 reads, '*Śrī-Abhayasīha-prabhṛtipañcakula-pratipattau*', whereas in the Bhinmal inscription (*Bombay Gazetteer*, I, pt. I, p. 480) of the year 1333 we have the passage '*tan=niyukta-Mahāgajasīha-prabhṛtipañcakula-pratipattau*'.
34. *SI*, p. 291.
35. *PHAI*, p. 561.
36. Ibid., p. 561.
37. *ASI*, 1903-4, pp. 101-20.
38. *HB*, p. 267.
39. Ibid.
40. *SGAI*, p. 210.
41. *CII*, III, pp. 68ff.
42. *EI*, XXIII, pp. 52ff.
43. *IA*, VII, pp. 72ff.
44. *SI*, pp 363ff.
45. *SI*, p. 368.
46. Ibid.
47. B.B. Mishra, *Polity In The Agni Purāṇa* (Calcutta, 1965), pp. 140-42.
48. Ibid., p. 161.
49. *EI*, IV, p. 243; *Gauḍa-lekhamālā*, p. 9.
50. The exact meaning of the term *jyeṣṭha-kāyastha* is not clear. U.N. Ghosal translates it as 'chief scribe', Pargiter as 'oldest official' and R.G. Basak as 'chief secretary'. There is also a view identifying the *Jyeṣṭha-kāyastha* with the *Sheristādār* of the Collector's office in a district of British India.
51. The *Viṣaya-mahattaras* or members of the district council are likewise mentioned in a sixth century Viṣṇukuṇḍin record from Andhra (*JAHRS*, VII, p. 17). The fact that the Khalimpur grant includes them in a list of persons, entrusted with the administration of the district, proves that these *Mahattaras* were not mere private individuals but were persons concerned with administrative functions.
52. *Gauḍa-lekhamālā*, pp. 147ff.
53. N.G. Majumdar, *Inscriptions of Bengal*, III, pp. 106ff.
54. *IE*, p. 369; *EI*, XXXI, pp. 284ff.
55. *CII*, IV, pt. I, pp. 178ff. The Anjaneri plates of Pṛthvīdeva I mention the Purī-Koṅkaṇa *viṣaya* as comprising 14,000 villages. This may indicate that some of the *viṣayas* were big in size. But generally speaking, *viṣayas* must have been much smaller in extent. Some of the *viṣayas* seem to have changed their names in the course of time. Thus when Broach attained a greater importance as the capital of the Gurjaras, the name of the Antarnarmadā-*viṣaya* was changed to the Bharukaccha-*viṣaya* (Ibid., CXXXIV).
56. The Chandravati inscription of the Vikrama year 1150 includes the *Viṣayādhikāri-puruṣas* in the list of officers to be informed in respect of a land-grant (*EI*, XIV, pp. 193ff).
57. *EI*, XIV, pp. 153ff.

58. The *Amātyas* Viṣṇupālita, Śyāmaka and Śivaskandadatta successively governed the Govardhana district in the time of Gautamīputra and Pulumāyi.
59. *Luders' List*, No. 1328.
60. *EHD*, p. 194.
61. *EI*, I, pp. 1ff.
62. *ASLP*, pp. 57ff.
63. *Ancient Deccan*, p. 344.
64. *ASLP*, p. 57.
65. *ASLP*, p. 61.
66. N.R. Ray (*IHQ*, IV, p. 470) draws our attention to the fact that in the Maitraka kingdom of Western India a *viṣaya* was a larger administrative area than a *rāṣṭra*, corresponding to a province. He refers in this connection to the Kavi grant (*IA*, V, p. 114) of Jayabhaṭa of the year 486 which mentions first the *Viṣayapati*, then the *Rāṣṭrapati* and then the *Grāma-mahattaras*. Sometimes, however, the terms *āhāra* and *viṣaya* were used synonymously as is proved by the Alina grant (*IA*, VII, p. 72) of Dharasena II of the year 270 where the expression *Kheṭaka-āhāra-viṣaya* is used.
67. *IA*, V, p. 17.
68. *RT*, p. 174.
69. Ibid., p. 177.
70. *EI*, VI, pp. 25ff.
71. Ibid., XVI, pp. 277ff
72. Ibid., I, pp. 55ff.
73. *SII*, IX(1), p. 101.
74. *EI*, XII, p. 154.

10

The Spy

I

Spies in the Vedic Period

The terms like *cāra*, *cara*, etc., are used in Indian literature to denote a spy in contrast with the word *dūta* which is generally employed in the sense of an envoy. In Vedic literature, there are some indications which would testify to the prevalence of the institution of espionage in the contemporary period. The *Ṛgveda* often speaks of the spies (*spaśaḥ*) of Varuṇa as sitting around their master at the time of his holding the court.[1] Varuṇa was urged to plant his spies everywhere so that they could visit every place and watch everything unceasingly.[2] Varuṇa's spies, surveying the two worlds, are extolled as being blessed with wisdom and piety.[3] Further evidence in regard to spies is supplied by the *Atharvaveda*. Thus Soma is described to have rays like spies that would never close their eyes and were present everywhere,[4] whereas Varuṇa's spies are said to have a thousand eyes to watch the whole world.[5] It may be suggested, on the basis of the employment of spies by Varuṇa, the divine counterpart of the human king, that spies were often employed by the Vedic monarchs with a view to keeping themselves well informed of the happenings of various kinds within their kingdoms. Macdonell and Keith[6] point out that such spies could be used in war also. From the application of such qualifying epithets as wise, holy, etc. to spies, R. Shamasastry[7] observes that the spies in the Vedic period were recruited from among the Brāhmaṇas. But it is highly debatable whether spying was approved of as one of recognised duties of the Brahmin community in the Vedic society.

II

The Testimony of the Jātaka Literature

Leaving aside the Vedic texts, we may now turn to Jātaka literature where secret agents are mentioned as *Upanikkhitta-purisās.* The Jātaka texts would create the impression that by the post-Vedic period there developed a regular network of spies in most of the Indian kingdoms. They reported to their kings, to whom they owed their appointment, the military preparations as well as the evil designs of foreign rulers.[8] It was evidently on the basis of such reports, secretly conveyed to them, that kings would decide their line of action to counteract enemies' movements. In the *Mahāummagga Jātaka*,[9] for instance, we hear of a spy who dispatched an important report to his master from a distant kingdom. Another Jātaka text[10] informs us how the secret agents of a king of Kampilla, even at the time of war, outmanoeuvred the enemies to enter the city of Mithilā by its postern gate, and successfully carried all sorts of useful news about the hostile camp to their master. Spies were also employed to thwart enemies' plans by creating a breach of trust between the latter and their army.

III

Evidence of the Classical Accounts and the Arthaśāstra

The combined testimony of the Classical authors and Kauṭilya proves beyond doubt the prevalence of the institution of spies in the Maurya kingdom. Arrian[11] refers to a class of officers called superintendents who 'spy out what goes on in country and town, and report everything to the king where the people have a king, and to the magistrates where the people are self-governed, and it is against use and wont for these to give a false report; but indeed no Indian is accused of lying'. To judge from the nature of their work one is tempted to identify the superintendents of Arrian with spies. Strabo[12] describes them as inspectors 'to whom it is given to inspect what is being done and report secretly to the king, using courtesans, and the camp inspectors, the camp courtesans; but the best and most trustworthy men are appointed to this office'. Megasthenes,[13] likewise, appears to have referred to spies when he says, 'The sixth class consists of the overseers, to whom is assigned the duty of watching all that goes on, and making reports secretly to the king. Some are entrusted with the inspection of the city, and others with that of the army. The former employ as their coadjutors the courtesans of the city, and the latter the courtesans of the camp. The ablest and most trustworthy men are appointed to fill these offices.' As would appear from the testimony of these writers, spies were the eyes and ears of the government, monarchical as well as republican, keeping watch on everything that happened in the kingdom, and reporting their discoveries to the king or to any other suitable authority, as the case may have been. The evidence of these spies would always bear the stamp of authenticity.

Kauṭilya has devoted four chapters[14] as well as a large number of isolated passages, here and there, to a gruesome description of spies who have been classified into two broad divisions, called the *Saṁsthas*, stationary spies, and the *Sañcāras*, wandering spies. The *Saṁsthas* have again been sub-divided into the following five heads:

1. The *Kāpaṭikas*, fraudulent disciples. The word *kāpaṭikaḥ* is derived from *kapaṭa*, deceit (*kapaṭena carati iti*). They were capable of guessing the mind of others (*para-marmajñaḥ*) and reported to the king and the *Mantrī*, to whom they were responsible (*rājānaṁ māṁ ca pramāṇaṁ kṛtvā*), whatever evils they noticed in any person (*yasya yad=akuśalaṁ paśyasi*). They were rewarded with honour and monetary grants[15] (*tam=artha-mānābhyāṁ pr-otsāhya*).

2. The *Udāsthitas*, apostate monks They were degraded ascetics (*pravrajyā-praty=avasitaḥ*), but were still endowed with intelligence and honesty (*prajñā-śauca-yukta*). 'Equipped with plenty of money and assistants, he should get work done in a place assigned (to him), for the practice of some occupation.[16] And from the profits of (this) work, he should provide all wandering monks with food, clothing and residence. And to those (among them), who seek a (permanent) livelihood, he should secretly propose, 'In this very garb, you should work in the interest of the king and present yourself here at the time of meals and payment.' And all wandering monks should make similar secret proposals to (monks in) their respective orders.[17]

3. The *Gṛhapatikavyañjanas*, householder spies. They were agriculturists, who had fallen from their profession but were possessed of foresight and pure character (*karṣako vṛtti-kṣīṇaḥ prajñā-śauca-yukto gṛhapatikavyañjanaḥ*). They had to carry on their duty as exactly as the *Udāsthitas* at a place assigned to them for agricultural work.[18]

4. The *Vaidehakavyañjanas*, merchant spies. They were traders, fallen from their profession, but possessed of intelligence and honesty[19] (*Vāṇijako vṛtti-kṣīṇaḥ prajñā-śauca-yukto vaidehakavyañjanaḥ*). They collected necessary information for the king with the help of fellow merchants, while carrying on the manufacture of merchandise on lands, allotted to them.[20]

5. The *Tāpasavyañjanas*, seeming ascetics. They were the hermits with a shaven head or with matted hair (*muṇḍo jatilo vā*), practising austerities. They lived in suburbs of a city in association with a host of disciples with a shaven head or braided hair and pretended as possessing preternatural powers to live on a handful of vegetables or meadow grass (*yava-muṣṭi*), taken once in the interval of a month or two and to foretell future events. 'And he should pacify with money and honour those who are resentful for good reason, those resentful without reason, by silent punishment, also those who do what is inimical to the king.'[21] The punishments in secret (*tuṣṇīṁ-daṇḍena*) which the *Tāpasavyañjanas* were capable of imposing obviously included assassination, poisoning, etc.

The *Sañcāras*, on the other hand, comprised the following:

1. The *Sattrins*, classmate spies. They were the orphans (*asaṁbandhinaḥ*), fed by the state (*avaśyabhartavyāḥ*) and they studied science, palmistry (*aṅga-vidyā*), sorcery (*māyāgata*), legerdemain (*jambhaka-vidyā*), the duties of the various orders of religious life (*āśramadharmaṁ*) and the reading of omens and augury[22] (*antara-cakra*).

2. The *Tīkṣṇas*, desperados. They were the bravadoes who had given up all thought of personal safety and would fight, for the sake of money, an elephant or a wild animal[23] (*ye janapade śūrās=tyakt=ātmāno hastinaṁ vyālaṁ vā dravya-hetoḥ pratiyodhaye yukte tīkṣṇaḥ*/).

3. The *Rasadas*, poisoners. They were the persons who had no trace of filial affection left in them and they were very cruel

and indolent[24] (*ye bandhuṣu niḥsnehāḥ krūrā alasāś=ca te rasadāḥ*).

4. The *Parivrājikās*, female mendicants. They were the poor widows of Brāhmaṇa caste, very clever, and desirous of earning their livelihood (*vṛttikāmā daridrā vidhavā pragalbhā*). Honoured in the king's harem, such women would frequent the residences of high officers[25] (*mahāmātra-kulāny=abhigacchet*).

The *Saṁsthas*, who were entitled to a higher emolument, as compared with the *Sañcāras*, appear to have been the superior of the two categories of spies. They were so called, because, they were stationed at a particular place for some time unlike the *Sañcāras* who, while discharging their duties, roamed about from one place to another. It is suggested that the *Saṁsthas* generally did not commit acts of violence, whereas the duties of the *Sañcāras* involved, according to the exigency of circumstances, such acts as murder, arson and looting. If this view be upheld, the *Saṁsthas* may be called secret informants, and the *Sañcāras*, secret agents. The *Sañcāras* may be compared with the *Krypteia*[26] or secret police in Sparta who, however, enjoyed a larger volume of freedom, being empowered to kill every helot whom they considered suspicious. Kauṭilya,[27] likewise, speaks of the *Ubhayavetanas*, persons in the pay of both, who would live with enemies, receiving wages from them, in order to find out secret information, each being unaware of the other, though from the same country. The king took charge of their sons and wives. In regard to the appointment of spies, Kauṭilya points out that the king appointed them as such in consultation with his ministers who themselves had been previously tried by spies.[28]

The duties and responsibilities of spies, as detailed in the *Arthaśāstra*, comprised the following:

To carry out the instruction of the government to assess the integrity of the candidates for posts in any of the state departments with the application of the four prescribed tests like those of piety (*dharm=opadhā*), material gain (*arth=opadhā*), lust (*kām=opadhā*) and fear (*bhay=opadhā*).[29]

To watch the movement of the councillor (*Mantrī*), the chaplain (*Purohita*), the commander-in-chief (*Senāpati*), the crown prince (*Yuvarāja*), the chief palace usher (*Dauvārika*), the chief of the palace guards (*Antarvaṁśika*), the director (*Praśāstṛ*), the administrator (*Samāhartṛ*), the director of stores (*Sannidhātṛ*), the magistrate (*Pradeṣṭṛ*), the commandant (*Nāyika*), the city-judge (*Pauravyāvahārika*), the director of factories (*Kārmāntika*), the council of ministers (*Mantri-pariṣad*), the superintendents (*Adhyakṣa*), the chief of the army staff (*Daṇḍapāla*), the commandant of the fort (*Durgapāla*), the commandant of the frontier fort (*Antapāla*), and the forest chieftain (*Āṭavika*).[30]

To collect information about the doings and policy of the enemy, the ally, the middle king, the neutral king, as well as of the eighteen high officers of each of these kings.[31]

To keep watch over both the citizens and the country people in the king's own dominions as well as in the enemy's territory.[32]

To collect information in regard to the number of fields, houses and families in villages—fields with respect to their size and total produce, houses with respect to taxes and exemptions and families with respect to their caste and occupation, and to ascertain the number of individuals in them and their income and expenditure.[33]

To 'find out the quantity and price of the king's goods produced in his own country, obtained from mines, water-works, forests, factories and fields'.[34]

To prevent foreign spies from carrying on their work within their dominions by causing them to be arrested.[35]

To spy on the counterfeiters of coins, adulterers, robbers, farmers, cowherds, traders, judges and heads of various departments.[36]

To assist the king in replenishing his treasury in times of financial stringency.[37]

And finally, to render useful service to the king in dealing with his external enemies by inspiring and encouraging the army before and during war, harassing enemies by setting fire to their camp and misleading them with false information.[38]

It is then evident that the safeguarding of the security of the kingdom against enemies, internal as well as foreign, and the elimination of corruption at all levels of government were the two principal factors behind the employment of spies. Even then, they were not granted unfettered authority. Kauṭilya was aware of human limitations and prudent enough to realise that personal likings and prejudices might stand in the way of the judicious discharge of duty on the part of a spy. He, accordingly, laid down that if the information, derived from three independent sources was in agreement, it would then be held authentic. If the sources were frequently found to be at variance, the reporters were punished in secret or dismissed.[39] Whenever spies put down anything in writing, they did it in a special form of writing, *gūḍhalekhya.* The idea was that even if it were miscarried, ordinary citizens could not make out its contents. The king was urged to set apart a few hours of his daily routine for attending to spies who were sent out early in the morning and received in the afternoon and the evening.[40] But such a direct contact between the king and spies, necessitating the parties to meet twice or thrice a day could have been maintained in a small kingdom but was impracticable in the case of a big empire like that of the Mauryas.

It is far from being known at present how far the *Arthaśāstra* reflects the actual condition of contemporary India. Accordingly, we may turn to the edicts of Aśoka for the true portrayal of the system of espionage in the Maurya kingdom. In Pillar Edicts I, IV and VII mention is made of a class of officers, called *Puruṣas,* divided broadly into high, middle and low ranks. Hultzsch,[41] following V.A. Smith, is inclined to equate them with the *Gūḍhapuruṣas* of the *Arthaśāstra.* H.C. Raychaudhuri[42] and R.G. Basak[43] have identified them with the *Puruṣas* or *Rājapuruṣas,* while B.M. Barua[44] takes them as corresponding to the *Amātyas* of the *Arthaśāstra.* B.M. Barua's view may be accepted on the ground that the *Puruṣas* were top-ranking officers as they controlled the *Rājūkas* who were the executive heads of districts. Again, as Pillar Edicts I and VII would suggest, one of their duties consisted of the dissemination of *Dhaṁma.* Open preachers as they were, it would remain inexplicable 'how they could remain undetected as they should, if they were to play the role of spies effectively'.[45] Aśoka speaks of the *Prādeśikas* who have been doubtfully identified with the *Pradeṣṭṛs.* They have sometimes been equated with spies or reporters[46] on the ground that the word *pradeśa* occurs in the *Arthaśāstra* in the sense of 'report'. But the *Prādeśikas,* who went out on tour every five years, as stated in Rock Edict III, could hardly have been spies who, while on duty, had to move regularly from place to place.

Rock Edict VI speaks of a class of royal agents, called

Prativedakas who were to keep the king abreast of the affairs of the people at all times, 'whether I am eating, or am in the harem, or in the inner chamber or in the cattle-shed (the station of herdsmen), or on horse-back (literally, on a trained or tamed horse), or in the garden.'[47] The *Prativedakas*, to judge from the nature of their work, as well as from the etymology[48] of the term itself, were evidently spies or informers, who were, no doubt, employed in large numbers to report to the king what was happening in the kingdom. But no further details about them are recorded in any of Aśoka's edicts.

IV

Spies in the Epics

An elaborate account of spies is to be met with in the *Rāmāyaṇa*. That the government of those days in eliminating corruption from within depended largely on the service of spies is evident from Rāma's enquiries of Bharata if the latter was keeping an eye on the fifteen *tīrthas* of the kingdom through *Caras*.[49] The *Ayodhyākāṇḍa* further shows that the king could not initiate any action on the basis of the report, submitted by a single spy. Actions could only be taken if the information received from three different sources, independent of each other, was found to concur.[50] The *Laṅkākāṇḍa*[51] speaks of spies, who were full of confidence, courage and zeal and were fearless[52] (*śūrān varān vigatasādhvasān*), being time and again sent by Rāvaṇa to know in secret the nature, number and movements[53] (*parimāṇañ=ca vīryañ=ca ye ca mukhyāḥ pla-vaṅgamāḥ*) of Rāma's forces, for, 'A wise monarch who discovers all that concerns his adversary through his spies, needs to exert himself only to a moderate degree to overcome his enemy on the field of battle.'[54] They were, however, recognised in the enemy camp where they were subjected to physical torture but were ultimately released by Rāma to whom they tendered their unconditional apology. The *Laṅkākāṇḍa* elsewhere speaks of a *Dūta*, named Śuka, being despatched by Rāvaṇa to Sugrīva but he was arrested on being suspected to be a spy[55] (*n=āyaṁ dūto mahāprājña cārakaḥ pratibhāti me*) who had come to count their forces. He was subsequently released by Rāma on the ground that he was really a *Dūta* and not a spy[56] (*vānarān=*

avravīd=Rāmo mucyatāṁ dūta āgataḥ). This would clearly show that spies did not enjoy any diplomatic immunity as was the case with ambassadors. It is worth noting that even in modern times spies are not granted any diplomatic immunity and 'every state punishes them severely if they are caught committing an act which is a crime by the law of the land or expels them if they cannot be punished.'[57]

The *Mahābhārata* provides us with a more elaborate account of spies, as compared to the *Rāmāyaṇa*. In emphasising the importance of the institution of espionage the *Śāntiparvan*[58] describes spies as constituting one of the eight limbs of the army. In the *Udyogaparvan*[59] they are described as the very eyes of the king (*cāraiḥ paśyanti rājānaś=cakṣurbhyām=itare janāḥ*). In referring to their qualities the *Śāntiparvan*[60] lays down that those who had undergone a thorough examination in respect of their ability, who were possessed of wisdom and were able to endure hunger and thirst, were capable of being appointed spies. The king was always encouraged to employ only devoted persons for these posts.[61] The *Śāntiparvan* further states that it was always advisable to send spies in the guise of atheists, ascetics,[62] the idiot, the blind and the deaf.[63] But spies were recruited so secretly that they were unable to recognise each other.[64] They were planted in every nook and corner of the kingdom, in shops, places of amusement, holy places, rural areas, public places, the king's assembly hall, the houses of citizens, business centres, secretariat, etc.[65] (*Udyāneṣu vihāreṣu prapāsvāvasatheṣu ca| pānāgāre praveśeṣu tīrtheṣu ca sabhāsu ca||*).

As revealed by the epic, the main duties of spies were the following:

1. To report[66] the opinion and conduct of the people to the king.
2. To keep a watch over the eighteen *tīrthas* of foreign states and the fifteen of their own kingdom[67] (*Kaccid=aṣṭādaś=ānyeṣu sva pakṣe daśa pañca ca| tribhis=tribhir=avijñātair=vvetsi tīrthāni cārakaiḥ||*). The commentator Nīlakaṇṭha enumerates the eighteen *tīrthas* and points out that a king was not required to spy on his own *Mantrī*, *Purohita* and *Yuvarāja*.

3. To harass the enemy either with the help of robbers, wild tribes, fire-raisers, poisoners and forgers or by sowing seeds of dissension among his principal officers.[68]
4. To spy on the plans and programmes of the opposite camp before and during the war and to watch the movements of other kings even at the time of peace.[69]

It is not definitely known whether spies were entitled to a systematic and regular emolument or were favoured with occasional rewards in return for the successful accomplishment of their mission. There occurs in the *Virāṭaparvan*[70] a passage which speaks of Duḥśāsana as granting an advance payment to spies with a view to finding out the Pāṇḍava brothers at the time of their living *in cognito*.

V

The Evidence of the Manu-Saṁhitā

Manu[71] speaks of as many as five categories of spies but unfortunately does not specify them. For the individual description of these spies we may turn to the commentary of Kullūka which states that they were the *Kāpaṭikas*, *Udāsthitas*, *Gṛhapatis*, *Vaidehikas* and *Tāpasas*. These divisions of spies would compare well with the five divisions of the *Saṁstha* group of spies, as enumerated by Kauṭilya in his *Arthaśāstra*. It remains inexplicable why Manu has passed over the *Sañcāras* in complete silence. The references to them in some later texts like the *Kāmandakīyanīti* would indubitably point to their existence even in later ages. Spies were posted in foreign lands as well as in the king's own dominions and were called upon to report to the king not only the duplicity amongst his adversaries[72] (*Budhyet=āri-prayuktāñ=ca māyāṁ nityaṁ svasaṁvṛtaḥ/*), but also the activities of village and town officials[73] (*teṣāṁ vṛttaṁ pariṇayet samyag=rāṣṭreṣu tac=caraiḥ//*). Even when a conqueror would set out on an expedition, spies were expected to acquaint him beforehand with the state of affairs, prevailing in the enemy's kingdom[74] (*cārān samyag=vidhāya ca*). To report their progress they would meet the king normally at night when the latter, holding weapons in hands, would attend to them in a special chamber.[75] It seems that Manu was aware of the conspiracy of spies, aiming at the murder of their masters. Manu does not mention how spies were appointed, what their caste was, whether they spied on the king's ministers as well, and the guises they adopted to mislead people while they were on duty.

VI

Spies as Depicted in the Tirukkural

The Tamil classic *Tirukkural*, about the date[76] of which there is divergence of opinion among scholars, mentions spies as constituting one of the king's two eyes and supplying him with all necessary information that happened in the kingdom.[77] N.M. Mudaliar[78] has summarised the accounts of spies, provided by Tiruvalluvar as follows: 'Spies can disguise themselves as ascetics and holy men and should wear an unsuspicious appearance. The spy should bring reliable information that is hidden, and the information brought by one spy should be got checked by that of another. Even spies should not know each other and if the reports of three agree, reliance could then only be placed on them.' The above account, it may be observed, is in agreement with the evidence of Kauṭilya in whose work, we, however, come across an elaborate treatment of the problem.

VII

Spies in the Gupta Period

The writings of Kālidāsa would bear witness to the prevalence of the system of espionage in India during the time of the Imperial Guptas. 'The system of spies,' writes S.A. Sabnis,[79] 'in those days was an essential part of the governmental machinery as it is even in the present times.' All over the kingdom was maintained a regular network of spies who were called upon to bring everything to the king's notice.[80] Such spies were asked to keep watch not only on hostile elements but also on friends.[81] Moreover, they were to report to the king as to what his subjects said about him and his doings. Rāma is represented in the *Raghuvaṁśa*[82] as questioning a spy, named Bhadra (*apasarpaṁ papraccha Bhadraṁ*) as to any rumour about his own conduct (*sva-vṛttam=uddiśya*). 'These spies themselves were unknown to one another and unknowingly carried on espionage against one another.'[83]

Yājñavalkya's account of spies, as appearing in the *Rāja-dharma-prakaraṇam* section, supplements the information, gleaned from the *Raghuvaṁśa*, since both the works were the products of the same age. It appears from Yājñavalkya's work that to keep the king well informed of the doings of his feudatories and other rulers (*sveṣu c=ānyeṣu*) and to watch his officers in order that they might be rewarded or punished as they deserved[84] (*Ye rāṣṭr=ādhikṛtās=teṣāṁ cārair=jñātvā viceṣṭitaṁ| sādhūn sam-pālayed=rājā viparītāṁs=tu ghātayet||*) were the main functions of spies. They were to report to the king every day, at noon as well as in the evening.[85] It cannot escape notice that both Kālidāsa and Yājñavalkya agree that spies enjoyed the rare privilege of being granted audience by the supreme head of the state.

A detailed account of spies is to be met with in the *Dūta-cara-vikalpa-prakaraṇam* section of the contemporary Sanskrit work *Kāmandakīya Nītisāra*. Following in the footsteps of his predecessor Kauṭilya, Kāmandaka has divided spies, who were unknown to each other[86] (*sarva n=āny=onya-vedinaḥ*), into two broad heads—the *Saṁsthas*[87] and the *Sañcāras*.[88] The former have again been subdivided into five groups, comprising traders, *vaṇik* (*vaṇig=vaidehaka iti dvitīya-nāmā*), farmers, *kṛṣīvalo* (*kṛṣīvalo gṛhapatir=iti dvitīya-nāmā*), ascetics, *liṅgī* (*liṅgī muṇḍo jaṭilo vā tāpasaḥ*), apostate monks, *bhikṣuka* (*tasy=odāsthita iti dvitīyaṁ nāma*) and teachers, *adhyāpaka* (*adhyāpakaḥ chātravṛtyā sthitaḥ*), while the five principal divisions of the *Sañcāras* were the bravadoes, *tīkṣṇa*, begging nuns, *pravrajitā*, classmates, *satrī* and poison-givers, *rasada*[89] (*tīkṣṇaḥ pravrajitā c=aiva satrī rasada eva ca|*). Pointing out how important these spies were Kāmandaka mentions that the king, having spies as his eyes, is awake even when he is asleep[90] (*svapann=api hi jāgarti cāra-cakṣur=mahīpatiḥ*). They were possessed of the ability to infer the inner thoughts of men from signs and gestures, a good memory, a sweet tongue, speed, capability of enduring privations, diligence, skill and ready wit[91] (*Tark=eṅgitajñaḥ smṛtimān mṛdur=laghu-parikramaḥ| kleś=āyāsa-saho dakṣaś=cāraḥ syāt pratipattimān||*). They gathered information as they roamed about in the guise of ascetics, *liṅginas*, hypocrites and merchants[92] (*Tapasvi-liṅgino dhūrtāḥ śilpa-paṇy=opajīvinaḥ| cāraś=careyuḥ paritaḥ pivanto jagatāṁ matam||*) and cautiously transmitted information among themselves with the help of a code, sign and gesture[93] (*Sanjñābhir=mlecchitair=lekhyair=ākārair=iṅgitair = api| sañcārayeyur=avyagrāś=cārāś=caryāṁ parasparam||*).

Important notices of spies during the Gupta period may be found in some other contemporary works like the *Mṛcchakaṭika* of Śūdraka and the *Mudrārākṣasa*, composed by Viśākhadatta. The *Mṛcchakaṭika*[94] speaks of spies as frequenting thoroughfares for scooping news to be reported to the king. The *Mudrārākṣasa* bears witness to the important role that spies used to play by bringing about discord among enemies and finding out what was going on in the kingdom. Mention is made in this text of a spy, employed by Kauṭilya, Nipuṇaka[95] by name, who moved through the city of Pāṭaliputra under the guise of a mendicant and related afterwards to his master his discoveries during the course of his wanderings. Siddhārthaka,[96] another spy of Kauṭilya, infiltrated into the service of Rākṣasa, and following the plan of his master, aroused suspicion in the mind of Malayaketu against Rākṣasa. Reference is also made to Virādhagupta who was deputed by Rākṣasa to collect information in the garb of a snake-charmer. Although Viśākhadatta has selected an event of the fourth century B.C. as the theme of his drama, there is hardly any denying that the author has drawn his materials from the age he lived in.

VIII

Spies in the Post-Gupta Period

For our knowledge about spies during the post-Gupta period, we may turn to the testimony of the *Kādambarī*, composed by Bāṇa and the *Śiśupālavadham* of Māgha where are to be found a few stray references to them. The former[98] speaks of the employment of many thousands of spies by a minister for keeping himself alive to every whisper of tributary kings in the kingdom, 'as though uttered in his own palace'. The *Śiśupālavadham* shows how spies (*praṇidhayaḥ*) obtained information on the enemy's strength by securing a footing in eighteen of his departments[99] (*tīrtheṣu*). Without the help of spies, no foreign policy would succeed, even though it followed the best approved line and was blessed with the most judicious employment of men and money.[100] Māgha also refers to a special class of spies called the *Ubhayavetanas* who would enter the service of other kings under disguise. They won the confidence of the principal officers there and estranged them from their kings at opportune moments by producing documentary evidence[101] (*Ajñāta-doṣair =doṣajñair=uddaśy=obhayavetanaiḥ| bhedyāḥ śastror=abhi-vyakta-śāsanaiḥ sāmavāyikaḥ||*).

IX

Spies in Early Mediaeval India

As we approach the early mediaeval period, we are delighted to find abundant materials on spies in contemporary literature. Highly important in this connection is the account of spies, as given in the *Agni Purāṇa*. As this *Purāṇa* mentions, spies were the eyes of the king[102] (*cāra-cakṣur=bhaved=rājā*), being appointed by him in such a way that they were not recognised by the people or even by one another[103] (*janasy=āvihitān saumyāṁs=tath=ājñātān parasparam*). They kept an eye over the strength and loopholes of other kings under the garb of merchants, physicians, astrologers and mendicants[104] and regularly watched the activities of various state functionaries like village headmen, lords of ten and hundred villages[105] (*nityam-eva tathā kāryaṁ teṣāṁ cāraiḥ parīkṣaṇaṁ*). The report of a single spy was not considered reliable[106] (*n=aikasya rājā śraddadhyāt*). They worked in close cooperation with the envoys of their country in foreign kingdoms. The spies were placed under the supervision of a superior officer called *Carādhyakṣa*.[107] It is interesting to note that such an officer is not mentioned even by the *Arthaśāstra*, 'which provides for the longest number of superintendents'.[108]

The *Kālikā Purāṇa*,[109] likewise, speaks of spies as being employed by the king to know what was happening within the kingdom, as well as to ascertain who amongst his subjects were pleased with or ill-disposed towards him. These persons, who were nightmares, wore various kinds of dresses and carried on their duty under different guises. They were neither inordinately tall nor were they dwarfish in stature. Great interest attaches to the information that spies moved at night and not by day, as gleaned from this *Purāṇa*, as this information is not to be met with in any other texts. It seems that the government did not stake the secrecy of the identity of these secret agents by allowing them to work by day when they ran the risk of being discovered by the public.

The author of the *Viṣṇudharmottarapurāṇa* was fully alive to the importance of the services of spies who have been identified as the very eyes of the king[110] (*rājānaś=cāracakṣuṣaḥ*). They helped him to ascertain the attitude of royal servants and the merits and demerits of ordinary men and reported to him what was beneficial or harmful[111] (*Rāg=āparāgau bhṛtyānāṁ janasya ca guṇ=āguṇān| śubhānām=aśubhānāṁ ca vijñānaṁ Rāma karmaṇām||*). Spies were generally those clever persons for whom hunger and hardship posed no problem[112] (*anāhāryān kleśasahān niyuñjīta sadā carān*). These men, who were planted both in the king's own dominions and foreign lands[113] (*sva-deśe para-deśe ca*), could not be identified by the public, nor were they known to each other[114] (*janasy=āvitatān saumyāṁs=tath =ājñātān parasparam*). They carried on their duty under the guise of traders, mendicants and physicians.[115] The validity of the statement of a single spy could hardly be upheld unless it stood confirmed by a different source[116] (*N=aikasya rājā śradhyāt cārasy=āpi ca bhāṣitam| dvayos=saṁvādam=ājñāya sandadhyān=nṛpatis=tataḥ||*). It is of interest to note that whereas other texts on ancient Indian polity are unanimous in upholding the agreement between three sources as the real proof of authenticity, the *Viṣṇudharmottarapurāṇa* departs from the traditional track by restricting the number of the corroborative sources to two.

Following the line of Kauṭilya, Somadeva in his *Nītivākyāmṛta* has provided us with a detailed account of spies who are compared to the eyes of the king[117] (*cārāś=cakṣūṁṣi kṣitipatīnāṁ*). As Somadeva[118] lays down, ungreediness, smartness, truthfulness and thoughtfulness were some of the qualities expected of these persons. Being disguised as ascetics, scholars, sorcerers, jugglers, physicians, soldiers, foresters, snake-charmers, singers, dancers, traders, artisans, astrologers, mathematicians and so forth, they roamed about throughout the country, keeping watch over the people and officers of the kingdom.[119] Spies helped the king in administration of justice and were paid regularly.

Somadeva[120] refers in his *Yaśastilaka* to spies roaming about under the garb of mendicants and reporting to the king the malpractices of his corrupt ministers. The kings who did not try to know their own situation and that of others through spies were divested of wealth and life by their officers and enemies.[121] The appointment of the superintendent of spies finds favour with Somadeva.

The *Mānasollāsa*, which was composed by king Someśvara III of the Western Cālukya dynasty in the twelfth century A.D. (A.D. 1129), mentions the *Gūḍhapuruṣas* and the *Ubhayavetanas* as being deployed by the king in foreign countries with a view to winning over to his side those subjects who were fearful, humiliated and embittered[122] (*Śatrusthair=ātma-puruṣair=gūḍhair=ubhayavetanaiḥ| bhītāpamānitān kruddhān bhedayec=ca nṛsaṁgatān||*).

The Sanskrit work *Narmamālā* of about the twelfth century A.D. shows that there was a regular network of spies in the Lohara kingdom in Kashmir where these agents were differently called *Carikās*, *Piśunas* and *Puṁścalakas*.[124]

Great importance has been attached in the *Śukranīti* to the appointment of spies, called both *Cāras* and *Sūcakas*. They were adept in ascertaining the designs of enemies, subjects and royal officers and they reproduced faithfully what they had noticed.[125] They traced the offences being committed in the kingdom, and brought them to the king's notice for necessary action to be taken against the miscreants.[126] Caṇḍeśvara,[127] whom K.P. Jayaswal has assigned to c. A.D. 1350, quotes in his *Rājanītiratnākara* the view of Yājñavalkya which urges the king to grant audience to his spies.

The *Prabandhacintāmaṇi*, composed by Merutuṅga, tells us how spies used to provide their masters during war with top secrets of enemies, and helped them to know beforehand any possible threat from outside. Thus when Siddharāja, king of Gujarat, invaded Mālava, he stationed his secret agents at various places like the junction of three or four roads, squares and temples in order to trace the clue as to how the fort of Dhārā could be captured. They collected the information that the fort could only be taken, if attacked at its southern gate-tower, and secretly communicated that to the king through a minister.[128] We are further told that Bhīma, king of Gujarat, was informed by his spies[129] (*sthānapuruṣaiḥ*) that king Bhoja of Dhārā was preparing for an invasion.

Notwithstanding the prominent mention that they find in literature, spies are almost passed over in silence in the contemporary official documents. Indeed, inscriptions seldom take any notice of them. The Hirahadagalli plates of the Pallava king Śivaskandavarman mention them as *Sañcarantakas*, the Sonpur[130] plates of the Somavaṁśī king Mahābhavagupta II Janamejaya speak of them as *Piśunas* and the Irda copper plate grant[131] of the Kamboja ruler Nayapāladeva refers to them as *Gūḍhapuruṣas*. The scant notice[132] of spies in epigraphic records would probably demonstrate that the government in those days displayed the wisdom to keep the identity of these agents secret, thereby enabling them to work undisturbed and unnoticed. As the circumstantial evidence shows, the intelligence department in several of the early mediaeval Indian kingdoms proved utterly inefficient in the wake of Muslim invasions. Muhammad Khaljī invaded Nadiya at a time when the Sena king Lakṣmaṇasena was hardly prepared to oppose him. The way the Muslim army reached Nadiya offers a sad commentary on the efficiency of the contemporary spies of Bengal. Again, what were the Cāhamāna spies doing in the second battle of Tarain when their king Pṛthvīrāja III, relying on a false assurance of a truce, went on merrymaking during the night when Mu'izzud-dīn Muhammad was peparing for a sudden attack on the unguarded Hindu force? The lack of efficiency and foresight on the part of Indian spies, along with some other factors, proved fatal for India which had to sacrifice her freedom so cheaply at the altar of Muslim domination.

References and Notes

1. I, 25, 13.
2. VI, 61, 8.
3. VII, 87, 3.
4. V, 6, 3.
5. IV, 16, 4.
6. *VINS*, II, p. 213.

7. *EIP*, p. 127.
8. *PBI*, p. 77; *JDL*, XX, p. 50.
9. *Jātaka* IV, pp. 390-93.
10. Ibid., pp. 399-400; *JDL*, XX, p. 50.
11. *AIDMA*, p. 41.
12. *CAI*, p. 268.
13. *AIDMA*, pp. 217-18.
14. I, 11-14.
15. I, 11, 2-3.
16. The term used in the text is *vārttākarma*. According to Meyer, *vārttā* is here the profession of spying, *karma* is the work of spying and *phala* denotes the remuneration for this work. This is hardly likely. *Vārttā* in the usual sense of agriculture, cattle-rearing and trade is quite all right. Both R.P. Kangle (*KA*, II, p. 24) and R. Shamasastry (*KA*, p. 18) have interpreted this term in its usual sense.
17. *KA*, II, p. 24; 1, 11, 4-9.
18. 1, 11, 9-10.
19. 1, 11, 11.
20. 1, 11, 12.
21. *KA*, II, p. 26.
22. 1, 12, 1.
23. 1, 12, 2.
24. 1, 12, 3.
25. 1, 12, 4.
26. *HG*, p. 132.
27. 1, 12, 17-19.
28. 1, 11, 1.
29. 1, 10.
30. 1, 12, 6.
31. 1, 12, 20.
32. 1, 13, 1; 1, 14, 1.
33. 2, 35, 8-9.
34. 2, 35, 11.
35. 1, 12.
36. 2, 21, 27; 2, 35, 13; 4, 4, 6-8; 4, 4, 20-22.
37. 5, 2, 41; 5, 2, 46.
38. 13, 3.
39. 1, 12, 15.
40. 1, 19, 13; 1, 19, 18; 1, 19, 22.
41. *CII*, I, p. xli.
42. *PHAI*, pp. 59, 75.
43. *AI*, p. 82.
44. *AAHI*, p. 175.
45. *Aśoka*, Calcutta, 1955, p. 57.
46. Thomas in *JRAS*, 1915, p. 112.
47. *AI*, p. 35.

48. The word *prativedaka* is derived from *prati-vid*, meaning 'to make known', 'to report', 'to inform'.
49. *Ayodhyākāṇḍa*, 100, 36.
50. Ibid.
51. 25, 1; 25, 15; 29, 16-29; 30, 1-35.
52. 30, 19.
53. 25, 4. Compare also the statement—*Kathaṁ svapiti jāgarti kim=adya ca kariṣyati* (30, 18).
54. H.P. Shastri, *The Rāmāyaṇa of Vālmīki*, London, 1959, III, p.72. *cāreṇa viditaḥ śatruḥ paṇḍitair=vasudhādhipaiḥ*.
55. 20, 29.
56. 20, 34.
57. L. Oppenheim, *International Relations*, I, p. 862.
58. 59, 41-42.
59. 34, 35.
60. P.C. Roy, *Mahābhārata, Śāntiparvan*, LXIX, p. 161.
61. Ibid., LXX, p. 167.
62. 140, 40. *Pāṣaṇḍāṁs=tāpasādīṁś=ca para-rāṣṭre praveśayet||*.
63. 69, 8.
64. Ibid., 69, 10.
65. P.C. Roy, op. cit., p. 161. *Śāntiparvan* 136, 41.
66. *Śāntiparvan* 89, 15-16.
67. *Sabhāparvan* 5, 38.
68. *Śāntiparvan* 54, 48-50.
69. P.C. Roy, op. cit., p. 217.
70. 25, 14-16.
71. VII, 154.
72. VII, 104.
73. VII, 122.
74. VII, 184.
75. VII, 223.
76. The date of Tiruvalluvar has not yet been finally settled. According to M.R. Ayengar, he flourished in the fifth century A.D., while in the opinion of V.R. Ramachandra Dikshitar (*STLH*, p. 54) Tiruvalluvar was not far removed from the close of the first century or the beginning of the second century A.D. Srinivasa Ayyangar is of opinion that Tiruvalluvar cannot be assigned to any date earlier than the sixth century A.D. (*TSELT*, p. 522).
77. *TSELT*, p. 592.
78. Ibid., p. 592.
79. *KST*, p. 220.
80. *Raghuvaṁśa* XVII, 48.
81. Ibid., 51.
82. Ibid., XIV, 31. *Apasarpaś=caraḥ spaśaḥ iti.*
83. *KST*, p. 219.
84. I, 338.
85. I, 332.

86. 19, 38.
87. 19, 36.
88. 19, 38.
89. Ibid.
90. 19, 29.
91. 19, 26.
92. 19, 27.
93. 19, 49.
94. *The Little Clay Cart.* Translated by S.K. Basu, Calcutta, 1939, Act IX, pp. 118-19.
95. Act I.
96. Act II.
97. Act II. Act V mentions one Jīvasiddhi who was known as a friend of Rākṣasa but was in reality a spy of Cāṇakya.
98. *The Kādambarī of Bāṇa,* translated by C.M. Ridding, Calcutta, 1896, p. 50.
99. II, 111
100. II, 112.
101. II, 113.
102. 221, 20.
103. 221, 22.
104. *PAP*, p. 119.
105. 223, 2.
106. 220, 22.
107. 221, 3.
108. *PAP*, p. 120.
109. *The Kālikā Purāṇa*, published by A.K. Ray and Company, Calcutta, 1293 (B.S.), p. 249.
110. II, 24, 63.
111. II, 24, 69-70.
112. II, 24, 64.
113. II, 24, 64.
114. II, 24, 65.
115. II, 24, 65.
116. II, 24, 66-67.
117. P. 172.
118. Ibid.
119. Ibid.
120. Book III.
121. *PAP*, p. 120.
122. 2, 18, 988. Śivaśekhara Miśra, *Mānasollāsa: Ek Saṁskṛtik Adhyayana,* Banaras, 1966, p. 130.
123. P. 6.
124. *EHCK*, p. 134.
125. II, 377-78.
126. II, 138-39.
127. Edited by K.P. Jayaswal, Patna, 1924, p. 50.

128. C.H. Tawney, *The Prabandhacintāmaṇi*, Calcutta, 1901, p. 86.
129. Ibid., p. 44. Forbes (*Rās Mālā*, p. 188) rightly interprets the term as meaning a spy. C.H. Tawney (op. cit., p. 44) has erroneously taken it in the sense of a representative.
130. *EI*, XXIII, pp. 251ff.
131. Ibid., XXII, pp. 150ff.
132. The expression *a-cāṭa-bhaṭa-prāveśya* occurs quite frequently in inscriptions from the Gupta period onwards. Opinions widely differ on the meaning of *cāṭa*. P.B. Desai (*EI*, XXVII, p. 290) equates the term with *chātra* of the expression *a-bhaṭa-chātra-prāveśyaḥ*. He is of opinion that the word *chātra* is originally derived from the root *chad* meaning 'conceal', 'hide', etc. He has, accordingly, taken *cāṭa* to mean a member of the secret service. But this goes against the view of Fleet (*CII*, III, p. 98) who has interpreted the term in the sense of 'irregular troops'. *Cāṭa*, according to lexicographers, means 'a rogue', 'a cheat', 'a swindler', etc.

11

The Village Headman

I

The Village Headman in the Vedic Age

The system of carrying on the village administration through a headman, which was a fairly popular institution in ancient India, seems to be as old as the *Ṛgveda*,[1] for it mentions the term *grāmaṇī* twice and uses it in the sense of a village headman at least in X.107.5. It is argued that the word *grāma* is used in the *Ṛgveda* in the sense of a group and that the *Grāmaṇī* might have been a captain of the army. That the word *grāma* is used in the *Ṛgveda* in the generality of cases to denote a village appears to be fairly certain. The office of the headman continued throughout the Vedic period, as is evident from the frequent references to the *Grāmaṇī* in the later *Saṁhitās* and the *Brāhmaṇas*.[2] It cannot be definitely ascertained whether the village headman owed his position to the crown or to a popular election by his co-villagers. The analogy from primitive society, the absence of any reference to him as a royal servant in the *Ṛgveda* and the etymological meaning of the term[3] (*grāmaṁ samūhaṁ nayati prerayati sva sva kāryeṣu*) may possibly indicate that during the early Vedic period the *Grāmaṇī* was elected by the community to which he was accountable. But in the later Vedic period, he no longer remained to be an elected officer of the people, for the *Śatapatha Brāhmaṇa*[4] describes him as one of the *Ratnins*, the Jewels, of the royal establishment.

Of his functions, the *Vedas* speak very little. Zimmer[5] opines that the Vedic *Grāmaṇī* was charged with military functions only. Since the Vedic texts represent him as leading the villagers to the battle-field, we may infer that one of his duties consisted of defending the village against aggressions from without and rendering military assistance to the king in times of need. But the sphere of his activities does not appear to have been so circumscribed; it possibly extended to civil operations also, as suggested by Macdonell and Keith.[6] There is no direct indication in Vedic literature that he was connected with the revenue administration. R.S. Sharma[7] is of opinion that he did not act in that capacity in those days, as the revenue function in the contemporary period was performed, according to him, by an officer called *Bhāgadugha*. The observation of R.S. Sharma is applicable to the later Vedic period, but not to the early age when the office of the *Bhāgadugha* was not yet in vogue. This is evident from the fact that the officer called *Bhāgadugha* finds mention only in the *Yajus Saṁhitās* and the *Brāhmaṇas*. Although the positive evidence is not forthcoming, the *Grāmaṇī* was probably connected with the fiscal function in the early Vedic age. The nature of his work implies that the headman normally belonged to the Kṣatriya caste. That the Vaiśyas, too, sometimes aspired for and obtained this post is testified by the *Taittirīya Saṁhitā*.[8]

The later Vedic literature mentions in several places some high functionaries of the state called *Ratnins*, Jewels, who probably constituted the king's council. The *Grāmaṇī* is said to have been one among them. The use of the singular number of the term presents some difficulties, because there must have been quite a large number of such officers in a kingdom. It is reasonable to suggest that the most prominent among such headmen was selected a member of the king's council.[9]

Scholars are not unanimous in their opinion in regard to the nature and functions of the Vedic *Sabhā*. There are reasons to believe that the *Sabhā* was a village assembly. A Ṛgvedic[10] passage states how the deliberations of the *Sabhā* time and again centred round the cow and its utility for human beings. Another passage of the *Ṛgveda* describes how the people indulged in gambling at the hall of the *Sabhā*, and staked the independence of themselves and their wives.[11] That gambling was played at the *Sabhā*-hall is further alluded to by the *Taittirīya*[12] and *Śatapatha*[13] *Brāhmaṇas*. The above references would make it abundantly clear that the Vedic *Sabhā* was a village assembly where the people met to discharge social functions and discussed a few items of village government, including the safety of the locality and cases of dispute. If our suggestion about the *Sabhā* is accepted, it would follow that the *Grāmaṇī* as the principal man of the village presided over its deliberations and guided its activities.[14]

Despite the meagreness of details about him, it seems that the *Grāmaṇī*, as one among the *Ratnins*, was regarded as an important functionary of the state in the Vedic period. That the post carried with it considerable power and position is further evidenced by the *Taittirīya Saṁhitā*[15] which observes that 'the prosperous are three indeed, viz., the learned brāhmaṇa, the village headman (*grāmaṇī*) and the *rājanya* (warrior)'[16] (*Trayo vai gataśriyaḥ śuśruvān Grāmaṇī Rājanyas=teṣāṁ mahendro devata*). A village judge called *Grāmyavādin* is mentioned in some of the Vedic texts.[17] It is not clear whether he worked independently or was placed under the supervision of the headman.

II

The Village Headman in the Post-Vedic Period

The *Jātakas* and a few Brahmanical texts afford us interesting glimpses into the office of the village headman. He is mentioned in most of the *Jātaka* texts as *Grāmabhojaka.* Then he was no longer an elected official of the villagers, as he had been in the early Vedic days, but was brought under royal control. That he was a royal nominee by this time is borne out by the *Kharassara Jātaka*[18] which describes him as an *Amacca* of the king and by the *Kaluvaka Jātaka*[19] which leaves the impression that such an official could be appointed or removed by the crown alone. In the post-Vedic period, we find the headman more concerned with the security of the people than anything else. That he could hardly have been indifferent towards law-breakers is evidently clear from the *Kharassara Jātaka*[20] which refers to an officer who was punished by the crown, 'as he with his own people went to the forest, leaving the villagers at the mercy of robbers'. He had hardly any opportunity to act despotically in the discharge of his duties. Sometimes the king used to exercise direct control over him as is testified by the *Vinaya Piṭaka* which states that king

Bimbisara once summoned all the 80,000 *Grāmikas* of his kingdom to instruct them in worldly affairs (*diṭṭhadhammike aṭṭhe anusāsitvā*). R.C. Majumdar[21] cites a few instances from the *Jātakas* to show that the *Grāmabhojaka* was not only controlled by the king but 'the popular voice operated as a great and efficient control over his decisions' as well. The *Jātakas* often represent the headman as exercising judicial powers, for we find him in these texts to settle disputes, make the guilty pay a fine,[22] issue prohibitions against the slaughter of animals (*māghātaṁ karapesi*)[23] and the sale of intoxicating liquors.[24] The *Gahapati Jātaka*[25] tells us how at the outbreak of a famine the inhabitants of a village approached their headman for help and were provided with meat by the latter on condition that 'two months from now, when they have harvested the grain, they will pay him in kind'.[26] As regards the income of the headman, A.N. Bose[27] rightly points out that 'he collects the king's tithe and sends it to the treasury unless the revenue is assigned to him by royal writ. The judicial fees and fines and the returns of liquor houses or excise dues are among his perquisites. He is the agricultural bank "par excellence". He may have had other incomes lawful or otherwise, for his assets are in cases gauged at eighty crores.'

Āpastamba, who is generally assigned to the pre-Maurya epoch, gives the following information about the village headman:

First, the headman should be pure and truthful and he should be recruited directly by the king from the members of the first three castes.[28]

Second, he should protect the village from thieves in every direction up to the distance of one *krośa* (*sarvato yojanaṁ nagaraṁ taskarebhyo rakṣyaṁ| Krośo grāmebhyaḥ||*).[29] If any theft occurs within these limits, the officer is required to make good the loss.

Third, he should collect lawful *śulka*.[30] The commentator Haradatta takes the word *śulka* to mean one-twentieth part of a merchant's gain. But as is clear from the *sūtras* immediately following it, *śulka* is used by Āpastamba as a synonym of *kara* to include all kinds of taxes.

Fourth, the headman in the discharge of his functions may

take the help of some subordinate officers who should be endowed with purity and truthfulness.[31]

III

The Village Headman in the Maurya Period

The *Arthaśāstra*[32] shows that in the Maurya period the headman was called *Grāmika, Grāmakūṭa, Grāmasvāmin* and *Grāmamukhya.* He is, however, not included in the text in the list of salaried officials[33] and this has given rise to the speculation that the village official[34] was not a royal nominee in the Maurya period. Such a theory does not appear to be tenable, because the *Jātakas,* as we have seen earlier, conclusively prove that long before the days of Kauṭilya, the headman had already been brought under royal control. It is interesting to note that the term *grāmika,* which is used in the *Arthaśāstra* as one of the designations of the headman, etymologically means, according to the *Vācaspatya,* an officer appointed to look after the village (*grāme tad-rakṣaṇa-niyukta ṭhañ| grāma-rakṣaṇāya niyukte grām=ādhyakṣe||*). In regard to the headman's functions Kauṭilya seems to imply that he was empowered to drive a thief or an adulterer out of the village and try some offences (*grāmakūṭam=adhyakṣaṁ vā satrī brūyāt).*[35] According to Kauṭilya the village headman was responsible for any loss suffered by the caravan within the limits of the village; the *Vivītādhyakṣa* was responsible for any loss on the village border and the *Corarajjuka* was held guilty for the loss in a place which was not pasture land.[36] A very similar idea has been expressed by Yājñavalkya[37] (*ghātite=pahṛte doṣo grāmabharttur=nirgate| vivītābharttus=tu pathi cauroddharttur=avītake||*) who flourished a few centuries after Kauṭilya. In return for his services to the government the headman was, no doubt, remunerated, but the early texts leave us in the dark about the way in which he was rewarded. Kauṭilya[38] appears to be the first among the ancient Indian writers to deal with this problem, and he prescribes that he was to receive rent-free land for his living. Besides, the villagers had to accompany the headman by turns at the time of his journey on village business. Those who could not do this paid a penalty of one and a half *paṇas* per *yojana.* A different interpretation of the corresponding passage of the *Arthaśās-*

tra implies that the headman could impose a fine between one *paṇa* and half a *paṇa* at his own discretion upon any person who did not accompany him at the time of his travel on account of any business. By the time of the Mauryas the *Grāmika* had evidently no direct contact with the central authority, and he was to work under the direction and supervision of the *Gopa*.

There is a passage in the *Arthaśāstra*[39] which suggests that the village headman was sometimes liable to be punished. The passage reads: *Grāmikasya grāmādas=tenapāradāraṁ nirasyataś=catuviṁśatipaṇo daṇḍaḥ*. R.P. Kangle[40] translates the passage thus, 'For the village headman ejecting from the village one who is not a thief or an adulterer, the fine is twenty-four *paṇas*.' It is evident from the above passage that the village chief, guilty of improper discharge of his duty, was punished with a fine.

IV

The Village Headman in the Post-Maurya Period

The office of headman continued to be popular in the post-Maurya age. In this period, we have for him a variety of designations; Manu[41] calls him *Grāmasyādhipati* and *Grāmika*, *Kāmasūtra*[42] *Grāmādhipati*, *Milindapañho*[43] *Grāmasāmika* and the Mathura votive epigraph,[44] *Grāmika*. About his appointment in this period we find the continuation of the same practice as in the previous epoch. Manu[45] informs us that the appointment of the *Grāmika* was a royal prerogative (*grāmasy=ādhipatiṁ kuryāt daśagrāmapatiṁ tathā*). Viṣṇu[46] also speaks of the appointment of a headman for each village by the king.

Our sources would tend to show that the office of village headship was normally hereditary in this period. A case of two generations of *Grāmika* is mentioned in a Jain votive inscription[47] from Mathura which records the dedication of a Jaina image by Sīhadattā, the wife of the *Grāmika* Jayanāga and the daughter-in-law of the *Grāmika* Jayadeva. It would, however, be wrong to suppose that the office of village headman was always hereditary. The protection of the life and property of the villagers was undoubtedly the most important duty of the headman. Manu[48] is not in favour of entrusting him with the defence of the locality. He ordains that in the midst of two, three, five or a hundred villages, the king should station military outposts which will look after the security of villages (*Dvayos=trayāṇāṁ pañcāṇāṁ madhye gulmam=adhiṣṭhitam/ tathā grāma-śatānāñca kuryād=rāṣṭrasya saṁgraham//*). Though relieved of his military duty, a village headman could hardly have been indifferent towards law-breakers. Gautama,[49] who is generally assigned to an earlier date, lays down that when a theft is committed, the king should recover the lost property and return it to the owner and if he fails to secure the stolen articles, he has to pay its value to the householder (*Corahṛtam=apajitya yathā-sthānaṁ gamayet/ koṣād=vā dadyāt//*). Manu[50] seems to imply that whenever a crime or theft was committed within a village, the headman had to enquire about it and take the necessary steps to detect the culprit. In case of his failure to apprehend the thieves, he, without undue haste, was to report the case to the chief of ten villages for better action (*Grāme doṣān samutpannān grāmikaḥ śanakaiḥ svayaṁ/ saṁśet grāma-daśeśāya daśeśo viṁ-śatīśinaṁ//*). Viṣṇu[51] enjoins that it was the duty of the head-man to quell the disturbances within the village and if his effort proved abortive, the lord of ten villages was to be contacted (*Tatra Grāmādhyakṣān=api kuryāt/ Daśādhyakṣān/ Śatādhyak-ṣān/ Deśādhyakṣāṁś=ca// Grāma-doṣāṇāṁ Grāmādhyakṣaḥ parīharaṁ kuryāt/ Aśakto Daśagrāmādhyakṣāya nivedayet/*).

In the post-Maurya period, the village headman was connected with revenue administration in most localities. Manu[52] definitely assigns to him the fiscal duty, for he was to collect royal dues in the form of grain, drink and fuels. The *Milinda-pañho*[53] also suggests that the village headman was empowered to realise royal revenue. As it has been shown already, the headman was entitled to get rent-free land for his living in the Maurya period. But the practice of assigning land to him has been opposed by Manu, according to whom, the articles of food, drink and fuel that were payable daily to the king by the villagers would be given to him (*Yāni rājapradeyani pratyahaṁ grāmavāsibhiḥ/ anna-pān=endhan=ādīni Grāmikas=tāny=avāp-nuyāt//*).[54] A headman could hardly become a tyrant under the system of Manu. From his statement that the *Grāmika* had to keep the *Daśagrāmapati* well informed of thefts and crimes (*caurādidoṣān*) within his jurisdiction, it appears that he had to work under the guidance of the latter. But that was not the only check to the power of the headman. Manu enjoins that the king should appoint a minister to keep a vigilant watch over the activities of this officer (*Teṣāṁ grāmyāṇi kāryāṇi pṛthak kāryāṇi c=aiva hi/ rājñ=onyaḥ sacivaḥ snigdhas=tāni paś-yedat=andritaḥ//*).

V

The Village Headman in the Gupta Period

As we approach the Gupta period, we notice that the village headman finds mention in the Supia pillar inscription[55] of Skandagupta and the Damodarpur copper plate[56] of the reign of Budhagupta. The former record speaks of a *Grāmika* named Varga whose father and grandfather were bankers (*śreṣṭhin*). Are we to infer on the evidence of this record that the post of the *Grāmika* was not hereditary in those days? The case seems to have been just the reverse, for in the Gupta kingdom most of the posts were hereditary. The mention of his name in connection with the gift of land in the above-mentioned Damodarpur grant implies that the *Grāmika* played an important role in the revenue administration of the localities where the office existed.

Saletore[57] holds, on the strength of an inscription of Hastin from Bhumra,[58] that one of the duties of the village headman of the Gupta period consisted in the setting up of boundary pillars. The relevant portion of the Bhumra inscription reads '*Indana-naptrā Vasu-Grāmika-puttra-Śivadāsena bala-yaṣṭi ucch-ritaḥ*' and it means that a boundary pillar was erected by Śivadāsa, who was not himself a *Grāmika* but a son of a head-man. The Bhumra record evidently does not conclusively prove Saletore's contention. Even then we may presume that as the state functionary in the village, the *Grāmika* might have acted as an arbitrator in case of any boundary dispute among vill-agers.[59]

Inscriptions prove that the Gupta *Grāmika* was not the sole authority in the village administration, but worked in consul-tation with the village council. A passage of the Damodarpur record[60] of the time of Budhagupta states that a notification was addressed by the *Aṣṭakulādhikaraṇa*,[61] headed by the *Mahattara*, the *Grāmika* and *Kuṭumbins* of Palāśavṛndaka to the Brāhmaṇas and other inhabitants of Caṇḍagrāma for the sale and grant of a piece of land. The exact meaning of the expression, *mahattar=ādy=aṣṭakulādhikaraṇaṁ Grāmika-Kuṭumbinañ=ca,* occurring in the inscription is far from clear. Some[62] have taken it to mean 'the village jury consisting of eight members and headed by the *Mahattara,* and the agriculturist householders who are village headmen'. It seems that in the expression, *Grāmika-Kuṭumbinañca,* the two terms should be treated independently to mean both the *Grāmika* and the agriculturist householders. It then appears from the above record that the *Grāmika* was associated with the *Aṣṭakulādhikaraṇa,* headed by the *Mahattara,* and the *Kuṭumbins* in the village administration, particularly in matters relating to the purchase and sale of land. The Dhanaidaha inscription states that the *Kuṭumbins,* several Brāhmaṇas and the *Aṣṭakulādhikaraṇa* in the village were informed by an officer, whose name ended with *viṣṇu,* of the details of a plot of land. It is worth noting that in this inscription, no mention is made of the village headman in connection with the transaction of land. This may be a proof of the fact that the body, known as the *Aṣṭakulādhikaraṇa,* was a more popular institution in Bengal during the Gupta period, as compared with the office of village headman.

In Central India and Bihar, too, we find the prevalence of village councils during this period. They were known as *Pañcamaṇḍalī* in Central India and *Grāmajanapada* in Bihar.[63] A study of a large number of seals issued in the name of the village councils which have been discovered at Nalanda shows that the councils would meet regularly in order to transact rural business. They would issue letters, bearing their own seals, to outsiders. Whether the members of such councils owed their position to their selection by the crown and higher authorities or to an election by the people cannot be deduced with certainty. It may not be unlikely that senior persons of different classes, who were reputed for their experience and character, 'were elevated to the village council by general approval'. A.S. Altekar[64] describes the functions of these councils in the following words, 'The village council looked after the village defence, settled village disputes, organised works of public utility, acted as a trustee for minors, collected government revenues and paid them into the treasury. Village lands were carefully measured and the boundaries were accurately fixed.'

In the localities where the councils were active, the headmen had to wield their authority with caution.

VI

The Village Headman in the Post-Gupta Period

The *Harṣacarita*[65] refers to a village official called *Grāmākṣa-paṭalika* who is said to have given Harṣa 'a new-made golden seal with a bull for its emblem'. We agree with R.S. Tripathi[66] who takes him to be a village notary.

Kalhaṇa mentions a large number of village officials, existing in the kingdom of Kashmir, the most prominent of them being the *Skandakas* and *Grāmakāyasthas*. The exact meaning of the word *skandaka* is far from certain, but this officer seems to have existed in Kashmir at least down to the reign of king Ananta, as the testimony of the *Samayamātṛkā* would indicate. Kalhaṇa's statement that 'by levying contributions for the monthly pay of the *Skandakas* and *Grāmakāyasthas*, Śaṅkaravarman drove the villagers to poverty' shows that the *Skandakas* were royal servants who were paid by the king. Stein identifies them with the village headman, the modern *Muquaddam* or *Lambardar*, who 'as the person directly responsible for the payment of the revenue, has since old days been an important factor in rural administration.'

Both the *Skandaka* and *Grāmakāyastha* acted in co-operation to run the administration. The functions of the *Grāmakāyasthas* were carried on by the *Grāmadiviras* at a later period. The position of the *Grāmadiviras* was similarly unstable, for Kṣemendra tells us that they could hold their post till they enjoyed the confidence of the *Mārgapatis*.[67]

During this and the following periods, the village headman was called by different names in different kingdoms in North India. In Bengal and Bihar under the Pālas, the headman was designated as *Grāmapati*, whereas in the Paramāra kingdom, he was known as *Paṭṭakila*. Under the Gāhaḍavāla kings in Uttar Pradesh, the title of the village headman was *Mahattaka*. The *Agni Purāṇa*, a work of the contemporary period, describes the village headman variously as *Grāmādhipati*, *Grāmeśa*, *Grāmaṇī* and *Grāmabhartā*.

The post of the village chief was usually hereditary, as was the case in the earlier days. He was a person of no mean importance as even the king used to consult him at the time of granting a piece of land in the village. A Gāhaḍavāla grant of A.D. 1109[68] tells us how Govindacandra consulted the village headman named Śrī Gāṅgeya when he made a grant of land, measuring four ploughs. The Kamauli grant[69] of the same Gāhaḍavāla monarch records that while granting the village of Usithā to a Brahmin named Vithākeyadīkṣita, Govindacandra took the consent (*sammati*) of the *Mahattaka* Vālhaṇa. The question why the village headman was consulted by the king at the time of making any land grant may be answered in the following words of P.B. Udgaonkar,[70] 'The village headman was a custodian of records and had an accurate information about the revenue of the village and of the ownership of the different pieces of land situated in it. It was therefore but natural that he should have been consulted at the time of land grant. The consultation was probably to ascertain whether there were any administrative difficulties; it does not suggest that the consent of the headman was a *sine-qua-non* for the grant of a village or a piece of land by the king.'

The post of the village headman does not appear to have been restricted to the Brahmin families alone. Some of the copper plate grants of the Gāhaḍavāla king Jayacandra refer to a Kṣatriya headman, while one of the Paramāra records speaks of the Paṭṭakila Jahṇa who belonged to the Tailika family.[71]

But the village headman could hardly be an autocrat in the discharge of his duties and responsibilities. The village elders like the *Mahattaras* and *Mahattamas* find prominent mention in the contemporary documents. They are referred to in connection with the land grant. The *Kuvalayamālā* refers to the *Grāmamahattaras* as playing an important part in village administration. It records that one Māyāditya, having done ill to a friend, approached the *Grāmamahattaras* and decided to throw himself into the blazing fire. But the chief *Mahattara* advised him to enter the holy water of the river Ganges and the other elders agreed to the proposal. In the Gāhaḍavāla inscriptions the *Mahattamas* are carefully distinguished from the *Puruṣas* or the king's officials. This distinction between the *Mahattamas* and the *Rājapuruṣas* proves that the former were not royal servants, but were probably elected by the villagers.

In any case, these village elders must have helped the village headman in carrying on the local administration and kept him under control. Lakṣmīdhara,[72] however, tells us that the king should appoint in towns and villages his own officers who should be endowed with many qualities of head and heart (*Grāmeṣu nagareṣu c=āryān śucīn satyaśīlaṁ prajā-guptaye nidadhyāt| teṣāṁ puruṣas=tathāguṇā eva syuḥ||*).

Inscriptions do not help us at all to ascertain how the appointment of the village headman was made. The *Agnī Purāṇa*,[73] however, states that it was the king who would appoint the headman of the village.

VII

The Headman in the Śukranīti

Śukra gives us useful information about the village headman, but how far his system of village administration was introduced in the contemporary period cannot be definitely known. Śukra enjoins the *Grāmapa*, who should be a Brāhmaṇa by caste[74] (*Grāmapo Brāhmaṇo yojyaḥ*), to be alert in protecting the villagers with paternal care from aggressors, thieves and greedy officers (*Ādharṣakebhyaś=caurebhyo hy=adhikārigaṇāt tathā| prajā-saṁrakṣaṇe dakṣo Grāmapo mātṛ-pitṛvad||*).[75] Thus the head of the village was primarily concerned with the preservation of law and order within the village. Śukra further says, 'Having determined the land revenue of the village, the king should receive it from one rich man in advance, or guarantee (for the payment) of that either by monthly or periodical instalments. Or the king should appoint officers called *Grāmapas* by paying one-sixteenth, one-twelfth, one-eighth or one-sixth of his own receipts.'[76] We thus see that the *Grāmapa* was sometimes entrusted with the collection of revenue payable to the king, and in return, he was entitled to receive a portion of the king's receipts (*Ṣoḍaśa-dvādaśa-daś=āṣṭaṁ tato v=ādhikāriṇaḥ| sv=āṁśān ṣaṣṭhāṁśa-bhāgena Grāmapān san-niyojayet||*). Again, the statement in Section V of Chapter IV[77] that the 'documents of gifts, sale and purchase about immovable goods are valid only when approved by the receivers and having the *Grāmapas* or village officers as witnesses' leads us to presume that the presence of the headman was needed at the time of the transaction of any gift, sale or purchase of immovable articles. The *Śukranīti* further states that trial of disputes was one of the main functions of the village headman.

Besides the *Grāmapa*, the other officers,[73] connected with the various functions of the village, were the following:

1. The *Sāhasādhipati*. He was the magistrate to deal with criminal cases and was of Kṣatriya origin.
2. The *Bhāgahāra*. This officer, a Kṣatriya by caste, was to collect the revenue and devote special care to the tending of trees.
3. The *Lekhaka*. This officer, who was well-versed in accountancy and several spoken languages, kept accounts of income and expenditure, corresponding to the *Kulkarnis* of the Deccan. He was a Kāyastha by caste.
4. The *Śulkagrāha*. The *Śulkagrāha*, who was a Vaiśya, levied tolls in such a way that producers did not incur any loss.
5. The *Pratīhāra*. He was the guard at the village-gate and was a Śūdra by caste. He was strongly built, skilled in the use of weapons and humble in conduct.

VIII

The Village Headman in Early South Indian Kingdoms

The office of the village headman was popular in South India also. He is described as *Grāmaṇī* in the *Gāthā Saptaśati*.[79] He was also designated as *Āyuktaka* (*grāmeyika ayutta*). He figures in an inscription, noted by Lüders,[80] as granting a piece of land with all immunities. Interesting information about him may be derived from the *Gāthā Saptaśati*[81] which implies that the office of the village headship was normally hereditary, for it contains a definite allusion to the succession to the office of the father by his son. It further narrates how a village headman led an expedition against some external forces which had endangered the peace of the locality.[82] Generally, the *Grāmika* was in charge of a village only; but, as the *Gāthā Saptaśati*[83] would make us believe, in exceptional cases his jurisdiction extended to five, and sometimes even to ten, villages.

The Kamukollu plates[84] of the Śālaṅkāyana king Nandivarman I mention a class of village officials, whose name is differently read by scholars. B.V. Krishna Rao reads their name as *Mutyada*, D.C. Sircar[85] *Muṭuda*, H.C. Raychaudhuri[86] *Muluḍa* and some[87] again as *Miluda* or *Munuda*. They were probably the heads of villages, one of whose functions, as inferred from these plates, consisted of distributing water for irrigating lands.

IX

The Village Headman in the Cālukya and Pallava Kingdoms

In the Cālukya kingdom the village headman was known as *Gāmuṇḍa*. But he was hardly allowed to act independently, for the administration and regulation of the social and economic life of the village were actually in the hands of the *Mahājanas*, village elders. A Cālukya record tells us that the *Mahājanas* governed the village of Benniyur in the reign of Vijayāditya, while in another record we are told that without their prior permission, no piece of land could be donated even to a temple.[88]

The village headman in the Pallava kingdom was known as *Viyavan*. Inscriptions furnish us with the following details about him:

First, the post of headman was normally hereditary.

Second, every senior member of the village contributed to his living by each paying a small fee.

Third, he was vested with power to try the culprits for their irreligious and anti-social activities and impose and collect fines and other penalties from them.

But in the Pallava kingdom the main bulk of village administration was borne by the *Sabhā*, the members of which were called *Perumakkal*, great men. The *Sabhā* was divided into various committees (*vāriyams*), which were named after the specific duties they discharged. The *Eri Vāriya Perumakkal*, for instance, was charged with irrigation and tanks. The *Toṭṭa Vāriya Perumakkal* looked after public gardens, etc.[89] The passage, *Avvavāṇḍu eri vāriya perumakkal*, occurring in an inscription[90] of Kampavarman, seems to suggest that there was an annual election of the committees with the result that fresh members were encouraged to get in and serve on the committees.

The works which the village *Sabhā* had to perform were, however, multifarious, including temple endowments, irrigation, local justice and the like.

X

The Village Headman in the Rāṣṭrakūṭa Kingdom

The Rāṣṭrakūṭa records provide us with a vivid picture of the village headman, and they show that the office was not only popular but carried with it enormous power and position. Inscriptions reveal that the most important duty of the Rāṣṭrakūṭa headman, called *Grāmakūṭa* in Maharashtra and *Gāvuṇḍa* in Karnataka, was to defend the village from both within and without. In order to discharge his duty properly, the headman had himself to be a good fighter and he used to maintain a militia which became the source of recruitment to the imperial army. Inscriptions refer to the headmen and members of the village militia as laying down their lives for the sake of defending their villages. In addition to his military function, the *Grāmakūṭa* was also associated with village revenue, as may be guessed from the fact that the Rāṣṭrakūṭa records invariably mention him in connection with land grants. As regards his remuneration, we have evidence to show that two systems were followed simultaneously—he enjoyed rent-free lands, in addition to taxes in kind which were payable to the king. It was hardly possible for the headman to carry on his duties single-handed; consequently he was aided by his subordinates. The Rāṣṭrakūṭa records time and again mention the *Yuktas*, *Āyuktas*, *Niyuktas* and *Upayuktas* between the *Grāmakūṭa* and the *Grāmamahattaras*. The position of these officers in the list of officials clearly suggests that they were all connected with the village administration, working, no doubt, in a subordinate capacity under the headman.

Some of the Rāṣṭrakūṭa records mention both the *Grāmakūṭa* and the *Grāmapati* in the list of officers who were informed of details of the grant. The separate mention of the two terms in one and the same record implies that they are not to be confounded with each other but denote two distinct persons. The government used to alienate villages in favour of military captains and Brāhmaṇa scholars; these alienees were accordingly called *Grāmapatis* in the Rāṣṭrakūṭa records. A.S. Altekar[91] observes that some Rāṣṭrakūṭa villages were governed by several headmen simultaneously and he refers to a few inscriptions in support of his contention. Since none of these records was issued by any Rāṣṭrakūṭa monarch, the theory of A.S. Altekar about the plurality of headmen for some Rāṣṭrakūṭa villages does not appear to be well founded.

As would appear from the Rāṣṭrakūṭa records, the management of village affairs in Karnataka was not entirely in the hands of the headman, but a great bulk of it was assigned to the *Mahājanas.* A.S. Altekar[92] has shown, with the help of a few epigraphic records, that the *Mahājanas* in ordinary villages included almost all the heads of the families living within the village. In the Brahmanical villages, however, they comprised all the heads of the families of the villages as well as all adults, as proved by an inscription[93] from Nadwadinge in Bijapur district. The *Mahājanas* are known to have discharged the duty of trustees and bankers, raised public subscriptions and government taxes, managed public schools, charity houses, temples and tanks and paid village dues to the central government. All the *Mahājanas* of a village were not directly connected with administration; it appears that the headman and the influential members of the locality carried on the various functions in the name of all.

The *Mahājanas* of Karnataka had their counterparts in the *Mahattaras* in Maharashtra and Southern Gujarat. But while the *Mahājanas* are represented in inscriptions to have discharged various functions, in the last two provinces these functions were carried on by an executive committee of the *Mahattaras*, the members of which were called *Mahattarādhikāriṇaḥ* and *Adhikārikamahattaras.* A sharp change is evidently noticeable in the system of village administration among the neighbouring regions. To use the words of A.S. Altekar,[94] 'In Karnataka the general assembly as a whole is saddled with the responsibility and never its executive body; in Maharashtra and Gujarat the case is just the reverse. It is not improbable that the general body of the village elders was accustomed to meet much less frequently in Maharashtra and Gujarat than was the case in Karnataka and had allowed its functions to be usurped by the executive council.' Inscriptions keep us in the dark about the strength of the executive body. Similarly, they give us no information as to whether its members were nominated by the king and his deputies or were elected by the general body of the *Mahattaras*. The *Mahattarādhikāriṇaḥ* as well as the *Mahājanas* of Karnataka could try and decide both criminal and civil cases. A.S. Altekar[95] points out that their criminal jurisdiction as compared with their civil jurisdiction was very limited.

XI

The Headman in the Raṭṭa, Eastern and Western Cālukya Kingdoms

The inscriptions of the Raṭṭa and the Eastern and Western Cālukya kings of Saundatti, Veṅgī and Kalyāṇī, respectively, refer to the office of headman. It seems that most of the localities in the Raṭṭa kingdom and a few villages in the Western Cālukya dominions had several headmen, instead of one. The five Raṭṭa records[96] discovered at Saundatti state that the villages of Sugandhavatī, Elerave and Hamdi had twelve headmen each, while Hirayakummi had six. Again, a record of the reign of the Cālukya king Vikramāditya VI claims twelve headmen for the village of Teridal. The existence of several headmen in these villages may be explained by the supposition that they were too big to be controlled by one officer or as A.S. Altekar[97] has said, 'there may have been prevailing in these localities the custom of allowing the senior representatives of the main branches of the original headman's family to officiate simultaneously.'

It seems that in the days of the Cālukyas of Veṅgī, the appointment of the headman was controlled by the centre.[98] The Pabhuparu grant of Śaktivarman shows how the king dismissed a headman on the ground of his disloyal and treacherous conduct and appointed a new headman in his place. That under the Cālukyas the village headman owed his appointment to the crown is further corroborated by the Kaluchumbarru grant[99] of Amma II which records that the king granted the office of *Grāmakūṭa* in perpetuity to an individual.

The village headman in the Western Cālukya kingdom was called *Gāvuṇḍa* or *Gāmuṇḍa* who appears to have been invested with executive and judicial powers. The office of the *Gāvuṇḍa* was generally hereditary and in the case of inefficiency on the part of the occupant, the post was transferred to the members of other families. His power was effectively limited by the *Mahājanas* whose influence was considerable. An epigraph of Vikramāditya VI records that 'at the request of the two hundred *mahājanas* of Mamgola, queen Padmāvatīdevī, who was enjoying that village as her *jāgir*, granted some land, free of taxes, to the temple of Narasimhadeva, through her agent Śaliyama Nāyaka.'[100] There are also references in the Cālukya inscriptions to the *Mahājanas* going on deputation to the king.

In the Raṭṭa kingdom the headman enjoyed rent-free land. A record from Saundatti[101] states that the *Gāvuṇḍa* of Kadole gave away a piece of cultivable land, 'when was his rent-free service land'. From this record it would obviously follow that first, the village headman enjoyed rent-free service land, second, this rent-free land of the headman was regarded as alienable, and last, if the suggestion of A.S. Altekar[102] be accepted, the alienees of the headman's land were required to discharge the duties of headman. This system under the Raṭṭas reminds one of a similar practice in the Maratha kingdom where rent-free lands and the privileges of headman were transferable.

XII

The Village Headman in Tribal Areas

The office of village headman was prevalent in the aboriginal villages also. Even now the tribal villages are governed by headmen who are known by different designations in different areas. Sachchidananda[103] observes, 'In the simpler societies the ordering of the social, political and ritual relations of the village are in the hands of one man. But in the more complex societies, we find a differentiation of function and authority vested in two headmen each with its own field of interest and prescribed duties. A primary differentiation of function splits village affairs into secular and sacerdotal spheres of activity with a headman responsible for each and among some tribes, this differentiation is further emphasized by the appointment of assistants to help each headman in the discharge of his duties.' In the Kharia villages there is only one headman who combines in his person the social as well as the religious leadership of the village.[104] The affairs of the Muṇḍā villages of Chota Nagpur are in the hands of the *Muṇḍā* and *Pāhān* who perform the secular and religious duties, respectively. We have, in addition to them, for each village a *Panchayat* which takes up important matters like punishment of offenders against tribal customs, settlement of serious disputes, partition of family lands, etc. In the Oraon villages the *Mahto*, the secular headman, the *Pāhān*, the religious headman, and the *Panch*, the village council, control the affairs. How these bodies discharged their respective functions will be clear from the following observations of R.C. Ray: 'The village *Panch* or council of village elders decide all disputes between the villagers and try and punish offences against the social and moral codes of the tribe. Partition of family lands according to tribal customs is one of the most important functions of the village *Panch*. Matters and disputes relating to marriage and sexual tabus and offences and cases of suspected witchcraft are still almost invariably referred to the village *Panch*. The *Mahto* or secular headman manages the secular affairs of the village and is the intermediary between the villagers and the landlord and Governmental authorities and the *Pāhān* (Oraon, *Naigas*) or village priest seeks to maintain harmonious relations between the village and the spirit-world.'[105] In Coorg, the management of the village rests with the headman called *Takka* and the village elders. 'They decide cases of violation of caste rules or social etiquette, cases of sexual immorality and so forth. Three to five *Takkas* constitute a *Nād* over which there is a headman called *Mukyastama* and a *Nād Panchayat* which decide disputes which the *Takka* cannot settle. The next higher organisation is the *Simatoka* of which there are four in Coorg proper.'[106] The office of headman is highly important among the Santals. P.O. Bodding[107] says, 'The *Majhi* is the head of the village people. All the people will have to follow his lead. In ordering and inviting, in calling and restraining, at the name-giving, at the initiating festivals, at marriages, when hunting and chasing, at feasts and festivals, at religious instruction and worship, in connection with rice and curry, with beer and liquor, with spirits and mountain spirits, in quarrelling and squabbling, in strife and dispute, when there is hunger and thirst, with landlords and moneylenders, when crime and misdeeds occur, in connection with theft and stealing, with medicine and witchcraft, with wenches and strumpets, when there is fighting and killing, murder and wickedness, in grief and sorrow, in calamities and dangers, in illness and pain, at dying and falling away, in ceremonies connected with death and disease, at cremation and at final funeral ceremonies, in connection with all this the *Majhi* has responsibility.' Referring to Indian villages, Lord Metcalfe observes: 'They seem to last where nothing else lasts. Dynasty after dynasty tumbles down; revolution succeeds revolution; Hindu, Pathan, Mughal, Mahratta, Sikh, English are all masters in turn; but the village communities remain the same.'[108] This statement may be applied with greater justification to the tribal villages in India. If the modern tribal headmen wield enormous power and influence in their villages, there can be no shadow of doubt that their forerunners discharged the same functions, perhaps more effectively, centuries earlier.

References and Notes

1. X 62.11; 107.5.
2. *Atharva Veda*, iii.5.7; xix.31.12; *Taittirīya Saṁhitā*, ii.5.4.4; *Maitrāyaṇī Saṁhitā*, i.6.5; *Kāṭhaka Saṁhitā*, viii.4; x.3; *Vājasaneyī Saṁhitā*, xv.15; xxx.20; *Taittirīya Brāhmaṇa*, i.1.4.8; 7.3.4; ii.7.18.4; *Śatapatha Brāhmaṇa*, iii.4.1.7; v.4 4.8; viii.6.2.1; *Bṛhadāraṇyaka Upaniṣad*, iv.3.37.38.
3. *Vācaspatya*, 2771-2.
4. V.3.1.5.
5. *Altindisches Leben*, p. 171.
6. *VI*, I, p. 247.
7. *APIIAI*, p. 108.
8. II.5.4.4.
9. *VI*, I, p. 247; *SGAI*, p. 153.
10. VII.28.6.
11. X.34.6.
12. I.1.10.6.
13. V.3.1.10.
14. Some scholars do not agree with the view that the *Sabhā* was a village assembly. B.A. Saletore (*AIPTI*, p. 391), for example, maintains that this theory, in view of a passage in the *Śatapatha Brāhmaṇa*, referring to a king as attending the assembly, cannot be regarded as tenable. Unfortunately, it is difficult for us to agree with Saletore. The Vedic texts refer to the presence of the king in the *Sabhā* only in one of their passages. This clearly proves that the king attended the *Sabhā* only under abnormal circumstances. In Vedic literature, we find terms like

sabhāpati, *sabhāpāla* and *sabhā cāra* but they have never been used as a designation for the king. Thus the view that the *Sabhā* denoted the assembly of the villagers does not appear to be unfounded. Ludwig (*Translation of the Ṛg Veda*, pp. 3, 253-6) is, however, opposed to the view that the *Sabhā* was a village assembly and maintains that it was an assembly of the Brāhmaṇas and Maghavans. Bloomfield (*VI*, II, p. 42) opines that the *Sabhā* was used for a domestic purpose. K.P. Jayaswal (*HP*, pp. 11-20) observes that the *Sabhā* 'was certainly related to the *Samiti* but its exact relationship is not deducible from the data available. Probably it was a standing and a stationary body of selected men under the authority of the *Samiti*.'

15. II.5.4.4.
16. *HD*, III, p. 153.
17. *Taittirīya Saṁhitā*, ii.3.1.3; *Kāṭhaka Saṁhitā*, xi.4.
18. I.354.
19. I.98.
20. *SONEI*, p. 162.
21. *CLAI*, p. 128.
22. I.483.
23. IV.115.
24. IV.115.
25. II.134.
26. *CLAI*, p. 143.
27. *IHQ*, XIII, p. 614.
28. II.10.26.4.
29. II.10.26.7.
30. II.10.26.9.
31. II.10.26.5.
32. III.10; IV.6; IV.4.
33. V.3.
34. But what was the extent of an Indian village in ancient times? An answer to this question can be found in the following statement of Kauṭilya, 'He should cause villages to be settled consisting mostly of Śūdra agriculturists, with a minimum of one hundred families and a maximum of five hundred families, with boundaries extending over one *krośa* or two *krośas*, (and) affording matual protection. He should fix, as the boundary lines a river, a mountain, a forest, a stretch of pebbles, sand, etc., a cavern, an embankment, a *Śāmī* tree, a *Śālmalī* tree or a milk-tree (like *Aśvattha*, *Nyagrodha* etc.)' (*KA*, II, pp. 62-3). The interpretation of the term *kula* in the original passage in the sense of a family, as has been suggested above, has been opposed by some scholars who observe that the term denotes land that can be ploughed by one, two or three ploughs. If this view is accepted, a small village would then have an area of 100 such fields with a boundary of one *krośa*, and a large village should comprise 500 fields with a boundary of two *krośas*. The commentator on the *Abhidhānarājendra*, a work of a much later date refers to ten different theories, then current, on the size of a *grāma*.,

A.S. Altekar (*RT*, p. 143) discusses them in the following words, 'The first theory maintained that it could comprise not only the area of settlement, but also the territory up to the limits of which the cows go out while grazing. The second theory contended that *grāma* could not denote so extensive an area, since cows often go out for grazing in the fields of contiguous villages. It maintained that only that much area, which is traversed by the grass and fuel gatherers in the course of the day, can be included in the meaning of the term in question. The third view maintained that even this interpretation is open to a similar objection and, therefore, *grāma* denotes only the area included in the boundaries of the village in question. The fourth view reduced even this extent and preferred to regard the *grāma* as comprising only the area up to the village well. The subsequent views go on curtailing the extent of *grāma* still further till the climax is reached when it is contended that *grāma* means that temple or village-hall which was first built in the village, and around which the settlement subsequently grew. The commentator further observes that *grāma*, in the opinion of some, meant the individual houses of the speakers; the last view cited by him is that the term can be used to denote the headman of the village as well' (*RT*, p. 143).

35. IV.4. P.V. Kane (*HD*, III, p. 282) observes in this connection, 'Even in the twentieth century in the Bombay Presidency under the Village Police Act (Bombay Act VIII of 1867), the village headman has the authority to try and on conviction to punish with confinement for a period not exceeding twenty-four hours any person charged with the commission of petty assault or abuse within the limits of a village and the person convicted has no right of appeal to any court or magistrate against such conviction and only the High Court has the power to entertain a petition for revision.'
36. II.34.
37. II.274.
38. II.1.
39. III.10.18.
40. *KA*, II, p. 258.
41. VII.115, 116.
42. V.5.5.
43. P. 147.
44. *Luders' List*, No. 48.
45. VII.114.
46. Jolly's Sanskrit Text, III.
47. *Luders' List*, No. 48. Another inscription from Mathura, belonging to the reign of Vāsudeva, refers to a *Grāmika* whose wife installed an image of the *Arhat* Ṛṣabha (*Luders' List*, No. 69a).
48. VII.114. While commenting on this passage, Kullūka says: *dvayor=iti| dvayor=grāmayor=mmadhye trayāṇāṁ vā grāmāṇāṁ pañcānāṁ vā grāma-śatānāṁ vā| gulmaṁ rakṣitṛ-puruṣa-samūhaṁ satyapradhāna-puruṣ=ādhiṣṭhitaṁ| rāṣṭrasya saṁgrahaṁ rakṣā-sthānaṁ kuryāt|*

49. X.46-7.
50. VII.116.
51. III.5-7.
52. VII.118.
53. The *Milindapañho* (D.C. Sircar, *Early Indian Political and Administrative Systems*, Calcutta, 1972, p. 123) speaks of a subordinate officer who used to make public announcements on behalf of the village headman.
54. VII.118. Kullūka points out that he was entitled to get the miscellaneous taxes in kind but not a portion of the annual revenue (*yāni annapān=endhan=adīn grāma-vāsibhiḥ pratyahaṁ rājñe deyāni, na tu avdakaraṁ-dhānyānām=aṣṭamo bhāgaḥ ity=ādikaṁ-tāni grām=ādhipatiḥ vṛtyarthyaṁ gṛhṇīyāt*/). R.S. Sharma (*APIIAI*, p. 172) observes, 'But we notice two important changes in the office of the village headman in Manu . . . Secondly, the *grāmika* was paid not in the shape of fines, realised from the villagers, as in pre-Maurya times, or in cash salary as the *grāmabhṛtaka* in Maurya times, but in grant of a piece of land.' This observation is based on the wrong interpretation of the relevant passages of the *Manusaṁhitā*.
55. *EI*, XXXIII, p. 307.
56. *EI*, XV, No. 7.
57. *LGA*, p. 298.
58. *CII*, III, p. 111.
59. H.C. Raychaudhuri (*PHAI*, p. 562) points out that the village functionaries were generally placed under the district officials but in exceptional cases they maintained direct dealings with the provincial governors.
60. *EI*, XV, pp. 135ff.
61. Much controversy has raged on the significance of *Grāmāṣṭakulādhikaraṇa.* The term has been explained by R.G. Basak (*EI*, XV, p. 137) to mean a local officer, 'appointed over eight *Kulas*, a technical term used to denote an inhabited country, especially as much ground as can be cultivated by two ploughs each driven by six bulls' (*HB*, I, p. 269). R.D. Banerji (*JASB*, *NS*, V, p. 460) interprets it to mean an officer exercising authority over a group of eight villages. N.N. Dasgupta (*IC*, V, pp. 110-1) opines that it was a judicial court comprising more or less eight judges. The Dhanaidaha copper plate inscription gives us a clue to the solution of the problem. The term is used there as a neuter singular and this is an indication that the term does not indicate an officer, big or small, for whom a masculine singular form would have been more suitable. *Grāmāṣṭakulādhikaraṇa* under these circumstances would signify a village board, invested with definite administrative power rather than an individual officer.
62. *SI*, p. 333.
63. *SGAI*, p. 224.
64. Ibid., pp. 342-3.
65. P. 274.

66. *HK*, p. 141.
67. *EHCK*, p. 131.
68. *IA*, VIII, pp. 15-17.
69. *EI*, II, pp. 359-61.
70. *PIA*, p. 161.
71. Ibid., p. 163.
72. *Kṛtyakalpataru, Rājadharmakāṇḍa*, pp. 79 and 81.
73. 223.1.
74. II.812.
75. II.343-44.
76. IV.248-52.
77. IV.348-49.
78. II.339-52.
79. 1.30-31; VII.24.
80. *Luders' List*, No. 1327.
81. VII.31.
82. VII.31.
83. *EHD*, p. 135.
84. *EI*, XXXI, pp. 1ff.
85. Ibid., p. 4.
86. *PHAI*, p. 524.
87. *EI*, IX, p. 58.
88. *EHD*, p. 237.
89. *ASLUP*, p. 126.
90. Ibid., p. 129.
91. *RT*, p. 190.
92. Ibid., p. 199.
93. *IA*, XII, p. 221.
94. *RT*, p. 206.
95. Ibid., p. 210.
96. *JBBRAS*, X, pp. 283ff.
97. *RT*, p. 190.
98. *EHD*, p. 499.
99. *EI*, VII.
100. *Karnataka Historical Review*, III, p. 13.
101. *JBBRAS*, X, p. 260.
102. *RT*, pp. 193-4.
103. *TVB*, pp. 69-70.
104. Ibid., p. 70.
105. *JBORS*, XVI, pp. 446-7.
106. Ibid., p. 449.
107. *TIS*, p. 104.
108. Charles Drekmeier, *Kingship and Community in Early India* (California, 1962), p. 275.

Bibliography

ORIGINAL SOURCES

(a) Vedic Works

Ṛgveda Saṁhitā, ed. by F. Max Müller, 1890-92.

——, ed. by Th. Aufrecht. Bonn, 1877.

Sāmaveda, ed. by Th. Benfey. Leipzig, 1848.

Taittirīya Saṁhitā, ed. by A. Weber.

Kāṭhaka Saṁhitā, ed. by L. von Schroeder. Leipzig, 1900-11.

Maitrāyaṇī Saṁhitā, ed. by L. von Schroeder. Leipzig, 1881-6.

Vājasaneyī Saṁhitā, ed. by A. Weber. London, 1852.

Atharva Veda, trans. by W.D. Whitney. Cambridge, Mass., U.S.A., 1905.

——, by M. Bloomfield. Oxford, 1897.

Aitareya Āraṇyaka, trans. by A.B. Keith. Oxford, 1909.

Aitareya Brāhmaṇa, ed by Th. Aufrecht. Bonn, 1879.

Śatapatha Brāhmaṇa, ed. by A. Weber. London, 1855.

Taittirīya Brāhmaṇa, ed. by R.L. Mitra. Calcutta, 1855-70.

Taittirīya Āraṇyaka, ed. by H.N. Apte. Poona, 1898.

Gopatha Brāhmaṇa, ed. by R.L. Mitra and H. Vidyabhusana. Calcutta, 1872.

Chāndogya Upaniṣad, ed. by Böhtlingk. Leipzig, 1889.

R.A. Hume, *Thirteen Principal Upaniṣads*. Oxford, 1921.

Max Müller, *Sacred Books of the East, I* and *XV*.

(b) Dharmasūtras, Dharmaśāstras and Arthaśāstra

Vasiṣṭha Dharma Sūtra, ed. by Führer. Bombay, 1883.

Baudhāyana Dharma Sūtra, ed. by Bühler. Leipzig, 1884.

Gautama Dharma Sūtra, ed. by Stenzler. London, 1876.

Āśvalāyana Gṛhya Sūtra, ed. by Stenzler. Leipzig, 1864.

Āpastambīya Gṛhya Sūtra, ed. by M. Winternitz. Vienna, 1887.

Kausika Sūtra, ed. by M. Bloomfield. New Haven, 1890.

Vaiṣṇava Dharma Śāstra, ed. by Jolly. Calcutta, 1881.

Yājñavalkya Dharma Śāstra, ed. by Stenzler. Berlin, 1849.
Nārada Smṛti, ed. by Jolly. Calcutta, 1885.
Mānava Dharma Śāstra, ed. by N.N. Mandlik. Bombay, 1886.
——, ed. by J.N. Vidyaratna. Calcutta, 1292 (B.S.)
Arthaśāstra of Kauṭilya, ed. by R. Shama Sastri, Mysore, 1919.
——, ed. by R.P. Kangle. Bombay, 1963.
——, ed. by R.G. Basak. Calcutta, 1964.

(*c*) *Grammatical Works*

Aṣṭādhyāyī of Pāṇini, ed. by S.C. Vasu. Allahabad, 1891-98.
Mahābhāṣya of Patañjali, ed. by Kielhorn. Bombay, 1906.

(*d*) *Epics*

Mahābhārata, ed. by H. Siddhanta Vagisa.
——, trans. by P.C. Roy. Calcutta, 1883-96.
——, trans. by M.N. Dutt. Calcutta, 1896.
Rāmāyaṇa, trans. by R.T.H. Griffith. Banaras, 1895.
——, Calcutta, Bangabasi edn. 1311 B.S.
——, trans. by H.P. Shastri. London, 1952.
Harivaṁśa, Calcutta, 1834-39.

(*e*) *Purāṇas*

Mārkaṇḍeya Purāṇa, trans. by F.E. Pargiter. Calcutta, 1904.
Vāyu Purāṇa, ed. by R.L. Mitra. Calcutta, 1880-88.
Viṣṇu Purāṇa, trans. by H.H. Wilson. London, 1864-70.
Matsya Purāṇa, Anandasrama Sanskrit Series. Poona, 1907.
Brahmāṇḍa Purāṇa, pub. by Venkatesvara Press. Bombay, 1913.
Kūrma Purāṇa, Calcutta, 1890.
Brahma Purāṇa, Anandasrama Sanskrit Series. Poona, 1895.
Bhāgavata Purāṇa, trans. by M.N. Dutt. Calcutta, 1895.
Agni Purāṇa, Anandasrama Sanskrit Series. Poona, 1900.
Padma Purāṇa, pub. by Venkatesvara Press. Bombay, 1895.
Liṅga Purāṇa, ed. by J. Vidyasagara. Calcutta, 1885.
Pargiter, F.E., *The Purāṇa Texts of the Dynasties of the Kali Age*. Oxford, 1913.
Yuga Purāṇa, ed. by K.P. Jayaswal. *JBORS*, XIV, 397-421.
——, ed. by K.H Dhruva. *JBORS*, XVI, 18-66.
Bṛhaspati Smṛti, ed. by A. Führer. Leipzig, 1879.
——, trans. by J. Jolly. Oxford, 1889.
Kātyāyana Smṛti, ed. by P.V. Kane. Bombay, 1933.

Nārada Smṛti, ed. by J. Jolly. Calcutta, 1885.
Varāha Purāṇa, ed. by P.H. Sastri. Calcutta, 1893.
Garuḍa Purāṇa, Bombay, 1906.

(*f*) *Other Sanskrit Works*

Kālidāsa's *Raghuvaṁśa*
Bṛhatsaṁhitā, ed. by J.H.K. Kern. Calcutta, 1865.
Bāṇa's *Harṣacarita*, trans. by Cowell and Thomas. London, 1897.
Bāṇa's *Kādambarī*, ed. by M.R. Kale. Delhi, 1968.
——, trans. by C.M. Ridding. London, 1896.
Daṇḍin's *Daśakumāracarita*, ed. by V. Satakopan and V. Anantacharya. Madras, 1963.
Kāvyamīmāṁsā, ed. by C.D. Dalal and R.A.K. Sastri. Gaekwad's Oriental Series, I. Baroda, 1916.
Ārya-Mañjuśrīmūlakalpa, ed. by Ganapati Sastri. Trivandrum, 1925.
Kuvalayamālākathā of Uddyotana Sūri, SJG, Bombay.
Prabandhakośa of Rājasekhara, Gaekwad's Oriental Series.
Prabhāvakacharita, SJG, Bombay.
Tilakamañjarī of Dhanapāla, NSP, 1st edn.
Yaśastilakachampū of Somadeva, NSP.
Kṛtyakalpataru of Lakṣmīdhara, ed. by K.V. Rangaswami Aiyangar Baroda, 1943.
Nītivākyāmṛta of Somadeva Sūri.
Nītisāra of Kāmandaka, ed. by T. Ganapati Sastri. Trivandrum, 1912.
Śukranīti, pub. by Ksemaraja Sri Krsnadasa. Bombay.
——, ed. by B.K. Sarkar. Allahabad, 1914.

(*g*) *Buddhist Works*

Majjhima Nikāya, ed. by V. Trenckner and R. Chalmers. London, 1888-1902.
Aṅguttara Nikāya, ed. by Richard Morris and Edmund Hardy. London, 1885-1900.
Dīgha Nikāya, ed. by Rhys Davids and J. Charpentier; *Dialogues of Buddha*, II, III and IV.
Vinaya Piṭaka, trans. by T.W. Rhys Davids and H. Oldenberg. Oxford, 1881-85.
Sutta Nipāta, ed. by D. Anderson and H. Smith. 1913.

Dhammapada, trans. by F. Max Müller. Oxford, 1898.
Mahāvaṁsa, trans. by W. Geiger, assisted by Mabel H. Bode. London, 1912.
Apadāna, ed. by Mary E. Lilley. London, 1925-27.
Cullaniddesa, ed. by W. Stede. London, 1918.
Jātaka, ed. by Faüsboll, I-VI. London, 1877-97.
Dīpavaṁsa, trans. by Oldenberg. London, 1879.
Divyāvadāna, ed. by E.B. Cowell and R.A. Neil. Cambridge, 1886.
Therī Gāthā, ed. by H. Oldenberg. London, 1883.

(*h*) *Jain Works*

Ācārāṅga Sūtra, trans. by H. Jacobi. *SBE*, XXII. Oxford, 1892.
Uvāsagadasāo, ed. by A.F.R. Hoernle. Calcutta, 1885-88.
Uttarādhyayana Sūtra, ed. by J. Charpentier. Uppasala, 1922.
Bhagavatī Sūtra, ed. by Weber. Berlin, 1866.
Bhavadeva's *Pārśvanāthacarita*, ed. by Pt. Hargovind and Pt. Bechardas.
Pariśiṣṭaparvan, ed. by H. Jacobi. Calcutta, 1932.
Prabandhacintāmaṇi, trans. by C.H. Tawney. Calcutta, 1901.
Kathākośa, trans. by C.H. Tawney. London, 1895.

(*i*) *Tamil Works*

The Sacred Kural, trans. by H.A. Popley. Calcutta, 1931.
Thirumathi Sornammal Endowment Lectures on Tirukkural, pub. by the University of Madras, 1971.
Śīlappadikāram, trans. by V.R.R. Dikshitar. Oxford, 1939.

(*j*) *Classical Works*

McCrindle, J.W., *Ancient India as described by Megasthenes and Arrian*. Calcutta, 1960.
——, *Ancient India as described in Classical Literature*. Westminster, 1901.
Schoff, W.W., *Periplus of the Erythraean Sea*. London, 1912.
Majumdar, S.N., *Ancient India as Described by Ptolemy*. Calcutta, 1927.
Majumdar, R.C., *The Classical Accounts of India*. Calcutta, 1960.
Loeb Classical Library Series. London and New York.

(*k*) *Tibeto-Chinese Works*

The Travels of Fa-hsien or *Record of Buddhistic Kingdoms.* Cambridge, 1923.

Hiuen Tsiang's Buddhist Records of the Western World, trans. by S. Beal. London, 1884.

On Yuan Chwang's Travels in India, I and II, trans. by T. Watters. London, 1908.

Tāranātha's History of Buddhism, trans. by F.A. Von Schiefner. St. Petersberg, 1869.

I-tsing's *A Record of the Buddhist Religion as practised in India and the Malay Archipelago,* trans. by J. Takakusu. Oxford, 1896.

(*l*) *Moslem Works*

Alberuni's *India,* trans. by E.C. Sachau. London, 1914.

Tarīkh-i-Firishta, trans. by John Briggs. Lucknow, 1905.

MODERN WORKS

Agrawala, V.S., *India as Known to Pāṇini.* Lucknow, 1953.

Aiyangar, K.V.R., *Aspects of the Social and Political System of Manusmṛti.* Lucknow, 1949.

Aiyangar, S. Krishnaswami, *Studies in Gupta History.* Madras, 1928.

——, *Hindu Administrative Institutions in South India.* Madras, 1931.

Aiyer, C.P.R., *Indian Political Theories.* Madras, 1937.

Allan, John, *A Catalogue of Indian Coins in the British Museum* (Ancient India). London, 1936.

——, *Catalogue of Gupta Coins.* London, 1914.

Altekar, A.S., *The Rāṣṭrakūṭas And Their Times.* Poona, 1934.

——, *State and Government in Ancient India.* Banaras, 1955.

——, *The Coinage of the Gupta Empire.* Banaras, 1957.

Bandyopadhyaya, N.C., *Hindu Polity and Political Theory.* Calcutta, 1928.

Banerjea, J.N., *Development of Hindu Iconography.* Calcutta, 1941.

Banerjea, P.N., *Public Administration in Ancient India.* London, 1916.

Banerji, R.D., *History of Orissa,* I. Calcutta, 1930.

——, *The Age of the Imperial Guptas.* Banaras, 1933.

Barua, B.M., *Aśoka and His Inscriptions*. Calcutta, 1955.
——, *Old Brāhmī Inscriptions*. Calcutta, 1929.
Basak, R.G., *The History of North-Eastern India*. Calcutta, 1967.
——, *Aśokan Inscriptions*. Calcutta, 1959.
Basu, P.C., *Indo-Aryan Polity*. London, 1925.
Beniprasad, *Theory of Government in Ancient India*. Allahabad, 1927.
Bhandarkar, D.R., *Aśoka*. Calcutta, 1925.
——, *Some Aspects of Ancient Indian Polity*. Madras, 1940.
Bhattacharya, S., *Select Aśokan Epigraphs*. Calcutta, 1960.
Chakraborti, H.P., *Trade and Commerce of Ancient India*. Calcutta, 1966.
Chakravarti, C., *A Study in Hindu Social Polity*. Calcutta, 1923.
Chakravarti, P.C., *The Art of War in Ancient India*. Dacca, 1941.
Chatterjee, G.S., *Harṣavardhana*. Allahabad, 1938.
Chatterjee, H.L., *International Law And Inter-State Relations In Ancient India*. Calcutta, 1958.
Chattopadhyaya, S., *Early History of North India*. Calcutta, 1968.
——, *The Śakas in India*. Santiniketan, 1967.
——, *Social Life in Ancient India*. Calcutta, 1965.
Choudhury, G.C., *Political History of Northern India From Jain Sources*. Amritsar, 1954.
Choudhury, P.C., *The History of Civilization of the People of Assam*. Gauhati, 1959.
Cunningham, A., *Ancient Geography of India*. Calcutta, 1924.
Dandekar, R.N., *A History of the Guptas*. Poona, 1941.
Das Gupta, R.P., *Crime and Punishment in Ancient India*. Calcutta, 1930.
Dikshitar, Ramachandra V.R., *The Mauryan Polity*. Madras, 1953.
——, *The Gupta Polity*. Madras, 1952.
Dharma, P.C., *The Rāmāyaṇa Polity*. Madras, 1941.
Drekmeier, Charles, *Kingship and Community in Early India*. California, 1962.
Ganguly, D.K., *Historical Geography and Dynastic History of Orissa*. Calcutta, 1975.
Ganguly, N.C., *Indian Political Philosophy*. Calcutta, 1939.
Gerini, *Researches on Ptolemy* (Asiatic Society Monographs, I, 1909).

Ghosal, U.N., *A History of Indian Political Ideas.* Bombay, 1959.

——, *The Beginnings of Indian Historiography and Other Essays.* Calcutta, 1944.

——, *The Agrarian System in Ancient India.* Calcutta, 1930.

——, *Contributions to the History of the Hindu Revenue Systems.* Calcutta, 1929.

Ghosh, J.C., *Principles of Hindu Law.* Calcutta, 1906.

Gopal, M.H., *Mauryan Public Finance.*

Gopalachari, K., *Early History of the Andhra Country.* Madras, 1941.

Hultzsch, E., *Corpus Inscriptionum Indicarum,* I. 1969.

Jayaswal, K.P., *Hindu Polity.* Calcutta, 1924.

——, *Manu and Yājñavalkya: A Comparison and a Contrast.* Calcutta, 1930.

Jha, D.N., *Revenue System in Post-Maurya and Gupta Times.* Calcutta, 1967.

Jha, G.N., *Hindu Law In Its Sources,* I. Allahabad, 1930.

Jolly, J., *Hindu Law and Custom.* Calcutta, 1928.

——, *Outlines of an History of the Hindu Law of Partition, Inheritance and Adoption.* Calcutta, 1885.

Kane, P.V., *History of Dharmaśāstra,* III. Poona, 1946.

Law, B.C., *Tribes in Ancient India.* Poona, 1943.

Law, N.N., *Aspects of Ancient Indian Polity.* Calcutta, 1960.

——, *Inter-State Relations in Ancient India.* Calcutta, 1920.

Leeuw, Von Lohuizen de, *The Scythian Period.* Leiden, 1949.

Macdonell, A.A. and Keith, A.B., *Vedic Index of Names and Subjects,* I and II. London, 1912.

Mahalingam, T.V., *Administration and Social Life Under Vijayanagar.* Madras, 1940.

——, *South Indian Polity.* Madras, 1955.

Mahtab, H.K., *The History of Orissa,* I. Cuttack, 1959.

——, *The History of Orissa.* Lucknow, 1947.

——, *History of Orissa* (in Oriya). Cuttack, 1948.

Maitra, S.K., *The Social Organisation in North-East India in Buddha's Time.* Calcutta, 1920.

Majumdar, B.K., *The Military System in Ancient India.* Calcutta, 1960.

Majumdar, R.C., *The Vedic Age.* Bombay, 1951.

——, *The Age of Imperial Unity.* Bombay, 1960.

Majumdar, R.C., *The Classical Age*. Bombay.
——, *The Age of Imperial Kanauj*. Bombay.
——, *The Vākāṭaka-Gupta Age*. Lahore, 1946.
——, *Suvarṇadvīpa*, II, Pt. I.
——, *History of Bengal*, I. Dacca, 1943.
——, *The Corporate Life In Ancient India*. Calcutta, 1969.
——, *The Struggle for Empire*. Bombay, 1957.
——, *History of Ancient Bengal*. Calcutta, 1971.
Mazumdar, B.C., *Orissa in the Making*. 1925.
Mehta, G.P., *Candragupta Vikramāditya* (in Hindi). Allahabad, 1932.
Mehta, R.N., *Pre-Buddhist India*. Bombay, 1939.
Minakshi, C., *Administration and Social Life Under the Pallavas*. Madras, 1938.
Mishra, B.P., *Polity in the Agni Purāṇa*. Calcutta, 1965.
Mishra, S.S., *Mānasollāsa: Ek Sāṁskṛtik Adhyayana* (in Hindi). Banaras, 1966.
Misra, B., *Orissa Under the Bhauma Kings*. Calcutta, 1934.
——, *Dynasties of Mediaeval Orissa*. Calcutta, 1933.
Mookherji, R.K., *The Gupta Empire*. Bombay, 1948.
——, *Harṣa*. Oxford, 1926.
——, *Local Government in Ancient India*. Delhi, 1958.
——, *Aśoka*. Calcutta, 1928.
——, *Chandragupta Maurya and His Times*. Madras, 1943.
Naik, B.B., *Ideals of Ancient Hindu Politics*. Dharwar, 1932.
Narain, A.K., *The Indo-Greeks*. Oxford, 1962.
Niyogi, R., *History of the Gāhaḍavāla Dynasty*. Calcutta, 1959.
Oppert, Gustav, *On the Weapons, Army Organisation and Political Maxims of the Ancient Hindus*. Madras, 1880.
Panigrahi, K.C., *Archaeological Remains at Bhubaneswar*.
——, *Chronology of the Bhauma-Karas and the Somavaṁśīs of Orissa*.
Panikkar, K.M., *The Origin and Evolution of Kingship in India*. Baroda, 1938.
Pargiter, F.E., *Ancient Indian Historical Tradition*. London, 1932.
Pires, E., *The Maukharis*. Madras, 1934.
Rao, M.V.K., *Studies in Kauṭilya*. Delhi, 1958.
Rapson, E.J., *The Cambridge History of India*, I (First Indian Reprint).

Ray, H.C., *The Dynastic History of Northern India*, I and II (Calcutta, 1931 and 1936).

Ray, N.R., *Vāṅgālīra Itihāsa*. Calcutta, 1359 (B.S.).

Ray, S.C., *Early History and Culture of Kashmir*. Calcutta, 1957.

Raychaudhuri, H.C., *Political History of Ancient India*. Calcutta, 1950.

Rhys Davids, T.W., *Buddhist India*. New York, 1903.

Sabnis, S.A., *Kālidāsa: His Style And His Times*. Bombay, 1966.

Sahu, N.K., *The Utkal University History of Orissa*, I.

Saletore, B.A., *Ancient Indian Political Thought and Institutions*. Calcutta, 1963.

Sarkar, B.K., *Political Institutions and Theories of the Hindus*. Leipzig, 1922.

Sastri, Nilakanta K.A., *A Comprehensive History of India*, II. Calcutta, 1957.

———, *The Age of the Nandas and Mauryas*. Banaras, 1953.

———, *Foreign Notices of South India*. Madras, 1939.

———, *Studies in Chola History and Administration*. Madras, 1932.

———, *The Theory of Pre-Muslim Indian Polity*. Madras, 1912.

———, *The Pāṇḍyan Kingdom*. London, 1929.

Sen, B.C., *Some Historical Aspects of the Inscriptions of Bengal*. Calcutta, 1942.

Shamasastri, R., *Evolution of Indian Polity*. Calcutta, 1920.

Sharma, D., *Rajasthan Through The Ages*, I. Bikaner, 1966.

Sharma, R.S., *Aspects of Political Ideas and Institutions in Ancient India*. Banaras, 1959.

———, *Indian Feudalism: c. 300-1200*.

Shastri, J.L., *Political Thought in the Purāṇas*. Lahore, 1944.

Shembavnekar, K.M., *The Glamour About the Guptas*. Bombay, 1 53.

Singh, R.C.P., *Kingship In Northern India*. Delhi, 1968.

Sinha, B.P., *The Decline of the Kingdom of Magadha*. Patna, 1954.

Sircar, D.C., *The Successors of the Śātavāhanas*. Calcutta, 1939.

———, *Indian Epigraphy*.

———, *Select Inscriptions*, I. Calcutta, 1965.

———, *Studies in the Society and Administration of Ancient and Mediaeval India*, I. Calcutta, 1967.

Sircar, D.C., *Indian Epigraphical Glossary*. Banaras, 1966.
Smith, V.A., *The Early History of India*. Oxford, 1924.
——, *Aśoka*. Oxford, 1919.
Spellman, J.W., *Political Theory of Ancient India*. London, 1964.
Stein, Otto, *Megasthenes and Kautilya*. Vienna, 1921.
Tarn, W.W., *The Greeks in Bactria and India*. Cambridge, 1938.
Tripathi, R.S., *History of Kanauj to the Muslim Conquest*. Banaras, 1959.
Udgaonkar, P.B., *The Political Institutions and Administration*. Delhi, 1969.
Upadhyaya, B., *Gupta Sāmrājya kā Itihāsa* (in Hindi), I and II. Allahabad, 1939.
Vaidya, C.V., *History of Mediaeval Hindu India*, I, II and III. Poona, 1921-26.
Varma, V.P., *Studies in Hindu Political Thought*. Banaras, 1959.
Vogel, J. Ph., *Antiquities of Chamba State*, I.
Yazdani, G., *The History of the Deccan*, Parts I-VI. 1960.
——, *The History of the Deccan*, Parts VII-XI. 1960.

ARTICLES IN PERIODICALS

Agrawala, V.S., 'The Use of a Scythian Title in a Mathura Image Inscription'. *JBRS*, XXXVIII, pp. 230-32.
Bakhle, V.S., 'Śātavāhanas and the Contemporary Kshatrapas'. *JBBRAS*, IV, pp. 39-80.
Basak, R.G., 'Pāla Sāmrājyer Śāsanapraṇālī'. *Pravāsī* (1343 B.S.), pp. 881ff.
——, 'Ministers in Ancient India'. *IHQ*, I, pp. 522-32; 623-42.
——, 'Indian Society as Pictured in the Mṛcchakaṭika'. *IHQ*, VI, pp. 290ff.
Bhattacharya, B., 'Ministers in Ancient India'. *New Indian Antiquary*, II, pp. 204ff.
Bhattacharya, S.C., 'Hindu Royal Titles and Kingship'. *University of Allahabad Studies* (*Ancient History Section*), 1963-64, pp. 61-74.
Bose, A.N., 'Early Industrial Organisation in North India'. *IHQ*, XX, pp. 167ff.
——, 'Gāmabhojaka in the Buddhist Birth Stories'. *IHQ*, XIII, pp. 610ff.

——, 'Indo-Aryan Land Revenue System'. *JBBRAS*, XV, pp. 53-71.

Champupati, 'Vedic Principles of the Constitution of a State'. *IHQ*, IV, pp. 646ff.

Choudhury, R.K., 'Administration Of Law And Justice In Ancient India'. *Journal of the Oriental Institute* (Baroda), II, pp. 153-60.

Dandekar, R.N., 'The System of Government under the Guptas'. *Munshi Indological Felicitation Volume*, pp. 340-54.

——, 'Sources of Ancient Indian Polity'. *Professor Birinchi Kumar Barua Commemoration Volume*, pp. 32-37.

Das Gupta, N.N., 'A Note on Aṣṭakulādhikaraṇa'. *IC*, V, pp. 109-11.

Desai, D., 'Local Organisation in Cālukyan Karṇāṭaka'. *Karnataka Historical Review*, III, pp. 10-14.

Deshpande, V.V., 'A Comment On Divinity Of King And Right Of Revolution'. *Purāṇa*, XIII, No. II, pp. 170-74.

Dikshit, R.K., 'Kośa in the Smṛtis'. *The Journal of the U.P. Historical Society*, V (New Series), pp. 48-82.

——, 'Kingship in the Vishṇu Smṛti'. *Munshi Indological Felicitation Volume*, pp. 340-54.

Dikshitar, Ramachandra, 'Notes on the Paura-Janapada'. *IHQ*, VI.

——, 'Public Opinion in Ancient India: A Bird's Eye View'. *Kuppuswami Sastri Commemoration Volume*, pp. 119-22.

Diskalkar, D.B., 'Designations of Public Officials in Ancient India'. *Journal of the University of Poona*, No. XIX (Humanities Section), 1964, pp. 107-33.

Gadgil, V.A., 'The Village In Sanskrit Literature'. *JBBRAS*, II (1926), pp. 150-66.

Ghosal, U.N., 'Some Notes on Ownership of the Soil in Ancient India'. *IHQ*, VII, pp. 658-63.

——, 'On Some Recent Discussions Relating to Ancient Indian Political Ideas'. *IHQ*, XXIX, pp. 64ff.

——, 'Ancient Indian Official Titles Explained'. *IHQ*, XIV, pp. 836ff.

——, 'Kauṭilya on Royal Authority'. *IHQ*, XXIX, pp. 286-92.

——, 'Authority Of The King As A Source Of Law In The Ancient Indian Literature On Law And Polity'. *The Journal of the U.P. Historical Society* (New Series), II, pp. 27-34.

Ghosal, U.N., 'Kingship in the *Ṛgveda*'. *IHQ*, XX, pp. 36ff.
———, 'Kingship and Kingly Administration in the *Atharvaveda*'. *IHQ*, XX, pp. 105ff.
Gopal, K.K., 'Assignment To Officers And Royal Kinsmen In Early Mediaeval India'. *University of Allahabad Studies* (Ancient History Section), 1963-64, pp. 75-103.
———, 'Pañca-Mahāśabda'. *Dr. Mirashi Felicitation Volume*, pp. 392-99.
Goswami, K.G., 'Appointment of Ministers and High Officials in Ancient India'. *IHQ*, XXIX, pp. 129ff.
Gupta, R.C., 'Democratic Element In Bṛhaspati's Theory Of Government And State Law'. *The Calcutta Review* (May 1965), pp. 139-48.
Hopkins, E.W., 'The Social and Military Position of the Ruling Caste in Ancient India'. *Journal of the American Oriental Society*, XIII (1889).
Jain, J.P., 'Political Thoughts In Pre-Muslim India'. *Journal of the Kalinga Historical Research Society*, I, pp. 71-74.
Jayaswal, K.P., 'The Terms 'Anusaṁyāna', 'Rājūkas' and 'Former Kings' in Aśoka's Inscriptions'. *JBORS*, IV, pp. 36-43.
Jha, Balabhadra, 'Village in Ancient India'. *Journal of the Bihar Research Society*, XLI.
Kamble, B.R., 'The Brāhmaṇas in *Rig-Veda*'. *Marathwada University Journal*, IX, pp. 103-18.
Karambelkar, V.W., 'Brahman and Purohita'. *IHQ*, XXVI, pp. 293-300.
Karmarkar, D.P., 'Administrative Systems of the Chālukya Empire'. *Karnataka Historical Review*, I, pp. 35-36.
Krishna Rao, M.V., 'The Prince In The Political System Of Kauṭilya And Machiavelli'. *The Half-Yearly Journal of the Mysore University* (New Series—Section A. Arts). March 1943, pp. 77-96.
Law, N.N., 'Machinery of Administration as depicted in the Kauṭilīya', *IHQ*, VI, pp. 441ff; pp. 614ff.
———, 'Notes on the Salaries and Allowances detailed in the Kauṭilīya'. *IHQ*, VI, pp. 780ff.
Majumdar, R.C., 'The Constitution of the Licchavis and the Śākyas'. *IHQ*, XXVII, pp. 327ff.

Mishra, B.V., 'The Administrative System of the Pratīhāras'. *Journal of the University of Gauhati*, III, pp. 105-15.

Mookherji, R.K., 'Ancient Indian Education From The Epics'. *Lucknow University Journal*, II, pp. 39-59.

Nigam, R.C., 'Rule of Law'. *The Journal of the U.P. Historical Society*, IV (New Series), pp. 70ff.

Om Prakash, 'Divinity of the King and the Right of Revolution in the Purāṇas'. *Purāṇa*, XIII, pp. 167-69.

Rangachari, K., 'Town-planning and House-building in Ancient India according to Śilpaśāstra'. *IHQ*, IV, pp. 102ff.

Rapson, E.J., 'Lord of Horses, Lord of Elephants, Lord of Men'. *Woolner Commemoration Volume*, pp. 196-99.

Saletore, B.A., 'The Sthānikas and their Historical Importance'. *The Journal of the Bombay University*, VII, pt. I, pp. 1-65.

Sarkar, B.K., 'The Political Ideas of Caṇḍeśvara, Mādhava and Vaiśāmpāyana'. *Woolner Commemoration Volume*, pp. 224-32.

Sastri, K.A.N., 'The Place of Arthaśāstra in the History of Indian Polity'. *Annals of the Bhandarkar Research Institute*, XXVIII.

——, 'Kautilya on Royal Authority'. *IHQ*, XXIX, pp. 286-92.

Sen, B.C., 'Administration Under The Pālas And The Senas'. *IC*, VII, pp. 203-19.

Sharma, D., 'Devānāṁpriya'. *IHQ*, XXVI, pp. 149-51.

——, 'The Significance of Two Old Historical Titles'. *IHQ*, XXVII, pp. 336-39.

——, 'Political Thought and Practice in the Agni-Purāṇa'. *Purāṇa*, III, No. I, pp. 23-37.

Sharma, R.S., 'Central Asia And Early Mediaeval Indian Polity'. *The Quarterly Review of Historical Studies*, IV, pp. 180-82.

Sinha, B.P., 'The King in Kauṭiliyan State'. *JBRS*, Vol. 40, pp. 277ff.

——, 'The Kauṭiliyan State and a Welfare State'. *JBRS*, Vol. 40, pp. 178ff.

Sircar, D.C., 'Dharmādhikaraṇa and Dharmādhikārin'. *Purāṇa*, VI, No. 2, pp. 445-50.

——, 'The Astrologer at the Village and the Court'. *IHQ*, XXVIII, pp. 342-49.

——, 'Nagara-Śreṣṭhin'. *Journal of the University of Gauhati*, VI, pp. 81-85.

Srivastava, Shakuntala, 'Rights of the Individual in Ancient India'. *Prajñā* (1969), pp. 144-59.

Thakur, Upendra, 'Forms And Features Of Governmental System In The Age Of The Rāmāyaṇa'. D.C. Sircar ed. *Early Indian Political And Administrative Systems* (Calcutta, 1972), pp. 67-75.

Tripathi, R.S., 'Pratīhāra Administration'. *IHQ*, IX, pp. 121ff.

Varma, V.P., 'Studies in Hindu Political Thought and its Metaphysical Foundations'. *JBRS*, XXXVIII, pp. 35, 294 and 449ff.

Verma, O.P., 'Espionage in Kauṭilya's Arthaśāstra'. *IHQ*, XXXVI, pp. 238-46.

——, 'Administrative Machinery Under The Yādavas'. *JOIB*, XVII, pp. 161-65.

Vyas, S.N., 'The Purda System In The Rāmāyaṇa'. *JOIB*, V, pp. 330-34.

Yadava, B.N.S., 'Chivalry And Some Aspects Of Warfare On The Eve Of The Muslim Conquest Of Northern India'. *University of Allahabad Studies* (Ancient History Section), 1966, pp. 1-28.

Index